Patrick Brennan

Secessionville

Assault on Charleston

Manufactured in the United States of America

All rights reserved. No part of this book may be reproduced or transmitted in any form or by any means electronic or technical, including photocopying, recording, or by any information storage and retrieval system, without written permission from the publisher.

SECESSIONVILLE:
Assault on Charleston

by Patrick Brennan

Printing Number
10 9 8 7 6 5 4 3 2
Second Edition

ISBN 1-882810-08-2

Copyright © 1996 Patrick Brennan
Maps copyright © 1996 Jim Coudal

Includes bibliographic references and index

Published by De Capo Press

To John C. Brennan
and his beautiful bride, Pauline

THE WAR IN SOUTH CAROLINA.—THE 3D RHODE ISLAND VOLUNTEERS, GEN. WILLIAM'S BRIGADE, DRIVING THE REBEL SHARPSHOOTERS FROM THE WOODS ON JAMES ISLAND, BY A BAYONET CHARGE, JUNE 16.—FROM A SKETCH BY AN OFFICER.

Table of Contents

Acknowledgements
i

Introduction by John Peterson
v

Prologue
x

Chapter 1
A Change in the Weather
1

Chapter 2
The Island and the Railroad
29

Chapter 3
Yankees Come to James Island
53

Chapter 4
First Blood
75

Chapter 5
Sparring
93

Chapter 6
Prelude
125

continued...

Table of Contents continued...

Chapter 7
Positions, Places
157

Chapter 8
Fields of Fire
195

Chapter 9:
A Disturbance There to Quell
241

Chapter 10:
After-Action
269

Chapter 11:
Exit
287

Epilogue
309

Order of Battle
314

Notes
317

Bibliography
368

Index
376

Interview
390

Illustrations

June 16 Battle (3rd Rhode Island)	Frontis
Brig. Gen. Henry Benham	2
Brig. Gen. Isaac Stevens	7
Maj. Gen. John C. Pemberton	12
Brig. Gen. Nathan "Shanks" Evans	13
Col. Johnson Hagood	15
Col. Clement H. Stevens	17
Lt. Col. Ellison Capers	18
Maj. Gen. David Hunter	21
Brig. Gen. States Rights Gist	35
Lt. Col. Simonton and Staff	37
Col. Dan Leasure	61
Brig. Gen. Horatio Wright	63
Lt. Col. John Jackson and staff	64
Brig. Gen. William Duncan Smith	98
Brig. Gen. Isaac Stevens and staff	107
Col. Thomas Lamar	122
Battle of June 10, 1862	128-129
Col. William Fenton	164
Attack on the Tower Battery	178-179
June 16 Battle (79th New York)	202
Secessionville 1865	286
Fort Lamar, 1890s	307

Cartography*

4	Southeast Atlantic Seaboard
30	Charleston and Vicinity (Theater of Operations)
77	Sol Legare Island, June 3, 1862
81	Sole Legare Island, June 3, 1862
124	James Island
131	Grimball's Plantation, June 10, 1862, Map 1
133	Grimball's Plantation, June 10, 1862, Map 2
149	Grimball's Farm Defenses
170	Battle of Secessionville, June 16, 1862: 4:30a.m.
175	Battle of Secessionville, June 16, 1862: 4:30–4:40a.m.
182	Tower Battery, June 16, 1862: 4:35–4:50a.m.
188	Battle of Secessionville, June 16, 1862: 4:40–4:45a.m.
192	Battle of Secessionville, June 16, 1862: 4:45–4:50a.m.
200	Battle of Secessionville June 16, 1862: 4:50–5:00a.m.
204	Tower Battery, June 16, 1862: 4:55–5:10a.m.
207	Battle of Secessionville, June 16, 1862: 5:00–5:10a.m.
210	Battle of Secessionville, June 16, 1862: 5:10–5:15a.m.
217	Battle of Secessionville, June 16, 1862: 5:15–5:20a.m.
222	Battle of Secessionville, June 16, 1862: 5:20–5:25a.m.
228	Battle of Secessionville, June 16, 1862: 5:25–5:40a.m.
235	Battle of Secessionville, June 16, 1862: 5:40–5:50a.m.
243	Battle of Secessionville, June 16, 1862: 5:50–6:00a.m.
249	Battle of Secessionville, June 16, 1862: 6:00–8:30a.m.

* Please note that the times set forth on the maps are approximations only, based on available evidence. They were included to assist the reader in understanding the progression of the battle.

Acknowledgments

In the six years I've worked on this project, one lesson among many clearly stands out. Although it may seem so, writing is no solitary effort. A great many people have helped make this work a reality, and I will attempt to thank them all. Please accept my apologies if I've forgotten someone.

I trace my interest in the Battle of Secessionville to a visit I made to Charleston in January 1990. I'm a musician by trade, and my band had been booked into Myskyn's, a music club in downtown Charleston. On the day I hit town, armed with *Blue and Gray Magazine's* tour of Civil War Charleston, I found Secessionville and the remains of Fort Lamar. Hurricane Hugo had recently devastated the area, and the fields looked like I had just missed the fight. Needless to say, I was tremendously moved. Standing on the right flank of the fort, I resolved to write something about the battle. So, as odd as it may seem, it was that performance of Dick Holliday and the Bamboo Gang at a club only five miles from the Secessionville battlefield that started the journey that ends here. My thanks go to Brad Nye, Greg Hayes, Grant Tye, Greg Marsh, and particularly Kyle Gustie, for affording me this opportunity.

In Chicago, the Abraham Lincoln Book Shop tends to be my center of interest, and proprietors Dan and Audrey Weinberg have always been great supporters and good friends. Thomas "Tom" Trescott at ALBS read the manuscript and offered valuable advice. Much of my research time was spent at the Newberry Library and the Chicago Public Library, and both staffs were tremendously helpful and pleasant to deal with, despite my many demands.

In Columbia, South Carolina, J. Tracy Power provided a tremendous amount of assistance. His own work on the battle provided a high standard for anyone following in his steps.

I would also be remiss if I did not thank the following individuals and organizations: the Newport Historical Society, the Rhode Island Historical Society, the Boston Public Library, James Fahey at the War Museum (Massachusetts), the Pattee Library at Penn State, the State of Louisiana Research Division, the Charleston Public Library, Nancy Birkheimer at the Georgia Historical Society, the Houghton Library at Harvard University, the Case Western Reserve Historical Society, the South Carolina Department of Archives & History, the Southern Historical Collection and Manuscripts Department at University of North Carolina at Chapel Hill, the Atlanta History Center, Michael Winey, Richard J. Sommers and Louise Arnold-Friend at the United States Army Military History Institute, the Michigan State Archives, John Bigham at the South Carolina Confederate Relic Room and Museum, Julia Parker at Cornell University, Trenton Hizer with the South Caroliniana Library at the University of South Carolina, and Gary Lundell with the Allen Library at the University of Washington in Seattle.

My thanks also extends to the following: Maggie and Dylan Brennan, Mary and Shane Howell, Sue and Terry Brennan, Mary and Mike Brennan, all the Brennan kids, the entire Burns clan, The Band, Ted Banta, Arthur Bergeron Jr., William Blair, Tim Bradshaw, the Bulls, William Burton, Don Butler, the Campbell family, Tim Callahan, Carol Chitaroni, Bill Compton, Richard Côté, Sam Crisafulli, The Daves, Jerry Lee Davidson, Kathy Dhalle, Roger Durham, Lou Evans, Mrs. James L. Ferguson, Kitty Fishback, Shelby Foote, Pete Fuller, Bill Gavin, Rod Gragg, Bob Greene, Elizabeth Hagood, John Hennessy, Jeffrey Hice, Larry Houghton, Phil Jackson, Terry Johnston, the Kilman's, Talley Kirkland, Larry Kohl, Mike Kraus, Judge John B. Lewis, Roger Long, A. Colin MacDonald, Mrs. Betty Mason, Dana MacBean, Mrs. Adeline McEnery, Cathy O'Hara, Cal Packard, Pete Peters, Betty Peterson, the Poulsom-Hosticka household, Warren Ripley, Mrs. Mary Robertson, Robert Rosen, CDR R. L. Schreadley, Carolyn Schriber, Gerhard Spieler, Mrs. Floye McEnery Smith, Barry Spink, Tom

Swift, Terry at the Mount Sterling Rebel, Steve Wise, David Woodbury, and of course all my good friends in the beautiful city of Charleston. All of them contributed in ways great and small to make this book what it is.

To two people especially, I owe much. The story of the 8th Michigan is central to the events of the James Island campaign, and one cannot follow the shadow of the 8th without the help of Mary Jo Verran. She has kept the flame of the Michiganders burning in her own pursuit of her great-uncle, John Burwell. Her tireless energy, unchecked enthusiasm, and gracious generosity stamped this book deeply.

The same must be said for Willis "Skipper" Keith. From my first unsure inquiries through every step of the writing process, Skipper provided the yardstick with which to measure everything I tried to accomplish. He generously shared his extensive personal archives and kindly spent an inordinate amount of time walking me across the contours of James Island and the Secessionville battlefield. Each visit to Charleston greatly expanded my knowledge of the campaign, thanks primarily to Skipper and his willingness to enlighten an inquisitive Northerner. It may sound trite to say I could not have done it without either of Mary Jo or Skipper, but quite often the trite is true.

I owe much to Tom Cleland, who helped develop a young reader's interest in the Civil War.

My gratitude goes to Jim Coudal, of Coudal Partners in Chicago. Besides being a fine writer and a driven Civil War buff, Jim did a wonderful job conceiving and designing the maps that accompany this work. I must also thank his co-workers—Kevin Guilfoile, Susan Everett, Robin Radke, and Jennifer Baer, for putting up with my incessant visits.

I am indebted to Theodore P. "Ted" Savas, of Savas Publishing Company, for getting this manuscript into book form. His energy and support over the past fifteen months has been tremendously gratifying. I still owe him a five-course Thai dinner in downtown Chicago.

I must also thank John Peterson for taking the time during a busy season at the Farnsworth House Book Shop in Gettysburg, Pennsylvania, to provide invaluable editorial counsel. We enjoyed many a linguistic skirmish in putting this manuscript together, and I greatly appreciate his assistance and friendship. Concerning his kind introduction and the question of whether there were Tennessee troops on South Mountain, I can only respond rather weakly with this point: I'm hopefully certain that although no units from the Volunteer State were present on South Mountain, some Tennessee men fought there as members of Hill's regiments. I also had to rhyme the word "family."

I offer my deepest thanks to my wife, Sheila, who suffered through every moment of this composition with good cheer and humor. The ranks of Civil War widows are blessed with such a patient and loving recruit. I was certainly blessed the day I met her.

I have learned one other thing writing this book. Most stories seem to take on lives of their own; they tend to burn their own hard track across the road, far beyond anyone's poor attempt at controlling them. In 1995, my wife Sheila managed to deliver our daughter, Dylan, two weeks before her due date. Notable enough I suppose, but this miracle of birth was accompanied by a sign that arcs well beyond the crossing of the stars. Originally, Dylan's due date was July the second, day two at Gettysburg. Instead, her birthday now falls on the sixteenth of June, the anniversary of the Battle of Secessionville.

Patrick Brennan
July 21, 1996

Introduction

Before commenting directly on this remarkable book, I feel compelled to provide a bit of personal testimony concerning Pat Brennan, one of the more remarkable characters of my acquaintance, who makes his debut here as one of the more promising Civil War battle scholars of his generation.

First of all, readers must understand that Pat is not an historian by trade, but rather a musician, a rock-blues and country keyboard player whom I met one day in the winter of '85 in the green pastures of the Abraham Lincoln Book Shop in Chicago. I had recently arrived at the Lincoln from the Military Bookman in New York, and on the afternoon that Pat strolled in, I was still feeling my way in becoming acquainted with the Lincoln Book Shop regulars.

Not that Pat had the slightest intention of making my job any easier. As I made my approach, he was not an easy read, as he well knew, clad as he was in galoshes, worn Levi's, down jacket, and a black and white piano keyboard scarf, topped with a hat that could only have been lifted from a Dublin chimney sweep, or maybe Billy the Kid. His longish hair lent a decidedly Bohemian Brigade air, and though the eyes twinkled in anticipation, his choir boy deadpan was giving nothing away. Obviously, I was headed into an encounter of sorts, more likely an ambush.

With thousands of books at my back, I took the plunge and asked if I could be of assistance. "Yeah," Pat Brennan replied, "I'm lookin' for something to read." Looking for something to read, was he? Taking the bait, I rose to the occasion as handsomely as a Civil War bookseller could, or so I thought. "Well, if you're looking for a good browse you can begin by reading your way through Shelby Foote's *The Civil War*, an excellent trilogy, at a thousand pages a whack." At this, Pat's eyes positively beamed. "I already have ...twice."

The ambush ended in laughs and Pat and I were soon to become fast friends. Along the way I was perpetually astonished at his zeal and the range of his Civil War interests. Lincoln proprietor Dan Weinberg and I once inventoried his library for fun and came away stunned, not only at the high percentage of magnificent dust jackets, but at the breadth and depth of the collection. Although a battle aficionado at heart, Pat was well versed in all social and political aspects. He was as comfortable in discussing Mary Chesnut or the fine points of Don Fehrenbacher's analyses of Abraham Lincoln, as in laying out the casualty count of the Antietam campaign.

I was further amazed at the way the war had managed to victoriously pervade every nook of Pat's life, even including rock 'n roll. One evening I journeyed to the West End Bar on Armitage Avenue to watch him and the Walter Williams Band strut their stuff, which included a Civil War rock tune of Pat's, a mournful lament titled "South Mountain." We afterwards sat around discussing not music, but Civil War research. In the tune he had alluded to the "Tennessee dirt poor" on South Mountain, and I wondered, was he absolutely certain that D. H. Hill's command contained Tennessee regiments? Pat answered with the look of a wounded hound. Far better to question his keyboard prowess than his knowledge of troop dispositions on South Mountain.

In addition, Pat monitored the Civil War magazines and kept furiously up to date on all doings of the national Civil War community. In the cause of battlefield preservation his fury was doubled, if not cubed. All Civil War battlefields were Hallowed Ground in Pat's eyes, and woe to the greedy developers attempting to convert them into condos and amusement parks. He not only contributed money and circulated petitions, but fought the good fight on a satiric rock 'n roll radio show that he co-hosted with Chicago personality Buzz Kilman. He battled on other fronts as well, enlisting

Charleton Heston during 1988's "Third Battle of Manassas," and making the Op-Ed page of the *Chicago Tribune* while arguing against the location of Disney's America. Pat even attained the fleeting celebrity of being featured in a Bob Greene column.

When I moved from the Lincoln to the Farnsworth House Book Shop in Gettysburg, Pat was sure to remain in touch. Every two to three weeks he would call to query the doings of Wayne Motts and other noteworthy Gettysburg Battlefield guides. How was Bill Frassanito and the Gettysburg Battlefield Preservation Association doing in their fight with Gettysburg College over the railroad cut property transfer? Sometimes he would merely want a report on the condition of the battlefield. How did it look? How was it doing? Was it OK?

Had anyone asked me in those years whether Pat Brennan would ever write a serious Civil War book, my answer would have been, in all probability, no. From everything I could see, he was far too busy—too busy as a family man, with one child in tow and another on the way; too busy running a commercial music house and recording studio, cooking up music for everyone from McDonalds to the Chicago White Sox, scoring documentaries for A&E television producers; too busy gigging with his new band, Dick Holliday & The Bamboo Gang; too busy with battlefield preservation; too busy traveling to places like Gettysburg, there to laze about the Farnsworth House Tavern sipping Guinness, playing Bob Dylan, and "knock, knock, knockin' on heaven's door." His wife Sheila—a younger, more charming version of actress Lindsey Wagner—was as bright and gracious as she was lovely. His life was full, his Civil War cup runneth over. He was having serious fun enough. There was golf to play. Why write?

Wrong. In Pat's extensive visits to national Civil War sites, there was one place that he had never seriously been. Charleston, South Carolina. In particular, James Island. Secessionville.

In January of 1990, he traveled there with his band and upon returning called me up in the tones of a man who had just undergone a mystical conversion. In the telling, it was obvious that the ghosts of Fort Lamar, south and north, were tugging at his heartstrings. Furthermore, there had been very little written on the subject, and in his view, the battle of Secessionville rated a full book-length treatment.

He returned to Charleston again and again with the band, and over time, the project took wings. After decades of neglect, it seemed that the men of Secessionville had at last found their author. In monitoring Pat's progress from Gettysburg, I was far more skeptical of the venture than I ever let on to him. And with good cause. Over the years I had seen a number of Civil War publishing projects begin in high hopes, only to founder on the shoals of inadequate research materials. In taking on the 1862 James Island Campaign, Pat was moving in uncharted waters. He badly wanted to tell their tale, but unless the soldiers of Secessionville provided sufficient first-hand testimony, all could come to naught.

When the manuscript arrived, it was apparent at first glance that my fears were groundless. The battle segment was studded with all manner of quotes from participants' letters, diaries, and memoirs, many of them unpublished. The rank and file of Secessionville had cooperated fully, had vied with one another in pouring out their hearts. Pat's secondary research was equally impressive. At a closer reading, it was obvious that the national Civil War community had much to learn concerning the James Island Campaign.

Civil War historians have long regarded this campaign as a minor, small stakes sideshow to McClellan's Peninsula Campaign. This book is an invitation to reconsider conventional assumptions. In point of fact, the Federals had assembled an awesome combination of naval and military might on the South Atlantic coast in the spring of 1862. In seven months, they had captured Port Royal and Florida's eastern seaboard, had fortified the barrier island north to Edisto, and had sealed off Savannah. In May they were handed an intelligence coup that all but guaranteed the success of a well-conceived and sharply executed assault on Charleston. Had they succeeded, it goes without saying that the fall of this major seaport—this rich symbol of Southern defiance—on the heels of the capitulation of New Orleans and Nashville, in the midst of the Peninsula campaign, would have shaken the Confederacy to its core. Charleston was a glittering prize, and in June of 1862, the stakes at Secessionville were high indeed.

Pat also does a skillful job in guiding the reader through the maze of command-level personalities. On the victorious Southern side, discounting the oafish Nathan "Shanks" Evans, there are a number of excellent officers in attendance—Thomas Lamar,

Duncan Smith, Ellison Capers, States Rights Gist, and Johnson Hagood—and even the much-maligned John Pemberton displays intermittent flashes of competence. The picture on the Federal side is somewhat darker, but even here, the courageous performance of Isaac Stevens shines through. Commanders Henry Benham and David Hunter emerge as the villains of the piece, and it is difficult to conjure up a pair of generals more bumbling than these two. Some scholars may feel that the author goes out of his way to blacken the reputation of Henry Benham, but from the evidence presented, Benham deserves everything he gets for later attempting to evade the consequences of his actions by charging Stevens' troops with cowardice. If there is an edge to Pat's portrait of Benham, it is because he has lived too long among the ghosts of the 8th Michigan, the 79th New York Highlanders and the 100th Pennsylvania Roundheads. Too many ragged privates have been tugging at his sleeves, cheering him on and begging for historical redress.

Which points to the real strength of this book, the author's empathy with the rank and file on both sides, and his ability to integrate their testimony into a smooth battle narrative. When Stevens' brigades jump off in the wee hours of June 16, 1862, in their assault on Colonel Lamar's artillerists manning the Tower Battery, the soldiers themselves take charge of the fight. Which is as it should be. For them, the fight for the Tower Battery is a descent into hell. In the author's mind, the resulting carnage—symbolic of all Civil War carnage—is redeemed by the tale of two brothers, two Scotsmen on opposing sides, who worry and grieve for each other, and manage to survive.

This book makes an extremely significant contribution to Civil War battle literature. As for its author, the next time I encounter an ersatz Civil War keyboard player "looking for something to read," I will skip Shelby Foote and point the lad in the direction of Pat Brennan's *Secessionville: Assault on Charleston*.

John S. Peterson
Gettysburg, Pennsylvania
March 6, 1996

Prologue

In many ways, the South Carolina coast in the Spring of 1862 retained the outward appearance of her ageless contours. Nature exploded in verdant display as wildflowers painted pastels across a landscape of near tropical beauty. Wildlife scoured the teeming swamps; along the oceanfront the screeches of seabirds mingled with the roar of the surf. But even as nature was reborn, startling changes marked this particular season of renewal. A profusion of wild blackberries now covered the cotton fields of the seacoast plantations, and the cotton itself, long the staple crop in the area, grew wild and untended if it grew at all. Instead of managing and overseeing their holdings, the landowners had fled their homes, leaving their slaves to fend for themselves. Young men from Michigan, Pennsylvania, and New England now camped and trained on those same fields. Still more men from Louisiana, Georgia, Tennessee and South Carolina lined the nearby entrenchments. Almost everywhere, fortifications gouged the fields. Offshore, the vessels of the Union Navy stood watch over the great harbors and hidden waterways of Carolina's coast. War had rooted on the South Atlantic coast.

South Carolina had already experienced the shock of combat. In the previous months, America was transfixed by the drama unfolding in Charleston harbor. Abraham Lincoln's November election provoked Carolinian leaders into elucidating a uniquely Southern view of states' rights. In December of 1860, they invoked what they saw as their constitutional prerogative and voted to secede from the Federal union. The Federal garrison at Fort Moultrie in Charleston, fearing imminent attack, was compelled to flee to Fort Sumter, situated on an island in Charleston's harbor. For months, political leaders in South Carolina's capital of Columbia tussled with their counterparts in Washington D.C. over the ownership of the masonry fort, while other Southern states followed South Carolina's lead and joined the nascent Confederate States of America. Eventually, the Carolinian fire-eaters and Confederate authorities tired of Washington's delaying game and, precluding Federal efforts to relieve the garrison at Sumter, launched a bombardment of the fort in the early morning hours of April 12, 1861. The fort surrendered a day later, and within hours, Abraham Lincoln called for 75,000 volunteers to put down the insurgents.

For months, the attention of the country had been centered on Charleston and her harbor. Suddenly, with the fall of the fort, the intense attention dissipated. South Carolinians and Georgians still rushed to man the emerging Confederate defenses along the coastline, and troops from other states arrived to bolster their numbers. But the strategic minds in both the North and South decided that the heart of the conflict would be north in Virginia and west along the Ohio and Mississippi Rivers, not on the Southeast Atlantic coast. As a consequence, South Carolina and Georgia quickly became little more than military backwaters while the "real" war evolved elsewhere. With the Federal Navy arriving in great strength to begin its blockade of the South's ports, the action in Charleston and Savannah centered on blockade-running, not fighting. Southern soldiers spent their days drilling and digging, but the prospect of crossing swords with the enemy seemed a remote possibility in this first summer of the Civil War.

Then, almost as quickly as the national attention had faded, the equation changed. In early November, a massive Federal fleet carrying three brigades of Northern infantry appeared off Port Royal, South Carolina. After a few days of ineffectual skirmishing, Federal Flag Officer Samuel Francis Du Pont led an attack squadron into the harbor itself and easily blasted the outgunned Confederate defenders out of their works. Northern troops poured ashore and claimed Hilton Head and Bay Point for themselves. In one brutally swift strike, Federal power re-established itself along the Southeast Atlantic coast.

The invading Federals quickly established a massive naval base on Port Royal harbor, then slowly began to extend their influence. Beaufort, the next major city north of Hilton Head, fell in mid-November. Soon thereafter, a Federal regiment landed on Tybee Island at the mouth of the Savannah River. Both movements went strangely unopposed. The Confederates in the area, commanded by recently-arrived General Robert E. Lee, initially intended to contest all enemy movements by fortifying the myriad barrier islands girdling the coastline. But the fall of Port Royal decisively proved the overwhelming strength of the Federal Navy, so Lee adopted a strategy of inland defense in an attempt to lure the Northerners away from their powerful naval guns. Accordingly, he strung his 13,100 troops along the line of the Charleston-Savannah railroad, effectively ceding the many barrier islands to the enemy. But the general refused to surrender the theater's two major cities. Sheltered by the massive Fort Pulaski at the mouth of the Savannah River, Savannah herself was soon ringed by intricate entrenchments. Charleston, with her townsmen manning defenses on nearby Coles and James Islands, also stood secure. And although limited thrusts continued, the Federals appeared unwilling to take the Confederate bait by either advancing inland or operating against the fortifications of the two great Southern ports. For the time being, a major Yankee incursion into this Confederate department seemed unlikely.

The Union command, which suffered from a number of inadequacies, served to confirm the impression. Brigadier General Thomas West Sherman assumed that his force would simply take and hold the designated coastal positions. When Port Royal fell quickly, Sherman was ill-prepared to organize aggressive movements inland. The army did mount a successful New Year's Day assault on a Rebel position at Port Royal Ferry on the Coosaw River, but the Federals were unable to capitalize on the moment. The attack proved to be nothing more than an isolated incident as Northern efforts angled south towards Savannah. There, too, operations bogged down as Sherman and Du Pont proved incapable of coordinating their forces. When delays prevented the Federals from taking Savannah in a coup de main, Fort Pulaski became the focal point for the Northern efforts. Combined operations slowly pinched the masonry work from north and south, but the glacial tempo of the campaign disturbed Washington's military planners. In an effort to energize the campaign, Maj. Gen. David Hunter and a subordinate, Brig. Gen. Henry Benham, were dispatched to the theater to supercede Sherman. Luck, which seemed to have abandoned Thomas Sherman, smiled on the new arrivals. Less than two weeks after they had assumed command, Hunter and Benham watched Fort Pulaski surrender on the afternoon of April 11, following a 30-hour Federal bombardment.

The fall of Pulaski had deep repercussions, demonstrating that the strength of masonry works was entirely compromised by the power of the rifled cannon. Captain Quincy Gillmore, the architect of the Federal artillery barrage that sealed Pulaski's fate, showed himself to be an excellent, perhaps brilliant, engineering officer. But more importantly, Fort Pulaski's fall gave Major General Hunter a free hand to try to make good on the bold promise he made when first he arrived in the theater: that the national flag would soon fly over the ramparts of Fort Sumter.

The nation's attention again turned to Charleston harbor, to follow a new drama played out on a familiar stage. After six months of preliminaries, Federal forces were finally prepared to launch their first assault on Charleston.

CHAPTER ONE

"(We) will put an end to this cursed Rebellion before next fall."

—Pennsylvania officer Henry Applegate

A Change in the Weather

As the victorious Federals filed past the battered walls of Fort Pulaski, word of the fort's reduction and surrender swept through the North. In a season tempered by the casualty lists of Shiloh, the fall of Pulaski was good news indeed. But for the Federals who had plotted the fort's destruction and labored hard to realize its fall, success at Fort Pulaski was nothing if not expected. These Northerners encamped on the barrier islands of South Carolina and Georgia had grown accustomed to the heightened emotions of victory. The collapse of Confederate resistance in early November at Port Royal and the resulting Northern occupation of Hilton Head had begun a series of triumphs that included the taking of Beaufort and Port Royal Island, the New Year's Day fight at Port Royal Ferry, and the retaking of the Florida coast. With the bottling of the Savannah River, Unionists knew full well their fighting was far from finished, but they looked ahead with a confidence born of experience. Corporal John Rice Burwell from the 8th Michigan wrote poetically, "May the time soon come when this wicked Rebellion shall bee put down...The Day star of Gladness Is

Brig. Gen. Henry Benham
Massachusetts Commandery, Military Order of the Loyal Legion
and the U.S. Army Military History Institute

beginning to dawn in the east." A Pennsylvania officer named Henry Applegate expressed himself more bluntly: "(we) will put an end to this cursed Rebellion before next fall."[1]

As cheering as the news was, not every Unionist shared in the emotion of the moment. From his Beaufort headquarters on Port Royal Island, Federal Brig. Gen. Isaac Stevens had come to question his superiors' efforts to reduce Savannah's citadel. Although he originally supported plans to take Savannah, Stevens recognized quite early in the campaign that the Charleston–Savannah Railroad, the iron lifeline that had anchored the Confederates in place, remained the most crucial strategic target in the area, not the Savannah River defenses. Ever since Stevens' Coosaw Ferry fight of New Year's Day, the general had been pushing small patrols up the myriad waterways deep into enemy lines, collecting intelligence concerning the Confederate works shielding the railroad between the Ashepoo and the Coosawhatchie Rivers. Based on the knowledge he gleaned from these efforts, Stevens worked out a complicated yet feasible operation that would destroy the rail link between the two cities and allow the attacking force to then turn on Charleston and force its capitulation. He chose the railroad at Pocotaligo, the closest station on the rail line to Stevens' forces on Port Royal Island, as his point of attack. Two columns would descend on the rail stop, one by land through Gardens Corner, the other by water via the Broad and Pocotaligo Rivers. Smaller support groups would ascend the Ashepoo and Combahee Rivers, uniting with the main force to lay waste to thirty miles of railroad tracks and bridges southwest of Pocotaligo. Phase two would push a full brigade to Church Flats via the North Edisto and Wadmalaw Rivers, providing a forward base for the final assault on Charleston. Once the railroad raiders united with the Church Flats force, these brigades could take the city with a rush or move to turn the Confederate defenses on James Island by way of the Stono and Wapoo Cut, depending upon the opportunities. Either way, Isaac Stevens was out to grab the enemy by the throat and take the harbor city of Charleston in the process.[2]

Stevens and former army commander Gen. Thomas Sherman had met to discuss this plan several times. Federal Flag Officer Samuel Francis Du Pont also entered into these discussions by proposing a feint on Bull Bay, north of Charleston, to further confuse the Confederates. Sherman gave his imprimatur to the operation and ordered it begun immediately after Pulaski's fall. With these assurances in mind, Isaac Stevens anticipated a speedy reduction of Fort Pulaski. Instead, he spent February and March observing the Federal efforts grind along at a snail's pace. Worse yet, Stevens' frail health broke under a chronic attack of yellow fever. Morale was indeed low when he wrote his wife, "I assure you, I am very weary at my position here. I have literally nothing to do, except to perfect the discipline of my Brigade."[3]

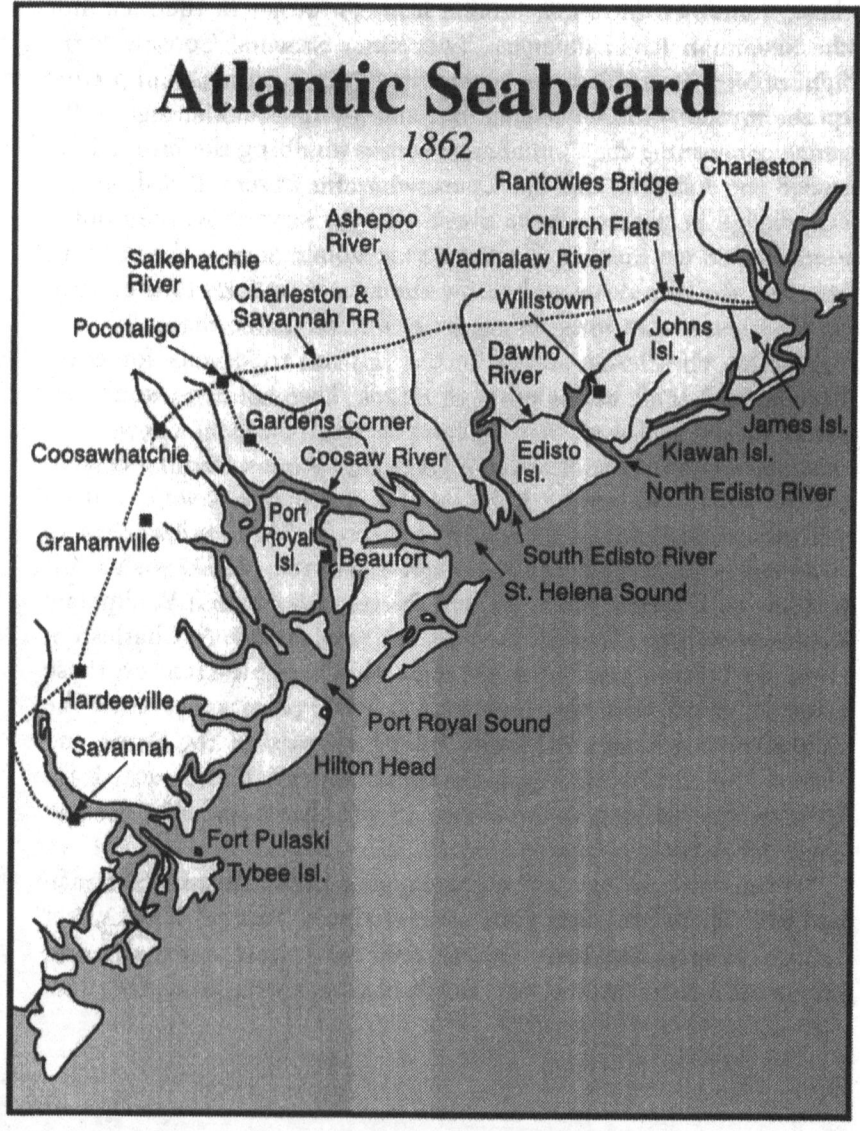

The arrival of the Hunter-Benham contingent and General Thomas Sherman's subsequent departure also caused wariness at Stevens' Beaufort headquarters, a concern that would prove well-founded. Stevens respected and admired Sherman and was truly sorry to see him go. Worse, he had crossed paths a number of times with the portly Benham in the pre-war army, and his relationship with his new commander was anything but cordial. This conflict could wait, however, for Benham had immersed himself in the Pulaski operations while Stevens wrestled with a knotty personal problem, namely the U.S. Senate's delay in confirming his rank of brigadier.

Earlier, Stevens had replaced his brigade quartermaster, a political crony named William Lilley, and Lilley retaliated by inundating Washington with lies about Stevens' behavior. Old charges that Stevens was questionable on the slavery issue, a charge that most Democrats had to face at one time or another, combined with Lilley's fabrications to hold up Stevens' confirmation. But Sherman arrived in Washington in time to undermine Lilley and shore up support for Stevens. On April 12, the Senate responded by confirming Stevens' new rank, allowing the newly appointed general to turn his attentions to more pressing military concerns.[4]

Benham seemed to raise the hackles of the entire Stevens family, as Isaac's wife was then visiting Port Royal and witnessed his arrival. She wrote to Coast Survey head and family friend Alexander Bache that Benham was "in high feather acting like a spread eagle." With amazing prescience she warned, "He is going to take Charleston at once. . . . I do not feel confidence in General Benham and regret his being placed in command at Hilton Head." Stevens' son Hazard served as chief of staff for his father, and he, too, remembered his introduction to David Hunter and Henry Benham. He considered the arrival of the pair "untimely and unexpected," and described the newcomers as "enfants terribles." In Benham, Hazard saw a "dense," egotistical blowhard, a whiner who was given this South Carolina command by Washington in an effort to silence him.

When Stevens' father presented the new commander with the outline for the proposed Pocotaligo operation, the plan "was rejected off hand by Benham," much to the elder Stevens' surprise and disgust. Hazard blamed the rejection on Benham's inability to listen "to any suggestions, or even information, that did not originate with himself." Isaac Stevens was angered by such treatment and shocked that the fortunes of war again had placed him under men he found wanting. At a crucial moment in what had been a successful if somewhat slow campaign, a change at the head of the Federal army on the South Atlantic coast had dashed Stevens' optimistic hopes for his strategy to take Charleston. Implementation of Stevens' operation had gone, as it were, north with Sherman.[5]

The object of Isaac Stevens' disgust, Henry Washington Benham, outwardly appeared to be a decent choice for this command. He certainly had compiled an antebellum record any regular army officer would envy, a record oddly parallel with Stevens' own. Both had graduated first in their respective classes at West Point, Benham in 1837 and Stevens in 1839. Both received wounds and honors in the Mexican War; 1st Lieutenant Benham earned a brevet captaincy at Buena Vista, while 1st Lieutenant Stevens was brevetted captain and major. But soon after the war, their paths diverged. Benham remained in the army and was promoted to captain, a rank he would hold for the next thirteen years in a number of posts along the New England shoreline, and as Stevens' replacement in the Coast Survey. Stevens resigned his commission in 1853 to enter politics and became governor of the new Washington territory. Secession found the two men literally and figuratively a continent apart.[6]

When Lincoln called for volunteers to suppress the Southern rebellion, Captain Benham found himself on the staff of Brig. Gen. T. A. Morris and received promotion to chief engineer of the Department of the Ohio. Serving under George McClellan, Benham participated in the campaign that threw Robert Garnett's small force off Laurel Hill in western Virginia and pushed it to Corrick's Ford. There, on July 13, 1861, Benham led the elements of Morris' Indiana Brigade that defeated the Confederates, killed Garnett, and launched "Little Mac" towards Washington and army command. Benham's action at Corrick's Ford earned him a brevet colonelcy which, in turn, led to line command as a brigadier, dated August 13, 1861.[7]

Quickly, the engineer-turned-infantry commander found himself in a feud with McClellan's replacement. William Rosecrans regarded Benham as insubordinate and privately accused him of drunken-

Brig. Gen. Isaac I. Stevens
Massachusetts Commandery, Military Order of the Loyal Legion
and- the U.S. Army Military History Institute

ness. When "Old Rosey" failed to bag the Confederate forces under John Floyd and John Wise at Carnifex Ferry, the feud between Rosecrans and Benham boiled over. On March 8, 1862, Benham left western Virginia under a cloud, heading for an assignment working on the defenses protecting Boston Harbor. However, in an attempt to clear his reputation and re-enter the war, he wrote voluminous correspondence to the War Department defending his actions in the Allegheny Mountains.

Hazard Stevens saw the business differently. He accused Benham of spending most of his time in Washington "claiming everything in the way of credit [for his western Virginia experiences] and loudly importuning the government for high command." The War Department relented, and line command again came to Henry Benham. In April of 1862, the engineer steamed to Port Royal to assume command of the department's Northern District, with Maj. Gen. David Hunter as his sole superior.[8]

Isaac Stevens' road to Port Royal proved equally winding. Although he attended the 1860 Democratic Convention in Charleston and then chaired John Breckinridge's presidential campaign, Stevens was a staunch Unionist who disliked slavery. When hostilities erupted, he immediately offered his services to the War Department. After a frustrating delay, Secretary of War Simon Cameron placed him in command of the fractious 79th New York. Stevens quickly molded the Scotsmen into a first-rate fighting unit, and his undeniable leadership abilities soon landed him in the Southern Expedition as commander of the Second Brigade. One colleague described Stevens as "a small, slight man, very careless as to dress and personal appearance, but the very best organizer and disciplinarian that I ever met. A genial, outspoken man, strong in his likes and dislikes, a warm friend and a bitter unrelenting hater." Commodore Du Pont spoke more pointedly: "Stevens is a tortuous man and very smart."

But besides his novel yet effective handling of the New Year's Day fight at Port Royal Ferry, Stevens stay in the South had consisted largely of outpost duty, and he chafed for action. When he departed the Army of the Potomac, Stevens rejoiced at being out from under the command of George McClellan, an officer the diminutive brigadier found both vascillatory and timid. Suddenly, with the arrival of Hunter and Benham, Stevens found himself in a similiar predicament. Benham's rude rejection of Stevens' Pocotaligo expedition left its designer angered and isolated. Hunter seemed more interested in promoting Radical policies than in promulgating aggressive military moves. Cotton speculators interfered with army business seemingly with Washington's blessings. Fed up with the direction of the Union efforts in the newly designated Department of the South, a distraught Isaac Stevens addressed Oregon Senator James Nesmith, "I rely upon your good offices to get me placed in some position where I can do service." On the eve of a major campaign, this fraying of the Federal command structure couldn't have come at a worse time.[9]

* * *

Such bickering in high command would normally give distinct advantages to an enemy across the way. Unfortunately for the Southern cause, here it wouldn't. Relations among the Confederate authorities in the Spring of 1862 mirrored the turmoil of the Federal command and, again, the problems began at the top. Since taking over the Department of Georgia and South Carolina from Robert E. Lee in early March, Maj. Gen. John Clifford Pemberton had found his new command less than appealing. He had inherited a rather unwieldy department of five geographical districts stretching from Georgetown, South Carolina, to Savannah, Georgia. Giving in to his bureaucratic instincts, the Pennsylvanian-turned-Confederate immediately began a departmental reorganization by dividing one district, combining others, redesignating infantry forces, and adding unnecessary complexity to his new command. Once he completed these reshufflings, Pemberton thrust himself into the machinations of theater command and quickly found himself in hot water.[10]

On March 25, Pemberton ordered 1st District commander Col. Arthur M. Manigault to dismantle the Georgetown batteries up the coast from Charleston and ship the guns and attendant troops to the latter place, thus leaving only 1,600 effectives for Georgetown's local defense. Two days later, he turned his attention to 2nd District Commander Brig. Gen. Roswell Ripley at Charleston. He ordered Ripley to retire the Confederate forces on Coles Island, which protected the mouth of the Stono River, and those on

Battery Island further upriver, and reposition them on James Island just south of town. Both moves were consistent with Lee's dictum to abandon the remote coastal areas in favor of interior defensive works. But both moves caught civilian authorities by surprise and caused heated exchanges between the two camps. When South Carolina Governor Francis Pickens heard that the Coles Island line was to be abandoned, he immediately wired Robert E. Lee, now Jefferson Davis' military advisor in Richmond. Complaining that the new lines of defense then forming on James Island were incomplete, Pickens wanted the Coles Island positions retained until they were fully prepared. Lee diplomatically informed the governor that such decisions were entirely up to the department heads. But concerning the Georgetown withdrawal, Lee felt moved to contact his departmental successor. He advised Pemberton to keep his forces there until the local planters could remove their property safely. Included in the communiqué was a lesson Lee himself had learned well. In the future, Pemberton should consult with the governor to better "preserve harmony between the State and Confederate authorities." Lee's counsel arrived too late to affect the troop movements. On April 5, Manigault reported that he and his 10th South Carolina had already abandoned Georgetown and had arrived in Mt. Pleasant, just north of Charleston. His ordnance would soon arrive by rail.[11]

Pemberton heeded Lee's advice in one respect. He alerted Ripley that the Coles Island armament might remain in place "until they can be fought at Elliot's Cut" on the Stono River. Concerning Georgetown, Pemberton assured Lee that the transferred guns had been too light to defend against the Union Navy, adding that he had kept Pickens fully informed of his intent to abandon the area through the South Carolina military liaison, Brig. Gen. States Rights Gist. Pemberton calmed Lee with assurances that relations between the army and the civilian leaders would be smoother, but closed his report by reiterating his desire to abandon Coles.[12]

One thing Pemberton couldn't control was Richmond's pressing need for additional troops. Confederate reversals and Federal movements along a broad front forced Davis and Lee to milk other less threatened districts for additional infantry. Unfortunately for Pemberton, his superiors regarded his district as just such a place. On April 10, the day Gillmore opened fire on Fort Pulaski, Lee ordered Brig. Gen. Daniel Donelson's Tennessee regiments to Corinth, Mississippi, to help bolster the bloodied Southern ranks in the wake of their sharp defeat at Shiloh. Pemberton complied but ordered Colonel Graham's local defense force from Georgetown to Charleston to offset the loss. Governor Pickens quickly stepped in, arguing that recent additions to Ripley's force, "two raw regiments and also twelve new Charleston companies," should more than compensate for the loss of Donelson's force and thus make Graham's move unnecessary. Moreover, Lee had requested two additional regiments from Ripley's command to accompany the Tennessee contingent. In an attempt to allay the Governor's fears, Pemberton ordered only one battalion of Graham's troops to Charleston. He, however, retained the right to remove the rest of the Georgetown infantry on his own authority. As these pressures mounted, word of the Federal attack on Pulaski forced the beleaguered general to order 4th District commander Brig. Gen. Maxcy Gregg to dismantle a small position on the Ashepoo River called Chapman's Fort and send its guns to Savannah.[13]

While these arguments simmered, Pemberton did what he could to keep district commander Brig. Gen. Nathan "Shanks" Evans in line with departmental strategy, but trouble brewed nonetheless. Both Pemberton and Evans had come to South Carolina in early December 1861 in an effort to bolster Robert E. Lee's officer corps. Where Pemberton was known as a bureaucrat with some engineering experience, Evans brought a hard fighting, hard drinking reputation to the table. Tensions may have risen because Pemberton, a major general since mid-January 1862, now commanded the Department of the South, while Evans only oversaw the 3rd Military District. On April 11, concerned with a possible enemy thrust up the South Edisto River towards the small hamlet of Willstown, Pemberton ordered "Shanks" to concentrate his forces at Rantowles Bridge, a stop on the railroad just west of Charleston. The next day, Evans responded with a reassuring report that dwelt specifically with his understanding of his tactical relationship with Ripley. While recognizing the new Federal presence at Edisto, Evans argued that the line covering his Adam's Run headquarters needed to be retained. So sure was he of his capabilities to defend the area that he actually expressed hope that the enemy would mount an attack near Church Flats. Evans confidently predicted

Maj. Gen. John C. Pemberton, commander of the Department of Georgia and South Carolina. Eleanor S. Brockenbrough Library, The Museum of the Confederacy, Richmond, VA.

that a combination of his own and Ripley's forces would either retard or cut off the attackers. Despite his obvious grasp of the local tactical situation, Evans received brusque orders from Pemberton dated April 15 to conform to the April 11 directive.[14]

As he redeployed his shrinking force to cover his strategic hubs, Pemberton was hit with another request for troops from Richmond. A huge Federal army had landed at Fortress Monroe on the peninsula southeast of the Confederate capital and had

Brig. Gen. Nathan "Shanks" Evans. Massachusetts Commandery, Military Order of the Loyal Legion and the U.S. Army Military History Institute.

marched upon the Confederate stronghold at Yorktown. Lee pressed Pemberton just as Jefferson Davis pressured Governor Pickens, both voicing the need for another full brigade to defend Richmond. Pemberton was feverishly busy dealing with the endemic lack of rifles in his department when Lee's directive arrived. Forced to comply, the Pennsylvanian ordered Maxcy Gregg with the 12th, 13th, and 14th South Carolina to prepare for immediate departure for Virginia. With another large chunk of his manpower about to disappear, Pemberton had to withdraw all of his men, save some cavalry units, from the area between the Ashepoo and the Oketie Rivers. Such action would necessarily lay bare a portion of the Charleston–Savannah Railroad to Federal probes, risking the severance of this important line. Since a planned rail line from Charleston to Augusta, Georgia lay uncompleted, taking such risks left Pemberton distraught; disappointment fairly radiated from his April 23 report to Richmond.[15]

Four days later on the 27th, at his new Charleston headquarters, Pemberton faced yet another crisis. Roswell Ripley, never a happy subordinate, had been lobbying behind the scenes for a transfer out of the department, preferably to a line command in Virginia. Lee wrote to Pemberton regarding Ripley's desires, but the department head responded quickly by begging that he be allowed to retain the irascible South Carolinian. He argued that Ripley's vast knowledge of Charleston's defenses, drawn from a full year of duty there, made him virtually irreplaceable. Pemberton could do with fewer troops, but officers like Ripley—however personally difficult—were desperately needed. For the time being, Ripley's request went unanswered.[16]

As April drew to a close, Pemberton could survey his command and see depleted regiments, quarrelsome subordinates, increasingly angry civilian authorities, and, perhaps worst of all, an enemy beginning to stir. Savannah was one of his few bright spots—notwithstanding the loss of Fort Pulaski. Brigadier General Alexander Lawton's two brigades, defending the newly-formed District of Georgia, exuded confidence and ability. Lawton's two brigadiers, Generals William Duncan Smith and Hugh Mercer, were able officers. But the area north of Savannah and south of James Island, namely the 3rd District under Evans and the newly combined 4th and 5th Districts under Col. Peyon H. Colquitt, had been gutted by

Col. Johnson Hagood, 1st South Carolina Infantry.
Eleanor S. Brockenbrough Library, The Museum of the Confederacy, Richmond, VA.

the recent troop transfers and were now dangerously undermanned. A forlorn Pemberton ended the month by ordering Evans to "Sink the obstructions at Church Flats immediately."[17]

* * *

Colonel Johnson Hagood and his 1st South Carolina had suffered the consequences of the Pemberton-Ripley-Pickens debates of late March. The colonel and his men, one of the first organized units to answer South Carolina's call, had garrisoned Coles Island along with Maj. J. J. Lucas' 3-company artillery battalion since August of 1861. Upon receiving orders to abandon Coles on March 25, Hagood went to work with zeal. Within 48 hours, almost all the batteries were prepared for removal. His speed was commendable, for the colonel had always believed that Coles Island should be defended and that additional batteries on Kiawah and Folly Islands would render the Stono Inlet impregnable. Thus, when his original orders were suddenly countermanded, a relieved Hagood doggedly pushed his men to remount the dismantled guns. As for the contradictory orders, Hagood blamed the business on "outside pressure from the state authorities."[18]

Johnson Hagood had grown used to the friction between the civilian and the military, for, during the course of his life, the colonel had kept a foot in both camps. Born in 1829, he had graduated with the "highest honors" from the South Carolina Military Academy—the famed Citadel—but opted instead to study law. South Carolina's then-governor John Means liked the young lawyer's military background and appointed him deputy adjutant general of the state militia. By the time South Carolina seceded, Hagood had risen to the rank of brigadier general in the militia. As war loomed, the state expected great things from her native son.[19]

Hagood helped to raise and was elected colonel of one of South Carolina's first 12 month regiments, and he marched them off to Morris Island to watch the reduction of Fort Sumter. Soon the unit was caught in a tug of war between Richmond, which wanted the regiment for Confederate service, and Columbia, which wanted to retain the men for state service. Although Hagood and his unit desired service in Virginia, Charleston commander Roswell Ripley regarded the regiment as "indispensable" for the city's defense. By mid-September 1861, Hagood's 1st South Carolina had marched out to Coles Island to man Charleston's southern flank, Hagood held as the Federals began expanding from their Hilton Head base.[20]

While Hagood kept an isolated watch out on Coles, various South Carolinians were raising three year regiments to face down the Federal threat. Clement Hoffman Stevens and Ellison Capers were two such citizens, fixtures of Charleston society who answered their state's call. Born in Connecticut in 1821, Stevens had built a flourishing banking career until the crisis in Charleston harbor unlocked his particular military genius. Generally regarded as the inventor of the ironclad battery that helped reduce Sumter, Stevens also designed and constructed the armored fortifications at Cumming's Point, south of Sumter on Morris Island. The Charlestonian banker accompanied his brother-in-law, Barnard Bee, to Manassas, where he served as a volunteer aide. In the carnage on Henry House Hill, Bee was killed and Stevens severely wounded. Following his recuperation, Stevens became a volunteer aide-de-camp on Roswell Ripley's staff and gained an abundance of knowledge of the harbor's defenses. In November of 1861, however, Stevens resigned his position to raise a new volunteer regiment. Joining him was Ellison Capers, a former lieutenant colonel in state service at the Citadel. Together they negotiated the pitfalls of forging a new military unit out of untrained though highly motivated volunteers. On April 1, 1862, the 24th South Carolina came into being, with Clement H. Stevens serving as its first colonel.[21]

Col. Clement H. Stevens, 24th South Carolina Infantry

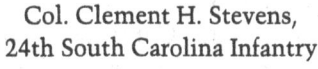

Generals in Gray.

Lt. Col. Ellison Capers, 24th South Carolina Infantry

The Citadel Archives.

In many ways, Ellison Capers epitomized the South Carolina tradition of the citizen-soldier. Born in Charleston in October of 1837, he followed a varied academic path that led to the Citadel, where he graduated first in the class of 1857. Appointed a full professor at his alma mater in 1860, Capers spent much of his spare time studying law and establishing a reputation as an astute legal scholar, although he never went into practice. At the time of secession, Capers was serving as a major in Pettigrew's 1st Regiment South Carolina Rifles, with whom he witnessed the bombardment of Sumter. When Pettigrew resigned to enter Confederate service in Virginia, Capers remained with the unit as lieutenant colonel, but left in November to assist Clement Stevens in the raising of the 24th South Carolina. When that regiment mustered in early April of 1862, Ellison Capers became its lieutenant colonel, an eager 24-year-old officer proudly serving his state and country.[22]

When the 24th arrived for duty in his department, General Ripley dispatched them to Coles Island to relieve Hagood's men. Stevens and Capers marched their regiment across James Island and its many causeways to the Stono Inlet works. There, they joined Lucas' Battery in the entrenchments facing the waterway, while Hagood's 1st South Carolina departed Coles Island and marched to Charleston. The men of the 24th South Carolina spent its first day in the field arranging new camps and acclimating to the surroundings, fully aware that heavily-gunned Federal warships cruised somewhere beyond the bar at the entrance to the river.[23]

Meanwhile, Hagood's regiment fell victim to what one writer recently described as a crisis "unprecedented in the annals of American military history." Units that had answered South Carolina's call in the winter of 1860 and the spring of 1861 were ending their enlistment periods. Such wholesale changes prompted the Confederate government to enact the Bounty and Furlough Act on 1 January 1862. In addition to offering $50 and a 30-to-60 day furlough to any one-year man who reenlisted for two more years, the Act also allowed those troops "to reorganize themselves into companies and elect their company officers, and said companies shall have the power to organize themselves into battalions or regiments and elect their field officers." Hagood's men took full advantage of these new provisions to radically change the body of the unit. Three of Hagood's companies, including the Wee Nee Volunteers and the Edisto Rifles, left the regiment to join the two companies of the famed Washington Light Infantry, an organization with a lineage tracing back to the Revolution. The Washington Light Infantry had served on Coles and Battery Islands side-by-side with the men of Hagood's command, so when the spring reorganizations occurred, the two groupings naturally came together under the title of the Eutaw Battalion. Two of Hagood's other companies that had trained earlier as heavy artillerists joined Thomas Lamar's Battalion of Artillery in manning Fort Johnson and the defense line on James Island. Obviously, such losses threatened the continued existence of Hagood's 1st South Carolina.[24]

Johnson Hagood saw all this movement as a chance for self-serving captains to gain advancement by joining new organizations. Despite the losses, which included the disbanding of one company, two of Hagood's remaining companies divided and recruited up to full strength while four new companies arrived to join the highly regarded regiment. After taking some advantage of the furlough offer, the fully reorganized unit rendezvoused in Bamberg, South Carolina. By May 4, Hagood's 1st South Carolina returned to Charleston, but its duty there was far from what the commander and his men had in mind.[25]

The growing Federal threat on coastal South Carolina led the civilian and military authorities to agree on at least one thing. At

Pemberton's urgings, Jefferson Davis ordered Governor Pickens and his council to declare martial law in Charleston. Pemberton gladly complied and ordered Hagood and his regiment to the city to take up provost duties. The South Carolinian didn't care for the assignment and let his feelings be known, but Pemberton curtly repeated the order. Significantly, one qualification was added: if the 1st South Carolina was needed for active operations, the provost duty would end, and end quickly. Thus, on May 4, Johnson Hagood returned to Charleston, and on the next day he assumed the role of Provost Marshall, with his 1st South Carolina Volunteers camped on the Citadel Green acting as the provost force.[26]

Another Confederate unit with a storied lineage was the 1st South Carolina Battalion, which most would refer to simply as the Charleston Battalion. At its head stood Lt. Col. Peter Gaillard, a 49-year-old graduate of West Point who had spent three years in the Regular Army. During the secession crisis he returned to military service to assume command of a number of Charleston's finest militia units. One such unit, The Irish Volunteers, had fought in the War of 1812. With the election of Lincoln in November of 1860, the Irishmen were moved to pledge their allegiance to the state of South Carolina, lest anyone doubt their loyalty. One of their companies went north with Maxey Gregg's 1st South Carolina, while the other joined the 17th Regiment South Carolina Militia. In the spring reorganization, the latter group returned to Charleston to join the 1st South Carolina Battalion, combining with such units as the Charleston Riflemen, the Union Light Infantry and the Sumter Guards to form the Charleston Battalion. Officially mustered on April 5, 1862, it marched off for James Island, where one witness was "highly gratified with the performance of their evolutions" on dress parade. Promised the writer, "The Battalion is admirably drilled and disciplined, and will doubtless make their mark on the enemy; and do honor to their mother city, if the chances of war shall afford them an opportunity."[27]

*   *   *

On April 22, Federal Gen. David Hunter sat in the department headquarters at Hilton Head and contemplated his prospects along the South Atlantic coast. From Fernandina, Florida, to Edisto

Island, he could count a variety of commands at his disposal. Lieutenant Colonel Louis Bell and a detachment from the 4th New Hampshire camped south of Fernandina, the southern tip of Hunter's flank. Garrisoning the port of Fernandina was Col. Richforth Rich and his 9th Maine. Hunter's main force lay further north. Quincy Gillmore at Fort Pulaski commanded 2,133 troops that included the 46th New York, the 7th Connecticut, and elements of the 3rd Rhode Island. Brigadier General Egbert Viele led 3,073 men on and near Daufuskie Island, regiments that included the 48th New York and the 6th Connecticut. Colonel Robert Williams of the 1st Massachusetts Cavalry commanded the 2,067 infantrymen occupying the massive military port on Hilton Head; among his brigade were the 76th Pennsylvania and the officially independent 28th Massachusetts. Isaac Stevens and his brigade covered Port Royal Island. His effectives from the 8th Michigan, the 100th Pennsylvania, the 79th New York, and the 50th Pennsylvania numbering 3,874. Hunter's northern flank was commanded by Brig. Gen. Horatio Wright, who had fully occupied Edisto, Little Edisto, and Otter Island on the 21st of April with the 3,616 men of the 3rd New Hampshire, the 47th New York, and the 45th, 55th and 97th Pennsylvania regiments.[28]

Maj. Gen. David Hunter
Massachusetts Commandery, Military Order of the Loyal Legion and the U.S. Army Military History Institute

Hunter had spent thirty-four years in the Regular Army and was an acquaintance of Abraham Lincoln, but he had come to the

Southeast Atlantic theater almost by default. A brigadier at First Manassas and a major general in command of the Western Department, Hunter eventually landed in the Department of Kansas when the Western Department was broken up. In March of 1862, Maj. Gen. Henry Halleck, who Hunter ranked, was placed at the head of the newly-formed Department of Mississippi. Protocol demanded action, and Hunter was recalled to Washington. His politics made him a darling of the Radical Republicans, and he soon found himself in command of the Union forces that made up the Department of the South.

On one hand, Hunter was somewhat reassured by the quality of the commands under his authority. Most of these troops had landed back in November of 1861 and were now entering their seventh month of campaigning and training on the South Atlantic seaboard. Only a few, the 1st Massachusetts Cavalry and the 28th Massachusetts, for example, had arrived relatively recently. Almost all had trained to a decent state of readiness and morale was high, although experience under fire was distinctly lacking. On the other hand, Hunter was perplexed as to Confederate intentions. His own intelligence estimates placed 25,000 enemy troops in the Charleston theater and another 10,000 near Augusta, Georgia. With the enemy massed in such numbers, Hunter could only assume that an attack was forthcoming. Indeed, in a letter to Secretary of War Edwin Stanton, Hunter wondered openly, "Why they do not attack us. . .is a mystery to me." And yet, an intercepted Confederate communiqué contained a line that signaled just possibly the opposite: "A profound quiet seems to have rested over our armies at all points the last few days." Did this cryptic line imply Southern passivity? Hunter's confusion as to Confederate intentions can be somewhat excused. He and his chief subordinate, Henry Benham, were recent arrivals themselves, so a certain period of adjustment could be expected. However, a second line in the captured communiqué suggested an ominous turn in the near future: "such profound quiet. . .may be and probably is the awful stillness that precedes the storm."[29]

One of the Federal soldiers in the area that May, the 8th Michigan's Pvt. Benjamin Pease, remembered that "The whole of the month. . .was spent very pleasantly." Besides the occasional artillery exchanges with small Confederate artillery units, life on

Port Royal Island had been nearly idyllic. Little fighting, light picket duty, and the rare scout made this a time of ease for the soldiers camping from Beaufort to Port Royal Ferry. On a warm Monday afternoon, May 13, some members of the 8th Michigan stripped off their uniforms and went bathing in the Coosaw River. In midswim, the soldiers caught sight of a smoke-belching steamer coming from the direction of the Atlantic. Realizing that Union vessels used smokeless anthracite coal, the swimmers feared that a Confederate transport had eluded the Federal blockade and was now bearing down on them. Private Pease recalled, "(w)e thought it best to make ourselves scarce." Scrambling out of the river water, the men were equally surprised as the vessel drew closer, for she flew the National colors. The steamer turned south into Brickyard Creek towards the riverfront of Beaufort, leaving the Michiganders wondering as to the identity of the curious ship. Time would supply the answer.[30]

* * *

One of the first tasks for Col. Clement Stevens and his 24th South Carolina on Coles Island was the construction of a second causeway connecting their isolated position to the mainland. When he and his men first arrived, they had been forced to march the length of Sol Legare Island just south of James Island, cross a low bridge to Battery Island, then follow a twisting causeway paralleling the Stono across a series of smaller rises in the thick marshland to Coles Island. If Battery Island somehow fell to a sudden Federal rush, the 24th would be completely cut off from the mainland. To avoid such a possibility, Stevens constructed a more direct walkway, proceeding by way of Dixon Island. Coles Island now had two escape routes to James Island.[31]

The 24th South Carolina had spent a rather uneventful four weeks in their new surroundings, but orders received on May 6 put an end to their routine. After the months of debate within the Confederate high command, Pemberton finally made good on his promise to remove Coles' valuable artillery to the mainland. The decision to abandon the island was met with widespread disapproval—especially among Charleston's citizenry. Carolinian politician and writer William John Grayson colorfully vented his disapproval: "This is another example of weakness and vacillation in our military rulers; one erects a fortification at enormous expense and another destroys it. Our waggon has a team hitched to each end and they draw in opposite directions—what will become of the waggon?" Despite the prevailing public opinion, Roswell Ripley reluctantly gave the orders to dismantle the positions and prepare the cannon for transport to other points in the region. Some of the pieces would go to the new defense works commanding the Stono near Elliot's Cut. Others would head for Charleston and the harbor defenses. Still others would be remanded to Major E. B. White to be distributed along the James Island lines. Wherever the guns went, Pemberton could finally rest easy knowing that they were now beyond Federal reach.[32]

Clement Stevens took a week to dismantle the 17 guns on Coles and the two pieces on Battery Island. With the guns' transfer from Stono Inlet, Major Lucas marched his three companies of artillerymen off Coles on the 10th and took up post in the new works near Elliot's Cut. Stevens' men remained, and by May 12, their work neared completion. On that day, a small vessel named the *Planter* arrived to transport four of the pieces to the Middle Ground Battery, or Fort Ripley, in Charleston Harbor. Once the pieces were loaded, the *Planter* moved off, belching a column of black smoke into the Carolina sky. With the armament gone, the soldiers of the 24th South Carolina needed little more evidence to realize that Coles would soon be abandoned. Strangely, at 11:00 a.m. the next day, those same men observed the *Planter* out in the Atlantic, steaming hard to the south. This sighting raised enough of a question that someone forwarded a report to headquarters. Why would the *Planter* be heading towards enemy territory? Again, time would reveal the answer.[33]

* * *

The *Planter* had been one of many Confederate vessels used for military transport in the Charleston Harbor area. Swift and of shallow draft, the steamer mounted a 32-pounder on a pivot complemented by a 24-pounder howitzer, but she could hardly be considered a true gunboat. The ship was used by Roswell Ripley to distribute dispatches, and she also transported both men and materiel around the harbor and along the coast. The captain, mate, and engineer led a crew of five black men that included an industrious and intelligent pilot named Robert Smalls. When the vessel left Coles Island on May 12 with the four guns aboard, she headed back to Charleston Harbor to her usual berth on the so-called Southern Wharf. There the crew loaded aboard 200 lbs. of ammunition and 20 cords of wood. Although general orders forbade a ship's captain and crew from spending the night ashore, those in charge of the transport did exactly that, leaving Smalls and his comrades aboard by themselves.[34]

Nearly a month before, one of the crew members had quipped that the *Planter* could be easily stolen if events fell just right. That remark had prompted Smalls to action, and after a series of clandestine meetings at his home, he and his crew developed a plot to pilot their ship out of Charleston harbor to freedom. On the night of May 12, Smalls put his plan into action. In preparation, he had secreted his wife and child, four other women, and another child aboard the *Etiwan*, a vessel that was docked at Charleston's North Atlantic Wharf. Around 3:00 a.m. the next morning, he ordered the crew to raise the Confederate and Palmetto flags, then fire the boilers. Although they did as they were told, the crew members voiced concern that the rising smoke would arouse suspicion. Smalls ignored their fears and backed the *Planter* out of her berth and into the channel, going so far as to blow her whistle to retain the appearance of routine. To everyone's relief, no one on shore, including a Confederate sentinel not 50 yards away, seemed to take notice of the unauthorized action. Smalls then eased the ship over to the North Atlantic Wharf and brought the women and children aboard. With that, he piloted the *Planter* into the darkness of Charleston Harbor.

Navigating the currents of the waterfront, the transport cleared Fort Ripley, the intended destination of her four guns. Again, no alarm was raised. They passed Fort Johnson where Smalls blew the steam whistle to retain the semblance of normalcy. With the screech of the signal echoing across the placid waters, Smalls murmured, "Oh Lord, we entrust ourselves into thy hands." Again, no one ashore took notice of the *Planter*'s movements. As early strands of light brushed the eastern sky, the vessel, now miles from

Charleston, steamed through the channel past Fort Sumter and headed for the open sea. The crew gave the normal signal—two long whistles followed by one short whistle—as they passed the fort. To complete the ruse, Robert Smalls donned his captain's straw hat and stood at the command post with his back to the fort and arms crossed, appearing for all to see as the master of a vessel embarked on routine business. The sentinel at Sumter reported the *Planter*'s presence to the officer of the day, but no alarm was raised by the vessel's appearance. Smalls' plan had worked perfectly.

Generally, a vessel heading out of Charleston Harbor would turn south past Sumter and run along the beach of Morris Island. Once Smalls had the *Planter* past the fort, however, he steered straight out the Swash Channel directly towards the Federal blockading squadron. In a quick motion, one of the crew lowered the Confederate and South Carolina flags and raised a white bed sheet. Suddenly, Smalls and his crew were beyond the reach of Confederate military authority, beyond the reach of South Carolina power. Suddenly, Smalls and his crew were free.[35]

Amidst the Federal blockading vessels, Lt. J. F. Nickels stood on the deck of his command, the *USS Onward*, and peered out into the faint morning light. It was 5:45 a.m. From the west, making a run out of Charleston Harbor, came a steamer heading directly for his ship. The skipper beat the crew to quarters and ordered the broadside brought to bear on the approaching vessel. Tension ebbed when the growing light revealed a flag of truce flying from the vessel's staff. Nickels allowed the steamer to draw up next to the Onward. When the unidentified vessel hove to, Nickels jumped aboard and immediately replaced the white flag with the national colors. Three cheers for the flag erupted from the group of blacks crewing the vessel. An astonished Nickels discovered that the vessel was the *Planter*, late of Charleston, and that these former slaves had evidently commandeered the ship, cargo and all, with the intention of surrendering it to the Federal blockaders. In addition, four large unmounted cannon lay on the ship's deck. Nickels left Acting Master Watson aboard the newly freed steamer, then contacted E. G. Parrott, the commander of the Charleston blockaders, to refer the matter higher up. In the meantime, Nickels sent the *Planter* with her bold captain to Port Royal to report directly to Flag Officer Du Pont himself.[36]

At 11:00 a.m., Robert Smalls piloted his ship past Stono Inlet in sight of Coles Island, where just the day before he and his crew had been engaged as slaves. Perhaps they could see the lookouts of the 24th South Carolina, for the lookouts certainly saw the steamer making her way across the waves of the South Atlantic. Later that day, the *Planter* turned into the Coosaw River where she startled the bathers of the 8th Michigan before heading south down Brickyard Creek towards Beaufort and Port Royal Sound.

At 10:20 on the evening of May 13, Flag Officer Samuel Du Pont was making a journal entry to his wife. An aide interrupted to request the officer's presence on deck, because an unknown vessel had just arrived from the Beaufort River. Du Pont went above to join a gathering of naval personnel, all busy trying to guess the identity of the mystery ship. In Du Pont's mind, the uncomfortable possibility loomed that this vessel was the phantom Confederate ironclad said to be based out of Savannah. But to the relief of all, a small transport identifying herself as the *Planter* out of Charleston drew up next to the Wabash. Soon the story of Robert Smalls and his crew of former slaves had the sailors on the *Wabash* marveling at the pluck of the brave band.

As the news spread among the Federal crew, Smalls began to reveal details of the Charleston defenses that no Federal intelligence had been able to ascertain. The declaration of martial law in Charleston raised eyebrows, but then Smalls began to really attract attention. Du Pont heard firsthand that "(b)ut a few thousand troops (were) left, all (the rest) drawn to Tennessee and Virginia." This was an astonishing piece of intelligence that strongly contradicted Hunter's estimates. And Smalls wasn't finished. He revealed that Coles Island and its batteries, the long standing protectors of Stono Inlet and Charleston's southern flank, had been abandoned! An avenue of attack to the very gates of Charleston now lay open and unguarded. In a few short moments, Robert Smalls and his group of former slaves handed an unsuspecting David Hunter and Frank Du Pont the key to Charleston's back door.[37]

CHAPTER TWO

"I think it literally impossible for him to conduct this military department."

—Federal Flag Officer Samuel Francis Du Pont

The Island and the Railroad

James Island has been colorfully described as land desperately seeking water and water desperately seeking land. Standing along the Stono River near Battery Island and gazing east across the island's ragged terrain, one can easily see how perfectly fitting that description really is. It is the confluence of water and land that defines James Island, that gives it its character, and as much as any soldier who came here to fight, it was the terrain that determined the battle for the island. On her northern extreme, James is separated from the mainland by Wappoo Cut and a small canal near the Stono called Elliot's Cut. From there, the Stono and Charleston Harbor guide the island's flanks southerly until another watercourse, the Newtown Cut/James Island Creek, intersects the terrain with its own marshy windings. While the Stono steers her western border almost directly south, on the harbor side the bell-like outline of the island fans easterly all the way to its southern border on Lighthouse Creek, a meandering tidal wash.

Two peninsulas marking the midpoint of the southern border rise up from wetlands fed by the Folly River's two adjuncts, Big and

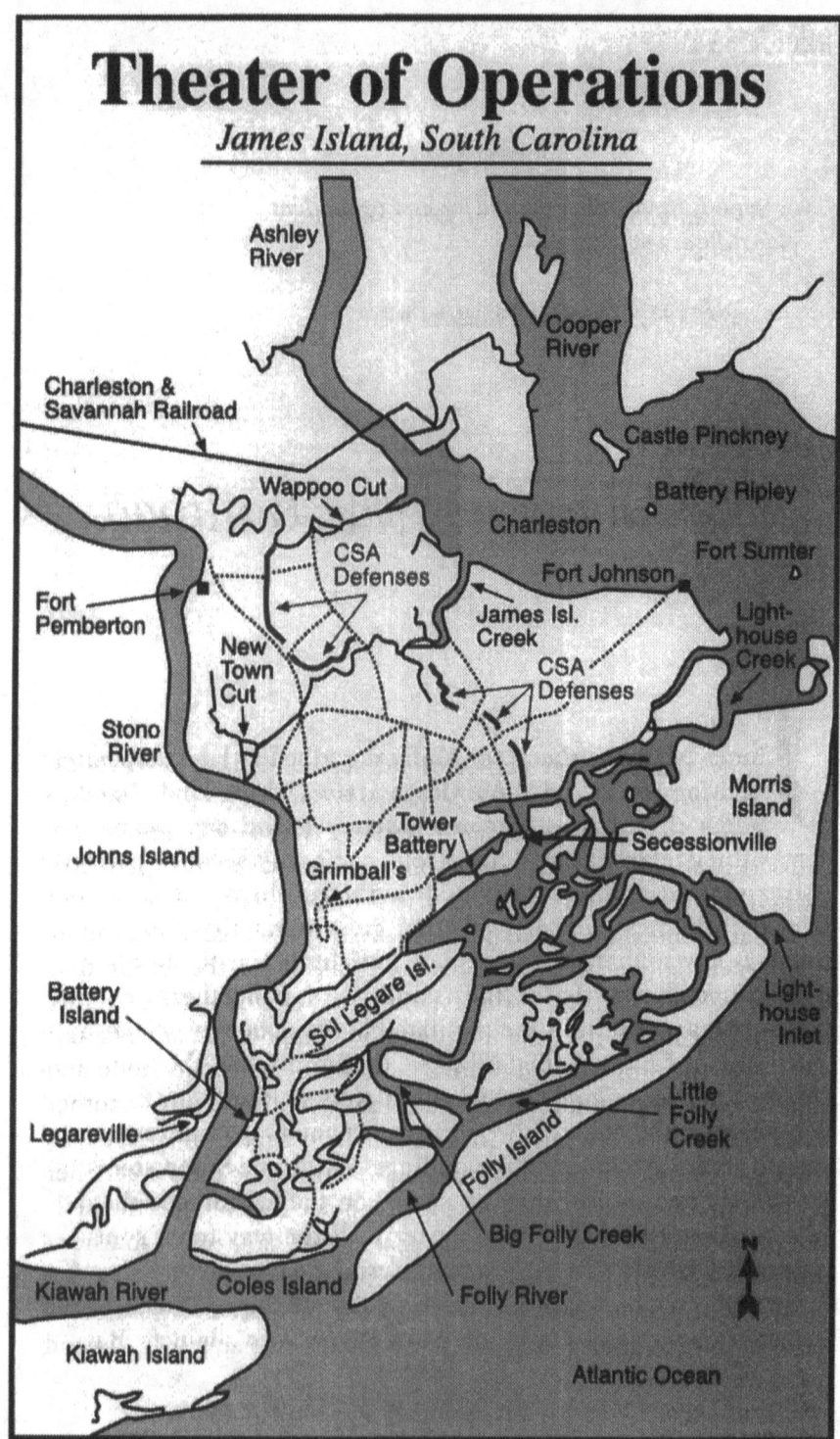

Little Folly Creeks; this same marsh separates James from the narrow Sol Legare Island to the south. From here, the island gives way to a confusing morass of wetland and sand ridges separating it from Morris Island to the southeast and Folly Island to the south. Battery Island lies on the Stono, just south and west of Sol Legare. Long Island stretches east of Big Folly Creek. South of Battery Island and northwest of Folly Island is Coles Island, a thin beachhead that forms the triangular mouth of the Stono with the eastern point of Kiawah Island. Innumerable smaller masses dot the creek-cut wetlands, all sustained by the Atlantic's tides.[1]

History has marked James Island. By the mid-1600's, generations of Indian tribes that had lined the shore of the Stono River gave way to English settlers. The newcomers carved farms and plantations from the tangled fields and forests covering the island. Soon, the names of the owners of these new establishments, names like Paul Grimball and William Rivers, began to appear on the rough maps of "Boone's" Island, in honor of an early inhabitant. In 1693, the island was re-named "James" for the brother of Charles II.[2]

When the infant colony of Charles Town was threatened in 1706 by a combined French/Spanish/Indian force operating from Florida, the need for harbor defenses led to the construction of Fort Johnson on James Island. Located at Windmill Point on the harbor between James Island Creek and Lighthouse Creek, the fort never came under fire but did witness the expansion of the nearby plantations, as an increasing slave population worked the fields producing indigo and rice. Indeed, by the time of the Revolutionary War, blacks comprised 60%-70% of the James Island populace.[3]

When war between the American colonies and the motherland broke out, the British viewed the area as a serious strategic target. In 1780, an English army operating from Seabrook Island crossed James Island near Wappoo Cut and marched on Fort Johnson, easily forcing its capitulation. Eventually the British marched north and crossed the Ashley River to invest Charleston from the rear. After a particularly bitter siege, the British forced the city's surrender on May 12, 1780, and Charleston would remain in enemy hands until the end of hostilities.[4]

After the war, the planters on James discovered what was to become known as Sea Island cotton, a longer-fibered crop that commanded six times the price of the upland strain. Suddenly, the value of James Island plantations skyrocketed, and the planters lucky enough to own land there grew wealthy overnight. Cotton production not only increased dramatically, but also demanded more slaves to work the burgeoning fields. James Island became a series of bald-cut, evenly tilled cotton rows, hemmed in by the ever-present marshlands, the winding creeks and rivers, man-made ditches and hedges, and the remaining stands of forest.[5]

As families like the Grimball's, the Clark's, and the Hill's ran these flourishing enterprises, another discovery created a more pronounced division in the area's social order. The residents of the barrier islands felt that the sea breezes helped negate the brutal summer fevers that seemed to rise up out of the swamps. Small villages built by the planters and located to take advantage of the ocean fronts sprung up on James, one such being founded at Stent's Point on the peninsula marking part of the island's southeastern edge. Originally called Riversville, the village was later rechristened Secessionville, although the exact reason for the name change is shrouded in legend. One story held that the James Island planters simply "seceded" from their plantations to the village for the summer. Another claimed that two youthful residents—Horace Rivers and Edward Freer—had "seceded" from the company of their elders, most of whom had settled near Fort Johnson, and established residence on the peninsula. A third source for the village's name, that it came "from the abortive secession movement of 1851-2," seems more fitting. There is even some evidence that the name came from the 1860 secession crisis. Whatever the reason, seven families had built well-to-do retreats along the peninsula's southern tip to take advantage of the "refreshing sea breezes." It might have been a place of "cool and salubrious summer residence(s)," but by the time of the Sumter crisis, the name of the summer village of Secessionville came to reflect perfectly the heated emotions of the time.[6]

By the spring of 1862, the Federal advance up the coast from Port Royal forced the evacuation of the planters and most of the slaves inhabiting James Island. For months, the Yankee threat had seemed remote to Confederate forces garrisoning the island. But Maj. Gen. David Hunter, like a gambler holding someone else's cards, played on with Brig. Gen. Thomas Sherman's old hand. Armed with Robert Small's intelligence, and driven by both

Benham's desire for action and the shadow of Thomas Sherman's failure, Hunter determined to march his force in the British footsteps of 1780, hoping to duplicate the English success.

War had come again to James Island.

* * *

Roswell Ripley had as little faith in John Pemberton as he had had in Robert E. Lee, but he was supremely confident in his own ability to hold the James Island defenses against any group of Federals in the world. Under his direction, an engineering force had constructed a defensive line that split the island in approximately equal halves. Captain J. W. Gregorie, who had had a difficult time managing the defenses at Port Royal, oversaw the buildup of these fortifications. From a point on the Stono near Wappoo Cut, Gregorie laid out an entrenched line supported by a series of redoubts that ran directly south to the banks of Newtown Cut. The lines re-emerged south of Newtown Cut, and further to the east another series of redoubts and an adjoining entrenchment facing south and west arched all the way to Lighthouse Inlet. Two fortifications anchored each flank of this line. Resting on the Stono in advance of the defenses' northern terminus stood Ft. Pemberton. To the south, Col. Lewis Hatch had placed a small fort on the neck of the Secessionville peninsula, well south and forward from the main line's left flank on Lighthouse Inlet.

To connect this isolated post with its supporting garrisons, Hatch had constructed a causeway running across the marsh from a point west of the main line near the Clark House to the rear of the peninsula. By necessity, the long causeway was narrow, allowing for only a single file, but Hatch realized that to properly maintain the outpost, something better than a water-based supply line would be needed. Unfortunately the colonel had taken some criticism for the location of the Secessionville work, which became known as the Tower Battery by virtue of the reconnaissance platform built directly behind it. Nonetheless, he stuck by his decision and wisely so. The Secessionville peninsula not only enfiladed the southern portion of the Confederate main defensive line but also provided access to a water route to the Confederate rear. Isolated though it was, the Tower Battery commanded a critically strategic piece of ground.[7]

Roadways crisscrossed both James and Sol Legare Islands. Two roads ran south from the Fort Pemberton area, one that roughly paralleled the Stono and another that lay behind the Confederate line and crossed Newtown Cut at Dill's Bluff. The former course crossed the Cut near the Stono, where one branch called Camp Road broke off in an easterly direction towards the Confederate lines, while the other continued south. Eventually this second branch curved east and became the King's Highway, the major east-west route across the island, which extended to Fort Johnson on Charleston Harbor. Just west of the Confederate works, the Camp Road reunited with the Highway.

At Battery Island on the southwestern extremity, a road snaked east from the Stono then passed over to Sol Legare Island where it eventually split into two tangents. One crossed north to James Island via the Grimball Causeway and continued on to the plantation of the same name. From Grimball's, a rough farm track broke from the main road and angled east towards Secessionville. Just to the north, the farm road split, with one branch running north towards Ft. Pemberton while the other veered northeasterly to connect with the King's Highway. The second tangent on Sol Legare, generally referred to as Battery Island Road, ran a half-mile along the southern border of the island then bent north, crossing to James Island on the Rivers causeway. Turning east, it approached to within 1,000 yards of the Secessionville works before working north. Running west of the Confederate lines, it, too, intersected the King's Highway and continued north to its terminus at a public landing on James Island Creek. A Federal assault force advancing on these roads would encounter any number of menacing earthworks. Could these entrenchments defend James Island against the Northern invasion and, by doing so, save Charleston from certain capitulation? Roswell Ripley was determined to find out.[8]

The abandonment of Coles Island meant that additional, badly needed ordnance and cannon would be available to James Island gunners. Ripley parceled out the guns to his battery commanders: Maj. J. J. Lucas now, at Fort Pemberton; Maj. E. B. White of White's South Carolina Battalion of Artillery, commanding east and west of

Newtown Cut; and Thomas G. Lamar, fresh from service at Ft. Johnson and now newly installed at Tower Battery.[9]

Placed in overall command of James Island was an officer of great promise, the newly commissioned Brig. Gen. States Rights Gist. As a young man, Gist had attended Harvard University, but had returned south after graduation to serve as the adjutant and Inspector General of the South Carolina militia until the war. His performance during the Sumter crisis greatly impressed his superiors. Gist then accompanied Barnard Bee north to Manassas, where, in the heat of battle, he was given command of the decimated 4th Alabama. Returning to South Carolina to organize new units, Gist was promoted to Confederate brigadier on March 20, 1862. A month later he reported to Ripley, and by May was headquartered in Secessionville commanding the James Island defenses.[10]

On May 14, the day after the *Planter* had escaped from Charleston, Gist pulled most of Colonel Stevens' 24th South Carolina off Coles Island and relocated them nearer Secessionville. He then placed two rifle companies under Lt. Col. Ellison Capers on Coles Island with orders to contest small enemy movements but to retreat before any larger ones. Gist also removed the guns from Battery Island and placed them on James Island, thus completing the evacuation of the original Confederate defense line. He buttressed the James Island works east of the creek with four companies from Thomas Lamar's battalion, and positioned an 18-pound artillery piece in the Secessionville works. Despite this difficult assignment, States Rights Gist wholeheartedly sub-

Brig. Gen. States Rights Gist

Eleanor S. Brockenbrough Library,
The Museum of the Confederacy,
Richmond, VA

scribed to Lee and Pemberton's defensive strategy and diligently went about implementing it.[11]

At Secessionville, the companies that had transferred from Hagood's regiment to the Eutaw Battalion arrived in early May under the command of Lt. Col. Charles H. Simonton. They found life here easier than their duty on Coles Island. One writer gushed, "The peninsula furnishes a most admirable and perfectly delightful camp ground. It is level, and affords a fine pasture for horses and cattle. The wild clover and other grasses grow there, spontaneously and luxuriently. Fish and crabs, (sea and stone,) of the finest kind and quality abound in the adjacent waters, and oysters (delicious bi-valve) crowd the mud banks, furnishing luxuries for both the planter and the soldier." But, Gist often assigned them "a most disagreeable and tiresome picket duty...which was done in small boats at night...with scarcely room enough to even change your position, for at least ten hours." But the men philosophically accepted such hardships, for they had completed a full year of duty on Coles Island and were well acquainted with the difficulties of service in the field.[12]

While their comrades labored with a group of impressed slaves to complete James Island's extensive works, Capers' men kept up a lonely vigil on Coles. The 15th and 16th of May had passed uneventfully, but ominous signs began to appear on the 17th. Enemy barges arrived at the mouth of the Stono and began sounding the channel. Confederate sharpshooters fired on one of the vessels and hastened its departure, but the increased activity indicated fresh Federal interest in the area. A day passed, and then on the 19th, a squadron of enemy gunboats attempted to enter the river. However, when one vessel appeared to ground on the bar, they all turned back. May 20 dawned, and the Confederates continued to scour the inlet. From the Atlantic, the gunboats appeared again. Swinging up from the south, they pushed across the bar, and, at 10:00 a.m., ran into the Stono River. The Confederates on Coles could do little but observe and send reports back to their commanders. There was little doubt now that the Federals, after a sputtering start, had begun their first sustained reconnaissance of James Island's southwestern flank.[13]

* * *

Lt. Col. Charles Simonton and members of the Washington Light Infantry, taken early in the war.

Washington Light Infantry, Charleston, SC.

Reacting to the intelligence borne by the *Planter*, a cautious Flag Officer Du Pont decided to test Confederate defenses. On May 15, he ordered gunboat Cmdr. J. B. Marchand to organize a probe of the Stono Inlet. With his usual strategic acuity, Du Pont guessed that if the Confederates had abandoned Coles Island, they also would have vacated Battery Island. Marchand moved quickly. On the 17th, he dispatched some barges across the bar to sound the channel. Two days later, he attempted to cross the bar with some deeper draft gunboats but was unable to find the channel. Despite the setback, the commander awaited the 20th, knowing full well that once he found the passage over the bar, he would finally come to grips with the distant Secessionists.[15]

With the dawn of the 20th, Marchand ordered Charles Boutelle of the U. S. Coast Survey to lead the *Unadilla*, the *Pembina*, and the *Ottawa*, all veterans of the November Port Royal engagement, across the bar and into the Stono. By 11:00 a.m., the three vessels successfully navigated their way to the confluence of the Stono and the Kiawah Rivers, where they dropped anchor. Across the shimmering waters, the watchful Northerners observed the Confederate buildings on Coles Island explode in flames, sending plumes of black smoke into the mid-day sky. Commander Marchand then arrived to join the trio of boats as they steamed up the Stono, the first Unionists to test this Carolina tributary. The flotilla passed the abandoned hamlet of Legareville standing off to port on Johns Island. Further up the Stono, near the bend opposite Johns Island lay the hump of Battery Island, the ships' gunners launched an occasional shot at a few enemy pickets. As the Federals approached, more flames swirled up from the former Southern works, confirming the position's abandonment. The vessels pushed past the smoking riverside and ran up to a line of sunken obstructions blocking the river. Although a brief inspection revealed a passage through the pylons, Marchand reversed the squadron's course and headed back to the river's mouth, satisfied with the day's work but eagerly anticipating the next thrust. In his mind, a quick rush of Federal infantry across James Island and a lightning assault on Fort Johnson would virtually ensure the fall of Charleston. On this 20th of May, anchored at dusk in the waters of the Stono, Marchand could envision a glorious conclusion to the Southern Expedition.[15]

* * *

Confederate Lt. Col. Ellison Capers counted himself fortunate that his Coles Island detachment hadn't been trapped by the Federal Naval sortie. With the appearance of the gunships, he had ordered his men to fall back. Since the enemy now commanded the Battery Island causeway, they were forced to make their retreat "on the qui vive" to James Island via the Dixon Island footbridge. Further north, the small detachment of Confederates manning Battery Island hustled across the short walkway to Sol Legare Island, just as the Union gunboats—"shelling in all directions at intervals"—steamed up the Stono. In parting, the Southerners fired what buildings they could. Columns of smoke drifted up from the two islands as the Southerners snaked across the marshes toward their new perimeter near Secessionville. During the withdrawal, Brig. Gen. Gist lingered near Battery Island to watch the Federal gunboats proceed all the way up to the obstructions blocking the Stono, where they turned and headed back down the river. Unknown to Gist, excited Confederate gunners at a marsh battery near the Folly River had panicked and heaved their carronade into the river, the only real casualty during the day-long withdrawal.[16]

That night at his Secessionville headquarters, Colonel Stevens of the 24th South Carolina received orders from Ripley to re-establish his regiment on Battery Island in order to keep track of the Federal activity on the Stono. Since Capers' men had already informed the colonel of the enemy's strength, Stevens sensed no immediate danger and put off action until the next day.[17]

The following morning, Stevens divided Captain Jones' Company F into four squads and placed them in positions ranging from Battery Island to the Rivers Causeway nexus. Six pickets were posted at the burnt fort on Battery Island. All was quiet until 11:00 a.m., when word from the pickets alerted Jones to both the reappearance of the flotilla and the approach of a smaller vessel launched from one of the gunboats. As the Captain moved to organize a relief for the suddenly threatened pickets, one of the enemy ships steamed slightly north of Battery Island and drew close to the shore in a position to enfilade the causeway connecting the island with Sol Legare's. To Jones's chagrin, the enemy opened a fire of shrapnel and grape, "completely cutting off all communication with the pickets and closing their line of retreat." Jones and his men could only duck.[18]

Eventually the Federals ceased firing and pulled away. The Confederates gingerly approached Battery Island and found severe damage. Not surprisingly, the six pickets had vanished, likely captured by the raiders. Jones posted another group of pickets at the charred fort and probably admonished them to be more watchful than the last. Through the rest of the day, the Confederates patrolled Battery and Sol Legare Islands, cautiously scanning the Stono for any sight of Federals. Towards evening, Stevens pulled Jones' company back to the safety of the entrenchments, putting them beyond the range of Federal naval guns. Unfortunately, nothing could undo the day's events: the Federals had forced the Stono and taken prisoners to boot.[19]

* * *

Charles Boutelle of the U. S. Coast Survey had resumed his sounding of the Stono on the 21st. His small gig and the *U.S.S. Bibb* followed the route the navy had taken the day before and eventually drew up to Battery Island. There Boutelle went to work marking the channel. Soon the *Unadilla* pulled abreast of the work party. As Boutelle boarded the steamer to pilot it through the river obstructions, he ordered the sailors in his gig, accompanied now by an armed party, to investigate the former Southern position on Battery Island. The *Unadilla* then pushed upriver and passed beyond the obstructing pylons. Suddenly, all attention was drawn to the *Ottawa*, which had maneuvered to a point just above the charred Rebel fort and had begun shelling the rear of the island. The *Unadilla* quickly reversed course to position herself for action. As she drew near, however, the small surveying vessel was seen pulling away from the shoreline and making swiftly for the gunboats. When the gig drew abreast of the *Unadilla*, the eight man crew shepherded aboard six shaken Confederates.[20]

John Bradford, the crew chief, stepped forward to relate the tale of the events ashore. When the gig had landed, he, his recorder Boyd, and a quartermaster named Thomas Davis, had approached a bushy area on the island. To their surprise, the trio spotted a Confederate soldier lurking in the underbrush. Working something of a bluff, Boyd called out for the soldier to surrender. To their surprise and relief, the Confederate did just as he was told. Moreover, he revealed that a number of his comrades were hiding in a magazine not ten feet away. This turn of events put the Unionists in a rather tricky position. Looking about, they could see a squad of enemy cavalry approaching a causeway from the high ground to the east. More Confederates were visible in nearby bushes. Thinking quickly, the trio called back to the gig for assistance. Five armed sailors appeared and helped hustle six members of the 24th South Carolina aboard the vessel. Fortunately, the gunboat *Ottawa* had observed the approaching enemy horsemen and held them off with an accurate series of salvos. Bradford was then able to steer for the *Unadilla*, and deposit his prisoners.[21]

The *Unadilla* and the *Bibb* worked their way back down the Stono to a point near Coles Island, where the *Unadilla* anchored while the *Bibb* continued on past the bar. With the first shots fired, the first positions taken, and the first enemy captives secured, the Union flotilla could relax for a moment. As had been the case with most of their earlier engagements, the opening Federal efforts in the battle for Charleston had met with success.[22]

But, Federal successes would continue only if relations remained harmonious between the army and the navy. Heretofore, the two services and their commanders had been able to coordinate transport and conduct small coastal operations with a minimum of friction. Unfortunately, at this critical juncture, cooperation between the two services collapsed. At the heart of the discord lay faulty communication among the three senior commanders. On the one hand, Brig. Gen. Henry Benham had begun to seethe over what he perceived to be naval indifference to the army's transport needs. By the same token, Flag Officer Du Pont had begun to bristle at Benham's brusque assumptions concerning the timetable of the assault. By delegating all planning responsibility to Benham, Maj. Gen. David Hunter had essentially removed himself from the communication loop. The result was chaos.

* * *

On the surface, Henry Benham's plan for the assault on Charleston seemed simple enough. Brigadier General Horatio

Wright would concentrate his scattered division on Edisto Island while Stevens' division boarded transports at Port Royal. Together they would, in Benham's words, "with a bound as it were...spring upon" James Island. After studying the intelligence estimates provided by Robert Smalls, Hunter approved the concept. All that was needed was an immediate conference with Du Pont to arrange for the necessary transports. Unfortunately for Hunter and Benham, Frank Du Pont had his own priorities. On the 16th, after engaging in a minor skirmish with the army over boarding procedures, the flag officer ordered Marchand to make the Stono reconnaissance. But by the 19th Du Pont had departed on a coastal inspection, leaving Capt. C. R. P. Rodgers in command at Port Royal. When Benham learned of the flag officer's absence, he exploded and immediately began to bombard Rodgers with a series of written requests which—in Du Pont's absence—the captain refused to honor. Stung by the rebuff, Benham decided to present his plans to Rodgers in person; if Du Pont's coastal inspection was more important than the organization of the attack force, so be it. Benham possessed enough rank to force a planning conference on the navy commander's second in command.[23]

The request put Rodgers in a delicate position, but he managed to extricate himself diplomatically. Rodgers wrote Du Pont on the 20th, "This [meeting], of course I have carefully avoided doing, nor shall I meet with him if I can help it during your absence." According to Rodgers, Benham had been outraged and had responded with extremely discourteous language. In his note to Rodgers, the general had complained that Du Pont's absence at such a critical point would force a suspension of the planned operation. He noted further that the withdrawal of the gunboats from the Savannah River to support the troop movements to James Island would no doubt alert the enemy as to the army's intentions and allow the Southerners to concentrate at Charleston. Should that happen, an operation that might have been quick and bloodless would become "difficult and bloody...perhaps impossible."[24]

Rodgers responded on the 22nd with a point-by-point rebuttal and claimed that the general had had plenty of time to meet with Du Pont before the flag officer left on his inspection tour. Furthermore, it was Benham's failure to appear at a previously scheduled conference with the naval commander that had prevented the plans from being discussed. Reminding Benham that Du Pont would return in two days, Rodgers signed off, assuming the affair had ended. It hadn't. In a remarkable breach of protocol, Benham bypassed Rodgers and directed Capt. John R. Goldsborough, the navy's local commander off Wassaw Sound, to put his squadron into action. Benham surely knew the seriousness of his course, as he weakly justified his orders to Goldsborough by stating that, "...you can aid me with your vessels which I feel assured will have the sanction of your flag officer now absent or I would ask him to write you." Luckily, by the time Rodgers learned of Benham's backhand, the affair was out of his control.[25]

While Goldsborough did what he could to divert Confederate attention, Du Pont returned on Saturday the 24th and waded into the fray. In an obvious effort to squelch Benham, the flag officer directed his correspondence to Major General Hunter and spared no one in his sharp denunciation of Benham's ways and means. Du Pont had read Benham's correspondence with Rodgers and found "its tone and character not such as should be addressed to an officer under my command." He then icily requested the army to provide him with all plans for the forthcoming operations and promised full naval cooperation. In closing, he emphatically stated that "I have never been addressed on the subject [of the operation] except in a very informal manner, and that verbally, some weeks back." Privately, Du Pont liked Hunter and thought him "calm, unimpassioned, dignified, courteous," even though he was an abolitionist. On this score, Hunter had issued a proclamation freeing all slaves that entered Union lines, and Du Pont feared that Lincoln might be forced to relieve him, thereby leaving Benham in charge. The flag officer found this scenario unnerving, for he described Hunter's subordinate as "coarse, pertinacious, heels over head." In Du Pont's view, if Benham rose to command, "I think it literally impossible for him to conduct this military department."[26]

* * *

The Northern troops comprising Hunter's command sensed that something big was in the offing. The few steamers that Benham had been able to muster were steadily, if slowly, transporting men from Hilton Head to Edisto Island. Companies B, E, F, H, and K of the 3rd Rhode Island Heavy Artillery boarded the *Delaware* from the Hilton Head wharf on the 23rd, and, by nightfall, the men trudged onto the bustling waterfront at Edisto. Once ashore, the Rhode Islanders were reunited with their own Company I, which had been detached to garrison nearby Otter Island the previous December. More changes were in store for the unit, as this converted artillery battalion returned to its original infantry role and spent much of their time on Edisto reviewing the manual of arms.[27]

As the troops steamed north, Benham organized the "First Division Headquarters Brigade," whose units included Capt. Edward Serrell's Engineers, the 3rd Rhode Island Heavy Artillery, the 3rd New Hampshire, and the 1st Massachusetts Cavalry. Commanding this new brigade would be Col. Robert Williams of the Massachusetts horsemen, a tough, highly regarded Regular Army officer who had ignored the claims of his native Virginia to remain with the Union. He had whipped a mutinous gaggle of volunteers into a decent cavalry regiment with a rough and highly autocratic hand. His troops begrudgingly regarded him as "a man who knew his business." Arriving at Hilton Head in mid-January, the 1st Massachusetts Cavalry had been broken up and its companies distributed to various posts in the theater, where they performed capably. Throughout May, the companies proceeded one by one to Edisto, until eight companies stood reunited in the burgeoning Union camp. One trooper remembered cavalry life in the South in less than glowing terms: "Dreary surroundings, dearth of news, poor food, and a wearisome round of camp duty, drill, and discipline." It was a sure recipe for low morale, but the New Englanders knew that a movement of great importance was underway, and they steeled themselves to perform their duty.[28]

Amid the quickening pace, Hunter was forced to make some command changes before he could trigger the assault on the Charleston defenses. Brigadier General Egbert Viele, the original commander of the 1st Brigade, had departed for Virginia in early May. Taking his place in command of Fort Pulaski was the 7th Connecticut's former colonel, newly commissioned Brig. Gen. Alfred Terry. Hunter then redistributed some of Viele's former troops for use in the coming campaign. On the 22nd, the 6th Connecticut and the 28th Massachusetts left their camps on Daufuskie Island, with the 6th proceeding to Edisto Island and the

28th returning to Hilton Head. The 48th New York, led by preacher-turned-Col. James Perry, broke camp on May 25, but an earlier order dated the 23rd directed "Perry's Saints" to Fort Pulaski for garrison duty. The New Yorkers were "greatly indignant at that order," but reported to the fort where they relieved the 7th Connecticut and its new commander, Lt. Col. Joseph Hawley. The Connecticut men boarded ship, and the "Saints" watched their comrades steam away to join the great push upon Charleston.[29]

Over on Port Royal Island, Brig. Gen. Isaac Stevens read Benham's general orders, and he immediately detected their inherent flaws. The most glaring miscalculations lay in the relative timetables. Stevens realized the impossibility of two separate forces, Stevens' by sea and Wright's by land, arriving on James Island at the same time if they started at the same time. When the brigadier mentioned this fact to his superior, Benham "took this friendly advice in dundgeon." Stevens then brought up the subject of the elimination of his own pet objective—an attack upon the railroad at Pocotaligo. Passionately persuasive, Stevens succeeded in convincing Benham of the efficacy of the move. Or so he believed. He left the meeting under the impression that an assault upon the Confederate railroad was now part of the general plan.[30]

Soon after Stevens began preparations for the action, Benham predictably had second thoughts. Fearing that Stevens' units would be unable to sail for the Stono at the prescribed time if they took part in the Pocotaligo thrust, Benham now imposed restrictive conditions on his subordinate. First of all, Stevens was to make his attack with only one regiment, the 50th Pennsylvania. Secondly, the mission must be accomplished in a single day so as to fall in line with the overall timetable. Stunned by the change of orders, Isaac Stevens reluctantly juggled his troop dispositions and reduced the mission's objective to the destruction of a single railroad bridge at Pocotaligo—a far cry from the extensive destruction he had originally envisioned. Stevens now realized that his abbreviated operation had become an unnecessarily desperate race against the clock.[31]

Stevens quickly assembled his force. He designated volunteer companies from the 79th New York and the 8th Michigan to act as supports, and he beefed up the assault regiment by adding a section of the 1st Connecticut Light Artillery and some horsemen from the

1st Massachusetts Cavalry. During the night of the 28th, flats and boats from the nearby islands were gathered at Port Royal Ferry. At the same time, the troops involved in the movement left their camps and marched to the area just south of the Ferry, arriving about 3:00 a.m. Just before daylight, Col. Benjamin Christ pushed his 50th Pennsylvania across the Coosaw, completing the crossing by 5:00 a.m. Unfortunately, trouble was already brewing. As the infantry disappeared north on the road towards Gardens Corner, Christ looked in vain for his artillery. The Connecticut gunners had left their camp at midnight, in plenty of time to reach the Ferry by 3:00 a.m., but had been plagued with a variety of problems. They couldn't reach the crossing until 8:00 a.m., a full three hours after the infantry had gone over the Coosaw. Clearly, the operation was off on the wrong foot.[32]

In the pre-dawn darkness, the 50th Pennsylvania passed the scene of their New Year's Day fight, but this was no time to savor past triumphs. Instead, they hurried up the road towards Gardens Corner, anticipating danger round every bend. Two miles beyond the Ferry, Confederate pickets fired into the head of the column. Christ deployed the lead companies to both sides of the road and returned the greetings, thus beginning a running skirmish that would last through the morning.[33]

Three times enroute, Southern pickets slowed the Pennsylvanians by goading them into full battle line. Major Higgenson and his single company of Federal cavalry had left the Ferry at 6:00 a.m. and caught up to Christ just as the infantry forced the last of the enemy west through the Corners towards Pocotaligo. The addition of the mounted arm allowed Christ to make better time, as he could now rely on the horsemen to outmaneuver the pesky Confederate pickets. Yet another running skirmish began on the road to Pocotaligo, with the larger Northern force forcing the Southerners closer and closer to the strategic railroad crossing. By 10:30 a.m., Christ and his column had reached the outskirts of their objective. With the railroad bridge but a short distance away, Union success seemed assured.[34]

To Christ's great disappointment, his column suddenly ground to a stop. The Rebels had found a shielded position overlooking a stream and causeway just outside the town. The Federals reconnoitered the watercourse in both directions and found it unfordable.

Moreover, the causeway itself had been dismantled by the retreating enemy. The Union colonel decided on a unique but time-consuming process: he would feed his men a company at a time across the remaining rope supports. Such an exposed balancing act could prove costly, although a blanket of Federal fire would greatly reduce the danger. The order circulated, and a detachment of Pennsylvanians under Lieutenant Colonel Brenholts was soon forcing a bridgehead by teetering on ropes while their comrades spread out to provide a covering fire. The Rebels did their best to counter the move, but before long 300 Unionists had passed to the far side of the swamp and, in two quick thrusts, dislodged the hidden enemy. Immediately, work parties moved to repair the causeway. Unfortunately, the balance of the force could do little more than stand and wait for the engineers to finish the task. Precious minutes ticked away as the work was carried out. While Christ prepared to assault the railroad, the Connecticut artillery under Lieutenant Cannon finally arrived, the irony of which was not lost on the Pennsylvania colonel. Had the artillery arrived earlier, the crossing could have been accomplished much more quickly. Now, the three hour delay forced Christ to reconsider his options. When field reports of his dwindling ammunition supply arrived simultaneously with the intelligence that Rebels in great force were detraining at the rail station in Pocotaligo, the colonel made up his mind. He quickly called off his tepid cavalry pursuit and issued orders for the entire column to return to the Ferry, leaving the destruction of the railroad bridge at Pocotaligo for another day.[35]

* * *

Brigadier General Isaac Stevens reached Port Royal Ferry early that afternoon. Here he received Benham's revised timetable for the embarkation of his division. Benham now wanted Stevens' troops on their transports on the 31st, a full 24 hours later than originally planned. The exigencies of the day prevented him from dwelling on what could have been, for word had reached him at 3:30 p.m. that Christ had met a superior force of the enemy and was retreating before them. Reacting with what he termed "abundant caution," Stevens first sent his support companies across the Coosaw to Gardens Corner and then ordered the 100th Pennsylvania forward to the south side of the Ferry. As he waited out the afternoon and evening, the thought of his entire brigade destroying the railroad bridge and miles of the track while cutting off Charleston from Savannah must have passed through Stevens' mind. Although Benham's revision of the brigade's timetable might have given Stevens the time he needed to accomplish at least some of these goals, his grand objective—the destruction of the railroad—remained out of reach.36

* * *

The local Confederate defenders had long assumed that Pocotaligo was a likely target for a quick enemy thrust. The railstop represented the nearest point of the Charleston–Savannah line to the Federal base on Port Royal Island. Still, when Confederate pickets alerted Maj. Joseph Morgan of the 1st Cavalry Regiment, South Carolina, sometime after 8:00 a.m. that the Federals were advancing in force on Gardens Corner, only a few Southern units camped near the railroad could answer the alarm. This smattering of pickets was to perform yeomen's work this day by repeatedly disrupting the Federals' march from just south of Gardens Corner all the way to Pocotaligo. Meanwhile, Morgan sent word of the enemy advance to Col. William S. Walker at Hardeeville and Pemberton in Charleston, and then went about organizing the defense of Pocotaligo with what troops he had. Captain Trenholm and his Rutledge Mounted Riflemen pressed forward from the railroad south through "Old" Pocotaligo on the road towards Gardens Corner. Immediately behind them were four companies of the 1st Cavalry Regiment, South Carolina, and Capt. Blake Heyward's Marion Men of Combahee. As the Confederate advance cleared the town, elements of the enemy's column appeared in the distance.37

Trenholm first sent a small party forward to destroy the causeway across the intervening marshland, locally called Screven's Canal, and then dismounted both his own troopers and the lead company from Morgan's command to deploy among some "old oaks." As the remaining Confederates rode up, Morgan fed them into line on both sides of the road while retaining three companies as a reserve. These undersized companies—a total of 76 men—were to oppose what was obviously an oversized Union regiment, but they went to their work "with great spirit" as the enemy approached. Colonel Walker reined up just as these troop dispositions were being completed and simultaneously with the first Federal attempt to cross what was left of the causeway. The Rutledge breechloaders and some Rangers' shotguns opened on the advance. "Soon the fight became general," stretching into a two-hour holding action that stalled the enemy within two miles of the vital railroad.[38]

Colonel Walker watched anxiously as his men expended their ammunition. At about 1:00 p.m., a daring Yankee flanking party hit the right of the Rutledge men, and threatened the causeway to their rear. The Southerners instinctively moved to their left, dragging their wounded with them. Perhaps aware that infantry reinforcements were due to arrive at the railroad, Colonel Walker decided to order a general retreat through Pocotaligo in the direction of the station. His small force pulled back from Screven's Canal, found their horses, and retreated nearly a mile "upon the banks of a ditch crossing the road." Here an ammunition train met the troopers as they formed perpendicularly to the roadway, where they awaited the next Federal thrust.[39]

When rail-borne reinforcements began to arrive in Pocotaligo at 4:00 p.m., the bluecoats had only moved a quarter of a mile from the causeway to Elliot's plantation. At this time, Capt. Stephen Elliot brought up the three guns from his Beaufort Artillery Battalion, which had just arrived via the rails, and was soon joined by two companies of the 11th South Carolina. Walker placed Elliot's guns in the roadway and added the infantry to his line of dismounted cavalry. Peering out over the "difficult" ground, Walker searched for signs of a renewed enemy advance. Soon, videttes came charging up the road with some welcome news: the enemy, instead of attacking, was retreating.[40]

Walker immediately organized a pursuit, but the fading daylight forced caution upon the Confederate column. Walker's force warily pushed through the darkness towards Gardens Corner. At about 10:00 p.m., when the Southern advance drew Federal fire just outside of the hamlet, Walker ordered a halt and decided to wait until morning to resume the chase. The lull allowed Col. John Hugh Means, the former governor of South Carolina, and 400 men from his 17th South Carolina, who had reached Pocotaligo Station by rail, to catch the pursuing column. Accompanying Means—"after a hot ride"—were Capt. Rutledge's Charleston Light Dragoons and a squadron under Major William Stokes. Walker moved to further bolster his force by ordering up Lt. Col. William Phillips and his Georgia Legion, which had just arrived at Pocotaligo Station. Come sunup, Walker would be ready to chase these Yankee intruders into the Coosaw River.[41]

* * *

With the two forces in such close proximity, the roadways near Gardens Corner were filled with danger. Late that night, two privates from the Rutledge Mounted Riflemen were sent with dispatches bound for Colonel Walker. Taking a supposed shortcut, the duo came upon elements of the retreating Federals in the darkness. Shots rang out, and one of the Confederates, Doctor P. C. Goddard, fell from his horse dead. The second rider, Private C. J. Lawton, found himself surrounded by shouting Northerners but managed to make his escape, suffering a lung wound in the process. Lawton eventually reached his camp, where he collapsed. Few who saw his wound held hope for his survival.[42]

* * *

For Christ's Union column, the return trip from the causeway had become a nightmare. The Connecticut artillery crews had exhausted themselves trying to make up the time lost during the morning delays, only to find their presence unneeded. Joining the retreat, the gunners struggled under a blazing sun to keep pace with the infantry. Men and horses, completely used up by the day's efforts, lined the roadway. Hog-wallowed water, "thick and sticky with mud," seemed the only available refreshment as the sun set on the weary column. File closers kept most of the men afoot, but a few of the artillerists joined those numerous infantrymen along the roadsides, too spent to continue the march.[43]

Fortunately, Colonel Christ foresaw one possible problem and, by taking appropriate action, saved his whole force. He sent orders forward for the New York and Michigan supports to clear the Ferry in advance of the retreating column. Christ wanted no delay in the crossing process once his Pennsylvanians finally reached the Coosaw. His orders were obeyed, and when the head of the column reached the ferry around 10:00 p.m., the Michiganders and the New Yorkers were already an hour on Port Royal Island. Christ made haste to cross his force over the Coosaw, and although groups of Union stragglers continued to cross the river through sunrise, most of Christ's people stood safely on Port Royal Island by 3:00 a.m. The colonel's casualties amounted to two killed, including the captain that led the swamp crossing at Pocotaligo, and nine wounded, a sacrifice hardly commensurate with the gains. One unimpressed Highlander wrote of Christ's performance, "The attempt was unsuccessful owing the incompetence of the officer in command." For his part, Isaac Stevens seemed satisfied with the operation, though the outcome had hardly proved the soundness of Stevens' original plan. He termed the affair a reconnaissance, and left it at that. In his heart, however, he still felt that full brigade would have done serious harm to the railroad, but for the vacillation of Brig. Gen. Henry Benham, a man Stevens was quickly coming to hate.44

* * *

At daybreak, Walker resumed the Confederate pursuit. His column passed through the small hamlet of Gardens Corner and pushed down the road towards Port Royal Ferry. Each stride brought the Southerners closer to the realization that the Federals had abandoned their objective. By the time Walker reached the Ferry, only a few enemy pickets lounged on the causeway opposite. Walker called up the two guns of the Beaufort Artillery, and they went into action on each side of the roadway. The belching cannon quickly dispersed the pickets with "a brisk fire of shot and shell." After watching the artillery destroy a number of buildings, Walker called a halt and directed his column back to Pocotaligo.45

As the column retraced its route, Walker welcomed Phillip's Georgia Legion and Major Jefford's cavalry squadron and placed them in line. Arriving in Pocotaligo, the commander was met by Col. William Slaughter, whose 51st Georgia had also been rushed to the scene by rail. Colonel Walker directed his forces to their former positions, all extremely proud of their staunch defense and spirited pursuit. As he did, he had one regret: a few more hours of daylight the previous afternoon would have enabled him to destroy the cheeky Unionists. Even so, the enemy thrust had been blunted by a lightning concentration of infantry, artillery, and cavalry. The "Lincolnites" were back on Port Royal Island, and the railroad bridge at Pocotaligo still spanned the Combahee River.[46]

CHAPTER THREE

"...give the orders that Charleston shall be defended even amid conflagration and blood..."
—South Carolina Governor Pickens, May 23, 1862

"Doom hangs over wicked Charleston, that vipers nest and breeding place of rebellion...deserving of holocaustic infamy..."
—New York Tribune, June 9, 1862

Yankees Come to James Island

The appearance of Federal forces in the Stono exacerbated the already strained tensions between the military and civilian leaders of South Carolina; the resulting pressure seemed to bring out the worst in everyone. John Pemberton continued to wrestle with nearly all parties. Governor Pickens kept a steady stream of complaints about Pemberton's methods flowing across Lee's desk in Richmond. Lee, for his part, discounted the Federal threat to Charleston and went so far as to request that a brigade led by Ripley be sent to Virginia. Predictably, Ripley remained as contentious as ever. Since he hadn't wanted to abandon Coles Island, he now simply requested instructions from Pemberton while venturing no opinions of his own. James Chesnut, chief of South Carolina's Department of the Military, heard reports that Ft. Sumter's garrison was near mutiny and asked for Pemberton's comments. Even simple things went wrong. An attempt to move the Stono River obstructions from Battery Island to Elliot's Cut was frustrated by the appearance of the Federal ships on the 20th. The desperation of the high command was revealed when Pickens and his council met to resolve to "repulse the enemy with the entire city in ruins" rather than evacuate or surrender. On this same day, Pemberton recommended dismounting the guns and destroying Moultrie and Sumter.[1]

Elsewhere, the constriction of the Confederate defense perimeter continued apace. Down the coast on May 21, Nathan Evans withdrew from Johns and Wadmalaw Islands, leaving but a small cavalry force to observe the developing Federal movements. Although this move opened a stretch of the railroad to enemy incursions, Pemberton remained more concerned about Federal movements up the Stono. He pushed Ripley to complete the new line of river obstructions to counter this possibility. At the same time, he urged Evans to be prepared to cooperate with a planned attack on the Federal ships in the Stono.[2]

All the while, Governor Pickens besieged Robert E. Lee with requests to send a replacement for Pemberton, stating "we want a new man." Pemberton's shortened lines, which actually kept with Lee's earlier strategy for Charleston's defense, scared the Governor. When the general reacted to Chesnut's inquiry by discounting civilian concerns about Sumter's garrison and arguing heatedly that Charleston should probably be defended from the city proper, the governor's confidence in this passive and seemingly disinterested general collapsed. Of course, exacerbating politician and warrior alike were the difficulties implementing martial law. At first, Charlestonians found that "(T)he provost and his subordinates were as inexorable as the ancient judges of the infernal regions." And although some leeway was granted as time went on, most of the city's inhabitants agreed that "The domestic tyranny would serve as a preparation for the stranger's oppression. We should get accustomed by times to being skinned."[3]

Even now, Pemberton faced another crisis that would further weaken his standing. The ever-critical Roswell Ripley was appalled by Pemberton's Fabian tendencies. When the commander's talk turned to abandoning Coles Island and possibly surrendering the masonry forts, Ripley's confidence in his superior was destroyed.

The quarrelsome subordinate had longed for a transfer away from Charleston and her Pennsylvania-born commander, and on May 23, when Lee requested a brigade and a brigadier, the door opened for Ripley's exit. Pemberton acted on Lee's orders the following day by plucking two regiments from Walker's Third District and ordering them to Richmond under Ripley's command. Pemberton then tapped General Hugh Mercer to replace the departing general. Mercer had spent the first year of the war on the Georgia coast, but he was a product of West Point, a seven-year army veteran who had been an active militia officer. Pemberton may have been delighted to see Ripley go, but Governor Pickens was appalled by the timing. Heretofore, state authorities regarded Ripley as their safety net. His departure, concurrent with Federal stirrings, left Pickens with a man he didn't trust and another he didn't know.[4]

Then there were those Federal ships still plying the Stono. Before Ripley left for Virginia, he resolved to give the Federals a parting shot by decoying the enemy into a trap. If one of the Federal gunships could be lured up the Stono to the waiting guns of Fort Pemberton, perhaps some damage could be done. (It is revealing that Ripley never could call the fort by its name, always referring to it as "the battery at Elliot's Cut.") As part of the plan, Capt. F. N. Bonneau and his small gunboat would be towed by the steamer *Chesterfield* from his position off Morris Island to the footbridge near Dixon's Island, where he could take the enemy in flank. General States Rights Gist was to support the naval pincer from the east bank of the Stono with musketry and a mobile siege train, in the hopes of surrounding the intruders in a ring of fire. On the morning of May 25, the Confederates put the plan in motion.[5]

* * *

Two Federal vessels, the *Unadilla* and the *Pembina*, began the morning of May 25 by steaming up the Stono past the Rebel piles near Battery Island. As they headed north against the current, one of the ships lobbed a few shells over James Island, reminding the Rebels that Federal naval power was nearby. They were approaching the clearings of the Grimball plantation stretching along the river's eastern bank when the lookouts spotted an enemy steamer upriver towing some kind of gunboat. Both Federal ships raised steam and gave immediate chase. But, as the enemy vessels ran further up, the Unionists decided to pause near Grimball's plantation, content to have forced the Rebels out of range. After this minor standoff, the Federal ships turned and rode the current south past the obstructions. Just past Battery Island another enemy threat was detected, this time to the east. Northern lookouts spotted a floating battery lying in one of the marshes' myriad creeks but still within range of the ships' guns. While the *Pembina* continued south, the *Unadilla* anchored and her gun crews came quickly to quarters, firing off two XI inch shells. Her commander, Lt. Collins, had expected the enemy to act normally and move out of range. But his confidence was shattered when three Rebel shots, then three more (two of which passed directly over the ship) came screaming from the marshes. Collins developed an instant respect for his brash opponent, so much so that he pulled anchor and steamed south. When he and his shaken crew reached the Stono's junction with the Kiawah River, they found the *Pembina* and the *Ottawa* fairly huddling near an onshore camp of freedmen. Collins quickly prepared a request for both reinforcements and heavier guns from Hilton Head; in lieu of such relief, the anxious lieutenant asked to be withdrawn from such a "tight place."6

* * *

Earlier in the day, the Confederate vessel *Chesterfield* had towed Captain Bonneau's gunboat to a point between Dixon and James Island. No sooner had two Federal steamers pulled into sight than a shell from one caused some slight damage to the ship. The *Chesterfield* beat a hasty retreat, but Bonneau, who had put his crew on shore under some cover, welcomed the Federal challenge. The Confederates rushed aboard to man their pieces and shot off fifteen rounds from their three guns, with at least two shots striking home. Bonneau had counted either five or six answering shots from the intruder when the Federal inexplicably lost interest in the duel and scurried south out of range. No ship had been sunk, and little damage had been inflicted, but the sight of an enemy gunboat retreating before the fire of a three-gun Confederate "mosquito" heartened the small crew and became easily the most cheering development in the week since the enemy had arrived.

With the Federals' sudden retreat, the *Chesterfield* returned from her safe harbor near Secessionville and towed Bonneau and his guns back to their post near Morris Island. The Confederates exulted in their small but stirring victory. Despite the ease of their success, they most surely knew this was but the first blow of many from a well-prepared and handsomely equipped opponent that was unlikely to give up easily.[7]

Hugh Mercer officially took over the 2nd Military District on May 27 and immediately opened communications with Roswell Ripley. As irascible as the departing officer could be, his knowledge of the Charleston defenses was extraordinary. Ripley briefed Mercer thoroughly on the string of earthworks that surrounded the harbor, the troops manning the defenses, and the defensive tactics he could expect from Pemberton. With that, Ripley departed, an argumentative yet able officer who had left a deep imprint on the defenses of his adopted home.[8]

Shortly thereafter, Pemberton received some cheering news: the obstructions in the Stono near the fort bearing his name were nearing completion. As usual, the general felt some unease about the command structure and, giving in to his doubts, set about reorganizing his department once again. On May 28, Pemberton announced the changes. Hugh Mercer would command the First District (the former First and Second Districts), and "Shanks" Evans would lead the Second District (the former Third). Col. William S. Walker was given the Third District (the former Fourth), and Thomas Drayton headed the Fourth District (the former Fifth). Brig. General Lawton was placed in charge of the Military District of Georgia, but the Louisiana troops located there would remain under independent command, as would the Georgia troops in South Carolina.[9]

When Mercer inspected Charleston's southern flank, he found a varied group of eager but untried troops. Colonel C. H. Stevens and his 24th South Carolina had established their camp east of the expanding defensive perimeter near the King's Highway, having been forced to move there when the *Unadilla*'s stray shots landed in their original campsite. Lieutenant Colonel Peter Gaillard and the Charleston Battalion shared the Secessionville peninsula with Thomas Lamar's 1st Battalion of South Carolina Artillery and Lt. Col. Simonton's Eutaw Battalion. The Palmetto Battalion under

Major E. B. White, Major J. W. Brown's 2nd Battalion of South Carolina Artillery, Company D of the 3rd Battalion South Carolina Cavalry, and the Macbeth Light Artillery made up the rest of James' defenders, manning an arc from Fort Pemberton on the north and west to the Tower Battery on the south and east.[10]

On the 29th at army headquarters, Pemberton received a message from Robert E. Lee that left no doubt as to what was expected of Charleston's defenders. The Virginian stated forcefully that the cities of Charleston and Savannah were to be defended "to the last extremity...street by street, house by house." Lee wanted particular attention to be paid to the relief of the forts so that equipment and morale would be sustained. At the same time, Lee informed Gov. Pickens that Pemberton would remain in command and that a competent officer would soon be sent to replace Ripley. Such news could scarcely have comforted the governor, who was beginning to regard Pemberton with a certain amount of terror. Pickens later accused the general of being "astonished" by Lee's directives concerning the intensity of resistance he expected from the Charleston defenders. The Governor long felt that it took this communication to awaken Pemberton to Charleston's predicament.[11]

Pemberton's latest biographer makes a strong case that, at this point in the campaign, Pemberton began to fear failure badly and lost much of his pre-war brashness in a wash of self-doubt. His Northern birth certainly didn't add to his standing in this most Southern of states, but Pickens' description of him as "confused and uncertain" during these days probably owes as much to the General's behavior as the Governor's prejudice. Pickens wasn't alone in his observations. Charlestonian William Grayson characterized Pemberton as being "irritable, petulant, and rude." A story was making the rounds that the General had treated a clergymen poorly—"(throwing) up his nose in the air like a wild ass' colt"—but all would be forgiven if he could gain success in the field. Pemberton had shown the occasional flash of spirit. After all, he had parried the Federal thrust at Pocotaligo, even though Walker and Drayton had acted at the point of attack. Pemberton had pushed for the placement of the waterway obstructions, especially in the channels near Moultrie and Sumter, and he no longer felt the need to respond to Richmond's requests for reinforcements. Perhaps the voice of a Federal braggart captured at Pocotaligo still rang in Pemberton's ear. If, as the soldier decreed, a large Federal force was collecting on Edisto Island, Federal interest in James Island couldn't be far behind. Pemberton wanted to be ready.[12]

As the situation fluctuated, Lee gave Pemberton an excellent piece of advice. On the last day of May, the Virginian counseled, "At this season I think it is impossible for the enemy to make any expedition to the interior. . .Charleston and Savannah must be held. Retain troops for that purpose." Forget the railroad, Lee counseled, for the Federals wanted the cities. Had Isaac Stevens been in charge of Federal strategy, such advice might well have proved fatal. With Hunter and Benham in control, Lee's advice was dead solid perfect.[13]

* * *

The Federal camps on Port Royal Island fairly crackled with preparations for imminent movement. On Saturday the 31st, the Michiganders got the call to break camp and march to the Beaufort wharf. There, they boarded a small steamer that transported the regiment down the Beaufort River to the Broad River. Afloat in Port Royal Sound, the high-spirited Westerners spent the first day of June shooting at sharks, much to their colonel's disgust.[14]

It was an interesting group, this Michigan regiment. Composed equally of rugged farm boys and patriotic townsmen, the 8th Michigan had sprung from towns such as Flint and St. Johns, Gratiot and Alma, Grand Rapids and Lansing. The regiment began a whirlwind month when it was mustered into Federal service on September 23, 1861, with William M. Fenton as its colonel. Within days the Westerners had shifted to Washington D. C. Three weeks later they were aboard the Vanderbilt heading for the Carolina coast as part of the Southern Expedition.[15]

As the only western regiment in this army of Easterners, the men of the 8th Michigan had taken considerable grief from their comrades. One private recalled that "Some of our men, a healthy & strong type of farmer lads, were not over clean about their person. The N. Y. boys mostly from the Bowery just the opposite, natty in dress and toilet, which caused our Regt. to be branded as the 'dirty Michiganders.' You can imagine that violent scraps and a free for all were of daily occurrences." The 8th's steadiness in the Port

Royal Ferry fight on New Year's Day had softened some of the hard feelings between the two units, and any that remained had dissolved by mid-April. On the 16th of that month, 300 Michiganders had been sent to Whitmarsh Island just southwest of fallen Fort Pulaski on a reconnaissance toward Savannah. In the afternoon, Colonel Fenton found his unit in a vicious little exchange with the 13th Georgia. Ten Michiganders died in the skirmish and thirty-five were wounded. The sight of the battered regiment returning to its Port Royal camps deeply moved their comrades who had gathered to honor them. After Whitmarsh Island, little if anything was ever said again about the Michiganders' coarse habits.[16]

When the 8th Michigan departed from the Beaufort waterfront, two sections of the 1st Connecticut Light Artillery stepped forward to unload the steamer *Honduras* to make room for their own cannon, carriages, and limbers. By the morning of the 1st, the artillerymen were aboard, ready to go. Also embarking that day were the troopers of the 1st Mass Cavalry, minus one company assigned to garrison duty. Taking up the rear were two units of great promise, the Scotsmen of the 79th New York and the Roundheads of the 100th Pennsylvania.

The 79th had evolved from an antebellum militia organization named Cameron's Highlanders, a proud Scottish unit well known in their adopted homes of New York City and Brooklyn. Already badly bloodied at First Bull Run, the low point of the Highlanders' enlistment occurred when, to their great displeasure, none other than Isaac Stevens had arrived to replace their fallen Colonel. The regiment mutinied, but Stevens rode out the uprising and guided the regiment back to stability. When he left in September to command the Second Brigade in the Southern Expedition, he specifically requested the Scotsmen's presence. The Highlanders had performed well at Port Royal Ferry, but like the rest of Stevens' brigade, they had done little since. On this last day of May, the New Yorkers sorted through their accumulated equipment and watched freedmen make off with the unnecessary impedimenta. Such pilfering meant little, for their spirits were soaring "at the idea of a change." Wrote Alexander Campbell, a member of the 79th's color guard, "We think its charleston we are going to or as near to it as we can get . . .I ust to wish when we were in Virginia how I would Like to be at the taking of charleston. I have every chance to be gratified. . ." The following morning the Highlanders struck their tents—late as usual, to Isaac Stevens' chagrin—and swung out onto the road with barely time for a gulp of coffee. The New Yorkers boarded a waiting transport and made for Hilton Head, arriving "early in the day."[17]

The final departing regiment was the 100th Pennsylvania, a unit with the venerable nickname of the "Roundheads." Led by doctor turned Colonel Daniel Leasure, these western Pennsylvanians brought a fervent religiosity and an intellectual industriousness to the ranks of Stevens' brigade. Early on they had established their own unique approach to army life when Leasure broke out a small press and began publishing a regimental newspaper. Although their participation in the Port Royal Ferry fight had been minimal, the Roundheads and their officers had impressed everyone with whom they had come in contact. There might have been some question as to the propriety of their nickname, for few of the Roundheads could claim any lineage to Cromwell and his followers. But, General Stevens liked what he saw of these Pennsylvanians.[18]

The remaining section of the 1st Connecticut Light Artillery and the 50th Pennsylvania had been chosen to stay behind, leaving the 50th's Col. Benjamin Christ in complete command of the island. Once the Roundheads cleared the dock, Isaac Stevens had his entire brigade waterborne. His troops were leaving camps they had inhabited for half a year, but the general knew that fresh adventure lay somewhere to the north.

* * *

Col. Daniel Leasure, 100th Pennsylvania Infantry, Stevens' 2nd Brigade.

Michael Krause Collection, U.S. Army Military History Institute, Carlisle Barracks.

At Hilton Head, two regiments awaited Stevens' brigades: Col. Rudolph Rosa's 46th New York and Lt. Col. McLelland Moore's 28th Massachusetts. Stevens' force—designated Benham's Second Division—now numbered five regiments, with the 7th Connecticut scheduled to join once it had reached the Stono. The Connecticut men would be brigaded with the Massachusetts Irishmen and the 8th Michigan, with brigade command falling to the 8th's Col. William Fenton. The 100th's Col. Daniel Leasure would lead Stevens' Second Brigade, which would consist of the 46th New York, the Highlanders, and Leasure's own Roundheads. Also steaming up was Thomas Sherman's old unit, Battery E of the 3rd U.S. Artillery, commanded now by Capt. John Hamilton. Hamilton had been Quincy Gillmore's Chief of Artillery during the reduction of Fort Pulaski, and his boys were the only regulars in the entire expedition.

Of course, few of Stevens' men cared a whit for the machinations of command. As the ship-borne Highlanders passed their old quarters on Bay Point opposite Hilton Head, some New Yorkers chanced guesses where they might be headed. Most, however, at least according to one observer, remained "totally indifferent as to where the fortunes of war might take us." Now, more than a year after they had enlisted, "the war seemed a great deal further from its ending than it did twelve months before." Anchors dropped into the waters of Port Royal and firmed the transports in place. In the quiet of the harbor's expanses, the first night of June fell on the anxious fighting men of Isaac Stevens' command. Anxious indeed, for something serious was afoot.[19]

On Edisto Island, Horatio Wright's Union brigades crackled with the tension of troops readying to move. On the 1st of June, his regiments finally received orders to prepare for a major campaign. For one group, the orders meant little if any movement at all. The 55th Pennsylvania and a squadron from the 1st Massachusetts Cavalry, supported by two artillery pieces manned by a detachment of the 3rd Rhode Island, would remain to garrison Edisto. For the rest of the troops, however, the early hours of June 2, 1862, signaled the beginning of the long road to Charleston. In the pre-dawn darkness, officers led their troops onto the roads leading to the Edisto wharf. The pace of the 3rd New Hampshire was typical. At 3:00 am, the men stepped off for a nine-mile, four-hour march to the loading zone. There, they found that Col. Edward Serrell's engineers had built "a floating pier, two hundred and ninety feet long and twelve feet wide. . . .constructed of the hulk of an old sloop and five life boats, lashed together and anchored. . .". They boarded the now-famous *Planter* and were ferried to the Seabrook Island landing, where the men tumbled ashore. The Hampshiremen were part of the new brigade commanded by Col. Robert Williams, which included six companies of the 3rd Rhode Island Heavy Artillery, two companies of Serrell's New York Engineers, such companies of the 1st Massachusetts Cavalry as were then on Edisto, and Hamilton's recently-arrived battery of light artillery. Colonel John Chatfield led the three regiments of Wright's First Brigade, his own 6th Connecticut, the 47th New York and the 97th Pennsylvania. Completing Wright's division was Col. Thomas Welsh's Brigade, which included his own 45th Pennsylvania and the 76th Pennsylvania.[20]

The 3rd Rhode Island Heavy Artillery had originally enlisted in August of 1861 as infantry, but when the unit arrived at Fort Hamilton in New York, they began immediate instruction in light and heavy artillery. As artillerymen, the Rhode Islanders became valuable additions to the posts along the newly liberated southern coastline. Various companies were dispersed on detached duty, and the sight of Rhode Islanders manning the new Federal gun emplacements became common. In February, the War Department codified the Rhode Islanders' status, and the regiment officially became the 3rd Rhode Island Heavy Artillery. Despite their new des-

Brig. Gen. Horatio Wright

Massachusetts Commandery, Military Order of the Loyal Legion and the U.S. Army Military History Institute.

64 SECESSIONVILLE

Lt. Col. John Jackson and members of the 3rd New Hampshire at his camp on Hilton Head, spring 1862.

Massachusetts Commandery, Military Order of the Loyal Legion and the U.S. Army Military History Institute

ignation, it was decided that the unit would be needed as infantry in the assault on Charleston. Major Edwin Metcalf led a battalion of six companies towards the wharf on Edisto, the 3rd Rhode Island Heavy Artillery marching once again as foot soldiers.[21]

Striding in their wake were their new brigade-mates, the 3rd New Hampshire. Led by Lt. Col. John H. Jackson, this group had yet to fire their weapons in earnest, although they had arrived at Hilton Head with the rest of the Expedition in November. Since then, the high-spirited Hampshiremen had done little but drill and dig. The men had longed to prove themselves in combat, and as they filled the roadway to the Edisto waterfront, it began to look like their chance would soon come.[22]

Almost immediately after Wright began crossing his force to Johns Island, conditions began to play against the operation. Despite hasty improvements, the wharves were incapable of handling the volume of traffic. Worse yet, the troops sweated under heavy packs as the rising sun stoked the temperature upwards. Still, as the units landed, officers formed them into columns and marched them out the road across Seabrook Island for Johns Island and Legareville on the Stono. Guided by "some Negro guides who were present," the 6th Connecticut led the advance on a march of "several miles" to a sugar plantation. There, Col. John Chatfield stirred his men with an emotional call "to victory or death" in this "hotbed of rebeldom." Their cheers rang across the fallow plantation fields. [23]

Strategist Henry Benham had assumed that this march would take one day, but the men struggling along the dirt road found such an assumption absurd. "Marched eight miles; hottest day I ever saw," recalled one unfortunate infantryman. As the thermometer hit 100, man after man fell out alongside the roadway eventually to be hauled aboard crowded ambulances. One hospital attendant remembered doling out five gallons of a quinine/whiskey stimulant, remarking that he "gave it very freely to the men till gone." As the semi-tropical sun baked the struggling lines, one rumor circulated that a soldier from the 76th Pennsylvania died from exposure. Frequent halts ground the marchers down, and blankets and overcoats, tossed away in vast numbers to lighten the loads, lined the road. Midway through the afternoon, with many of the Northerners reeling like drunks, a final halt was called. The severe straggling had whittled some companies to as few as five men, but the severe heat wasn't the only story. Back at the Edisto wharf, the steamer *Cosmopolitan* had slammed into the makeshift pier and carried part of it away, causing further delays in the crossing. Colonel Serrell estimated that only a third of Wright's troops had crossed to Johns Island at the time of the accident. Meanwhile, at the head of the advance, elements of the 1st Massachusetts Cavalry stood picket, supported by two infantry companies and a group of overworked engineers. Far behind them, commissary wagons stacked up and, in the congestion, failed to find their regiments, thereby adding hunger to the burden suffered by the troops. By this time, however, few of the men cared, for most had collapsed where they stood, surrendering to a sleep of exhaustion. The day ended with Wright's division brutally sapped and badly strung out across Edisto and Johns Island.[24]

Although awaking refreshed on the morning of June 3, the troops gazed out at the gray heralding of a summer storm, South Carolina style. The buildings of nearby sugar mill plantation disappeared as the men used the wood to prepare rude shelters to combat the elements. Luckily, Wright had suspended the march to complete the crossings from Edisto and concentrate his dispersed columns, so most of the Unionists on Johns Island simply stayed put. The inklings of the storm proved to be no mirage. When the weather broke, torrents of rain and a severe wind buffeted the troops, drenching the division to the bone. "(I)t really seemed as if it had never rained before," commented one Hampshireman. This raging day gave way to a black night that enveloped the strung out formations. Again, the rations remained little more than a promise, but now Confederate cavalry began to nip at the edges of the rude camps. Since commissary support had failed again, hardtack began to sell for a quarter a biscuit. Not surprisingly, hungry Northerners ranged over the nearby areas, searching for food and shelter, prompting one local refugee to pin a note to an abandoned house: "If you d____d Yanks can't beat us fighting, you can in stealing." Even with the copious amounts of standing rainwater, fresh water remained scarce, forcing the assignment of guards to protect the springs from overuse. As a result, most of the soldiers went to sleep thirsty, hungry, and wet. Benham's plans had literally drowned in the downpour.[25]

The rain let up on the 4th, prompting Horatio Wright to order a review of the troops. Exhausted pickets who could barely drag themselves into the camps bristled at the news, but early that afternoon, soon after the first rations of the march were finally issued, the troops filed by columns into the muddy roadway and marched a two mile course. Predictably, the road soon became a quagmire and movement grew increasingly difficult. As the regiments struggled through some slippery evolutions, the exercise effectively organized the troops for the second phase of their march. In the early evening of June 4, the forward elements of Wright's division pushed off for the Stono. The column was moving again, and the brass could only hope the delays of the first two days were behind them.[26]

Skirmishers fanned out across the front of the troops and quickly found the going tough. Tangled bushes and briers slowed the struggling advance while the main column snaked along the muddy road in the growing darkness. For hours the Northerners crawled through the night. By 2:00 a.m., the rains returned, filling the sunken roadway with standing water. Major Edwin Metcalf of the 3rd Rhode Island Heavy Artillery observed, "My horse did not drown, perhaps because he was born to be shot." In the downpour, the men continued their search for anything to eat, and someone reportedly caught an unfortunate dog.

The remaining hours of darkness passed with the Federals struggling mightily against mud, rain, and hunger. Finally, in the morning gloom, the 3rd New Hampshire arrived at a sizable creek swollen by the previous week's rain. The Unionists splashed into the foaming, waist-deep water and emerged soaked on the far bank. Beyond the river's edge lay the village of Legareville, and at 8:00 a.m., June 5, with their comrades stretched out for miles behind them, the leading elements of Wright's division reached their objective. Benham's supposed one-day march would eventually take almost four, and each day tested the mettle of its unfortunate participants. One Northerner who made the difficult trek later wrote that, "Our little army was floundered. . .I saw the hardiest in my command, proud, self-reliant officers and men, sit down and cry like children while they cut off their shoes, and then dragged themselves along to shelter."[27]

Legareville stood deserted, and yet with its numerous homes and two churches it struck many of the arriving troops as "quite a village." Company B of the 3rd Rhode Island Heavy Artillery occupied one of the houses of worship and speedily converted it into a bivouac, with one officer commenting facetiously on the ease with which "good Federal citizens seemed to take to sacrilege, if the way they crowded pulpit and pew alike, was sacrilegious!" Slowly, Wright's columns slogged into the town to scrape together rude shelters, but many found their quartermasters strained beyond effectiveness. One marcher recalled, "(We) arrived without food, tents, or cooking utensils. The only cooking utensil the field and staff of the Sixth (Conn.) had was a gallon camphere can, with nozzle & top cut off. In this were cooked potatoes, pork, beef, coffee, tea—food of every sort. . ." Most dealt with their situation as best they could. When the 97th Pennsylvania arrived at 3:00 p.m., the rain had just stopped, so the men began to brew some coffee, "making themselves comfortable as possible after their tiresome, disagreeable march."[28]

Out in the nearby Stono, Federal steamers and gunboats plied the river. Across the river opposite Legareville protruded the humped outline of Battery Island. Beyond it rose the smoke of Unionist camps now established on nearby Sol Legare Island. No doubt many of Wright's infantrymen envied the soldiers who had arrived at the Stono via comfortable steamers, and had thus been spared the miserable and hungry march across Johns Island. No doubt the grass is always greener on the other side of the river.

* * *

Early on June 2, while the Wright's advance crossed from Edisto to Johns Island, the Federal transports carrying Isaac Stevens' division weighed anchor from Port Royal Sound. Gunboats screened the transports and led them north up the coastline. The ocean's sea breezes provided relief from the heat, but some of the landlubbers received a rude reminder of their previous voyage through these waters. "(O)ld Neptune presented his bills and demanded the usual tribute," waxed one participant, as many of the men got seasick on the journey. For most of the men, however, "the trip was a pleasant one."[29]

The gunboats pushed forward, leaving the slower transports behind. The barrier islands of South Carolina slipped astern as Kiawah Island loomed ahead. Soon the flotilla swung westward, angled past the northern tip of Kiawah, and entered Stono Inlet. Finally the objective of the expedition became apparent. Word spread along the decks and among the ranks that the Northerners were bound for an assault on Charleston. Charleston would be the objective, Charleston would be the prize.[30]

The formation passed between the deserted fortifications of Coles Island and a "corral" of freedmen on Johns Island. As some of the ships snaked up the Stono, the deserted Legareville, "fifty houses and a church," appeared off to starboard. Here, two companies of Roundheads were disembarked to secure the town and reconnoiter the vicinity. The flotilla resumed its course past some ineffective river obstructions then anchored in the channel on the right bank of the Stono. Smaller steamers began darting around the larger ships, transferring Stevens' eager troops to the gates of Charleston.[31]

At Stevens' suggestion, the 79th New York Highlanders landed first, splashing ashore at Battery Island around 3:00 p.m. The deserted earthworks and spiked guns drew the interest of the New Yorkers—especially when they learned, as one New Yorker described it, that the "fiery southrons had deserted the place without firing a shot." As more troops came ashore, Lieutenant Colonel Morrison ordered his trusted Captain Elliot out on a scout towards neighboring Sol Legare Island. Elliot threw out a strong skirmish line, crossed the intervening causeway and wetland, then drove his detachment forward across the oblong-shaped island. The skirmishers picked their way through swamps, cotton fields, and woodlots until they reached a causeway bridging a creek and marsh that separated Sol Legare from James Island. Suddenly, a number of Confederate pickets made an appearance on the opposite side, but no shots were exchanged. Elliot posted a "strong picket" at the causeway and led the remainder of his men east along the line of the marsh until darkness forced a halt. Concluding that no Rebels inhabited Sol Legare's, the captain returned his men to the causeway picket position and settled in for the evening.[32]

Four companies of the 100th Pennsylvania and the 28th Massachusetts followed the Highlanders ashore and made camp as best they could on the torturous terrain. One Roundhead recalled, "It was with difficulty we could find enough dry ground to sleep on." The proximity of the swamps, especially when the sun went down, introduced a new enemy to the Northerners, as ". . .the countless long nosed mosquitos bled us. . ." But camp they did, amid the buzzing insects of the tractless marshes, the first Federal infantry to threaten Charleston.[33]

Out on the picket line, Elliot's detachment was awakened when some Rebel cavalry inadvertently wandered into the New Yorkers' position. Shouts and rifle shots exploded in the oppressive night, but the Rebels managed to make their escape. As a murky daylight broke, the Federal sentries moved forward to examine the scene of the night alarm. According to one Scotsman, on the ground lay "a cap clotted with blood, and a cavalry sabre lying near it." The first blood of the campaign was "claimed and allowed for the Highlanders."[33]

* * *

For the Confederates holding Charleston's southern flank, June 2, 1862, began much as any other. During the previous two weeks, Federal gunboats plied the numerous waterways, and small squads of Southern infantry and artillery attempted to drive the intruders off. Just the day before, some sharpshooters from the Eutaw Battalion fired at Northern sailors as they guided their ships up the Stono. On this day around 10:00 a.m., one gunship pushed up the Folly River and engaged a Confederate battery on Sol Legare Island, while tossing a few shells in the direction of the Secessionville works for good measure. One Federal shell overshot the battery and destroyed an outhouse behind the Seabrook house, General Gist's headquarters, breaking a horse's leg in the process. Despite the fire, the horse remained the only casualty of the hour-long engagement. As the afternoon wore on, more Northern ships ascended the Stono as far as Grimball's and bombarded the Secessionville area. Gist, in an attempt to spread his force out a little more, ordered Simonton to relocate the Eutaw camp. By evening, the Battalion had crossed the Secessionville causeway and encamped 300 yards east of the main defensive line between the King's Highway and Dill's Branch roads.[35]

Carlos Tracy, a captain on Gist's staff, had spent most of his time on the island keeping track of the enemy movements. That afternoon, alarming reports from the pickets near Battery Island began to filter back to the command post. Someone counted twenty Northern vessels near Stono Inlet. Another report placed the Federals in force on Battery Island, with elements aggressively advancing eastward across Sol Legare Island. Tracy and a cavalry officer went to the scene to observe the movements for themselves and quickly drew rifle fire. Gist himself rode up and the Federals sent some shots at him as well. The group returned to headquarters, well aware that the defensive struggle for Charleston was entering a new—and much more dangerous—phase.[36]

As the situation slowly unfolded, Pemberton sat in Charleston tracking the Federal buildup through Gist's reports. The exact nature of what was transpiring was confusing, however, and he did not yet know the identity of the enemy force. As the descriptions of Union gunboats and transports made their way to his desk, the commander wondered whether the invaders were Ambrose Burnside's forces, fresh from their victory in North Carolina. Pemberton warned two of his brigadiers, Drayton at Hardeeville and Lawton at Savannah, to be prepared to move troops to Charleston at a moment's notice. Ironically, Jefferson Davis chose this day to wire the beleaguered commander to send more troops from South Carolina to Richmond. Pemberton replied tersely that the Federals were in the Stono River in force and compliance with the requested troop movement would be "dangerous." As late as 9:30 p.m., Pemberton was still unaware that enemy troops had actually landed, but he realized that the Stono incursion would threaten communications along the railroad. He therefore telegraphed "Shanks" Evans to move his headquarters to Adams Run.[37]

The Federal presence on Sol Legare Island made for a second long night for one group of Confederate artillerymen. Captain C. E. Chichester and the 70 artillerists of the Gist Guards had been ordered forward to engage the Federal ships cruising the Folly River. Since his four 42-lb. pieces only had an effective range of 1,000 yards, he knew he would have to position his battery well in advance on Sol Legare Island to effectively engage the enemy. Chichester had spent Sunday June 1st reconnoitering his new position and erecting an earthwork, which his crew completed that afternoon. At dark, the captain began the long process of crossing his train from James to Sol Legare Island via the Rivers Causeway. Teams of eight horses pulled each of the four guns, with four mules pulling each of two heavy ammunition wagons. Near 10:00 p.m., in the midst of the crossing, disaster struck. At a narrow portion of the long bridge, the second gun in line tumbled off the causeway, embedding itself in the muck and damaging the bridge's flooring. Through the remainder of the night, Chichester's entire force labored with "(e)very available appliance at hand" to extricate the gun, but the heavy iron piece remained stuck fast in the mud. At dawn, a frustrated Chichester was forced to leave the cannon in the marsh and continue on to the earthwork.[39]

When the remaining guns were finally positioned and mounted, the crews collapsed "and were soon lost in sleep." Their rest was but a brief one. A Federal gunboat appeared in the Folly River at 10:00 a.m. and forced the men from their slumbers to battle stations. With States Rights Gist observing from the Secessionville area, the Southerners traded shots with the vessel for an hour until the gunboat drew off voluntarily and ended the engagement. With the above-mentioned outhouse and horse the only casualties of the day, Gist later commented, "Your command behaved well under a heavy fire." The proud artillerists held their position for the balance of the day, but at 5:00 p.m., were ordered to pull back across the Rivers Causeway under the cover of darkness.

Disturbing rumors were circulating that a Federal thrust had cut them off from James Island. Fearing capture, the exhausted crews awaited nightfall to evacuate their remaining guns north to safety. Darkness arrived, and after a short march the Rivers Causeway loomed ahead of them. As the trains wound up the road and onto the narrow bridge, luck ran out again for the Confederates. In the midst of negotiating the narrow structure, the crews lost control of the first and third guns. The heavy pieces plunged into the sticky muck near the vicinity where they had earlier lost their first cannon. Chichester, conscious of the seriousness of his predicament, sent for fresh hands to help extricate the pieces, but all efforts were in vain. At daylight, the unlucky officer led his spent men back to Secessionville, leaving three of his four guns stuck in the marsh near the causeway.[40]

When Gist learned of Chichester's misfortunes, he assigned Lt. Col. Ellison Capers the job of retrieving the valuable pieces. It was one more crisis for the Southerners to face, for word of the pickets' sightings and the Tracy/Gist encounter with the enemy had swept through the Southern camps on James Island. Every Confederate defender, from General Gist to the lowliest private, now knew that the inevitable had occurred: the Federals were on James Island.[41]

CHAPTER FOUR

Letter From Hilton Head, June 3, 1862: "With Gen. Hunter at the helm, the long-expected attack on Charleston is about to take place, and I have no doubt of the success of our brave fellows in the field. You can put it down as a dead certainty."[1]

First Blood

Colonel Daniel Leasure arrived at Sol Legare Island on the morning of June 3 and accompanied the remaining four companies of his 100th Pennsylvania to their new campsites. The confusion of the landing zone made Leasure less than hopeful about uniting his immediate command with those Roundheads already camped somewhere out on the island. But soon after he arrived, while perusing his new surroundings, he noticed some unexpected activity. Crews were transporting dead and wounded soldiers back to the landing area, and many of them were men of Leasure's own regiment. Arriving with these bleeding unfortunates was news of a sharp fight up ahead on the island, and the Roundheads were reportedly in the thick of it. The sight of these gravely wounded men, some of whom the colonel knew well, surprised the unsuspecting officer. He rounded his four companies up and moved them forward to their comrades' relief.[2]

* * *

Before he could continue the process of unloading his division, Isaac Stevens resolved to open the landing area by advancing those first troops ashore across Sol Legare Island. Therefore, at midnight on the 2nd, the 100th Pennsylvania received orders detailing 40 men from each company to report to Captain Elliot of the 79th New York at his picket post. Captain James Cline departed with the Roundhead detachment at 4:00 a.m., and soon discovered the Highlander pickets in the pre-dawn darkness. As the Pennsylvanians stacked arms to prepare breakfast, Cline found Elliot and received a briefing on the forthcoming operation, a proposed sweep of the length of Sol Legare Island. The Roundheads would join two companies each of the 28th Massachusetts and the 79th New York in spearheading the movement. As Cline shook his men out for action, Elliot aligned the Irish right on the Battery Island Road, which ran along the southern border of the island, and pushed them forward into the underbrush as skirmishers.[3]

After advancing a short distance, the Northerners found themselves among the buildings of the Legare plantation, a clustering of structures at a bend where the road turns north towards the Rivers Causeway. The Legare house stood in the northwest quadrant of the bend. Immediately to the east, some slave quarters rested between the marsh and a hedgeline that ran parallel to and north of the swampline. North and east of the Legare buildings lay a large cotton field bisected by the Battery Island Road. A stand of woods girded by a heavy hedgeline marked the northern border of the field. The entire force paused briefly around the Legare buildings to survey the area before Elliot advanced the Massachusetts detachment over the field toward the woodlot. As the Irishmen disappeared into the beltline, the Roundheads, forming a battle line near the Legare buildings, ominously noted "unmistakable signs of the enemy."[4]

Popping rifle fire announced Rebel resistance to the movement. The Irish had made contact with the enemy somewhere north in the woods, so Cline advanced his troops to the plantation and formed a line of battle. The sounds of the firefight echoed through the woods and across the field, warning the Pennsylvanians that hard work lay ahead. As the riflefire grew closer, the Roundheads tightened their grips on their rifles and peered into the distant trees for signs of their Massachusetts comrades. Within a half hour of disappearing into the woods, the Irish reappeared looking very much the worse for wear. Singly and in squads, the raw troops tum-

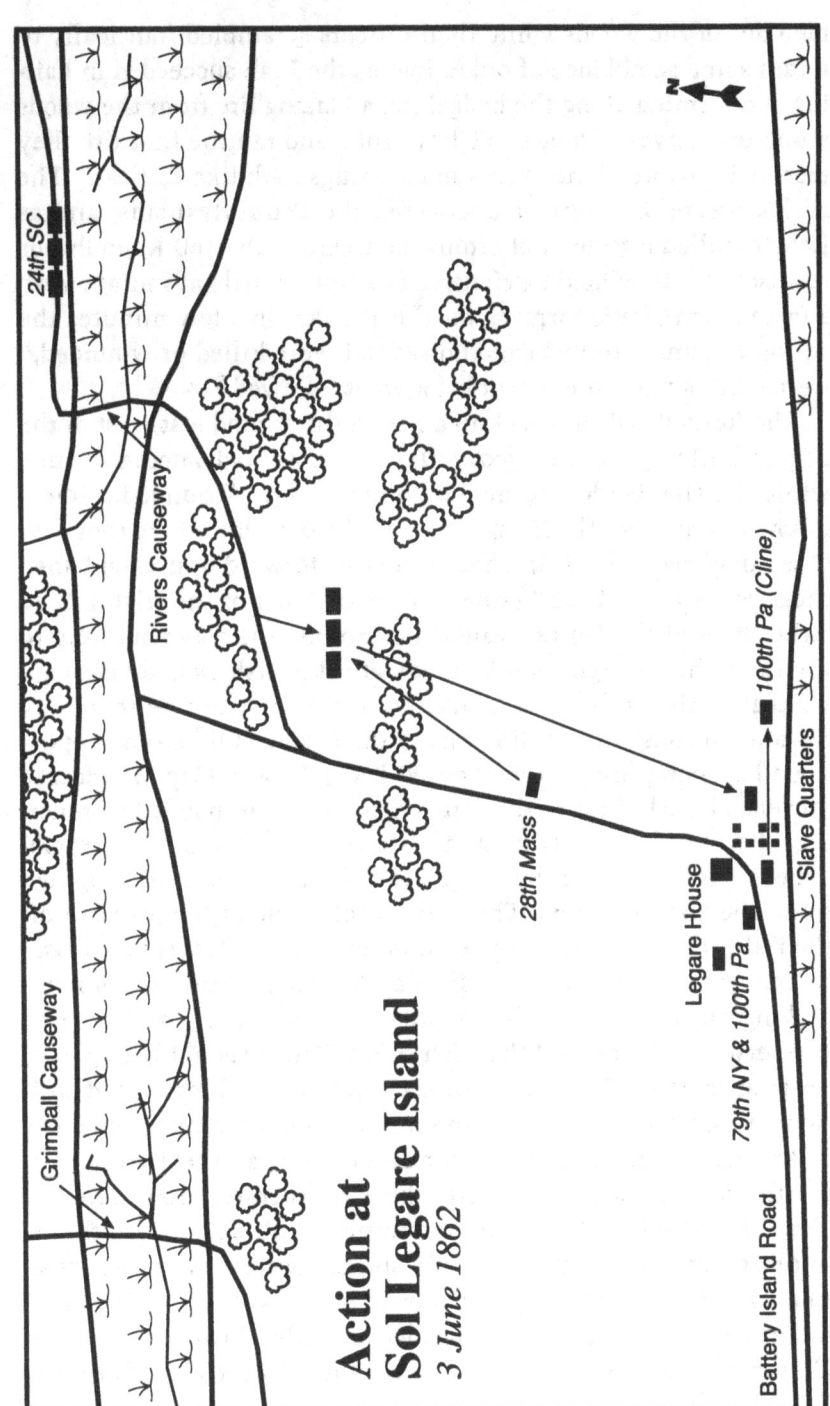

bled out of the woods while their officers scrambled frantically to retain some semblance of order. Just as the Irish succeeded in halting and forming along the hedgeline, a blazing fire from the woods stung the nervous troops. "(T)hey broke and ran the first fire they received," wrote Cline. "This made things look like earnest." The Irish's precipitous retreat uncovered the Pennsylvanians, and as Rebels spilled into the field from the treeline, the 160 Roundheads realized that they held a defensive position of little advantage with a large enemy force forming for the attack. "In a few minutes the action became quite warm, and several were killed or wounded," were Cline's understated words for what followed.[5]

The Roundheads fell back to a rise in the ground just west of the Legare buildings and traded volleys with the advancing enemy, while the Highlanders formed up on their left. Wounded soldiers lurched away from the firing line, and the dead lay where they fell. One small party of Roundheads pushed forward and established themselves around the Legare buildings. Most of the Irish rallied either behind the Pennsylvanians or among the slave quarters to the Roundheads' right, but Confederate skirmishers had taken advantage of the 28th Massachusetts' retreat by working their way towards the bushy marshline east of the Legare buildings and opening a harassing fire on the exposed Federal right. Captain Hazard Stevens alerted Elliot to this danger, and Elliot responded by ordering Cline to advance about 20 men to cover the flank. Cline established a position along the hedgeline in front of, and extending east from, the slave quarters. This move took some of the pressure off the Federal line near the Legare buildings, for the Rebels now began to concentrate their fire on the smaller Roundhead detachment, making things warm for the isolated Pennsylvanians. With a small gap between his left and the Irish right, Cline was not happy with his predicament. He could easily see the danger of his exposed position and sprinted back to the main line to obtain reinforcements.[6]

The fight remained static for some time as the two sets of Northerners traded shots with the Confederates now bunched along the woodline. When Cline returned to his squad with the reinforcements, the enemy suddenly sprang forward from their positions in two distinct wings and advanced across the field. Led by a mounted officer, one group headed straight down the road at Cline's men, while a larger group made for the Legare buildings and the gap in the Federal line. Despite the increasing pressure, Cline held his men in control, for he naturally assumed Elliot would fill the gap with the reserve from the 79th New York. As the charging Southerners closed the distance between themselves and the isolated Pennsylvanians, Cline discovered, much to his horror, that no Federal troops were moving to plug the dangerous rift in the line. Worse, both the Roundheads and the Irish around Legare's and were falling back before the Rebel thrust, leaving Cline and his men, as he later described it, "to our fate."

Sergeant Robert Moffatt remembered Cline's shouted order for the men to "cut our way through" the encircling enemy. Cline's pocket began a fighting retreat, but the Rebels easily curled around their flank and bracketed the Northerners against the marsh. "They kept pouring volley after volley on us till within 10 paces of us," Moffatt recalled. "We were cut off and compelled to surrender," was Cline's memory of the trap. As the small but hot engagement continued to rage, the Confederates hustled the 22 dejected soldiers of the 100th Pennsylvania—the first Union captives of the campaign—to the rear.[7]

* * *

Lieutenant Colonel Ellison Capers had led four companies of his own 24th South Carolina west from their camps in the pre-dawn darkness with Gist's orders to retrieve Chichester's marsh-bound guns. When Capers learned from Col. Thomas Lamar at Secessionville that the Federal pickets covered the Rivers Causeway, he sought further instructions from General Gist. The general ordered Capers to advance on Sol Legare island "until the fire of his boats obliged me to withdraw," Capers later reported. The South Carolinian placed his men in line and marched west. Near the Rivers House, where the rugged Secessionville path met the Battery Island Road, Capers hailed the two companies of the Charleston Battalion that had drawn picket duty the night before. These outposts confirmed the increased Federal activity just over the Rivers Causeway on Sol Legare Island, so Capers moved quickly. Ordering the pickets to fall in, Capers directed his entire force first south and then west on the Battery Island Road, eventually drawing up before the Rivers Causeway. The Confederates found the upturned barrels of Chichester's cannon sticking out of the muck, but Capers knew he would have to clear the area of the Federals before he could possibly remove the guns. He ordered his command into attack formation just north of the causeway and advanced Captain Sigwald and the Marion Rifles across the bridge to act as skirmishers. As Sigwald developed the enemy's position, Capers rushed his remaining five companies by flank across the causeway and deployed them into battleline, where Capers watched as they "engaged the enemy warmly." The Confederates pushed the retreating Federals southward into a large stand of trees. In spite of the cover provided by the timber, the South Carolinians charged into the trees and fired into the increasingly disorganized collection of Federals, who were desperately attempting to rally along the southern edge of the woods behind a hedge. For a short time they managed to hold on in this position, but eventually the well-directed fire of Capers' men broke the line, sending them scurrying south across an open field towards the distant Legare plantation buildings.[8]

Ellison Capers reached the front and made some hurried observations. Near the Legare buildings, an enemy battleline "poured in a strong fire" on the assembling Confederates, "most of which passed entirely over us," he later related. Separated from this main line along a hedgerow just east of the buildings stood a smaller force, whose apparent isolation made for a tempting target. Capers immediately determined "to cut off the advance from the support," by assaulting the fissure in the Federal line. Aware that the Legare plantation was well within the range of the enemy gunboats in the Stono River, Capers felt unwilling to expose his men to such fire. But the isolated Federals dangled like forbidden fruit, and the young officer's fighting blood was up. As he later put it, "I resolved to attempt it."[9]

Just at this moment, as both sides traded volleys, Capers received some welcome reinforcements. Learning that Capers was engaging a large enemy force, Lt. Col. Peter Gaillard led the remaining five companies of his Charleston Battalion from their Secessionville camps to the scene of action, mirroring Capers' earlier route. Gaillard and his men pulled up just as Capers had resolved to attack. Capers returned what he called the "borrowed" picket companies to Gaillard, and ordered him to attack the isolat-

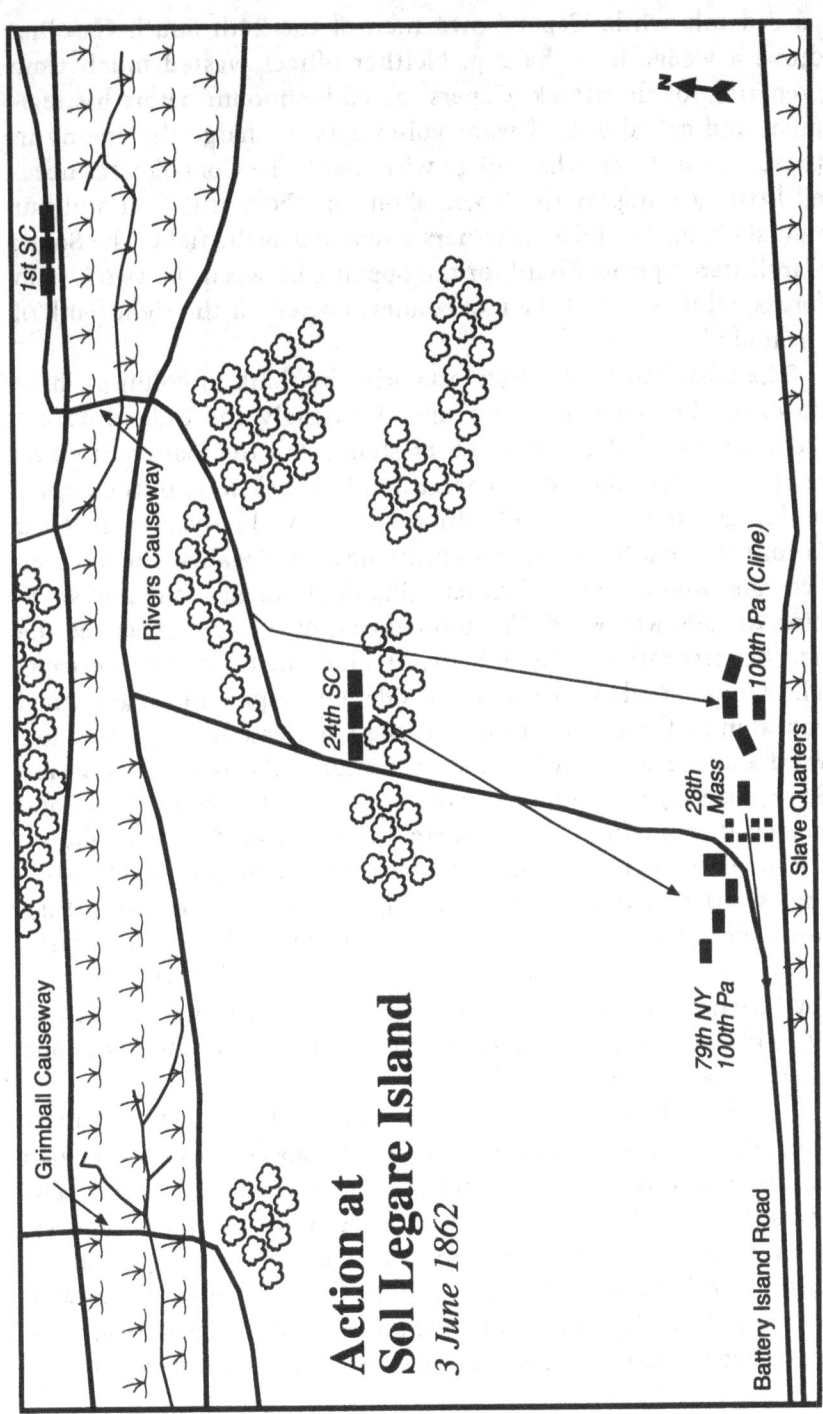

ed Federals while Capers' own men of the 24th South Carolina drove a wedge into the gap. Neither officer wasted much time preparing for the attack. Capers reined his mount before his regiment and called out, "I want volunteers to charge the enemy in those cabins. Boys, who will go with me?" The Confederates needed little goading. With Capers shouting "Forward! God and our rights! Charge!," the Southerners swept across the field. The South Carolinians sprinted hard for the opening between the two Union forces, while some of the foot soldiers angled for the right flank of the main line.

The Charleston Battalion, attacking by flank in columns, bore down on the isolated enemy unit. Amazingly, the Federal pocket stood firm and offered signs of resistance, but the main battle line retreated before the 24th's charge and fell back west of the Legare buildings. One of Gaillard's officers, Capt. W. H. Ryan of the Irish Volunteers, led his company on the dead run against the isolated Federals, who were just then realizing their predicament and beginning to sidle westward. The momentum of the charge carried the Southerners into the gap, effectively blocking their line of escape. The Unionists demonstrated considerable esprit and maintained cohesion in their dire straits, but the Charlestonians pressed forward and squeezed the Northerners against the swamp. Captain Ryan, seizing the moment, raised his sword over his head and lunged at an enemy officer, demanding his surrender. As he did so, a Federal he later described as "a strapping Pennsylvanian" rushed the startled Ryan. Rody Whelan, a private from the Irish Volunteers, quickly jumped in front of the burly Federal and twisted his bayonet "like wire." They locked in a deadly struggle until the "Irishman's trip of the foot" laid his opponent on the ground. With that, the Federal officer surrendered his remaining troops and effective resistance ceased.[10]

As the Charlestonians were mopping up the unfortunate Federals near the swamp, the mounted Capers led his own men against the retreating Roundheads near the Legare buildings. The Federals had fallen back to a point west of the plantation houses, but when the pursuing Southerners reached the buildings, Capers' earlier fear became reality. Shells from the Federal gunboats spun over the suddenly firm enemy line and landed with alarming accuracy near the Confederates. Capers recognized the futility of continuing the attack, and, satisfied with the success on his left, decided to retire his force to the woods. With the Charleston Battalion providing support, Capers pulled the 24th South Carolina back from the buildings and reformed under the cover of the timber. Having blunted the Federal advance while capturing a number of the enemy, Capers and his men felt confident that they had made the most of their morning's work.[11]

* * *

When the firing initially erupted around Legare's that morning, the balance of the 79th New York was busy establishing their base camp. Rattled horsemen reined up with news of the battle, and quickly-shouted orders called the New Yorkers to "fall in at once and hurry to the front." The Highlanders arrived on the field about the same time that the Roundheads stabilized their line west of the Legare buildings. It was too late to save Cline's detachment, but there was time aplenty to pitch into the advanced Confederates. According to one New Yorker, two cheering New York companies rushed forward just as the Southerners around the structures "scattered. . .like chaff." The Highlanders pressed forward, but with so few troops in reserve, their pursuit was called off. The Federal Navy, however, had added the weight of its metal to the fight, and high over the 79th's heads, naval shells sailed through the overcast sky and landed with some precision on the enemy positions. The well-placed artillery chased the Confederates across the field and into the woods, and with that the firing along the line petered out.[12]

The accurate artillery fire was made possible by superb communications between Signal Corps spotter Lieutenant Keenan and the *Unadilla's* gunners. Keenan had advanced with the Federal infantry and positioned himself to observe both the Confederate lines and gunnery officer O. H. Howard aboard the ship. With their newly-devised signal system, the officers could direct the shell fire with amazing accuracy. Even as the enemy disappeared into the woodlot, naval artillery continued to pour forth a harassing bombardment, proving again the efficiency of the system that had been developed and tested back at Port Royal Ferry.[13]

* * *

As the Federal gunboat fire crashed down on the Confederates along the Legare field woodline, Ellison Capers knew that it was time to withdraw. With enemy reinforcements advancing to bolster their position, he ordered a retreat to the James Island defense perimeter. Herding the Federal prisoners ahead, Capers drew his force together and headed across the island en route to the Secessionville earthworks. But mocking their retreat near the Rivers Causeway in various states of muddy repose lay Chichester's guns, mute reminders of the failure of the Southerners' primary mission. Evidently, no one seriously considered that the Federals might make a dash for the guns and succeed where the Southerners had failed, an oversight for which the Confederates would pay dearly. Assuming someone else would effect their release, Capers left the guns where they lay.[14]

* * *

Soon after the Confederates quit the field about 11:00 a.m., the threatening skies unleashed a drenching downpour. From then until 3:00 p.m. that afternoon, the 79th New York and the 100th Pennsylvania watched the woods across the Legare field for any sign of enemy activity. Finally, just as distant Rebel guns began to fire from extreme ranges at the Union positions, two Highlander companies were ordered forward to reconnoiter the woodlot. The New Yorkers plunged into the dripping timber and followed the tortured curvings of the rough roadway. Not quite advancing a mile, they broke out of the woods and came upon a startling sight. Sitting in what appeared to be an open field were three upturned artillery pieces with nary a Confederate in sight. Flankers were deployed as the Federals, suspecting a trap, warily moved forward. Along the marsh they found a wounded Highlander, "Clark of Company G." The New Yorker was nearly dead from loss of blood. He had lain near Rivers Causeway since the night before, when his reconnaissance party had come under Confederate fire. The New Yorkers tended to their friend as best they could.[15]

Just as Capers had recently left them, the Highlanders found the three cannon firmly ensconced in the marsh next to the causeway.

Some pulling and tugging freed two of the pieces, and both were soon rumbling westward on a pair of improvised caissons with the wounded Clark along for what was probably a bumpy and painful ride. Efforts to free the third weapon were complicated when an enemy force appeared from the north across the marsh. An accompanying Southern battery opened on the Scotsmen from only 500 yards, forcing the Federals back to the cover of the trees. Fortunately for the New Yorkers, the enemy artillerists were forced to divide their fire between the retreating train and the hunkering infantry, inflicting no real damage on either. Support for the New Yorkers was readily at hand, as naval gunfire—again aided by land-based spotting—crashed near the outmatched Confederate battery. No harm was done to either group. The Highlanders withdrew in good order and the Confederates seemed uninterested in pursuit.

Just as the retreating Highlanders overcame the slower train, a section of the 1st Connecticut Light Artillery came galloping up to support the operation, much to the New Yorkers' delight. The Connecticut gunners had spent most of the morning unloading their pieces on Battery Island. When Lieutenant Porter's section was finally landed and readied, it took off for the front to see what good might be accomplished. With the Rebel guns still barking at the Highlanders, Porter brought his section to bear and exchanged fire with the distant Southerners. "(A) few well-directed shots silenced the enemy," wrote a somewhat biased Scotsman.[16]

As the New Yorkers rolled toward camp with their prizes, Connecticut artillerists took their turn trying to extricate the lone remaining marsh-bound gun. Joined by a small detachment of Roundheads, Porter guided his men to the piece while Confederate sharpshooters made life difficult for the persistent Northerners. Three times the Unionists managed to hitch up the cannon to pull it out, and as many times the harness broke. Finally, in a shower of bullets, Porter ordered his disappointed men to abandon their coveted prize. The artillery section pulled back from the causeway and wound westward towards the landing zone, but in the confusion a detail of artillerists lost their way. They were wandering about in the drenched woodland when an enemy bullet nearly clipped the flesh from a sergeant's nose. He announced "with considerable earnestness...'I guess we had better get somewhere pretty quick.' " Eventually the gunners managed to rejoin their comrades in the withdrawal. Porter's soaked and hungry men slowly made their way back to their camps, arriving just at dark.[17]

* * *

When the fighting first began on Sol Legare Island, the Eutaw Battalion was ordered to march for Secessionville. Although it arrived too late to join Colonel Capers in the fight, the men could hear the sounds of the engagement. The Carolinians fidgeted as they waited for orders, but it wasn't until Capers and his men returned with a group of Federal prisoners that the Eutaws finally got their turn to join the action. General Gist split the men between Captain Simonton and Maj. John Pressley, and then ordered them forward. Simonton's group was deployed to cover the Rivers area, while Pressley and his four companies marched north on the Battery Island Road about a quarter mile before filing west towards Grimball's Plantation. After passing through a woodlot, Pressley's men formed in a ditch facing the Stono River just a mile away. They remained in the soggy depression until noon, a rainstorm all the while offering them a thorough drenching, until finally orders were received to re-dress the line to face south towards Sol Legare Island.

As Pressly's men marked time in a muddy ditch, Simonton's soldiers had lingered near the Rivers House before moving north to join Pressley's detachment in its new position. This alignment was soon deemed unsatisfactory, however, and the original position facing Grimball's was again assumed. Through the course of these movements, Federal naval fire fell haphazardly along the front but did little damage. As late afternoon arrived, a report reached Simonton that the enemy was attempting to force the Rivers Causeway. Amid what one Confederate described as "perfectly furious shelling" from the gunboats in the Stono, the Eutaws moved directly south to a position in support of the Preston Light Battery, which had deployed in sight of the Federal activity near the bridge.

With their musketry and artillery fire aided materially by Colonel Lamar's Confederate guns in front of Secessionville, the Southerners thought they had repulsed a Northern assault on the causeway. Unfortunately for the Confederates, however, the poor visibility caused them to misread Federal intentions. In fact, they were not repulsing an assault but witnessing the theft of Southern bronze by some enterprising Federals, who were making off with two of Chichester's stuck guns after a valient but unsuccessful attempt to pilfer the third. The Confederates never realized what was happening, and their misjudgment allowed the Federals to abscond with the two freed cannon.[18]

After the causeway threat subsided, the Eutaws reacted to a report of another Federal advance from the Grimball area by returning for the third time to their original, ditch-lined position. In the gathering darkness, a well-aligned battleline appeared in the field to their front. Before the frazzled Eutaws could fire off a volley, someone fortunately discovered the advance to be Maj. W. H. Duncan and Johnson Hagood's equally bewildered 1st South Carolina Infantry. The enemy landings had proved crisis enough to relieve Hagood's men from their provost duty, although Hagood himself had remained in Charleston to tie up loose ends. As the two units commiserated on the near-exchange of friendly lead, they received orders from General Mercer "to hold the front during the night" and act as shock troops against the enemy advance that was "confidently expected early the next morning."[19]

Fearing that the wet weather had rendered many of the defender's firearms unserviceable, Mercer also ordered his front line troops to discharge their weapons. Only about one in ten rifles were able to fire. Even this modest fusillade revealed the location of the advanced Confederate line to enemy gunboats, and a nagging naval artillery barrage resulted. The condition of the men's muskets also jolted the Confederate officers into requesting fresh troops to bolster the line against the expected morning attack. Major Pressley drew the unenviable task of locating Mercer to make the plea. After what he described as "a very fatiguing ride and much inquiry," the major found the general at the Reverend Mellinchamp's house, just east of the northern terminus of the Secessionville causeway. After describing the condition of the 1st South Carolina and Eutaw men, Pressley was asked by Mercer if the soldiers had bayonets. The Major replied in the affirmative. Mercer responded, "Well Major, tell Captain Hagood to use the bayonet in the morning." Pressley rode until daylight to report Mercer's firm command to the exhausted infantrymen at the front.[20]

While Pressley endured a soaking night in the saddle, the Confederates in the front lines, according to one tired participant, were "wet, weary, and hungry-slept on their arms. The night tempestuous."[21]

* * *

When they were relieved at dark from front-line duty by the now-suspect 28th Massachusetts, the various companies of the 79th New York were finally reunited in their new camps. The rough accommodations made it a memorable evening for one Highlander. Andrew Fitch recalled his first night on Sol Legare Island for his father:

> I spent the most fearful night. . . .On my arrival at our tent, which was used at that time as a hospital as well as quarters for ourselves, I found four wounded men stretched out on the floor occupying at least half the space. The remaining was crowded with boxes containing our baggage and medicine stores. . . . The men were severely wounded and required constant attention. During the night the storm increased in severity the wind blowing a gale and the rain coming down in torrents. Finally the wind increased to threatening to blow off and leave the poor wounded exposed to the drenching. In the midst of all this confusion one poor fellow was breathing his last—attended hourly by a woman who is acting as nurse for the 100th Pennsylvania regiment.

Fitch closed his letter by noting that it took "all the force we had at hand" just to secure the tent. The men finally succeeded in their efforts, but spent a sleepless first night on Sol Legare. More sleepless nights would follow.[22]

The Highlanders had taken but one prisoner during the day's efforts, a fellow Scotsman from the Charleston Battalion. Sergeant Alexander Campbell, one of the 79th's color bearers, asked the prisoner about his own brother, James, who had served in the Charleston militia before the war. To Campbell's surprise, the prisoner replied that James Campbell had been in the fight just that day. Continuing the brotherly exchange with the Highlanders, the Southerner blithely remarked, "Had I known I was to be taken prisoner, I would have worn my kilts." But another Rebel prisoner spoke in harsher and less fraternal terms. "In the inland towns, in every mountain pass and rugged ravine," he warned, "at every crossing of the road, and at every fording place, your people will be met, and harassed if not overcome, till you will be glad to close the war and leave us in possession of our rights." In the pouring rain on this drenched island, soldiers from both sides stood reminded of family and friends, of nation and nationality. The roaring fires fought off the rain as fried bacon and fresh coffee served to revive the tired soldiers.[23]

Such camp comforts were not available to Captain Cline and his captured Roundheads, now consigned to captivity in Charleston. Their captors had hustled the Pennsylvanians across the Legare field at the double-quick through both Federal rifle fire and exploding naval shells. At least one captured Roundhead fell in the attempt, pierced by his own comrades' fire. Sergeant Moffatt observed an artillery explosion that killed several of the enemy, although the Northerners remained unharmed by the barrage. The Roundheads, after being led across the Rivers Causeway and past the Secessionville works, eventually arrived at Confederate headquarters. After their names were taken, an escort marched them across the island to Fort Johnson, where the Pennsylvanians enjoyed their first dramatic look across the Charleston harbor at Fort Sumter. Enduring the taunts of some gathered Rebels, the men were piled onto a ferry and were conveyed to Charleston. One more of these Roundheads would later die in captivity from typhoid, but for now, for Cline and the rest of his Pennsylvanians, the Charleston campaign was over.[24]

* * *

Not far from where the captured Federals were taken, John C. Pemberton had just concluded one of the more trying days of his life. As the reports of Federal landings filtered across his desk, he immediately started to re-distribute the troops under his command. From Brig. Gen. Alexander Lawton in Savannah, Georgia, Pemberton ordered up both three regiments and the talents of Brig. Gen. William Duncan Smith. From Drayton at Hardeeville, the beleaguered Pemberton directed one regiment to be transferred to Nathan Evans' right at Adams Run. As far as Evans himself, Pemberton ordered the enigmatic "Shanks" to advance immediately upon the enemy. The orders to Evans were symptomatic of

Pemberton's confused state of mind. The general wanted Evans to advance simultaneously on Seabrook Island and Legareville. "Shanks" had sufficient men to attack one or the other, but certainly not both simultaneously. Ironically, on this same day, Robert E. Lee had requested Alexander Lawton's Brigade of Georgia troops for service in the Richmond theater. He justified the request by explaining to Pemberton that the enemy troops opposing him around Charleston were being siphoned off to reinforce McClellan's growing juggernaut positioning to capture the Southern capital city. Pemberton had hoped reinforcements from other theaters might be available, but Lee's request doused that dream. One can only surmise the tenor of Pemberton's reaction to such news. It could not have been good.[25]

The northern-born Pemberton also ordered some of the Citadel's guns into the lines west of Newtown Cut, although he later allowed General Gist some latitude as to their placement and disposition. This exchange pointed out a serious flaw in the Confederate chain of command. In his excitement to organize a solid response to the Federal incursions, Pemberton continuously passed over General Mercer's head (the district commander), and gave orders directly to States Rights Gist (the local commander). Mercer and Pemberton met earlier that morning (June 3), and soon thereafter Mercer had left for the front, where he and Gist directed operations from the Secessionville area. Such a sloppy command structure could only breed more confusion, as illuminated by both the Eutaw Battalion's recently-completed gyrations and the loss of Chichester's three guns. The major general did his best to juggle his resources and assure his men at the front that reinforcements—including the Citadel Cadets under Major J. B. White—were on the way. However, June 3, 1862, despite the late morning capture of 22 Federals, had been a chaotic, exhausting day for the defenders of James Island.[26]

* * *

While Confederate and Federal alike spent the third day of June blasting away at each other over the Legare fields and the Rivers Causeway, harrowing adventures occupied the Northern soldiers attempting to disembark during the fierce summer storm. The 8th Michigan spent Tuesday morning out near the bar, trying to transfer from the *Alabama* to a smaller vessel, the *General Burnside*. The high seas made the transfer impossible, so a flotilla of smaller boats buzzed back and forth between the two vessels, ferrying Michiganders now forced to face the prospect of drowning. When the transfer was finally completed, the *General Burnside* fought rough water and driving rain to deliver the regiment to Battery Island. As the troops disembarked, ten men from each company were detailed to ride the ship back to Stono Inlet to obtain rations from the *Cosmopolitan*. Michigan private Benjamin Pease joined the group that drew this assignment. The *Burnside* steamed south but had to turn back when the heavy swells made docking with the larger ship impossible. Again, Pease and his compatriots weathered the ride to Battery Island only to be ordered again to ply the Stono to get rations. Near 4:00 p.m., as the ship approached her rendezvous, the captain of the *Cosmopolitan* shouted over the raging torrent to stay away. The *Burnside's* captain turned to tell the hungry men that there was nothing he could do, but changed his mind when the 8th Michigan's quartermaster put a pistol to his head. The beleaguered captain chose expediency over the obvious alternative and ran his vessel alongside the *Cosmopolitan* while his opposite shouted, recording one observer, "until he was black in the face: 'Keep away from me. Keep away from me.'" Suddenly, a wave lifted the smaller craft high in the air and crashed her into the massive *Cosmopolitan*, crushing the *Burnside's* starboard forequarter while slamming the captain and the quartermaster to the deck. The *Burnside* gave up the effort and left empty-handed.[27]

The steamer returned to dock at Battery Island and waited out the raging storm. Private Pease found some comfort by dozing on a coil of rope, but his detail was soon roused to march off to the 8th Michigan's new camp. The private searched for his comrades while wading through standing water up to two feet deep before he finally found his regiment with "no tents up and the rain just pouring down." At midnight, Col. William Fenton rode up to his miserable charges and asked for volunteers to bolster the picket line. Evidently suffering little from his exploits, Pease gamely shouldered his rifle and joined the detail struggling off into the gloom, a very long way from the comfort of the Beaufort environs, and a lifetime from the farms and forests of Michigan.[28]

CHAPTER FIVE

"Landing on John's Island and James Island—those awful Federals!"

—Mary Chesnut

Sparring

Within sight of the church spires of Richmond, Virginia, George McClellan and the massive Army of The Potomac had creased the neck of the Peninsula, their seemingly unstoppable march on the Southern capital nearly complete. As President Jefferson Davis and his chief military advisor, Robert E. Lee, searched the Confederacy for troops to help stem the inexorable Federal advance, John Pemberton awoke on the morning of June 4 with General Horatio Wright's Federals struggling across Johns Island, and Isaac Stevens' men wading about on Sol Legare Island. The first serious challenge Charleston would face in the bloody course of the Civil War was rapidly heading to a climax.

Wednesday
June 4

The *Charleston Mercury* ran a somber two-paragraph article under the title "Our Day of Trial at Hand." Mistakenly identifying the Federals as Maj. Gen. Ambrose Burnside's force, the newspaper grimly placed the responsibility for the city's defense from "imminent attack" upon the men manning the earthworks on James Island. "We trust the defense of Charleston in 1862 will be ever memorable for its heroism and its effect upon the country. It must be worthy of the cause, and of the old City, and of the Palmetto State." As the editors attempted to stiffen fighting morale, the streets of the city were choked with refugees desperately transporting their belongings away from the growing danger. Recalled one eyewitness, "The talk in the streets is when do you go; where are you going. Every one take care of himself and the enemy take the hindmost..."[1]

In a bit of timing worthy of the most notable of actors, Governor Francis Pickens picked this moment—the breaking of the enemy storm over James Island—to reassert South Carolina authority. Pickens had discovered that Davis and Lee were considering further stripping the state's defenses in favor of Richmond, and the governor had had enough. On June 3, he wired Davis to strongly express his frustration with the president's policy, and Davis played perfectly into Pickens' hand. While Davis' telegram with Pemberton early on the 4th reflected an unyielding demand for additional Palmetto State's defenders, later messages fairly brimmed with concern for Charleston's desperate situation. On the morning of the 4th, Pemberton gave in to Davis' demand for four regiments, but by that afternoon, the major general received notice that he could retain the Georgia troops for his own use. Although gunpowder was running low and reports from the front remained confusing at best, Pemberton was heartened by the addition of the Georgia brigade to his defense force. In another encouraging development, Pickens promised Pemberton a liaison officer to better coordinate state efforts with the Confederate military. Despite the lopsided odds, Pemberton's confidence slowly grew. Perhaps these Federals could yet be beaten.[2]

* * *

Dawn had barely lit the cloudy morning skies over James Island when Major Duncan and Colonel Simonton deployed their weary Confederate troops in an arc covering the approaches from Sol Legare Island. The Union gunboats had mercifully stopped their barrage, but the rains had further fouled the defender's weapons.

According to one officer, General Mercer's order of the previous night to resort to the bayonet, if necessary, suited the troops fine. "The men showed no hesitation," he later noted. All present expected a general engagement sometime that day.³

* * *

About 7:00 a.m., having been relieved from picket duty by a Pennsylvania unit, Pvt. Benjamin Pease dragged himself back to the 8th Michigan's water-logged camp on a sand knoll near the troop landing. The company cooks could only offer the private some coffee, so Pease enjoyed a cup before wrapping himself in a blanket in an attempt to somehow steal a little sleep during a break in the weather. Soon thereafter, an orderly sergeant inexplicably awoke the private and asked him to help butcher some cattle. Pease groggily arose to assist and eventually returned to the regiment carting a load of fresh beef. Oddly enough, his fellow Michiganders seemed more interested in standard army rations than the newly slaughtered cattle, but Pease cared little for his comrades' taste. For the first time in days he dug into a good meal of fresh beef and, with the rainfall resuming, contentedly lay down again. Sleep was not in the cards for the hardworking private however, for assembly was called soon thereafter.

The Michigan men formed and advanced as a regiment to the Legare plantation fields, where a demonstration by enemy cavalry demanded attention. Action was expected, but the two sides did little more than face each other down, and eventually the Confederates departed. The Michiganders then broke into groups of 4-man picket parties and lined the hedgeline girding the field. With no sustained sleep for 36 hours, Pease fought off the seductions of slumber until 9:00 p.m., when he began taking 5 minute catnaps. Despite a comrade's considerable efforts to keep Pease awake, the private remembered the evening fondly: "Although I probably did not sleep more than three to five minutes at a time, I managed to sleep considerably more than half the time."⁴

The 79th New York had also answered the same afternoon assembly. Responding to musketry fire near the Legare plantation, the Highlanders marched to the front "to see what was wanted," forming near their position of the day before. Rebel artillery fire kept the Scotsmen's heads down, but counter-battery fire by the gunboats in the Stono soon silenced the Confederates. A celebration of sorts occurred when Capt. Ralph Ely and a number of Michiganders emerged from the woods dragging a Rebel cannon similar to those captured the day before. Unfortunately, the ubiquitous rain returned and dampened the jovial mood. The 8th Michigan remained on the line, but late in the day, the Highlanders returned to their camps to try to catch some sleep amidst the continuing showers.[5]

The poor weather did more than simply dampen Northern ardor. Daniel Leasure of the Roundheads complained, "There is a failure on the part of Wright's Brigade to form a junction with us today. . ." George Leasure, the colonel's son and acting adjutant, even wondered that "somehow or other he (Wright) has gone to Savannah." Nonetheless, heartened by his troops' steadiness the day before ("They fought like horses," the senior Leasure had noted), the colonel confidently hoped the planned attack upon Charleston would begin on the morrow.[6]

* * *

General Mercer's good news came not in the form of a captured artillery piece, but rather in a message from Pemberton specifically intended to bolster his soldier's fighting spirits. Pemberton promised Mercer both whiskey "to revive your fatigued troops," and reinforcements to add numbers to the stretched defenses. The cheering missive from Charleston's commander also included a warning to his subordinate to keep his men in front of their entrenchments: under no circumstances was he to abandon Secessionville. At 11:00 a.m., Mercer disobeyed Pemberton's orders and pulled his troops back behind the main defensive line, but he gave no indication of a willingness to leave the Secessionville peninsula. Captain Carlos Tracy, Gist's staff officer, wrote in his diary of Secessionville's growing importance, penning the terse observation, "Design of the enemy to occupy (the peninsula) apparent." Despite the usual skirmishing on Sol Legare Island, the Federals continued to baffle the Confederate defenders by failing to follow up the fight of the 3rd with anything resembling aggressive action.[7]

In his continuing quest to gather reinforcements, Pemberton reached down to Camp Mercer, just outside of Savannah, Georgia. Late in the day, he informed President Davis that he would draw Harrison's Brigade, which included the 32nd and 47th Georgia and the 4th Louisiana Battalion, from Savannah's defenses to serve at Charleston. When word of this transfer found some of the Louisiana artillerymen, they were in the act of constructing a floating battery near Ft. Jackson on the Savannah River. The men quickly packed their spare belongings for the trip north, leaving behind most of their camp equipment under a skeleton guard. The battalion left Savannah under the impression that it would be stopping briefly in Charleston enroute to Richmond. Their "temporary" sojourn would prove to be otherwise, for the Louisianans detrained in Charleston and were immediately marched for Secessionville.[8]

Thursday
June 5, 1862

Once again, the *Charleston Mercury* rang out with martial ardor. The invading Federals—now identified only as something other than Burnside's expedition—were to be thrown off James Island at the point of the bayonet. Charleston would be no Yorktown or Corinth, where earthworks and artillery held sway. Charleston would be Ball's Bluff and Winchester, where Confederate cold steel invariably broke Northern ranks. The *Mercury* also lashed out at new undercurrents being introduced to the conflict by the enemy. Both Benjamin Butler's proclamation equating female resistance to the Federal occupation of New Orleans with prostitution and David Hunter's arming of former slaves were lambasted by the paper. According to the *Mercury*, these actions were "criminal and atrocious. It is merciless and murderous. Self preservation and the laws of nations require retribution." But one female observer boiled the situation down to its most basic element: "Landing on John's Island and James Island—those awful Federals!"[9]

As the *Mercury* waxed patriotic, Jefferson Davis seemed to reverse or at least temper his position of the preceding day. Most of his previous friendly concern for John Pemberton's feelings dissipated under McClellan's continued advance on the Peninsula. In the president's mind, the war would be decided on Richmond's doorstep, not in Charleston's harbor. General Lee was even advising the Confederate President to strip Pemberton's department to reinforce Thomas J. "Stonewall" Jackson, whose army was baffling and battling Federals in the Shenandoah Valley. Davis curtly wired Pemberton with questions as to whether his dispatch of the 4th had reached him, evidently forgetting the latitude granted by his last missive. Pemberton, for his part, was regaining his poise in the face of enemy quiescence. With the Federals contentedly huddling under the protection of their gunboats, he informed the president that he hoped to be in a position to send Alexander Lawton and his brigade to Richmond that evening. Incredibly, Pemberton was beginning to discount the gravity of the Northern threat.[10]

The departure of Lawton, who would later prove his capacity as a solid battlefield leader, would create another vacancy in the Confederate command structure, and to Pemberton's credit he moved quickly to fill it. The obvious choice to take command in Savannah was General Mercer, an officer with extensive knowledge of the city's defenses. Unfortunately, Mercer had only been in command of his district since May 26, 1862, and present in the field for only two days. Removing him would continue the institutionalized flux in the chain of command on James Island. Lawton, however, was as good as gone, and Mercer seemed to be the only rational choice for Lawton's replacement. Pemberton sent Mercer south.

Brig. Gen.
William Duncan Smith

Virginia Historical Society

Mercer's replacement turned out to be a newly-arrived Georgia officer, Brig. Gen. William Duncan Smith, and Pemberton tapped him for command on James Island. Smith's credentials certainly were impeccable. An 1846 West Point graduate and former colonel of the 20th Georgia, Smith rose through the field ranks of Jubal Early's Brigade in Virginia where, on March 14, 1862, he was promoted to brigadier and transferred to Savannah. In Georgia, he commanded the 1st Brigade under Alexander Lawton, the post he held when Pemberton sent for him to replace Mercer. Smith arrived sometime on June 5 and established his headquarters at Secessionville. With the timing of Hugh Mercer's and Alexander Lawton's departures still up in the air, Smith's formal ascension to command was necessarily delayed. This unfortunately caused considerable tension, especially with three brigadiers headquartered within shouting distance of each other. As matters stood, the vacillating Pemberton was waiting for intelligence from States Rights Gist on the latest enemy movements before he would release Lawton for duty north. The dominos would have to fall before the command anomalies on James Island could be resolved.[11]

In the meantime, the commanding general treated Smith as though his new position was a foregone conclusion. Colonel Harrison and his 32nd Georgia also arrived in Charleston on the 5th, and Pemberton sent them to Secessionville to be posted near Smith's headquarters. Pemberton also offered Smith some advice about picket postings and informed him of a number of arriving artillery pieces, among them an 8-inch Columbiad. The major general also offered a remarkable bounty to Smith: any man under his command that could set fire to the causeway linking Coles to James Island would receive $200. Whether any Confederate arsonist ever collected the prize money is unknown, but the causeway was never reported damaged by fire.[12]

By June 5, Sol Legare and much of James Island had turned into a quagmirish no-man's land. Despite the tensions of the close quarters, the incessant rain did give rise to some soldierly humor. According to one observer, a "half-drowned Federal" picket questioned his Confederate counterpart, "I say, does it ever get dry in this country?"

Humor notwithstanding, tension was building. The fact that this campaign represented the first large-scale clash of arms for most of the participants helps explain the taut nerves and confused state of affairs that prompted indiscriminate firing along the lines. Colonel Johnson Hagood remembered this continual skirmishing, which he attributed to the inexperience of the fighting men. Rumor and alarm also ruled the day, prompting many futile patrols. Captain Tracy of Gist's staff recalled, "Enemy said to be advancing this evening. Our troops marched to the front. Everything quiet by sundown."[13]

The June rains were influencing the evolving campaign in more ways than just discomforting the soldiers. The attendant marshy terrain gave the roadways that crisscrossed James Island a strategic significance they lacked in drier times. As it was, those roads became important factors with which both commanders would have to grapple. Straight west on King's Highway, about 1,000 yards from the Confederate defenses, was the intersection of that road with the Battery Island Road, a position referred to as Artillery Crossroads. A mile and a half to the south sat the Rivers House and the Southern pickets fronting the Secessionville works. The James Island Presbyterian Church was 1,000 yards west of the intersection of the Fort Johnson and Battery Island roads. Just west of the church, hemmed in by a heavy woods, lay a critical split in the road. One tangent ran southwest towards the Grimball plantation, while the other ran due west almost to the Stono River before swinging north in the direction of Fort Pemberton.

By June 5, Confederate pickets lined the woods near this fork, while reserves used the area around the church as a support base. This ground daily attracted the opposing forces, and exchanges of picket fire often developed across the confusing terrain. Elements from both the Eutaw Battalion and the 24th South Carolina became involved in one such confrontation on June 5, when a rapid advance of enemy pickets compelled the South Carolinian infantry to fall back. The men of the Eutaw Battalion held the Federals in check, and when the 24th South Carolina finally rallied, many of its members mistook their comrades as the enemy. In a sudden change of circumstances, the Eutaws found themselves in a dangerous crossfire, with Federal lead from one direction and friendly metal from another. Demonstrating much battlefield aplomb, they drove the Federals off and then signaled the South Carolinians. Lieutenant F. J. Lesesne affixed a handkerchief to his sword and, in the words of one witness, "surrendered with his command, to his friends." These types of hit-and-run probes were generally bloodless, as they were designed more to gather information than inflict casualties. In this case, only one Confederate private was slightly wounded, prompting Maj. John Pressley to report laconically, "No other casualties."[14]

* * *

At this stage of the campaign, one of the singular failings of the Confederate commanders was their inability to form a coherent picture of Federal intentions. As it was, Nathan Evans, the hard charger at First Manassas and the hero of Ball's Bluff, was letting one of the truly golden opportunities of the campaign slip from his grasp. As the first elements of Brig. Gen. Horatio Wright's division slogged into Legareville, "Shanks" sat in his headquarters at Adam's Run and misinterpreted most of the intelligence that reached him concerning enemy movements. By Evans' estimate, 1,500 Federals were at Seabrook's, and only a small detachment was located at Legareville. To counter this supposed threat, he kept three regiments at Church Flats and planned an advance of Dunovant's regiment against Seabrook's. Good intelligence and a balanced command structure might easily have identified the sorry state of Wright's exhausted bluecoats and the opportunities for aggressive action. Instead, Evans could only announce, "I have the honor to report that I have yet been unable to ascertain the exact intentions or design of the enemy."[15]

* * *

On James Island, the fighting men of Isaac Stevens' division spent the day coping with the uncooperative weather. The rain fell "at intervals" the entire day, leading one Highlander to wonder "Would it never stop? We found ourselves in the most unpleasent and uncomfortable camp we had ever occupied, it was surrounded by swamps, and the miasma rising from the saturated ground was thick enough to 'cut with a knife'...Whew! how sour and mouldy everything about our tents smelled."[16]

After a day of picket duty broken by but one brief alarm, the 8th Michigan finally withdrew around 5:00 p.m. and marched to their camps. For the first time since they arrived, the Westerners finally pitched their tents, but their comfort was negligible. The ground was soaked, their clothes were soaked, and as night approached, the rain began to fall yet again. One Michigander recalled the orders to "make ourselves as comfortable as possible, which consisted in lying down or standing up in the rain." Captain Ely agreed, noting that "The night quite rainy and everything wet, the war horrible."[17]

Once his front had solidified, Isaac Stevens turned to the pressing needs of supporting his two brigades. Landing supplies and equipage and establishing camps for 3,000 men required a great amount of logistical energy, and Stevens went to work with his usual speed and focus. While attending to his laborious efforts, the general no doubt paused briefly to consider the men that made up his brigades. By and large, he was satisfied with the quality of his troops, but a few unsettling questions remained. The 79th New York he could trust, and the 8th Michigan had proven itself on Whitmarsh Island. Similarly, the 100th Pennsylvania (Roundheads) had performed well at Port Royal Ferry. The 46th New York had displayed some disciplinary problems on Tybee, but tested material filled its ranks.

The Irish of the 28th Massachusetts presented a serious problem. As the second Irish regiment to muster in their state, the 28th had been recruited for service by the commander of the Irish Brigade, Brig. Gen. Thomas F. Meagher. Meagher's plans went awry when Massachusetts feared the loss of state designation if the regiment joined the primarily New York organization. Instead, in fulfillment of Massachusetts' promise of an infantry regiment for the Southern Expedition, the men of the 28th departed Boston for New York on January 11, 1862, under the command of Col. William Monteith. Almost immediately rumors of mismanagement began to hound Monteith. After a few months of undistinguished service near Hilton Head, the colonel's incompetence finally cost him his command when, on May 20, David Hunter arrested the officer on unspecified charges. Dublin-born Major George Cartwright, a former private from the 12th New York State Militia and lieutenant in the 12th New York, had commanded a wing of the 28th in Monteith's absence and was a fine officer. However, command of the regiment fell to Lt. Col. MacLelland Moore, a former captain in the 11th Massachusetts. One prescient Bay State cavalryman who came into contact with the Irish liked what he saw, writing "We have found very pleasant neighbors in the 28th Mass. Regiment and have witnessed their drills with a good deal of attention and gratification... It will be decidedly a fighting regiment." Another Hilton Head observer brayed, "The Faugh-a-Ballahs are the pets of the Commanding general—so saith the report—and 'wo to secesh' when...they charge bayonets." But the 28th had turned in a poor performance on Sol Legare Island during the June 3 fight. Blamed by both the Roundheads for the loss of Cline's detachment and the Highlanders for not being Scottish, the 28th Massachusetts had failed to live up to their advance billing. Now, it had become an outcast regiment and a worrisome one at that.[18]

* * *

By the afternoon of June 5, the cautious Pemberton had seen enough of the enemy's timidity to approve Alexander Lawton's move to Richmond as well as confirm the other changes in the command structure. Hugh Mercer would return to Savannah and take over the Department of Georgia, while Brig. Gen. William Duncan Smith assumed command of the 1st Military District of South Carolina with headquarters at Secessionville. In one last move, Pemberton voiced a desire that would reap bitter fruit: he wanted a battery constructed below Fort Pemberton that could command the Stono River. Details were sketchy, but the major general was displaying a dangerous tendency to fight this campaign on a map rather than the actual terrain. A large, well-supported work like Fort Pemberton was one thing; an isolated battery located well ahead of the defensive lines was inviting disaster.[19]

At night, the rain began to fall.

Friday
June 6, 1862

With Horatio Wright's division resting and refitting at Legareville, Henry Benham—who was awaiting confirmation of his promotion to brigadier general—turned to Isaac Stevens for some action. Although David Hunter's vision for the James Island campaign rested on rather conservative underpinnings, Benham wanted to see an armed reconnaissance follow up the Union occupation of Sol Legare Island. Stevens, however, distrusted Benham's precipitancy and was determined to avoid the blunderings of rash action. Accordingly, he urged caution, informing Benham that any movement towards the mainland would demand at least 24 hours preparation. Stevens also argued that Wright's entire division should be ferried over to James Island to participate in the action. In his mind, the next Union move should be nothing less than a well-prepared, two-division sledgehammer that would blast open the Confederate lines. But Benham's orders stood, and Stevens resignedly reported, "We shall probably be as well able to make it (the attack) day after tomorrow (daylight) as at any other time."[20]

* * *

At some point on June 6, John Pemberton issued Special Orders No. 70, the announcement of Mercer's departure and Smith's arrival. Although the Federals had spent the day probing his lines with small groups of skirmishers, the tweakings bore little semblance of a large movement. In fact, Confederate intelligence reported the majority of the enemy strangely quiet under their naval guns. While dealing with bureaucratic military minutiae such as filling the positions of chief of ordnance and chief engineer of the department, Pemberton spent at least part of the day wondering what the Federals really had in mind if they hadn't come to Charleston to fight. But his own resolve to fight them building by building certainly seemed to strengthen. Those Charlestonians remaining in the city watched as "military authorities" began to construct bombproofs in the middle of Meeting Street in front of the ruins of the famed Circular Church.[21]

William Duncan Smith also had fighting in mind. Upon assuming command of James Island, he quickly implemented his concept of what he termed "Advanced Forces," a mobile brigade that would picket the area from New Town Cut on the north to the Hill's peninsula just north of Secessionville on the south. Smith chose Col. Johnson Hagood to command this brigade, which included

Hagood's 1st South Carolina, Stevens' 24th South Carolina, Simonton's Eutaw Battalion, and the recently arrived 4th Louisiana Battalion under Lt. Col. John McEnery. An artillery battery would report daily as two regiments at a time took turns supplying the pickets. Three bases provided forward support for the force: the Episcopal Church just south of New Town Cut, the Presbyterian Church on Kings Highway, and a position off Battery Island Road near the Rivers House. In turn, these outposts were supported by two "grand guards": one at Artillery Crossroads, and the other further north near Freer's Store. The supporting artillery sections generally accompanied these "grand guards," ready to advance when and where their presence was necessary.[22]

To the benefit of the Southern arrangements, Smith had finally brought a unified defensive concept to James Island. The use of Hagood's force provided both organization and flexibility, and soon proved an excellent tactical accommodation for the fluid state of affairs on the island. Hagood was certainly pleased with the assignment. He regarded the troops under his command as the best men on the island.[23]

But such regard had yet to be tested in battle.

*　　*　　*

While Stevens' Federals spent the day drying out their belongings, the last of Horatio Wright's troops straggled into Legareville on Johns Island. Wright ordered one small reconnaissance north from Legareville across the Aberpoolie Creek, but otherwise allowed his men abundant time to recover from their ordeal on Johns Island. The respite was doing the exhausted men a world of good. The wooden structures of the village were sacrificed to the campfires of the Northerners, as a chaplain from the 6th Connecticut counted 83 fires in the area. The reverend estimated 5 cups to a fire "cooking pork, bacon, and coffee," victuals necessary to cast off the gloom of the previous four days. The 3rd Rhode Island Heavy Artillery's Lt. Col. Edwin Metcalf humorously recalled that, "Battalion Headquarters . . .were sumptuously supplied with a bedstead, condemned as unfit for firewood. . .upon which the commanding officer was compelled to sleep." The sun added its power to the proceedings, driving temperatures up and baking the dampness and mold from Federal equipage. A Michigander wrote, "In camp... drying clothes and fixing camp-cleaning streets, etc.," while a Hampshireman recalled the day as "fine...we continued the drying process." Indeed, the spirit of the Northerners shuffling about the Carolina swamps began to revive.[24]

At 2:00 p.m., the 3rd New Hampshire received a summons to report to the primitive wharf that spanned the marsh between Legareville and the Stono River. There, the Hampshiremen boarded the steamer *Mattano* for a quick ride across to Battery Island. The regiment disembarked and marched about a mile inland on Sol Legare Island, halting in an overgrown cotton field. The new surroundings caused great uneasiness among the men. They knew little about their position except that they were close to Charleston, that Rebels shared their surroundings, and that Stevens' division lay nearby. Unaware that they were within the Federal picket cordon, the Hampshiremen allowed rumors of powerful Confederate earthworks to disrupt their ranks, leaving the men highly on edge. Since no baggage accompanied them, the 3rd New Hampshire made a rough camp and settled down for an uneasy night.[25]

After they spent their morning drying their camp equipage, the New York Highlanders used the afternoon to prepare for picket duty. Near 5:00 p.m., as they marched to the front to relieve pickets from the 100th Pennsylvania, the Highlanders passed Isaac Stevens and his staff surveying the Union lines. Suddenly, a Rebel shell crashed into the area and forced the general and his entourage to find less exposed ground. This random shell proved to be the only disturbance of their evening. Later, at 3:00 a.m., after eight hours at the front, the rains began to fall anew. The Scotsmen wrapped their rubber ponchos around themselves and tried as they could to keep their musket caps dry. One New Yorker philosophically accepted the heavens pouring on the just and the unjust alike. Despite such slight shelter, this cumulative exposure continued to undercut the morale of the men.[26]

Saturday
June 7, 1862

Others were up late that night. An hour after midnight, Pemberton thought enough of a talkative prisoner to wire Jefferson

Brig. Gen. Isaac Stevens and staff, Beaufort, SC, spring 1862. From left to right: Capt. B. F. Porter, W. T. Lusk, Hazard Stevens (Isaac's son), Abraham Cottrell, General Stevens, Lt. Wm. Taylor, Maj. George Kimble, and Lt. Benjamin Lyons.

Massachusetts Commandery, Military Order of the Loyal Legion and the U.S. Army Military History Institute.

Davis with the results of the Federal's interrogation. The garrulous captive provided a rather accurate appraisal of Northern strength on the island and, for the first time, Charleston's chief defender had a good idea of what he and his men were up against—if the Federal was telling the truth. Believing that the enemy were in deadly earnest, Pemberton made preparations for the fighting that was sure to come. He reminded William Duncan Smith that the Secessionville works needed a bombproof, inasmuch as the enemy artillery would soon be within range of the southernmost section of the defenses. Pemberton also requested a full accounting of all the artillery along the lines, assuring Smith that anything needed would be quickly supplied. Of the small earthwork intersecting the bottleneck of the Secessionville peninsula, Pemberton's opinion was firm: "This work is important and its speedy completion necessary."[27]

* * *

The threatening weather conditions that had broken early Saturday morning continued into the daylight hours as the jittery men of the 3rd New Hampshire arose to inspect their new surroundings. To the rattled newcomers, every movement, every distant object, appeared to be "a real live reb 'for shuah,'" noted one soldier. They formed ranks and marched another mile to the east. Once, for a brief moment, a real Confederate picket did wander into view, but that remained the extent of their contact with the enemy that morning. As with almost every day since the campaign began, the skies continued to pour.[28]

Saturday's rain converted Sol Legare's back into a cramped, wet environment, but now most of its limited high ground was covered by milling blue uniforms. Isaac Stevens decided to extend the pickets in order to open up more of the island for camp space, and as a consequence, the 79th New York received orders to advance their line farther east. Gathering what little baggage they had brought to their outposts, the Highlanders pushed across the open Legare field and into the woods and fields beyond, with little resistance from the Confederate defenders. Eventually, the New Yorkers established their new line a mile beyond the old one, thereby opening up campsites around the Legare buildings and fields. Arriving Federals took quick advantage of the new clearings.[29]

One of the regiments headed for a fresh camp was the 7th Connecticut. Having rested up in the Legareville area, the Connecticut men were ordered across the Stono to join their new brigade. Like the 3rd New Hampshire before them, the 7th landed on Battery Island and marched across Sol Legare's. They finally came to rest "in a muddy cotton field with rain pouring on our devoted heads,"wrote one of the unfortunate foot soldiers. Soon thereafter, a foraging party located a drove of cattle and hustled them into the new camp for butchering. With the fresh beef passed about, the men roasted the "tender morsels...using their bayonets for spits." Neither salt nor pepper were to be found, but the meal had all the elements of a delicacy for the water-logged men from New England, camped in what one of them described as "a floating cotton field" their first day on Sol Legare Island.[30]

While the 7th Connecticut busied themselves with the crossing of the Stono and the establishment of their new camp, other Northerners crowding Sol Legare's saw a unique sight hovering over their camps. Near Battery Island, an observation balloon commanded by a Captain Starkweather was inflated and slowly rose towards the cloudy heavens. Over the next two days, the aeronaut "discovered two camps...and defined the picket line" from his perch while enjoying a clear view across the island all the way to Wappoo Cut. The Highlanders enjoyed their introduction to the art of air reconnaissance from their advanced positions two miles away, but one nearby Roundhead had more pressing matters on his mind. "It was raining all the time & the mud was knee deep," he complained. "I tell you we were wet!" The precepts of war continued to evolve with the advent of the rifled artillery and the land-to-sea signaling system. But the nature of war remained much the same, with the hardships of camp and the frayed nerves of the front lines, changing, yet immutable, amidst the swamps and sand hills of South Carolina.[31]

* * *

Since his stay in Legareville was proving somewhat longer than expected, Horatio Wright realized he would need updated intelligence concerning the Rebels on Johns Island. He organized a reconnaissance north along the Stono to examine the area above Legareville. Colonel Edward Serrell, commanding a force that included the 97th Pennsylvania and two companies of the 1st Massachusetts Cavalry, pushed up the muddy road paralleling the Stono. When contact was made with the mounted enemy pickets, a cavalry squadron formed and attacked the Confederates, driving the pickets before them. The Northerners reformed and continued their advance north to a causeway, where they encountered a masked Rebel battery supported by a company of Confederate horse. Two companies of the 97th Pennsylvania deployed with the Massachusetts cavalrymen to engage the Southerners. As the fighting slowly developed, Serrell duly noted the Confederate positions, but word came "that large bodies of infantry and cavalry" were moving on the Union rear. Serrell wisely decided to halt the advance. While some Federal cavalry witnessed two enemy forces firing at each other, other Northerners probed what was described as "a long line of natural or artificial earth defenses in front and manned by a large force."

Towards sunset, after capturing two unsuspecting Confederate pickets, the Federal reconnaissance began to retrace its route with an enemy mounted patrol nipping at its heels. The rain, as usual, was falling, but the downpour slowly grew into a ferocious, pounding storm, accompanied by booming thunder and blinding lightning. The Federals snaked through the difficult and dangerous terrain, feeling their way along the flooded roadway until 9:30 p.m., when they finally made Legareville. Wright thanked the troops for their "promptness and success" in the face of such difficulties. For their part, with but two wounded men to show for the day's work, the men were just happy to get back alive.[32]

Another Unionist who led a reconnaissance into uncharted terrain was Lt. Col. Joseph Hawley. He and Lt. Benjamin Lyons of Stevens' staff moved north across the Grimball causeway sometime in the afternoon with three companies from the 7th Connecticut. Eventually they crossed the head of a small creek that ran west to the Stono River, before passing a farm road running west to the Grimball plantation buildings, which consisted of the family home, a barn, a gin house, and two groupings of slave quarters. Although the Grimball farm lane continued due east, the patrol chose to head north then northeast as their route veered towards the Rebel lines. They drew the attention of some enemy pickets, but the bad weather added confusion to the situation, which allowed them to withdraw without loss. Hawley returned to report on the area around Grimball's, but his was no ordinary reconnaissance. With all the campsites on Sol Legare Island taken, David Hunter and Henry Benham needed more space if Wright's troops were to take part in the assault on Charleston. The Union generals also knew that the springboard would have to widen if the assault was to be over a broad front. Grimball's plantation provided answers for both concerns.[33]

As night fell on Sol Legare Island, the 3rd New Hampshire marched east to relieve the 79th New York and the 8th Michigan, both serving on the picket line. No sooner had the men from New Hampshire assumed their positions than the same storm that had seared the Johns Island reconnaissance with claps of thunder and bolts of lightning broke in all its fury over Sol Legare's. "(B)linded by the excessively white light and deafened by the meteoric explosions," explained one Federal, the men actually confused the storm blasts with shell fire and feared a pending Confederate attack. A few Northerners sought shelter from the storm in some sheds and corn cribs, but they paid for their comfort with a bad attack of fleas, described by one sufferer as the "permanent" occupants of the structures. Out on the line, startled soldiers instinctively felt for the next man in line for the simple assurance that they weren't alone. One Hampshiremen, stunned by the ferocious launchings of nature, simply wrote, "Language cannot describe the event."[34]

* * *

For the front-line Confederates, the rainy day proved uneventful except for an enemy push on Sol Legare Island. Oddly, the fierce storm that so struck the Federals barely raised an eyebrow among the Southerners. Perhaps they were used to the intensity of Carolina storms, but they penned nary a word about the thunder and lightning of this night. Whatever the reason for their silence, the Confederates settled down to another night in the driving rain.

Back at his headquarters, John Pemberton continued his fevered exertions as he attempted to summon reinforcements. He ordered

Mercer in Savannah to be ready "to move at the moment's notice." He also requested that Mercer's best artillery battery be forwarded immediately to Charleston. He pressed the head of the Charleston Arsenal to prepare a large shipment of percussion caps, shells, and friction tubes for General Smith at Secessionville. From Smith, Pemberton requested a complete accounting of the Confederate armament and ammunition lining the James Island perimeter. Already, Pemberton was beginning to sense that the battle for James Island could very well happen in the fields west of Secessionville.[35]

* * *

In an incident typical of the nature of this war, Private Patrick Hayes of the 1st Massachusetts Cavalry and a Confederate captain named Jenkens came to blows at some anonymous point on Johns Island. The officer shot the private and demanded his surrender, but the spunky Irishman refused to halt his mount. It took a second round of shots into the private again, as well as his mount, before the determined captain finally trapped his quarry. He carried the badly wounded Hayes back to his camp, where they attempted to make the man comfortable. The private lasted 24 hours.[36]

Sunday
June 8, 1862

For the Northerners on Sol Legare Island, the pace of the campaign began to quicken. During the morning, the 46th New York and elements of the 1st Massachusetts Cavalry came ashore as Stevens' division continued to spread from Battery Island to well past the Legare buildings. More importantly, in response to Benham's urgings, Stevens formulated a series of movements—one north towards Grimball's, the other east towards Secessionville. By applying pressure across a broad front, Stevens intended to stretch the Confederate defenses while providing increased space for the growing Unionist camps. On this, the 6th day of the occupation, Benham and Stevens were clearly preparing to raise the stakes of the invasion.[37]

That morning, Col. J. H. Morrow, a member of General David Hunter's staff, came ashore to lead the 46th New York and one company of the 1st Massachusetts Cavalry north across the Grimball causeway. Morrow divided his command and accompanied one wing along the rough dirt road towards the Grimball plantation, the same route Hawley had taken the night before. Like that officer, this grouping moved past the plantation houses and angled towards the interior of the island. The roadway, wide enough to allow three horses to ride abreast, passed through a mottled cornfield before turning to the northeast. At that point they encountered a dense wood that rose up on the road's left and eventually dominated both sides of the route until an open field with "girdled and felled trees," as one soldier described the fallen timber, extended off to the road's right. The field was divided by a hedge and drainage ditch that ran perpendicularly to the roadway's direction. The route then plunged into a second forest as it continued to angle more east now than north.[38]

By mid-afternoon, Colonel Morrow and his group arrived at the second stand of woods after a ride of some one and one-half miles. As they came within sight of a church sitting placidly among the trees, a galling fire erupted from both sides of the road. The Federals had run directly into a Confederate picket line, described by one of the Unionists as "a heavy force of skirmishers." Morrow's soldiers quickly paid the price for their mistake. Panic swept through the ranks as the Germans of the 46th New York fell into a fit of "unexplained wild shooting." Within moments, many of Morrow's men began to break for the rear as the line wavered before the enemy fire. In an attempt to rescue the deteriorating situation, Morrow furiously spurred his mount along the line to steadied his rattled troops, but a Confederate minie slammed into his horse and dismounted the rider. Although lucky to have avoided a serious wound, the fall sprained the officer's ankle. Adding to the confusion, another officer, Major Wright from General Horatio Wright's staff, took a bullet to the thigh, but despite the wounding managed to remain at his post to help steady the panic-stricken Germans. Slowly, the ambushed Federals overcame their initial shock and returned the Southern missiles.[39]

Somehow, one of the Union gunboats discovered that Morrow's reconnaissance had found trouble and began to launch shells over the heads of the struggling Northerners. In the sudden, frighteningly blind engagement, only the flash of rifle fire betrayed the presence friend and foe. In his claustrophobic surroundings, Morrow could only count his own casualties of two dead and five shot. Facing an unknown number of Rebels in uncharted territory, Morrow deemed "it prudent to withdraw" from the smoking woodlot.

Although apparently bloodied for no good purpose, Morrow's reconnaissance gleaned one bit of critical intelligence: the Confederates meant to hold the area northeast of Grimball's.[40]

* * *

Morrow's heavy probe had initially run into four companies of the Eutaws, stationed near the Presbyterian Church, around 4:00 p.m., but the size of the enemy force surprised the Confederates, who were more used to cavalry patrols and small unit tactics. Word went back to Artillery Crossroads of the enemy thrust, and soon Preston's Light Artillery came roaring down the road, followed by two supporting companies of infantry. The Eutaws took up the challenge offered by Morrow's sudden appearance, as spitting fire flew across the woodlots, but the Federals hadn't the stomach to keep up the fight and soon melted back into the woods towards Grimball's. Several Confederate patrols inched carefully forward to assess the damage inflicted on the intruders. They assumed the price the Federals paid for their impudence would be high, but in the afternoon light they could find but one dead Federal. The curious Rebels examined the corpse's effects and discovered during the gruesome process that the soldier was a German—and a poorly dressed one at that. Two days later, the *Charleston Mercury* reported the Federal's death, commenting that "the sorry plight of the uniform in which he was clothed scarcely sustained the generally accredited assertion of the excellent character of the clothing and equipments of the Federal army."[41]

* * *

In the meanwhile, with Stevens' brigades under arms "in readiness to march in a minutes warning," the right wing of the joint

Federal reconnaissance pushed east from the plantation across cotton and corn fields, woods and wetlands. The Federals eventually reached a slight rise of ground, from which they got their first good look at the Secessionville area. One of the observers later wrote that "(p)lainly discernable" across the intervening fields was a lookout tower. "It is a skeleton one, neatly built, not unlike a New York fire observatory in construction," he noted, ". . .almost if not quite 200 feet high." Even at this distance, they could make out "the red line of the fort, on the further side of a deep fosse. . ." Further east, a floating battery holding what the Federals described as "two heavy guns," could be seen in a waterway next to the village, which consisted of "perhaps a dozen to 20 houses." To the north about 1,000 yards, another battery covered Secessionville's right flank. Pleased with this intelligence, the Federals withdrew to report their findings to General Stevens, whose curiosity was instantly piqued. In late afternoon, he sent his son Hazard, together with Lt. P. H. O'Rorke, three companies of the 3rd New Hampshire, and some Massachusetts horsemen, to pressure the Secessionville area a bit and see what, if anything, might give.[42]

The 3rd New Hampshire detail, commanded by Captain Donohue, moved out from its picket position and rushed the Rivers Causeway. The Hampshiremen moved east on the Battery Island Road, while the Massachusetts cavalry fanned out north towards the distant woods. Thanks to the speed of their advance, the marchers gobbled up four Rebel pickets near the Rivers House before pausing to divide into two wings. The left wing moved north up the road, advancing about a half mile before it halted. Donohue and the right wing headed due east from the Rivers House and crossed into a cotton field fronting the Secessionville works. After covering perhaps 300 yards, the men suddenly drew fire from what appeared to be Confederate rifle pits covering the approaches. Artillery erupted from the earthwork and the floating battery, the barrage described by one who suffered through it as "(w)ell directed and well sustained fire." The Southern shells exploded near the men from New Hampshire, but despite the danger, some of the more observant Federals caught a sight they would never forget.

Across the marshes, well beyond the buildings in the village, the low profile of Fort Sumter could be glimpsed through the rising powder smoke. The masonry work had become a telling image of the South's resistance and a symbol of the North's objectives. One can sense the suppressed excitement of a Hampshireman's simple diary entry: "(W)e saw Ft. Sumter for the first time."

The view from the field was brief. Donohue pulled his wing back from the barking cannons just as Southern infantry sallied out from their lines to give chase to the retreating Unionists. The pursuit became so spirited that two more companies of the 3rd New Hampshire were called out to blunt the Confederate advance and cover the retreat. The left wing of the reconnaissance also withdrew about the same time and joined their comrades crossing the Rivers Causeway back to safety. One Northerner concluded that "two or three battalions" manned the Rebel lines before Secessionville. Without doubt, the enemy's aggressiveness demonstrated their will to hold the ground near Secessionville. Donohue's group returned to camp chastened by the bristling Confederate response.[43]

* * *

The Charleston Battalion had supplied the pickets for the area fronting Secessionville on this Sunday. The four privates from the Charleston Riflemen who had manned the picket post just west of the Rivers House found themselves at the mercy of the flying Federal column. In an instant, they were herded across the causeway to Sol Legare Island and captivity. For four more soldiers, the battle for Charleston was over.[44]

* * *

Supporting this entire Federal operation in a secondary role were the 7th Connecticut and the 28th Massachusetts. A skirmish line from the Connecticut regiment was deployed poorly in the thick undergrowth of James Island, causing a number of the men to become disoriented and lose contact with the main line. When a bugle call announced retreat, Private Milton Woodford of the 7th Connecticut continued to fire at the Rebel pickets, unaware of the bugle's meaning. Thus isolated, Woodford was easily surrounded by three aggressive Southerners who demanded his surrender. The Federal bravely advised them to come and get him, but an enemy officer calmly talked him out of his suicidal challenge. Woodford surrendered, and the Confederates confiscated his rifle.[45]

*   *   *

The important information collected from these two thrusts allowed Benham to implement the second phase of James Island's occupation. When the 3rd New Hampshire resumed their picket line on Sol Legare's, they received immediate word to march west. As the 79th New York moved to take the 3rd's place on picket duty, with supports provided by the 8th Michigan, the Hampshiremen trailed rearward then angled north to cross the Grimball causeway. Soon they found the open stretches of the Plantation and located a seemingly safe place where they "did valiant service by sitting down and staying right there," noted one of the men. At nightfall, however, a barrage of Rebel shells sent the Hampshiremen ducking for cover. One witness recalled, "the diaries were not disturbed by pen or pencil." They may not have struck the most martial of poses, these "valiant" sitters of the 3rd New Hampshire, but they accomplished one more important objective that day: Benham now had his new northern flank on James Island.[46]

*   *   *

As the sun set on Sunday June 8, the Confederates out on the lines didn't seem terribly concerned with the new Federal movements. One of General Gist's staffers, Captain Tracy, described the day with the seemingly harmless journal entry, "Alarm in the evening. Troops to the front. Everything soon quiet. Enemy moving about Grimball's, on the Stono."[47]

The same could not be said for the Confederate commander-in-chief. Pemberton ordered Hugh Mercer at Savannah to dispatch "a strong, well-armed regiment" to Charleston. The Georgians resented having their defenses stripped in favor of South Carolina, but Pemberton had ceased to worry about such matters. He had finally accepted that the majority of David Hunter's forces were now operating in the vicinity of the Stono River, and it was there they would have to be stopped. In obtaining men for the city's defense, the major general was at least acting aggressively. Yet, when it came to using those men, Pemberton was proving somewhat timid. He did little more than remind William Duncan Smith on James Island to hold the woods west of the works and "endeavor to capture his (the Federal's) artillery." The Federals had done little to entrench their position on Sol Legare Island, and a single enemy regiment sat isolated near Grimball's. Quick action might have yielded substantial results and wrested the initiative away from the enemy, but Pemberton had fallen into something of a static defense, a strategy that once again pleased few around him. Even the civilians that had cheered the construction of the bombproofs on Meeting Street were shocked when the work was suddenly halted. One frustrated Charlestonian groused a telling indictment of Pemberton's leadership: "So we go with feeble vacillating councils, a ship tempest tost with irresolute or ignorant pilots in command."48

* * *

If Pemberton was expecting great results from his force on Johns Island, he would have to wait for another day. Brigadier General Nathan "Shanks" Evans still couldn't provide his superior with any kind of useful intelligence concerning the Federals near Legareville. In fact, one of his confrontations with the enemy ended in tragedy. Evans reported that on the previous evening, one of his cavalry patrols ran straight into a hail of friendly fire as it returned from a scouting operation. A company from the 17th South Carolina misunderstood an order and blasted eight returning cavalrymen from their saddles, four dead and four wounded, in what "Shanks" termed "a sad catastrophe." Meanwhile, the enemy on Johns Island remained a dangerous unknown.49

Monday
June 9, 1862

On Monday morning, June 9, Evans attempted to retrieve the situation. While he would later term his action an attack, in truth it might be more accurately termed an oversized reconnaissance. For almost the entire day he marched his whole command across Johns Island until it reached a point within three miles of Aberpoolie Creek, a watercourse north of Legareville. There,

"Shanks" sent a detachment across a footbridge towards the village. When the advance returned, members reported that "the enemy had returned to Legareville." A satisfied Evans settled his men down along the creek for the night.⁵⁰

* * *

Information that "the enemy had returned to Legareville," was in fact the transfer of Horatio Wright's troops from Legareville on Johns Island to Grimball's on James Island—and it had taken place under "Shanks" Evans nose. Wright had posted two companies of the 97th Pennsylvania at Legareville, along with one company of the 1st Massachusetts Cavalry and a two-gun section of Hamilton's battery to act as a covering force against possible incursions from above the village. With that done, Wright began the tedious process of moving his entire division across the Stono. The remaining companies of the 97th Pennsylvania joined the 6th Connecticut aboard a transport and cruised up the Stono to Grimball's, where they disembarked on James Island proper. The 6th Connecticut moved forward immediately and relieved the weary "valiants" of 3rd New Hampshire on the picket line. With neither tents nor baggage, the Pennsylvanians set up a rude camp just south of the landing area while General Wright established his headquarters in the Grimball plantation house. The Hampshiremen arrived from their night at the front to observe the troops, horses, and cannon crowding onto the landing. The high command had obvious and serious designs on James Island.⁵¹

Back at Legareville, five companies of the 3rd Rhode Island boarded the *Mayflower* for the two mile run up to Grimball's. They landed there at dusk "covered by the Federal gunboats," noted one Federal soldier. With their arrival, Wright's camps now spread northerly for almost a mile along the Stono and arched south to the neighborhood of the Grimball causeway. Haphazard construction of a low parapet running the length of the line began almost immediately, and outposts extended into the woods beyond the cordon. That evening, the 3rd Rhode Island Heavy Artillery joined the 6th Connecticut on picket duty. Major Metcalf had difficulty moving his Rhode Islanders across unfamiliar territory with night fully fallen. One of his captains drew the ire of General Wright when he and his company got lost trying to find their assigned position. For his part, Metcalf was relieved that he could even find the front.[52]

To the surprise of no one, it began to rain.

Confederate response to the Federal occupation of Grimball's elicited differing responses from a variety of witnesses. Colonel Chatfield of the 6th Connecticut recalled landing "in the face of a severe fire from the enemy." The Rhode Islanders only remembered drawing a fire from a single enemy picket that mortally wounded one of their comrades, "a sturdy old sergeant in the British army." One Northerner recalled that his battalion "played militiamen and fired into the air, and kept on firing until...they started the long roll in every rebel camp south of Charleston." Years later, Metcalf wondered whether the British sergeant was killed by friendly fire, such was the confusion out on the picket line this first night on James Island. With Hamilton's guns coming ashore, it seemed Wright's division experienced little pressure from the Southern infantry save some slight action northeast of the camps. As a consequence, by the night of June 9, Horatio Wright and much of his division were safely ensconced on James Island. The Federal noose was drawing tighter.[53]

* * *

Colonel Simonton's Eutaw Battalion had drawn picket duty on the morning of June 9, and advanced to their usual posts near the Presbyterian Church. Preston's battery joined the battalion at the religous site where, soon afterwards, pickets spotted Federals in the woods to the west. The alarm was raised, but the enemy just as quickly disappeared from the front. The Eutaws sensed nothing out of the ordinary and manned their posts all day and into the night, but reports from the picket line made them all too aware that the Federals were camped at Grimball's not two miles away.

Farther south, staff officer Carlos Tracy penned a calm understatement in his diary: "Enemy evidently in force at Grimball's."[54]

* * *

Over on Sol Legare Island, the 7th Connecticut relieved the Highlanders on the picket line. The 8th Michigan had spent the morning in camp before advancing to the front to serve as the picket reserve. Confederate artillery around Secessionville, however, could observe the newly-expanded Federal front that now covered the Rivers Causeway, and the Southern position began resemble a stirred-up beehive. One Michigander wrote, "The enemy throwing shell and ball at us." Indeed, by increasing the pace of their fire, Southern heavy metal had picked up the Northern gauntlet. Watching the effects of the Confederate barrage from his post inside the Tower Battery was the officer who had accepted the Federal challenge, Col. Thomas G. Lamar, the commander of the 1st South Carolina Artillery.[55]

Like many Southern officers, Thomas Gresham Lamar had developed into an aggressive leader from a less than military background. Born to a prominent plantation owner from the Edgefield district of South Carolina, Lamar was a planter-turned-politician who had been elected to the State General Assembly in 1860, where he became a hearty supporter of the Secessionist movement. As the Sumter crisis developed, Lamar received an appointment to Governor Pickens' staff, but he chaffed at the inaction and opted to go on his own to Morris Island, where he gained command of an artillery battery. After Sumter's surrender, the promising officer returned to Edgefield, where he raised an artillery company and became its captain. Returning to Charleston, the captain and his men served at Fort Johnson. Over the months, his company grew into a battalion, and his battalion soon expanded into a regiment, a tribute to Lamar's popularity and ability. Eventually, the 1st South Carolina Artillery manned most of the Confederate defenses east of New Town Cut, and the James Island artillerists were fired by the energy of their colonel.[56]

For Lamar, the Federal invasion of James Island had become a challenge that needed answering. Given the enemy's boldness on the June 8, Lamar decided that it was time to give notice that further advance would not go unpunished. During the rainy afternoon, his responses thundered across the island and slammed into one Federal position after another. Word of Lamar's bombardment got back to Pemberton, who tore off a quick dispatch to General Gist at Secessionville: "Don't allow your command, and especially your

Colonel Thomas Lamar
Clemson University

batteries, to waste ammunition. They must not fire merely because they are fired at. The large guns must not waste their ammunition." Lamar's response unfortunately went unrecorded, but the Federals spoke less of the Confederate artillery fire over the next few days than they did on this Monday. Colonel Lamar and his men had been restrained by the cautious Pemberton and would have to wait for a greater crisis to again unleash their aggression.[57]

As night fell, "Shanks" Evans camped his command north of Legareville after their brush with Federal pickets. He had informed Pemberton of his planned "attack" to take on the enemy at Legareville, but did little to keep his commander abreast of the developing situation. Of course, Pemberton assumed Evans' assault was proceeding apace and informed Gist that plans were underway for offensive action on Johns Island. At the appropriate time, Gist was to make a demonstration against the Federal camps to prevent enemy reinforcements from crossing the Stono.

On the night of June 9, States Rights Gist listened intently for "Shanks" Evans to duplicate his success at Ball's Bluff, where he had driven hundreds of Federals over a steep incline and into the waters of the Potomac River just a handful of miles from Washington D.C. Instead, the night passed with neither sound nor word from Johns Island. Rain again pelted Rebel and Federal alike.[58]

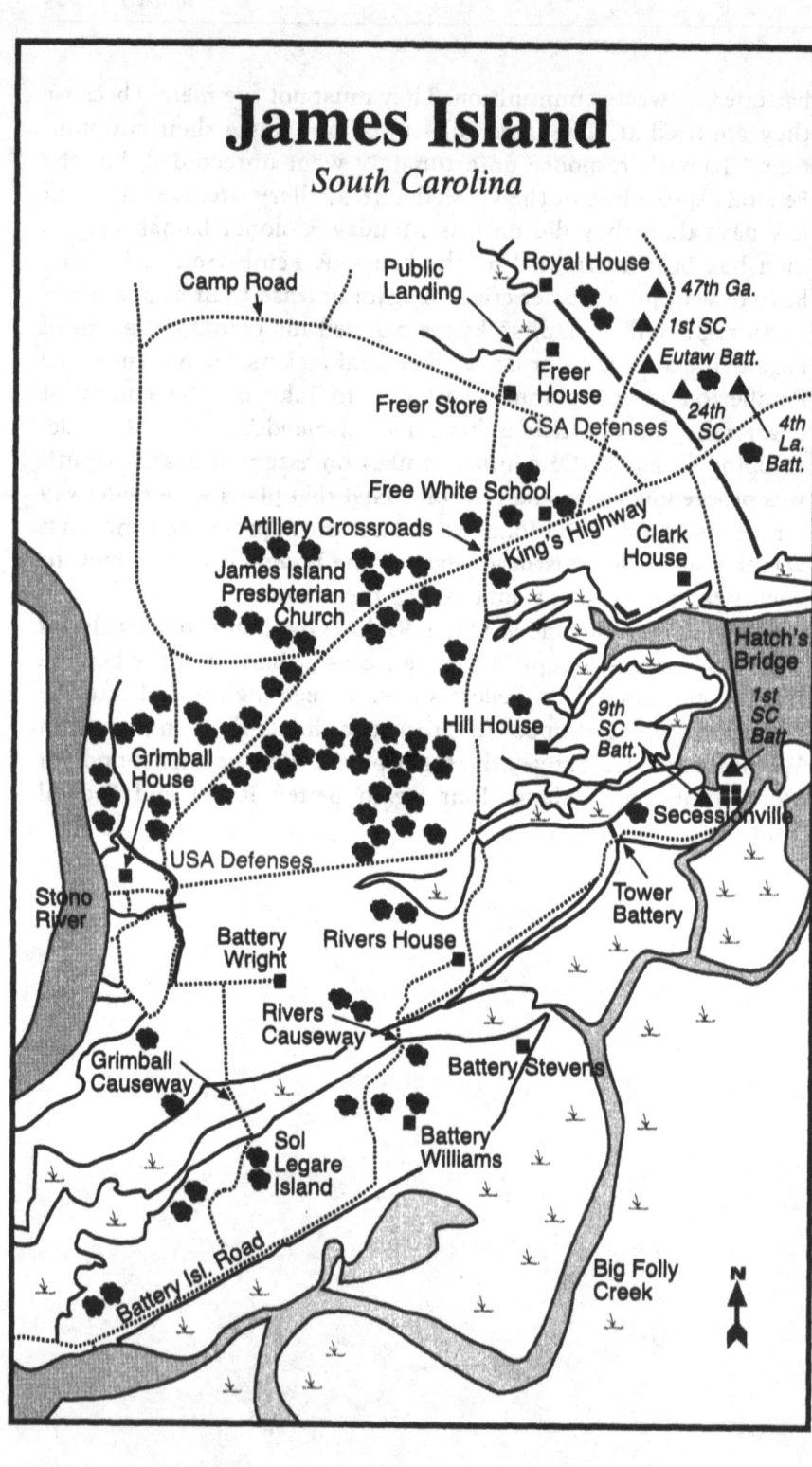

CHAPTER SIX

"(Y)ou will make no attempt to advance on Charleston or to attack Ft. Johnson."

—Maj. Gen. David Hunter to Brig. Gen. Henry Benham

Prelude

Tuesday
June 10, 1862

With Brigadier General Horatio Wright's three undersized Federal brigades finally ensconced on the right bank of the Stono River, establishing and defending the camp perimeter became the primary concern for his front line officers. Responsibility for the northern flank of the defenses fell to Col. John Chatfield, the new commander of Wright's First Brigade. To counter the enemy's obvious interest in the roadway running northeast from the Stono camps, Chatfield decided to strengthen his own position by organizing his picket forces in-depth. Since the 97th Pennsylvania was just completing a long night on the picket line, Chatfield ordered Col. H. R. Guss, the 97th's commander, to place a detachment of the 47th New York some distance in advance of the main picket line. Chatfield then sent two companies of the 45th Pennsylvania—Companies I and H—under Capt. Francis Hills, and Captain MacDonald's Company D of the 47th

New York, on the left of three companies of the 97th Pennsylvania stationed near the roadway. Soon after dawn broke, active Confederate skirmishers began probing this new Union formation and continued their activity through the morning. Around noon, while the camp equipage continued to land back by the Grimball buildings, Federal lookouts detected a group of Confederate skirmishers crawling forward under the cover of dense grass and chaparral. Members of the 97th Pennsylvania drove them off, but the Unionists remained edgy, anxiously aware of the unusually aggressive Southerners operating just beyond the perimeter.[1]

Three hours after the 97th Pennsylvania sent the crawling Southerners back to the cover of the woods, an artillery barrage covered Colonel Guss' defenses. Shells crashed into the picket area, sending some Unionists scrambling for cover, but "the men remained steady at their posts," reported one officer. One shell flew far across the lines and landed in the empty camp of the 97th Pennsylvania very near the Stono. The Northerners could do nothing in response to this bombardment, which one picket termed "a terrific storm." When the end finally came, the Federals peered expectantly into the woods north and east of their lines as an uneasy calm prevailed.[2]

* * *

At his headquarters aboard the transport *Delaware*, Henry Benham held a meeting with his divisional commanders. Benham was disturbed by two recent developments: the placement of the Confederate batteries that had lit up Grimball's the previous night, and the threatening Confederate positions to the northeast of Wright's camps. To deal with these nuisances, the former engineer proposed an extremely complicated operation. Isaac Stevens was to throw two regiments across the Rivers Causeway and sweep north up Battery Island Road, while Horatio Wright simultaneously moved one regiment east from Grimball's to hook up with Stevens' advance. Theoretically, the united columns would would capture any Confederate field artillery in the area. The final portion of Benham's scheme had two regiments from Williams' brigade sweeping around Confederate positions northeast of Grimball's, in an effort to either outflank or surround them. In either case,

Williams would then link with the other two Federal thrusts somewhere to the east. The navy would support the operation with land-directed gunfire. Much of the early action was to occur in the pre-dawn darkness, so signal flares would be used to coordinate communications. Benham directed the movement to begin at 3:00 a.m. the morning of June 11. Both Wright and Stevens received copies of the orders and, whatever their misgivings, dutifully went ahead with their own preparations. It was a plan fraught with peril.[3]

* * *

The appearance of the Federals at Grimball's further frustrated John Pemberton. Despite ceding the landing area to the enemy, the Confederate commander decided to place a heavy battery southeast of the Presbyterian Church to contest further enemy incursions in the area. Such thinking was cloudy at best, for no battery—no matter how heavy the guns—could maintain itself in such an isolated position, far removed from its supports. Moreover, no single battery could possibly take on the Federal gunboats on any footing approaching equality, much less the burgeoning infantry force now shadowing the Stono River. But Pemberton ordered it, so his new subordinate, William Duncan Smith, took on the nearly impossible task.

Smith placed Johnson Hagood and his 1st South Carolina, together with McEnery's 4th Louisiana Battalion and a section of Preston's guns, at the Presbyterian Church. Colonel Gilbert W. M. Williams' 47th Georgia was deployed south of Hagood in the thick woods west of the Battery Island Road. Smith planned an artillery barrage to precede the infantry assault, an attack intended to take and hold the area bracketing the northern and eastern forest edge of the Grimball clearing. As a precaution, he called out the Eutaw Battalion to support the assault and stand ready to exploit any opportunity.[4]

The Confederates took the morning to assemble the troops near the church. While small patrols pricked at the Federal outposts, Hagood split his force into three sections, one on each side of the road facing Grimball's, and the third further back in the road itself. The Georgians deployed south of Hagood's Carolinians in a particu-

REPULSE OF THE REBELS AT JAMES ISLAND, NEAR CHARLESTON, S. C., JUNE 10, 1862

Prelude 129

CAPTURE THE PICKETS OF GEN. WRIGHT'S DIVISION.—FROM A SKETCH BY AN OFFICER.

larly dense section of timber, while the 4th Louisiana Battalion formed in column on the roadway. The Eutaws, fresh off picket duty, had just reached camp when orders called them back to the front. The battalion reversed itself and took up a supporting position near the church grounds. At 2:00 p.m., as the infantry slogged towards their assigned positions, Confederate artillery from Secessionville north along the line opened fire. For a full hour and a half the Southern guns thundered at the enemy lining the Grimball defenses, until 3:30 p.m., when the barrage tempered, then ceased. As the front quieted, Smith ordered the gray infantry forward.[5]

As Col. Gilbert Williams pushed his 47th Georgia soldiers in a southeasterly direction, the low tracts of swampy ground, "almost a jungle" as one Confederate remembered it, ruptured his formation. Although Hagood's men advanced slowly but steadily along the road, Williams' wing pushed forward well beyond Hagood's left, rousting a Federal outpost in the process. The nearly-overrun Unionists fired a hurried volley and fell back, heartening those Confederates witnessing the precipitate retreat of the enemy.

As the Georgians advanced through the woods, all Federal resistance seemed to melt under their steady pressure. When elements of Williams' advance burst exultantly out of the swampy tract into a large clearing, however, astonishment replaced Confederate confidence: a sweeping volley ripped into the uncovered, isolated Southerners. Captain William Williams, the brother of the colonel, cried out over the explosion, "Here are the Federal sons of bitches; now then, boys, give them hell." The captain had indeed found a line of Federal rifles, well posted and well defended. Unfortunately for the officer, the enemy rifle explosion cut down the charging Confederates in a scything, fiery blast. Seven bullets hit Captain Williams almost simultaneously, toppling him to the ground badly wounded. The momentum of the charge brought many of the Georgians past the writhing Williams to within ten yards of the blazing enemy line, but the sweeping volleys prevented them from driving any further. Isolated in a position bereft of cover, the small band of Georgians recoiled before the hail of musketry and dragged off many of their fallen comrades to the relative safety of the just-departed woodline. The Federal retreat turned into a stinging repulse as Georgia blood puddled on the South Carolina fields northeast of the Grimball plantation.[6]

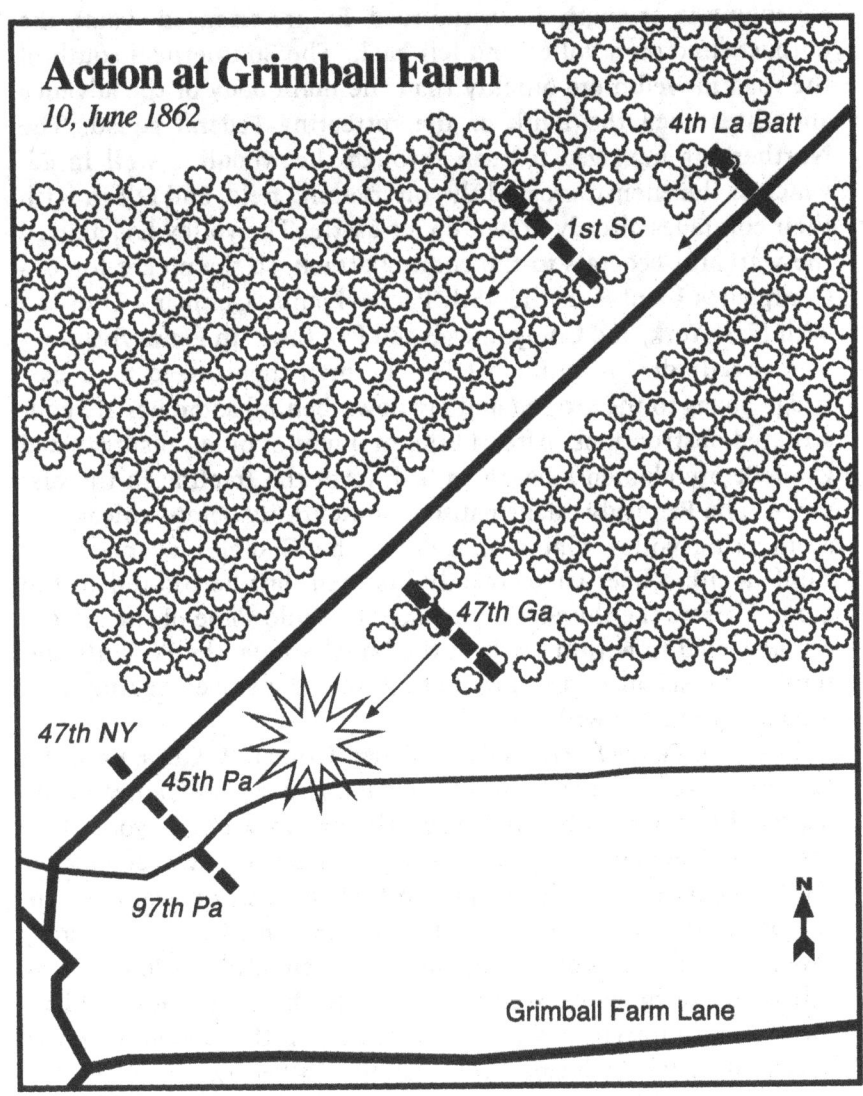

* * *

The fifteen-man outpost from the 47th New York were the first to see the ragged Confederate line pushing through the woods and advancing in strength down the road. By pre-arranged signal, the outpost fired off a volley and fell back. The Southerners south of the road moved more quickly than the main body of the advance and threatened the flank of the retreating Federal squad. The Northerners managed to rush through the woodline well in advance of the enemy, crossed the intervening field, and fell in with their comrades already drawn up for battle. The volley had alerted the watchful Federals to the coming attack, so the picket force—Companies I and H of the 45th Pennsylvania, Company D of the 47th New York, and Companies B and F of the 97th Pennsylvania—was already drawn up for battle. The men then tossed their cartridge boxes to the ground and lay down behind some hastily constructed obstructions. After a brief moment of quiet, disorganized Confederate elements began to leak from the treeline in the distance. The Pennsylvanians paused momentarily before unleashing a shivering volley that struck down the Georgia advance. One Confederate officer tried to rally his men, but he too fell to the ground before the thundering musketry. While some of the attackers struggled to within yards of the Northerners, the Federals' determined resistance forced them back into the woods, taking their dead and wounded with them.[7]

The 97th Pennsylvania's commander, Col. H. R. Guss, used the lull to secure his right flank by advancing three companies of his regiment to the right before angling the line forward. Beyond that, the Northerners did little but await the renewal of the enemy assault. Twenty minutes later, the Southerners came on again. As the enemy pressed their assault with, as one defender remembered, "great vigor," the entire Federal front exploded. Colonel Guss called out for his boys to fire, and "the flashing guns seemed like the voice of a torrent irresistible in force." For the second time, the Southerners fell in heaps. Guss calmly walked the line, and his men responded in kind, having been "rendered cool and brave" by his example. The charging Southerners again closed to within yards of the 45th's line, but the Pennsylvanians poured forth a deadly and

Prelude 133

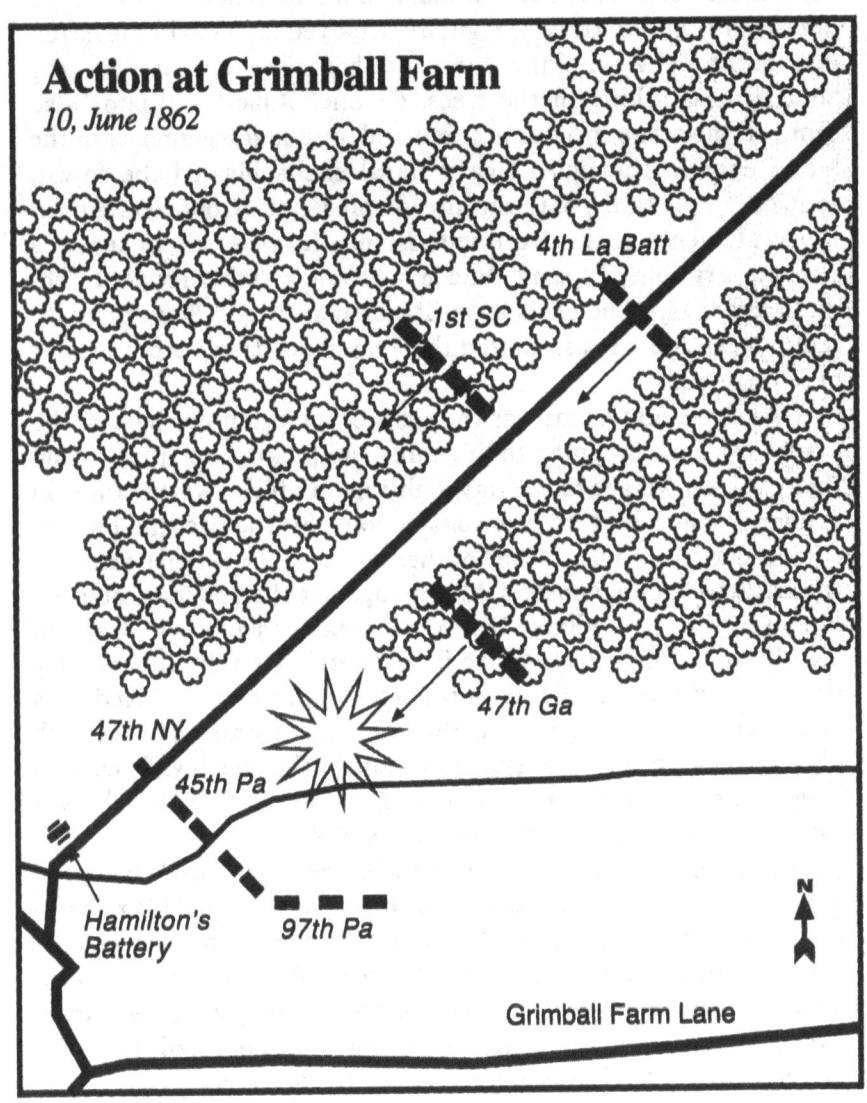

destructive fire that spread confusion and death among the attackers. The survivors fell back into the woods a second time.[8]

Now, however, the defending infantry was joined by elements of Federal artillery. With Captain Ransom in command, part of Capt. John Hamilton's battery of regulars deployed on a slight elevation just behind the smoking line and began to hammer at the Southerners lurking in the trees. Colonel Robert Williams also came on the scene to assume command, just as the gunboats in the Stono entered the fight. Heavy naval shells blasted the forest, showering tree limbs onto the already precarious Confederate positions. Elements of the 3rd Rhode Island Heavy Artillery set up a light battery behind a sand dune and, as one member recalled, "administered grape and canister in liberal quantities." From three directions, Union guns saturated the enemy position with a torrent of flying metal.[9]

One scene few forgot was the sight of the drummer boys of the 47th New York dropping their snares and picking up rifles to add their bantam weight to the fray, fighting for all the world "like old soldiers." Their bravery was conspicuous, for the fire line had become a dangerous place. The Southerners used the relative safety of the trees to open a considerable fire against the Federals, and the blue-uniformed soldiers began to take casualties. Captain Hamilton left his guns to move forward and help rally the infantry line, but suffered "a slight contusion" when he was winged by a Confederate ball. Further along the line, three members of the 97th also went down: Pvt. Henry Dunn, shot in the chest; Cpl. Edward Corcoran took a bullet in the forehead; and Pvt. George Wright was hit in the neck. All three died on the field.[10]

While the elements of these three Federal regiments exchanged volleys with their adversaries, Horatio Wright deployed his remaining regiments in a line of battle about 400 yards to the rear. But the frontline troops never approached the breaking point, and after what some estimated to be a two-hour battle, the enemy musketry fitfully weakened and the Confederates disappeared into the gloomy woods. Darkness crept over the fields and forests, frustrating any pursuit, but the Northerners, keenly aware that they had just stood, and stood well, their first test of fire, were content to let the enemy go.

* * *

Colonel Williams had come upon his reeling Georgians, blasted back into the woods by their first contact with the Federal firing line and rallied two of the battered companies inside the woodline. Taking almost twenty minutes to knead them into an assault formation, Williams sent them back into the field at the enemy lines. The Georgians bravely charged the flaring musketry, but the enemy rifle fire was now supported by a sweeping artillery barrage, which turned the open area into a killing field. The murderous blasts carved up the unsupported Confederates attackers. Those Georgians still standing had little choice but to fall back once again to the protection of the woods. Advance elements of the 4th Louisiana Battalion met the bloodied 47th Georgia there, and together formed a pitted line among the trees and undergrowth to answer the stinging enemy fire. A new danger began to threaten the hastily-assumed Confederate line when falling limbs and chunks of tree trunks, blasted into wooden shrapnel by the plunging artillery fire, showered the Southerners. To make matters worse, those Georgians holding Williams' left now felt rifle fire on their flank. Unable to get a good look at the enemy line, most Confederates simply struggled to hold on, desperately attempting to equalize what had rapidly degenerated into a decidedly one-sided affair.[11]

Aware of the heavy nature of the fight developing ahead of his men, Johnson Hagood tried to hustle his regiment to the front through the dense undergrowth. But the Federal artillery fire—especially the naval shells from the gunboats—made any sort of advance extremely hazardous. Learning of Williams' bloody rebuff, Hagood determined to withdraw, despite having taken no casualties himself. Orders snaked to the front pulling Williams' Georgians and McEnery's Louisianans back towards the church. In the growing dusk, the bloodied Southerners disengaged from their unequal contest, leaving wounded and dead comrades sprawled across the open field that fronted the Federal lines.[12]

Colonel Williams was no doubt jolted by the casualty report offered by his subalterns. The 47th Georgia's casualties—somewhere between 60 to 70 dead and wounded—represented the total for Hagood's entire assault. About 25 men were left on the field, including Williams' own brother, and the two companies that spearheaded the second attack had practically ceased to exist. William Duncan Smith was furious when he learned of the debacle. Finding his troops decimated for no apparent reason, he informed Pemberton that the battery he wanted constructed "would occasion great sacrifice of life, & if he still insisted on it, he (Smith) wished he (Pemberton) would give him a written order." Later rumors held that Pemberton became so irate he ordered Smith arrested. If true, he either did not carry out the directive or else quickly released the officer. Either way, Pemberton had suffered a double setback: he managed to lose a vicious little fight *and* alienate an important subordinate, all with the enemy at his gates.[13]

* * *

As the Southerners melted into the smoky forest, the excited Northerners realized that they had just won, however small, a tough fight. Detachments cautiously examined the field and woods for wounded Confederates, and eventually collected and buried 17 bodies while capturing eight wounded Southerners, including a mortally struck Captain Williams. The captured Southerners admitted that the retreating force had dragged away many more and that the Confederate casualty total was much higher than the body count indicated. On their own side, only three Northerners, all members of the 97th Pennsylvania, died, and but 13 others were wounded. Numbers, however, weren't the only measure of the engagement. In sight of almost the entirety of Wright's division, "the men fought like veterans, standing up before the enemy's galling musketry without wavering," reported one Federal officer. Colonel John Chatfield, the commander of Wright's First Brigade, wrote in his report that "too much cannot be said in praise of the conduct of the troops engaged." Even over on Sol Legare Island, a Michigan man admitted that "General Wright. . .had quite a battle." Later, the press would heap much praise upon the 97th Pennsylvania, describing the bravery of the "tenacious, determined, and gallant" heroes for the folks back home. Although the Unionists heavily outnumbered the Confederate attackers, thus helping to account for the lopsided victory, this affair cemented mutual respect among the participating Federal regiments in the fight, a bonding that would serve the men well down the line. A supposed conversation between a New Yorker and a Pennsylvanian illustrates well the post-battle spirit of the victors:

New York: "Well, colonel, that was quite a brilliant affair."
Pennsylvania: "Yes, the 97th did well."
New York: "The 47th, you mean."
Pennsylvania: "No, I mean the 97th."
New York: "No sir, you are quite mistaken; the brunt of the action fell upon the 47th."
Pennsylvania: "How comes it, then, that the only men killed were those of the Pennsylvania Regiment?"
New York: "Yes that is a fact; they were in the reserve."
Pennsylvania: "Odd that they should have began by attacking our reserves; but who was in command of our forces? Was it not Col. Guss of the 97th?"
New York: "Bully for you, colonel, you have got me there. But the 47th did nobly."
Pennsylvania: "So they did and all honor to them."[14]

As night fell, the 76th Pennsylvania moved forward to take the 97th's place on the picket line. Despite the losses, June 10, 1862, was a day to remember for those young Pennsylvanians and New Yorkers who had seen and survived their first action in the war. Reflecting on the day's events, a Rhode Islander observed that the Southerners "smarting from the wounds received," knew now that the Federals intended more than simply holding to one end of the island. It would soon be the Federals' turn to take the battle to the Rebels.[15]

* * *

Captain Percival Drayton, the commander of the Stono naval squadron, didn't share the good cheer then warming the infantry camps. In analyzing the military preparedness of the Federal forces, he had become extremely discouraged by the state of affairs—and wrote Flag Officer Samuel Francis DuPont as much. His pointed memorandum concluded that now, seven days after the first troops had landed, the men were hardly in any condition to fight. Drayton characterized every attempt to penetrate the Confederate-held areas as futile. More importantly, he feared that Benham had lost the confidence of his officers and that the soldiers themselves had grown what he described as "despondent." He informed DuPont that the enemy had moved their floating battery near Secessionville to shallow water, thus making it impossible to reach from the Stono. Fortunately, two of his gunboats, the *Ellen* and the *Hale*, were now stationed in Lighthouse Creek, and therefore in a position to protect Stevens' right flank. Captain Drayton mentioned Benham's plans for a grand reconnaissance, but expressed doubts that the troops could operate far from the protection of the navy's guns. Now, perhaps most dishearteningly for Drayton, those very guns were showing wear. His large Parrott rifles were "completely used up," and the supplies of shell and powder were dwindling rapidly. As for the effect of naval gunfire on the enemy: "I am satisfied that half of our shells fired are wasted." Adding that ammunition and coal would need replenishing soon, Drayton closed his dreary report.[16]

That night, Alexander Campbell, the color bearer for the 79th New York, wrote a telling letter to his wife. It was the first time he had written from the Highlanders' new camp, located, he informed his wife, on "a small Knoll of Land, all surrounded with swamp." After describing the battle of June 3 ("our men stood like bricks"), he related the amazing story of his brother, James. One of the Rebel captives had revealed to him that James was a lieutenant in the Charleston Battalion and had been in the fight on the 3rd. The prisoner related that brother James thought Alexander wounded and captive in Richmond, but his inquiries had proved the rumor false. Alexander took some solace in how the war had brought the two brothers so close together ("so you see we are not far from each other now"), but he had grown fearful of the nature of this conflict—"This is a warr that there never was the Like of before Brother against Brother Jane all (I) wish is that it wont Last much Longer and that god will spare us all to return to our homes in safety." Campbell then shifted gears, adding that "when we make the grand advance on Charleston, the fire from our gunn Boats and field Batteries will teach them a Lesson that they wont apt to forget." Almost as an afterthought, he noted that, "this is the first dry day we have had since we Landed here."[17]

* * *

Federal theater Commander Gen. David Hunter was pondering his James Island invasion aboard his headquarters gunboat *Delaware*. Henry Benham's ambitious plan originally had envisioned a lightning rout of the Southerners, the capture of Fort Sumter, a mortar attack on Charleston itself, followed by the city's capitulation. But his grandiose vision had degenerated into a nightmare of cramped camps and bad weather. In a reversal of expected roles, the Southerners had seized the initiative, having launched two attacks on his camps in less than a week. Worse, intelligence revealed that Confederate reinforcements were arriving almost daily, and Hunter now feared that taking Charleston with his present force was becoming an impossibility.

Benham, however, aggressively attended to the myriad details, as Hunter grew cautious to the point of regarding his army as a garrison rather than strike force. As a result, when Hunter decided to return to Hilton Head for a few days—"matters affecting the safety of the command in other portions of the department called for (his) presence," he explained— he felt compelled to rein in his rash second in command. "(Y)ou will make no attempt to advance on Charleston or to attack Ft. Johnson," Hunter specifically ordered Benham, unless reinforced or directly instructed by Hunter himself. "You will however provide for a secure entrenched encampment" covered by the gunboats. When the camps were completely secured and provisioned, Benham was to report to Hunter in person at Hilton Head. Otherwise he was to report daily as to the progress of his efforts. With that, Hunter prepared to leave for Hilton Head, secure in the belief that Henry Benham understood exactly what was expected of him.[18]

Wednesday
June 11, 1862

Almost to a man, the Federals celebrated Tuesday's smart little repulse of the Southerners. Unfortunately for the Union cause, one of the few who regretted the action was Henry Benham. Horatio Wright had informed him that his men were "much fatigued" by yesterday's fight and, as a consequence, while his troops could assist any operation, they could not now be regarded as "fresh." Benham used Wright's report as an excuse to cancel his "grand" reconnaissance, and, in doing so, destroyed whatever slight regard Isaac Stevens might have had for him. In a letter to his wife dated June 11, Stevens poured out his anger at the two men who controlled his destiny. He described Hunter and Benham as "imbecile, vascillatory, and utterly unfit to command." Once more, as with McClellan, he was forced to serve under incompetent commanders, and he feared his own reputation would be tarnished by the shortcomings of his superiors. While expressing hope that Maj. Gen. Joseph Mansfield might be sent to take over the department, Stevens depicted Benham as "an ass—a dreadful man of no earthly use except as a nuisance and obstruction."

Stevens knew he wasn't alone. He had heard camp rumors that Benham had whipped up a grudge against Horatio Wright, whose week-long transfer of his division from Edisto to James Island ruined Benham's timetable for a speedy advance on Charleston. Wright's dallying had supposedly fouled Benham's timetable—as unrealistic as it was—and turned Hunter against an aggressive continuance of the campaign. Benham "never forgave that officer for the delay."

Despite his private misgivings, Stevens still needed Benham's support on a number of matters, especially in the area of medical supplies. Simply put, the health of his command was slowly, but steadily, deteriorating. Stevens had learned the day before that "The Surgeon of the 7th Regt. C.V. reports 100 sick on his list alone." Since Hunter had spent much of his time organizing a regiment of freemen back on Hilton Head, Stevens saw a way to make the former slaves useful while benefitting his own weary troops.

He wrote Benham,

> "The men of my command are getting sick from the severe fatigue duty which has been devolved upon them. The loading and unloading of vessels, the repair of roads, the throwing up of works can better be done by men accustomed to the climate, and they are duties which in my judgement can with great advantage to the public service be devolved upon the Carolina volunteers. I desire that this communication be laid before the Major General Commanding the Dept. and I trust that you will be able to give it your earnest endorsement."

Privately he minced few words: "Hunter has 400...nigger soldiers basking in the sun on Hilton Head whilst white soldiers are doing enormous labor here. It is a crying shame..."[19]

Benham and Hunter met one last time where, perhaps along with Stevens' concerns, they discussed the security arrangements for the camps. When the meeting ended, Hunter departed for Hilton Head, leaving Benham in command of the James Island forces. By now, dissatisfaction with Benham had grown widespread through the Federal camps. Benham's imperious ways—the haughtily sputtered "Those are my orders, sir"—sat badly with officers struggling with steep difficulties. Typically, this attitude had blinded the general to the realities Wright had faced on Johns Island and now placed him at odds with his subordinates. Lieutenant William Thompson Lusk of Isaac Stevens' staff echoed the emotions of many when he wrote to his mother:

> "I believe General Rosecrans was not far from wrong when he charged Genl. Benham with cowardice, drunkenness, and lying...Right or wrong all despise him. No one trusts him. If we take Charleston it will not be his fault. This is rather bitter, but it is a shame to put such men in command."[20]

* * *

The people of Charleston assembled at the hospital on Trapmann Street to view the wounded of the 47th Georgia as they arrived after their Tuesday afternoon fight. Curious citizens questioned the soldiers about their battle experiences, and the Georgians obliged by describing the strength of the Federal line, the marshy ground, and the "heavy and continuous fire from the unseen foe." In describing the scene, the *Charleston Mercury* reminded its readers that these "gallant men who have shed their blood" were deserving of the "many little comforts and delicacies" so needed by wounded soldiers. No doubt, Charleston opened her arms.[21]

In another part of town, John Pemberton felt the rising pressure of command. Earlier in the day, he had ordered Nathan "Shanks" Evans to send immediately as much infantry as possible to Charleston. Pemberton wired Richmond that his 15,000 effectives were inadequate for the job of defending Charleston and Savannah. Ironically, Secretary of War Randolph had just ordered Pemberton to send more troops to Richmond "if you possibly can." A frustrated Pemberton shot back in response, "I not only cannot spare any more troops from this department, but there is danger here unless I am re-enforced."[22]

The rattled Pemberton then turned his attentions to William Duncan Smith, an officer still smarting from their run-in the day before. He suggested that Smith use the Eutaw Battalion to attempt to take the new Federal batteries deployed near Grimball's. Inexplicably forgetting that Col. Johnson Hagood couldn't accomplish this objective with three times the men, and discounting the slight intelligence gleaned from Hagood's assault, Pemberton must have been incredibly ill-informed to request such action from a seething subordinate. He hoped that such efforts would "accustom the men to fire. . .if it effects nothing else." Pemberton then asked Smith, "Is it possible to burn the woods I have been so anxious to hold? You can get resin and turpentine and the wind is favorable. Give me your own and General Gist's views." Given the swampy nature of the island, the damp weather, and the prickly whims of the wind, Pemberton's suggestions struck his James Island subordinate as preposterous. It was no wonder that Smith risked arrest by requesting further orders from General Pemberton in writing.[23]

Duncan Smith was not alone in his mistrust of his commander. Charleston citizen William Grayson watched as both military stores and bank documents were transported out of town, prompting him to write, "Doubts are entertained whether the government intends to defend the city." William Porcher Miles, a former United States and now Confederate Congressman, wrote a letter to Robert E. Lee begging the Virginian to replace Pemberton. Miles asserted that the commander "does not possess the confidence of his officers, his troops, or the people of Charleston," due to reasons supposedly too numerous for the writer to list. He explained that he wrote to avoid the appearance of a petition, hoping that official action in Richmond might forego such embarrassment. Miles thought William Duncan Smith could do the job, but he pleaded with Lee to act with "early and earnest consideration."[24]

* * *

With the canceling of Benham's "grand reconnaissance," the Northerners spent an uneventful day on Sol Legare and James Island, if dodging the occasional shell and bullet can be called uneventful. Stevens' camps had reached their physical limits, extending now from Battery Island all the way to the Legare House and fields. Although the 8th Michigan had been ordered to the front soon after daylight, it stayed only a short time before returning to its camps. Instead, the 7th Connecticut moved to the picket line after spending a pleasant night in camp, their first in their recently arrived tents. The 7th's Company G made a dash on the Confederate pickets around 3:00 p.m., accompanied by a member of Stevens staff, in an effort to uncover a hidden earthwork and its artillery supports. Confederate cannon boomed in response, wounding one man. Satisfied with their intelligence work, the company volleyed once and retired.[25]

* * *

Up at Grimball's, Col. Edward Serrell's engineers joined the infantry strengthening the 1,220 yard line of entrenchments surrounding Wright's camps. Of particular importance was a bastion that would soon mount the two 42-lb. James guns and the single 30-lb. Parrott Rifle that had just arrived from the recently-completed Fort Pulaski operations. The emplacement extended out from the main line and effectively covered both the left flank of the camps and the roadway heading northeast towards the Southerners. When finally placed, the guns would add their weight over the contested ground of the day before, thus adding an extra deterrent to further Confederate efforts in the area.[26]

To aid their observations, the men of the Federal signal service commandeered a tall pine tree "fully a half a mile in front of our lines," wrote one soldier. Signalmen had nailed slats into the bark of the tree to form a rough ladder to a lookout perch one hundred and twenty feet in the air. From this vantage point, lookouts could see the Confederate positions from Secessionville north to Fort Johnson and Charleston Harbor. Signal Officer Henry Tafft made the climb and promptly swore that "once was enough for me. I made a solemn vow that if I ever reached mother earth alive, I would never again be guilty of such a foolhardy act."[27]

But life in the camps on James Island was proving dangerous. In the evening, a spent ball felled a private from the 3rd New Hampshire, the first Hampshireman wounded in the campaign. Word also spread that two more of the captured enemy, including Captain Williams of the 47th Georgia, had died of their wounds. Williams was discovered to be a Mason, so some Rhode Island brethren prepared to transport his remains through the lines under a flag of truce, a strange but common courtesy acted out many times in the midst of the war.

* * *

Towards the end of the day on June 11, Pemberton fired off another wire to "Shanks" Evans: "Have you received my telegram? Send at least one good regiment, more if you can. It is evident that the enemy is not in great force before you." The answer to Pemberton's stinging rebuke, which implied some degree of negligence on Evans' part, went unrecorded. As both Smith and Evans seethed, Pemberton was allowing the pressure of his command to badly taint his official relations with his subordinates.[29]

Thursday
June 12, 1862

One the morning of June 12, the Eutaw Battalion was marched to Artillery Crossroads and south onto the Battery Island Road. After a mile or so, the Carolinians stopped at a finger of timber that crossed the roadway and continued east towards the marshes. The woods were an extension of the forest that bracketed the Grimball fields near the Stono—the same timber that had disrupted the Confederate attacks two days earlier on June 10—and covered most of the intervening area to the Battery Island Road. The fields south of the timber line were separated from the Secessionville peninsula by a swampy tidal basin, but aggressive Federals venturing north from the Rivers House could easily use the cover of these trees to mask their movements. To eliminate this advantage, the new arrivals of the 22nd South Carolina drew the unenviable duty of felling the timber east of the roadway, and the Eutaw Battalion was positioned to cover their comrades' efforts.

The 22nd South Carolina spent the day hacking away at the trees and arranging the fallen logs to form a thick abatis facing south. These obstructions freed a line of fire that could play on the flank of any force assaulting Secessionville. Unfortunately, some of the abatis proved inordinately thick, blocking a clear view of the fields south of the former timber line. But visible through much of the obstruction were a cluster of slave quarters, hugging the tidal marsh, that belonged to the Hill plantation. Other than these shacks and the Hill's house further east, this stretch of land now lay open and flat—an almost perfect field of fire.[30]

The Clark house stood northeast of the newly formed abatis, across further juttings of the harbor-fed marshland on a point just west of the main Confederate defense line. Erected on a slight elevation west of the house was the earthwork designed to sweep both the field in front of the Tower Battery and the area south of the newly-felled abatis. If well served, the two 24-lb. artillery pieces mounted in the battery could counter any attack on the Secessionville works with a battering flank fire. Each chop of the wood by the 22nd South Carolina opened more of the area west and north of the Tower Battery, a back-breaking revelation of possible, if not probable, Federal attack routes. Federal pickets were interested in the Confederate efforts but did not attempt to harrass or stop the work. As the axes rang out, one member of the Eutaw Battalion recalled, "The enemy did not fire, though they were quite near."[31]

Another member of the Eutaw Battalion wriggled his way through the woods and underbrush to the Federal camps near Grimball's. In his fanciful words, he counted 70 coffins "for the killed in the engagement yesterday." He also claimed to have heard some Federals admit that "they got the worst of the fight," an admission perhaps good for the Confederate morale but terribly untrue.[32]

* * *

John Pemberton made a crucial decision early on the June 12: "Shanks" Evans and two of his regiments would transfer from Adams Run to Charleston. Having desired this consolidation for some time now, Pemberton was more convinced than ever that the main Federal attack would fall on James Island. Thus, he risked exposing the vital railroad near Adams Run to bring even more troops to Charleston. Pemberton must have realized that this troop transfer would raise another knotty command problem, for Evans ranked William Duncan Smith and would thus be entitled to command on James Island. The almost ludicrous spectacle of another change at the top of the James Island officer corps might be offset by the additional soldiers, but Pemberton was willing to risk this possibility. He needed every man he could get his hands on.[33]

* * *

That evening, the woods around the Presbyterian Church saw yet another engagement. Late that afternoon, three companies from the 97th Pennsylvania drew outpost duty and advanced towards the crossroads west of the church. Confederate shelling had broken desultorily across the island all day, and the Federals were experiencing almost incessant picket fire. The Pennsylvanians spread out in the woods expecting action, and, around 10:00 p.m., they got it. For the better part of a half-hour Confederate rifles sprayed the 97th's position, killing one man and wounding four. The gunfire ceased as quickly as it had begun, and the Pennsylvanians held their ground until the morning. Back at Grimball's plantation, the remainder of the Pennsylvania regiment slept fitfully on its arms in a line of battle along the length of the camp. With the enemy so near and active, serious action was expected nightly. The various pleasures of Hilton Head had become but a dim and distant memory.[34]

Somewhat more cheering was the experience of the 3rd New Hampshire. Having manned the picket lines from 2:00 a.m. until noon, the Hampshiremen discovered that their equipment and their "Sunday clothes" had arrived on a steamer docked at the wharf. Despite the early evening interruption of the 97th's run-in with the enemy, the men of the 3rd were in a state of joy at finally having obtained their knapsacks. Small comforts obviously mattered greatly to these front-line infantrymen.[35]

* * *

Life on Sol Legare was much the same. "(T)here was more or less (firing) each day on the picket line, and occasionally our batteries and gun boats would throw a few shells," remembered a Highlander of his now monotonous existence. Even picket duty had become somewhat mundane. A Michigander on outpost duty the night of June 12 could only recall that he was "up all night—saw several of the Confederate Pickets." One 100th Pennsylvania Roundhead, however, recalled the first ruminations of the coming battle: "We have orders to have 24 hours rations ready. . ."[36]

For Henry Benham, the action was just beginning. David Hunter had left for Hilton Head, and Benham now stood alone in command at the front. His overall campaign—originally designed to be a lightning amphibious operation culminating in a quick dash across James Island—had degenerated into a veritable but porous siege. It had taken a full week to get Stevens' and Wright's brigades ashore, and now both subordinates, having judged the Secessionville approaches as impracticable, were urging an assault on the Confederate right. Benham's planned combinations for the morning of June 11 were further frustrated by the surprise Confederate attack on the afternoon of the 10th. Isaac Stevens was reporting the construction of new Confederate works and the appearance of extensive abatis blocking the approaches inland. By this time, Benham's troops were crowded into swampy camps within artillery range of the Confederate emplacements. What was worse, Hunter left for Hilton Head and forbade any attack in his absence. He did specify that Benham was to provide for a "secured entrenched encampment."

As the occasional Confederate shell crashed to the ground near Grimball's, Henry Benham debated with himself the meaning of the word "secured."[37]

*　*　*

In Charleston, the bells in the steeple of St. Michael's Church were removed for transport upcountry to Columbia.[38]

*　*　*

Friday
June 13, 1862

Friday the 13th. Soldiers tend to be a superstitious lot, but to the Northerners grown accustomed to the wet Southern spring, this was, noted one blueclad warrior, "an unusually fine day." More importantly, preparations moved apace. Additional siege guns arrived from the Fort Pulaski environs, and men from the 3rd New Hampshire, noting the excellent "planting" weather, helped mount the new armament in three batteries fronting the Grimball plantation. Colonel Serrell had his engineers strengthening the infantry parapet that surrounded the Grimball camps while adding two more gun emplacements to the line. At least one Hampshireman, however, was shocked at the state of affairs, noting, "I find we have got into a dangerous place; the rebel shells burst near our camps."

The large, level cotton and corn fields that made up much of James Island opened up some uninterrupted sight lines from the enemy at Secessionville to the low-lying Federal encampments radiating out from the Stono. The woods continued to offer some protection, especially on Wright's left and Stevens' front, but the forward positions of both opponents were now within easy range of each other. A Pennsylvanian near Grimball's reported, "The rebel batteries continue to shell the lines...The picket lines, being about six hundred yards apart, also kept up a constant firing at the front." James Island was indeed a dangerous place, and growing more so by the day.[39]

* * *

A squad of the New York Highlanders broke camp early in the morning and marched east on Sol Legare Island towards the now familiar picket line. But as they approached the advanced posts, their officers kept them in line and moved them further along the marshline. Passing a small earthwork mounting two 30-lb. Parrots Rifles, the New Yorkers suddenly came into full view of the Confederate Tower Battery some 2,000 yards to the northeast. They rushed past the open field to a line of bushes not 200 yards from the eastern extreme of the island, where they went to work constructing a new battery. The earthwork's design was formida-

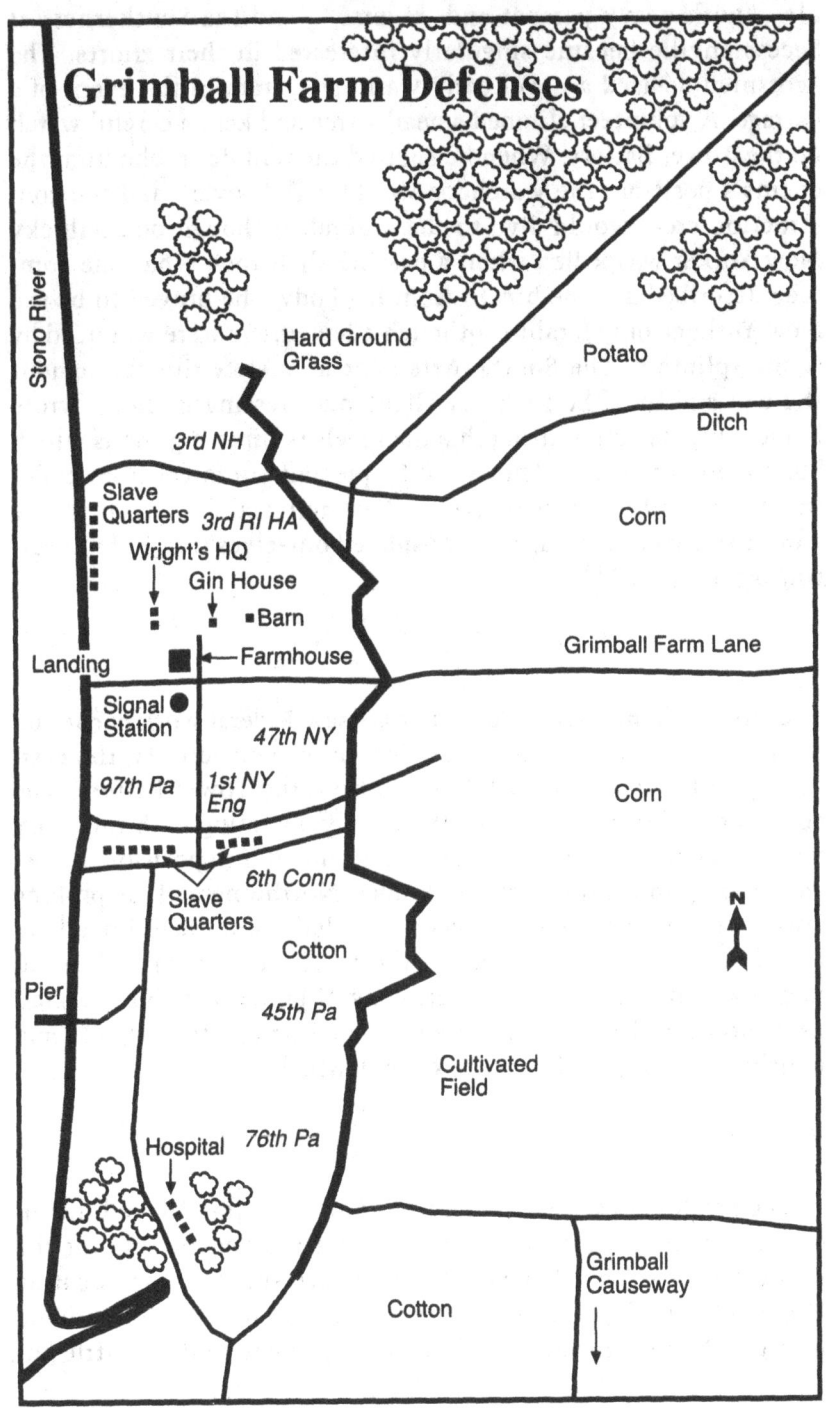

ble—"with heavy parapet and traverse"—and the Southerners at Secessionville became singularly interested in their efforts. The Scotsmen devised a novel early warning system in the event of a barrage. A volunteer climbed a nearby tree and kept a careful watch on the Tower Battery. When he spotted the telltale smoke from the enemy's position, the watchdog would yell "Cover" and the construction crew would dive to the ground. Although one unlucky New Yorker was killed when a passing shell took what one comrade described as "the breath from his body," he proved to be the New Yorkers' only fatality, although a few others were wounded by flying splinters. The Southerners kept up a slow fire throughout the day and into the night. A Highlander resting in camp wrote home, "Just as I am writing this the rebels is throwing shells which burst high in the air...They want to prevent our forces from building earth worke but they can't." One relieved Scotsmen in the work party commented, "we considered ourselves fortunate in getting off so easily."[40]

* * *

Colonel Thomas Lamar's artillerists saw Federal work parties on Sol Legare's in an area previously barren of such activity, the eastern tip of the island not 2,000 yards from the Tower Battery. The colonel could not stand to see the enemy operating with impunity within his eyesight. Wheeling his Columbiad into position, he began zeroing in on the partially hidden Northerners. This probing stirred up a hornet's nest, as Federal artillery from the Grimball entrenchments to the gunboats in the Stono responded in kind to Lamar's challenge. The reverberations of gunpowder blasts, shell explosions, and screaming metal echoed across the islands and marshes, pausing neither at dusk nor dawn.[41]

* * *

The 8th Michigan had drawn picket duty on June 13, and the increased artillery activity made the day a memorable one for the Midwesterners. The Confederate shells, overshooting the sweating Highlander work party, plowed into and exploded over the ground near the Rivers Causeway, and the Michiganders could do little but dive for cover each time a shell arched in their direction. Even when the 8th marched back to camp, they still felt the effects of the incessant enemy barrage. Most of the day and into the night, the roar of artillery and the cracking of rifle fire rent the air with cacophonous report. Some members of the 7th Connecticut, resting as best they could, reported a rumor then filtering through their camp. This increase of heavy exchanges could only be a prelude to an advance against the Southern defensive network. Those that heard the gossip began to prepare accordingly.[42]

★ ★ ★

On this day, only 600 troops garrisoned the extensive Federal works on Hilton Head—such was Hunter's commitment to the James Island campaign. The small numbers, however, did not prevent the occasional aggressive action. A combined group from the 45th Pennsylvania and the 3rd Rhode Island Heavy Artillery used the cover of darkness to attack and burn a collection of Confederate boats near Pinckney Island, thus frustrating a possible amphibious assault. The Unionists pulled off the night operation perfectly, "a small affair. . .of itself not of much importance, yet in its results quite so."[43]

Saturday
June 14, 1862

As the sun rose on the 14th of June, it fell to the Highlanders of the 79th New York to mount and arm the battery they had just constructed. Despite their weariness, they enjoyed the chance to help their comrades "jaw back," as they called it, at the enemy battery that had so troubled them the day before. The New Yorkers mounted two 30-lb. Parrots and a 64-lb. James Rifle, then cheered when the guns began what one Highlander termed an "interchange of compliments" with the Tower Battery. One Union observer noted with satisfaction the "considerable effect" the Federal fire had on the Confederate position. But by now, most of the infantry had grown accustomed to the din of the barrage. Captain Ely of the 8th Michigan, not a mile away in camp, slept through the exchanges, blissfully unaware of the booming artillery duel.[44]

The new Grimball's battery that was taking on Lamar's position had been armed courtesy of the 3rd New Hampshire. A detachment had risen early to continue their second day of mounting artillery pieces. They hauled a heavy gun to the earthwork "pretty well out to the front," where one Hampshireman observed, "Both sides were busy as bees, getting ready to kill each other." Another sign of impending action, this one more chilling even than the thundering artillery, struck one member of the work detail: a hospital had been established "in some Negro houses."[45]

* * *

North of Colonel Lamar's Tower Battery position, Lt. Col. Charles Simonton led all 8 companies of the Eutaw Battalion to the picket posts near the Presbyterian Church. Three companies under Major John Pressley advanced to the fork in the road, where they spent the day as spectators to the raging artillery exchanges. To the south they could observe Lamar's shells arching through the sky and slamming into Federal positions in front of Grimball's. Some shots actually cleared the enemy camps and thundered among the vessels in the Stono. With a certain sense of awe, one of the battalion's members wrote that he and his comrades watched the sun set with "(t)he shells from the gunboats above Grimball's...passing over our heads."[46]

As the artillery barrage continued into its second day, camp life near Secessionville was proving dangerous. A second Confederate unit now shared the plain between the village and the fort with the Charleston Battalion. Commanded by Lt. Col. Alexander D. Smith, the newly-arrived 9th South Carolina Battalion answered to the nickname "Pee Dee Battalion," its companies having been raised in the rugged Pee Dee district of the state. Their new surroundings must have proved shocking. As enemy shells thudded into the earthen walls of the Tower Battery, many more overshot their target and spun through the camps behind the work. Amid the what one Confederate labeled the "old game of mutual and promiscuous shelling," a projectile crashed through five tents of the Charleston Battalion, killing Pvt. John Andrews as he lay reading. Though many of the soldiers on both sides had grown accustomed to the noisy exchanges of iron, death could come instantaneously in this raining of shot and shell.⁴⁷

Colonel Lamar's men had taken up the Federal gauntlet and poured out their own responses to the incoming barrage. "Vigorous replies of Colonel Lamar's guns," noted Colonel Tracy of Gist's staff in his diary, "(F)iring nearly all day." Despite Pemberton's June 11 directive to keep artillery use at a minimum, Lamar was proving to be quite the fighter, more than willing to mix it up with the heavier enemy guns. All day, from Legare's, Grimball's, and the Stono, the Federals blasted shot and shell at Lamar's cannons atop the Tower Battery. And all day the colonel gave as good as he got, even keeping up a slow rate of fire during the night. Although the exchanges served to bolster Confederate morale on the island, they were having a second, more sinister effect. The Southern artillerists were already drained by the physical efforts of building and improving their defenses. The additional strain of this continuous barrage was quickly pushing the men to the limits of their endurance.⁴⁸

That evening, the men of the Eutaw Battalion edged their outposts progressively nearer to the enemy lines until one last needling triggered an eruption of rifle fire. The Confederates fell back, regrouped, then moved forward again. In the confusion, two pickets from the 4th Lousiana Battalion were captured by a roving Federal patrol. For the balance of the night, dead silence alternated with swift, bitter explosions, testing the soldiers' oft-frayed nerves. Shortly before 10:00 p.m., off to the north, the Dill's House—a sometimes post for Federal pickets—burst into flame and burned to the ground. Confederate brass had ordered its destruction to prevent such use. The flames lit the night sky.⁴⁹

* * *

The northern section of the Federal picket line was manned that night by the 6th Connecticut. Forced to face the increased number of enemy rushes, the Federals regarded what one soldier called the Confederate "sudden dashes" as nothing compared to the sharpshooting that downed their comrades "without giving us a chance to fire back." While at the front, members of the 6th had laughed at an unnamed Pennsylvania regiment that had staggered away from a small force of "Johnnies" that had "ventured near our lines to see what material Uncle Sam's boys were made of." Such moments of dark humor had become quite rare, for the incessant picket fire was taking casualties with little real purpose. Men were dying, as one Federal put it, "without extending the line on either side."[50]

* * *

Pursuant to Pemberton's order, Nathan "Shanks" Evans arrived on James Island with his two regiments and assumed command of all the troops in the First Division, First Military District of South Carolina. One officer, disturbed by Evans' ascension to the James Island command, was Johnson Hagood, who observed his new commander with Generals Smith and Gist at the Royall house, the new island headquarters. Hagood could feel what he called the "consideable unpleasantness" that developed amongst the high-ranking trio, and the colonel blamed Pemberton for creating the "anomalous relations in command." Hagood's distaste for "Shanks" was unfortunately obvious. After the war he would as much as accuse his former commander of drunkenness, a charge seconded by many of Evans' colleagues. One witness described Evans as "the best drinker, the most eloquent swearer (I should say voluble) and the most magnificent bragger I ever saw." Here at Royall's, Hagood would chin up and spend the balance of June 14 accompanying the brusque Evans on an inspection tour of the island's defenses.[51]

The new headquarters at Royall's stood just south of New Town Cut at the very northern flank of the area's defense line. Hagood and company rode south from the cut, passing several redans connected by a "slight" infantry trench that formed the bulk of the works snaking south towards Secessionville. Evans could also observe the camps of the advanced forces, which stretched east from the defenses. The 47th Georgia tented near Royall's. Next to it was Hagood's 1st South Carolina. Beyond the Dill's Bluff Road successively stretched the camps of the Eutaw Battalion, Stevens' 24th South Carolina, and McEnery's 4th Louisiana Battery, posted further east on the King's Highway. The party crossed the footbridge to the Secessionville peninsula, where they passed the camps of the Charleston Battalion and the Pee Dee Battalion before arriving at the Tower Battery. Despite the best efforts of the men involved, Hagood found the Confederate defenses faulty in design and incomplete in construction. Besides the four guns mounted in the Tower Battery and the armament frowning from Fort Pemberton, "the redans and redoubts...had no guns mounted or platforms laid." Evans' opinion is unknown, but Hagood was far from satisfied with the Confederate dispositions on James Island.[52]

In Charleston, meanwhile, stories of Pemberton's frailties as a commander continued to make the rounds. One had the beleaguered commander admitting that "he ought not to have given up Cole's Island...But...there was nothing for them to do but fight to the death. He had no way of getting them off (James Island), in case of defeat."[53]

* * *

Hazard Stevens recalled an incident that occurred "a few days after the battery" at Legare's point "was completed." Henry Benham and Isaac Stevens were inspecting the picket lines near the Rivers Causeway when Benham announced that he wanted to see the earthwork at the eastern point of the island. As the generals and their staffs approached an open field near their destination, Stevens suggested proceeding on foot to avoid drawing Confederate fire. Hazard Stevens recalled that Benham reared up and "repelled the suggestion with a rude exclamation," and as the cavalcade emerged from the shielding woods into the clearing, a distant enemy battery unloaded a shot that shrieked past the startled horsemen and splashed into the adjoining marsh. Stunned and seemingly frightened by the close call, Benham drew about and hastily led his staff to the safety of the trees. At the same time, Stevens and his people continued on at a moderate trot under heavy fire, until they reached the earthwork safely. Hazard Stevens had no trouble calling Benham's action that of a coward.[54]

* * *

At dusk, the sun set on two remarkably similar armies. The preliminary phase of the invasion of James Island had cost both commanders the respect of their subordinates. Both command structures had sagged under their own self-inflicted weaknesses—the Confederates being top heavy with too many generals, and the Federals floundering without one. The rank and file filling the camps and lining the defenses south of Charleston had little to do with such bickering. They were simply fighting men, facing the specter of battle.

CHAPTER SEVEN

"We shall try to prevent any disaster occuring. This is all I can say at present."

—Isaac Stevens to his wife, June 15, 1862

Positions, Places

Sunday
June 15, 1862

The previous 48 hours had been an exhausting stretch for Colonel Lamar's gunners. Their batteries had engaged the Federals almost constantly, and each break in the barrage only gave the Confederates more time to toil on the Tower Battery's defenses. By Sunday, the two artillery companies manning the Secessionville works were stretched to breaking point. As a consequence, even in the face of continued Federal pressure, Lamar finally called for a slackening of fire. Captain Samuel Reed of Company B and Capt. G. D. Keitt of Company I complied. "Similar firing upon Secessionville," recalled one witness to the day's operations, but "Lamar replies more deliberately."[1]

Lieutenant Iredell Jones hadn't planned to witness this artillery duel first hand. An artillery officer then stationed at Fort Sumter, Jones spent this Sunday accompanying a number of his comrades on an inspection tour of James Island. At an outpost opposite Grimball's, Jones decided to amuse himself by climbing a tree to observe the Federal pickets, but he found the enemy outposts just

600 uncomfortable yards away. Amazed at finding the enemy so close, he carefully shimmied down the tree then moved with his party to Colonel Lamar's headquarters at Secessionville. Although they had expected to depart immediately for Sumter, the officers now learned that Lamar had ordered a reply to the Federal fire that had been pounding the earthwork all morning. "(L)ed on by curiosity, rather than by wisdom," Jones wrote, he and his party decided to observe the duel up close.[2]

Eight hundred yards separated the hamlet of Secessionville from the Tower Battery. As Jones and his comrades moved west toward the earthwork, they passed the camp of the Charleston Battalion near the terminus of the footbridge connecting the peninsula with the main Confederate line to the north. Further west lay the camp of Lt. Col. Alexander D. Smith's 9th South Carolina Battalion, and beyond it stretched an open expanse that narrowed abruptly to the neck of the peninsula. Here in Big Folly Creek, Capt. F. B. Bonneau's gun boat kept watch over the marshy southern approaches to the peninsula. To the north, a few buildings and a small stand of woods covered a stretch of high ground forming the bank of the marsh. Dominating the area was the skeletal frame of the lookout tower, rising some seventy five feet over the battery's northern flank.[3]

At the narrowest point of the peninsula rose the walls of Lamar's battery, an incomplete but already formidable work. Constructed in the shape of the letter M, with the ditch fronting the walls, the battery reflected the fortification style of the day. Both segments of the front wall stretched 175 feet and angled inward to usher any Federal attack force towards the center of a plunging, enfilading fire. In some places the walls rose as high as 16 feet, with the southern leg of the fort stretching rearward further than the lighter northern leg. Almost directly behind the left front wall lay the magazine, located close enough to the parapet to give the gunners quick access to ammunition. The southern flank of the fort faced the marshes of Savannah Creek and Big Folly Creek, and the northern flank faced the tidal flats of Simpson Creek, with a "thick growth of myrtle bushes" lining the banks both front and rear of the works. A "gooey, bottomless" muck which the locals called pluff mud constituted much of the swamps, making the flank areas impassable. Along the length of the southern wing, a narrow farm track called the Savannah Road ran along a causeway that linked the fort's interior to the fields west of the work. With the Tower Battery completely choking the peninsula at this point of the neck, an attacking force would have to take the work dead on.[4]

Upon entering the battery proper, Jones and his group found the 8-in. Columbiad positioned to the right of the centerpoint of the front wall. To the Columbiad's left sat a rifled 24-lb. piece. Several 18-lb. guns and another rifled 24-lb. piece made up the remaining front line armament, with a mortar battery positioned to the rear of the magazine. By the time Lieutenant Jones and his comrades arrived to view Lamar's handywork, Federal artillery fire was already "striking the battery or grazing the top." Many of the shells "bursted mostly in the rear," noted Jones, so many in fact that a few Confederates wondered whether the Federals were trying to hit the distant footbridge. One shot, however, exploded directly over the works, taking down two of Lamar's men. "It was very unwise of us to have exposed ourselves thus recklessly, and the more so that we should have done so merely out of curiosity." Actually, the entire peninsula had become a dangerous place, as a wide arc of enemy fire engulfed the open plain and drove much of the infantry to the safety of some protective trenches. Nonetheless, the five officers remained an hour under fire, "looking at the mortar practise."[5]

To the west of the battery, the peninsula widened considerably. The border of the southern marsh angled in a southwesterly direction, but the northern edge ran directly west about three hundred yards until it curved sharply to the north, then west again, for another six hundred yards. Two fallow cotton fields, sectioned by a drainage ditch and hedge running on a north-south axis, stretched from marsh to marsh. The patch of pluff mud to the north finally ended about 1,000 yards from the battery, where another heavier hedge separated the peninsula from the Battery Island Road. Beyond the nearby Rivers House, Lamar had stationed his pickets to cover the Rivers Causeway, which linked the Battery Island Road to Sol Legare Island and the Federals beyond. With the battery of two 24-lb. pieces posted near the Clark house north across the marsh, Lamar could cover the two cotton fields and make them a killing field for anyone reckless enough to test the Confederate position.[6]

* * *

While the 47th Georgia fanned out to cover the continued tree-felling operation near Battery Island Road, the Eutaw Battalion returned from picket duty early Sunday morning, and "spent a quiet day in camp," their first in quite a while. As it was the Sabbath, the Carolinians participated in a service led by the battalion's chaplain, Rev. A. Toomer Porter. Hymns and prayers rose above the booming reports of the Federal artillery hammering at the Secessionville area. The men found great solace the words of their chaplain. As one Eutaw member noted, "(H)is addresses and sermons are much enjoyed, and are doubtless productive of much good." For one day at least, the the men of the battalion were off the line and out of harm's way.[7]

While Johnson Hagood spent a second unpleasant day with Nathan Evans, the battle between Charleston civilian and military leaders continued to rage. Governor Pickens had wired Gen. P. G. T. Beauregard imploring the Creole to assume command of the beleaguered city. Since Beauregard declined the offer to return to the site of his former glory, Pickens wired Jefferson Davis directly for a replacement for Pemberton. "I fear great confusion, and all may be lost," the governor sputtered, suggesting in the process some possible replacements: William Hardee, Earl Van Dorn, Benjamin Huger, John Magruder—even James Longstreet. As for Pemberton himself, it scarcely helped that he had just complained to Pickens that his troops were "inadequate" for the defense of Charleston. The harried general had asked the governor "(t)o furnish such aid in men and arms as may be within your power." By this time, Pickens was literally begging for someone, anyone, to come and take Pemberton's place.[8]

In a last desperate appeal to Richmond, Pemberton that day wrote, "I am very scarce of ammunition; want more powder."[9]

* * *

In the Union camps, the rumors of an impending attack persisted and grew. Many more attended morning religious ceremonies than usual, and officers like Captain Rockwell of the Connecticut Battery conducted services in a lay capacity. For other soldiers, the concerns were of a more worldly nature. Pay had arrived for Stevens' division, reminding one Highlander of the remark, "They pay us the day, and shoot us the morn."[10]

That morning, Colonel Serrell reported that the three batteries lining the Grimball parapet were "revetted with sod" and complete, with one gun mounted on the left flank and three guns—"two 42 lb. James' and one 30 lb. parrot"—mounted on the right. To one observer, this Sunday seemed "(t)he same as yesterday—several fires exchanged between our's and the Rebel's batteries." Another soldier recalled that "Battery Lamar having irritated our camps with shell, General Stevens ordered all his batteries to open fire on the troublesome work, and the fire was kept up through the day." Still another had more personal concerns: "I have the headache and diarhea and am not able to be out."[11]

In the early afternoon, word of a pending assault raced from camp to camp. The Highlanders of the 79th New York were ordered to draw 40 rounds, prepare one day's rations, and be ready to move at a moment's notice. Such orders spawned numerous rumors. One tale had it that there was to be an assault on the Rebel works, possibly at the point of the bayonet, a prospect that worried the battle-tested Scotsmen. The Highlanders knew how easily Confederate pickets could sound the alarm, and they didn't relish making the attack with unloaded weapons.[12]

Over at Grimball's, similar scenes were played out. As word of the attack spread, 60 rounds of ammunition were issued to the 3rd New Hampshire, prompting some of the men to wonder at what one called their "dreadful hurry" to get to Charleston. Within minutes, every Federal soldier had become aware that the army would pitch into the Confederates at daylight on Monday. One Hampshireman viewing the rushed preparations observed, "It really looked like war."[13]

* * *

Isaac Stevens later called it "an evil hour"—the moment that Henry Benham decided to attack the battery fronting Secessionville. Benham had concluded that the safety of his camps was seriously compromised by the nearness of the Tower Battery. Since Hunter ordered him to provide for his troops' security,

Benham felt justified in ordering an attack upon it. Opinions seemed to differ regarding Benham's analysis. Hazard Stevens thought that "they (the Rebel guns) could almost reach Wright's camp." Isaac Stevens, on the contrary, felt that the Confederate guns could reach only the Union picket lines and the batteries at the east point of Sol Legare Island. Nonetheless, Benham issued the orders to prepare for the assault and called for his officers to convene on his floating headquarters for an evening council. Fearing what was to come, Stevens wrote his wife, "We are now attempting an enterprise for which our force is entirely inadequate. The want of a proper commander is fearful. We shall try to prevent any disaster occuring. This is all I can say at present."[14]

What was said at this meeting later became a matter of intense controversy, for each participant tended to remember only what suited his own purposes. The few facts that each agreed upon were these: that on the evening of June 15, the army's brigadiers, Stevens and Wright, the acting brigadier, Colonel Williams, and the navy's Percival Drayton, joined Benham aboard his headquarters ship *Delaware*. There, Benham informed the assembled commanders that he wanted two divisions and a brigade to combine in an attack upon the enemy battery fronting Secessionville. The Unionists would hit the works at 4:00 a.m. in the pre-dawn darkness of June 16. Isaac Stevens' men would hammer the assault home while Horatio Wright's division and Colonel Williams' brigade would provide support. After Wright directed a few questions to Stevens, the conference broke up and the officers retired to brief their commands.[15]

The fire-lit camps teemed with soldiers grimly preparing for action. At Grimball's, the 3rd New Hampshire picked up its gear and moved east to camp near the shielding woods, where the Hampshiremen could get a quick start in the morning. Four companies of Hampshire troops filed off for picket duty, well aware that they would be called back to join the assault. A firm posting of the scheduled jump-off— "Two AM tomorrow"—passed from regiment to regiment and from soldier to soldier. Throughout the night the hushed Northerners around the smoldering campfires grew "exceedingly thoughtful," noted one Federal. Similar scenes occurred on Sol Legare Island. Even as a detachment of Roundheads shifted east to support the new battery and man the picket line near the Rivers Causeway, a pensive silence descended as the men stirred about their smoky fires. Officers strode from group to group, reminding their troops in low tones of the need for rest. Soldiers darkly glanced about, wondering which of their friends might be missing from the next evening's roll. Despite their misgivings about the manner of the attack, the Highlanders voiced faith in Isaac Stevens, whom they affectionately called their "little General." Whatever was to come, the veterans of First Bull Run were prepared to follow Stevens anywhere. The campfires burned low and darkness enveloped the restless soldiers. As sentries paced to and fro, thousands of Northerners dozed fitfully on the eve of battle.[16]

* * *

As was his habit, Eutaw chaplain Toomer Porter organized a Sunday evening hymn service. It was lights out for most of the Confederates, but over by Porter's tent the voices of a dozen Eutaws rose above the dark campsites in praise of their God. When they concluded the service with "Bow Down Thy Ear, O Lord," Porter led the assembled in the Lord's Prayer and bestowed benediction. "We then shook hands and bade good-night," remembered the reverend.[17]

Monday
June 16, 1862

At 2:00 a.m., Union orderlies scurried through the darkness and awakened the men to the work of the day. Small knots of soldiers gathered together, chewing hardtack and gulping freshly-brewed coffee. The weather was cool and somewhat drizzly, but the men barely noticed. All eyes peered east through the gloom towards the enshrouded Southern defenses. For days, enemy artillery had made the earth tremble. Now came the Northerners' chance to take and silence those very guns.[18]

Weakened by exposure, William Fenton, colonel of the 8th Michigan and commander of Stevens' 1st brigade, struggled to get his regiments moving into line. His beloved 8th Michigan, guided by Lt. Col. Frank Graves, led the way. Graves designated two companies, C and H, to form the advance. They would be accompanied by staff officer

Col. William Fenton
8th Michigan Infantry
Stevens' 1st Brigade

State Archives of Michigan

Lt. Benjamin Lyons, Co. E of Serrell's Engineers, and a local black guide. This group had been given distinct orders: after the engineers cleared the field of obstructions, the infantry was to move through and charge the fort with the bayonet. Commonly referred to by the men as the "forlorn hope," these two advance companies were to distract the battery's attention long enough to allow the weight of the brigade to hit the wall relatively unmolested. In other words, these companies were to act as the bait that would absorb the intial onslaught of Southern metal. Behind the 8th Michigan strode Lt. Col. MacLelland Moore and eight companies of his Irish 28th Massachusetts, followed by Lt. Col. Joseph Hawley's 7th Connecticut. Stevens must have felt some trepidation and concern for the Irish, for he dispatched staff officer Captain William Lusk to guide them into column.[19]

Captain Alfred Rockwell of the 1st Connecticut Light Artillery gave orders to muffle the wheels of the caissons, further alerting the gunners to the gravity of the situation. As he did so, the captain was no doubt considering an earlier exchange he had had with his commander. Stevens had given Rockwell verbal as well as written orders, but the two sets of instructions had left the artillerist confused. When Rockwell sought out the general to seek clarification—"General, may I ask what is the plan of battle?"—Stevens lashed out, "Damn it, sir, there isn't any plan. You will fire when you get a chance, and be careful not to hit any of our own men." Rockwell left the brief meeting with the distinct impression that Stevens strongly disapproved of Benham's operation. As his battery fell in behind Colonel Fenton's Brigade, the captain rode alone with his thoughts, and no doubt with his misgivings as well.[20]

Colonel Daniel Leasure, the commander of Stevens' 2nd Brigade, confidently placed Lt. Col. David Morrison and the 79th New York in the van. Although the 100th Pennsylvania was placed second in column, only a fragment of the regiment was able to begin the march. It would be joined enroute by the detachment of Roundheads that had spent the night manning the new battery on Sol Legare, where they were awaiting relief by a company from the 3rd Rhode Island Heavy Artillery. The remaining Roundheads, strung out along the picket line, were to join the column as soon as they could. Third in line marched Col. Rudolph Rosa and his German 46th New York, followed by Co. H of the 1st Massachusetts Cavalry under Capt. Lucius Sargent. One hundred and fifty-four officers and 2,806 effectives of Isaac Stevens' division snaked their way towards the Confederates through the murky Carolina night.[21]

Colonel William Fenton had ridden ahead of the column. When his troops drew up, he decided to re-shuffle the marching order. He ordered the 28th Massachusetts and the 7th Connecticut to exchange places in the line so that Hawley's men would follow the 8th Michigan in the attack. As the division halted to accomplish this maneuver, some of the Michiganders loaded their weapons in contradiction of orders. When the men of the 7th Connecticut learned of it, they too loaded and capped their pieces, causing Hawley to seek the advice of staff aide Lt. Horatio Belcher. "Do as you please...in self-defense," was his simple reply. As the regiments completed their re-alignment, Hawley made a quick decision. He would not enforce the bayonet-only order and allowed his men to load up. That done, the column lurched forward.[22]

* * *

General Horatio Wright's troops at Grimball's roused to the 2:00 a.m. wake-up and joined in hurried meals as final instructions were given. At least one regiment—the 3rd Rhode Island Heavy Artillery—received its orders to move before it could prepare even the simplest breakfast. Another unit—the 3rd New Hampshire—was scattered about on picket duty and received orders only at the last moment. Most of the troops ate on the move. By 3:00 a.m., Wright's division was on the march and had assumed the following order: Col. Robert Williams led the van with an expanded brigade consisting of five companies of the 3rd Rhode Island Heavy Artillery, the 3rd New Hampshire, six companies of the 97th Pennsylvania, all followed by Co. E of Hamilton's U.S. Artillery. Next came two undersized brigades under Wright's personal direction: Col. John Chatfield's Brigade, composed of two companies of the 6th Connecticut and eight companies of the 47th New York, and Col. Thomas Welsh's Brigade, made up of six companies of the 45th Pennsylvania and three companies of Serrell's engineers. The remaining sections of Hamilton's battery and two squads of the 1st Massachusetts Cavalry brought up the rear of Wright's division.[23]

Since his column was to provide support for Stevens' assault, Wright decided to move forward about a mile to await the beginning of the attack. As the men pressed eastward across some open fields, picket detachments from the 3rd New Hampshire rushed to join the advance. By 4:00 a.m., most had located their regiment and, in the pale light of a cloudy dawn, one soldier surprisly noted that "quite a large force was at hand."

The regiment had assembled in a large field, and most of the men were busily discarding their surplus equipment into small piles to be guarded by a select squad. Orders were circulated to stack arms, and most of the soldiers dropped to the ground, anxiously awaiting the beginning of the battle. One sergeant, Elbridge Copp, drew a biscuit from his haversack, but nerves prevented him from summoning enough spittle to eat it. Despite the clouds, faint light began to filter through and illuminate the surroundings more distinctly. Suddenly, a series of short rifle bursts caught the attention of everyone within hearing range. Somewhere off to the south, shots had been exchanged, followed by an eerie silence, as if an engine had started, then stopped, unable to sustain its spark.[24]

* * *

Colonel Thomas Lamar had worked his men hard over the last week, preparing his position for the attack he realized was inevitable. The night of June 15 was no different. General "Shanks" Evans had ordered Lamar to mount Bonneau's water-based guns in the Tower battery, "although it might require super human exertions." Lamar knew that he couldn't accomplish the task with the men at hand, but he still ordered the gunboat moved from its mooring south of the fort to the wharf in the rear of the peninsula. Reinforced by elements of the Charleston and Pee Dee Battalions, one detachment of artillerists unloaded the cannon from the small gunship. Meanwhile, Lamar worked his remaining men at strengthening the battery's earthworks. His gunners responded with all their might, straining until 3:00 a.m. to prepare the position for action before Lamar finally ordered them to rest. All were exhausted, and when word of the respite spread, the gunners collapsed beside their cannon and alongside the parapet. Indeed, for the first time since the Federals had landed on James Island, the defenders of the Tower battery carelessly slept without their arms.[25]

Lamar had momentarily expected a detachment from the 22nd South Carolina to assist him in manning his battery, but as of 4:00 a.m., the reinforcements still had not arrived. Four men from Smith's Pee Dee Battalion stood picket near the Rivers House 1,000 yards to the west. Others manned outposts north along the Battery Island Road. Lamar assumed that they would detect any Federal movement from that direction and quickly spread the alert. Even without Bonneau's guns, the hard-working colonel figured his position to be as ready as it was going to be. In a slight drizzle, fully spent, Thomas Lamar sank into sleep on the parapet of his battery.[26]

* * *

North across the fields and through the woods of James Island, a cordon of Confederates had spread out to man the rest of the defensive perimeter. Seven companies of Clement Stevens' 24th South Carolina, six companies of Johnson Hagood's 1st South Carolina, and one company of Gilbert William's 47th Georgia covered the entirety of the Southern line, save for Lamar's pickets left at the Rivers House. Out on the perimeter, the night had been particularly dark, interrupted by occasional showers of light rain. Colonel Stevens, the picket line commander, had not received any reports of unusual Federal activity, and even the area around the Presbyterian Church remained quiet—abnormally quiet. Hagood had spent the night near the camps of Simonton's Eutaws and McEnery's Louisianans. The colonel was no doubt relieved that "Shanks" Evans had shifted his headquarters from Royall's to the Lawton House, back near Fort Johnson on the banks of Charleston harbor. Hagood experienced a night free from the distasteful presence of the island's new commander.[27]

Around 4:00 a.m., off to the south, a handful of shots rang out, followed by silence.

* * *

At the Rivers House, three privates from the Pee Dee Battalion had passed an unpleasant evening standing picket under the watchful eye of Lieutenant Sarvis. The dark, drizzly night was slowly giving way to the first light of a gray, cloudy morning, when a wave of Federals burst out of the darkness in a rush. Two of four pickets squeezed off hurried shots and began a sprint for the battery. These two escapees covered considerable distance before a thundering horseman ran them down. The mounted Federal officer demanded their surrender, and the winded Confederates had little choice but to comply. They were led to join their crestfallen comrades, now surrounded by what appeared to be the entire Federal army. Stunned by the suddennes of their change in circumstances, Lieutenant Sarvis and his detachment were marched off to captivity past the ranging Federal columns.[28]

* * *

Up until now, Isaac Stevens' orders to maintain strict silence had worked beautifully. No Confederates had caught sound of his division winding its way through the darkness to the Rivers Causeway. Once there, one section of Rockwell's battery—Lt. Seward's rifled pieces—dropped out to fall in at the tail of the 2nd

Brigade. The division was then marched across and brought to a halt to allow scattered elements and stragglers time to catch up. Although there was never an official explanation for this halt, it appears that the column had become somewhat broken up. Certainly Stevens was disposed to wait for more light to better observe the ground ahead. Whatever the reason, the lead elements of the 8th Michigan lay down to rest just yards away from the Confederate pickets.

This halt lasted no more than a quarter hour, and when the advance was resumed, the "forlorn hope" rushed forward to smother the unsuspecting Confederate pickets, while the remainder of the regiment marched up behind. Shots rang out and five men from Company H went down, struck by Confederate fire. Their comrades quickly captured two of the surprised Confederates, while the others made a dash for the fort. Realizing that the secrecy of the attack depended on the capture of the sprinting pickets, Lt. Col. Frank Graves spurred his mount in pursuit. Fortunately, he was able to run them down before they could sound the alarm, and within a few moments he was herding them back to the line. As a consequence, many of the Michiganders took heart in the belief that they still retained the element of surprise. Older and wiser heads assumed that all the noise accompanying the pursuit and capture of the pickets must surely have alerted the sleeping Confederates. In any case, the avenue of attack now lay open.

The 8th Michigan pushed up the Battery Island Road for a short distance. As the road curved to the north, the regiment began filing to the right through an opening in a hedge separating the roadway from a cotton field stretching to the east. Companies C and H fanned out, stumbling over the two and a half foot wide furrows that cut across the line of advance. Captains Ralph Ely and Richard Doyle aligned their respective companies, and then rushed the boys forward.[29]

As the "forlorn hope" companies jumped off, precious moments passed as Frank Graves formed his remaining eight companies into line of battle. The Michiganders filed in columns of fours through the hedge opening. Struggling against the uneven terrain, the men from Michigan fanned out as they entered the field—the first companies obliquing to the right, the middle companies forming in the center, and the trailing companies angling to the left. As the regi-

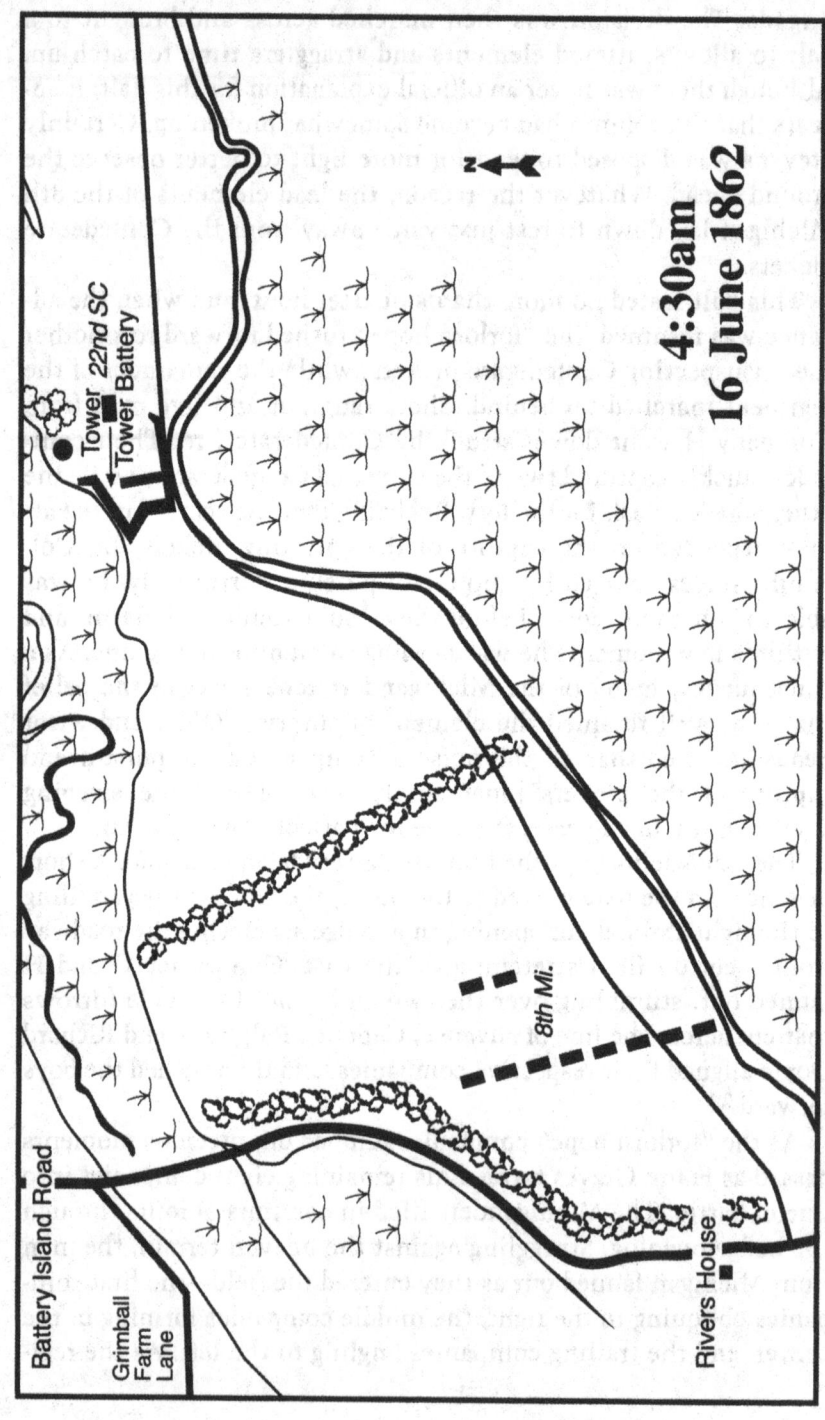

ment lurched forward, Graves peered out across the cotton rows and got his first view of the objective of the assault. Just ahead, perhaps a half mile away, squatted the Tower battery. The lieutenant colonel was immediately concerned, because the 8th's formation seemed to cover the entire front of the fort, leaving the trailing regiments little room for maneuver.

About this time, Colonel Fenton rode up and made his first observation of the point of attack and quickly decided to order Graves to oblique his charge to the right—he too was concerned that the following regiments would not have enough room to support the 8th Michigan's left flank. Graves called out the corrective orders, and the Midwesterners shifted their alignment accordingly. Ominously, some of the Michiganders reported hearing "the long roll in the enemies camp" off in the distance. Stumbling feet propelled the men across the furrowed field. Yards passed under straining legs and sweating brows. Ahead, Graves witnessed the "forlorn hope" racing towards the enemy battery. Up on the walls, even at the distance of 500 yards, Graves could make out the Confederates scrambling to their guns, making "ready to receive us."

With a lusty cheer the Michigan line charged forward, passing over a combination ditch and hedge that some of the men mistook for rifle pits. As the Federals drove forward, the front face of the Confederate battery erupted in a series of fiery explosions. A deafening roar rent the air, then another, then a third. In one terrifying moment, the center of the Michigan line melted before a hissing spray of Confederate shell and canister. Broken and bleeding bodies shivered by the blasts littered the patchy cotton rows, while those still standing pressed forward into the metal storm. "Every discharge of their old churn (as we called it) would pass through the ranks of our brave boys and mow them down like grass before a scythe," recalled one veteran, "but with dogged persistence they closed ranks and pushed on with the federal yell." But even as the main line of the 8th Michigan was rocked by the artillery blasts, elements of the "forlorn hope"—Companies C and H—were covering the final yards fronting the battery.[30]

* * *

Captain Joshua Jamison and his 100-man fatigue party from the 22nd South Carolina had marched into the Tower Battery after a three hour trek. What should have been a relatively short trip from their camps on James Island to Secessionville had turned into a confusing journey through the dark, rainy night. Above them on the wall of the battery, a Confederate sentinel kept watch over the field stretching to the west. Exhausted gunners lay slumbering, scattered along the parapet. Somewhere to the west in the gloom, movement made hazy by the half-light of the morning attracted the watchful attention of the sentinel.

In a few seconds the distant forms took focus: a mass of Federals was forming not a half mile west of the battery. Worse yet, a smaller group was already charging across the intervening fields. Some winded Confederate pickets who had manned a position north of the Rivers House panted as they entered into the fort, but theirs was hardly a proper advance warning.

The sentinel roused the slumbering Colonel Lamar, who rose to see the distant blue formations gelling before his eyes. Already, the 150 cannoneers of the two companies that had slept along the parapet were being awakened by the shouts of excited orderlies. The colonel turned to a waiting aide and issued firm orders: Get Gaillard's and Smith's battalions from their Secessionville camps up to support the battery immediately, then find General Evans and inform him of the attack. Lamar then turned to Lt. J. W. Moseley at the Columbiad and ordered him to load the 8-inch gun with canister (a metal container holding dozens of small round iron balls). Lamar himself sprang onto the chassis and aimed the piece, setting the sights on the center of the surging Federal line. To the left of the Columbiad, Sgt. James Baggott swung his 24-lb. artillery piece into action, aimed it, and blasted off the fort's first response to the attack. Lamar, beaten to the draw by Baggott by just a few seconds, tugged the Columbiad's lanyard and sent a storm of canister screeching into the enemy's line. The battle was joined.

The aim of the pieces was true, as the Federals—at least those not hit by the explosion—veered wildly left and right as they instinctively shied away from the deadly missiles. Lamar ordered more canister and began to re-sight the piece while elsewhere along the parapet other gun crews took up the challenge. Two rifled 24-lb. pieces—commanded by Lieutenants J. W. Lancaster and William Johnson from Lamar's Company B—quickly found the range and launched shot and shell across the cotton field. On the fort's right flank, Lt. J. A. Bellinger had his 18-lb. guns pouring what one officer described as "a murderous fire into the approaching line." Having miraculously arrived in the nick of time, Jamieson's fatigue party rushed to the parapet and filled in wherever they could find space, thus adding musketry to Lamar's artillery. Within a few short moments from the sentinel's first warnings, the front of the battery had erupted with shell and smoke, a demonic explosion in the murky dawn of shouted orders, straining crews, and a charging and cheering enemy.[31]

When Lamar finished his second sighting of the Columbiad, he turned to Lt. J. B. Humbert, the gun's commander then standing just paces away, and ordered him, as he recalled it, to "give them canister freely, which he did." The artillery continued to roar as Lamar directed Capt. T. Y. Simons to hurry forward the infantry, for he knew full well that the enemy, although hurt, could not be stopped with artillery alone. Lamar also knew that the momentum of the charge would bring the Federal rush to the walls of the battery, and the Confederate gunners were at risk of being overpowered. Captain Simons raced rearward to find the reinforcements, but for now, Lamar realized that it would be he and his artillerists, supported by Jamieson's hundred or so men, that would take the brunt of the assault.

As Simons searched for supporting infantry and the battery's guns continued to belch smoke and shot, Federals—some singly, others in groups—started appearing along Lamar's left front and flank. Moments later, small knots of the enemy jumped down off the wall and charged into the battery itself, and Southern gunners began going down before flashing Union bayonets. Other Federals poured rifle fire at point blank range into the nearly defenseless crew members. Additional Federals appeared further along the left wall, where another scything fire erupted into the fort.

The outnumbered Confederates withered before the killing volleys. Thomas Lamar watched what he described as a "murderous" flanking fire tear into his men, all the while turning to search the rear areas for signs of reinforcing infantry. Despite his best efforts, not five minutes had passed from the time he had tugged the Columbiad's lanyard, and yet the Federals were inside his walls and threatening to capture the fort that would open the door to the city of Charleston.[32]

Where were the reinforcements?

* * *

Private Philip Coleman, Co. I., 8th Michigan Infantry, certainly felt the power of the Confederate guns that morning. Belying the notion that all the Michiganders loaded their weapons, the private recalled that, "The order was to charge, with unloaded guns and fixed bayonets," when halfway across the field, the three artillery volleys ripped into the Unionists. A swath of Michigan men, Coleman included, went down in a bleeding heap, either stunned or maimed by Southern iron. Dazed, Coleman sat up to find his blasted left arm dangling gruesomely from the muscles across his back and shoulder. Watching his comrades race forward, Coleman could only wonder "how was I to save my life." With little consideration for rank, the fire also raised havoc among the Michigan officer corps. Lieutenant Colonel Graves was blown from his horse by a passing shot, but managed to remount and continue to give orders in the inferno that was growing around them. Major Amasa Watson's horse and the mounts of two of Fenton's aides-de-camps also went down before the blasts, bleeding from the spray of canister. All three men continued on foot.[33]

As the dead and wounded lay strewn across the cotton furrows, Lieutenant Lyons led the charging "forlorn hope" companies in a race for the right wall of the parapet. Instead of the wall of earth, they found a deep and hitherto unknown ditch running the length of the fort's front. Approaching this final barrier, the lieutenant shouted, "Come on, Boys," and leaped forward, earning the honor of being the first Unionist across the obstruction. With Confederate artillery blasting away just a few feet above his head, Lyons clawed at the packed dirt of the earthen wall and pulled himself nearly halfway up the embankment. Suddenly, a missile shattered his arm and he sank down against the berme on the earthwork's angled side while other Michiganders surged past in a violent effort to mount the parapet. Reaching the top of the wall, they pitched into the stubborn Confederates lining the position. More Unionists curled around the southern flank of the fort by following

Positions, Places 175

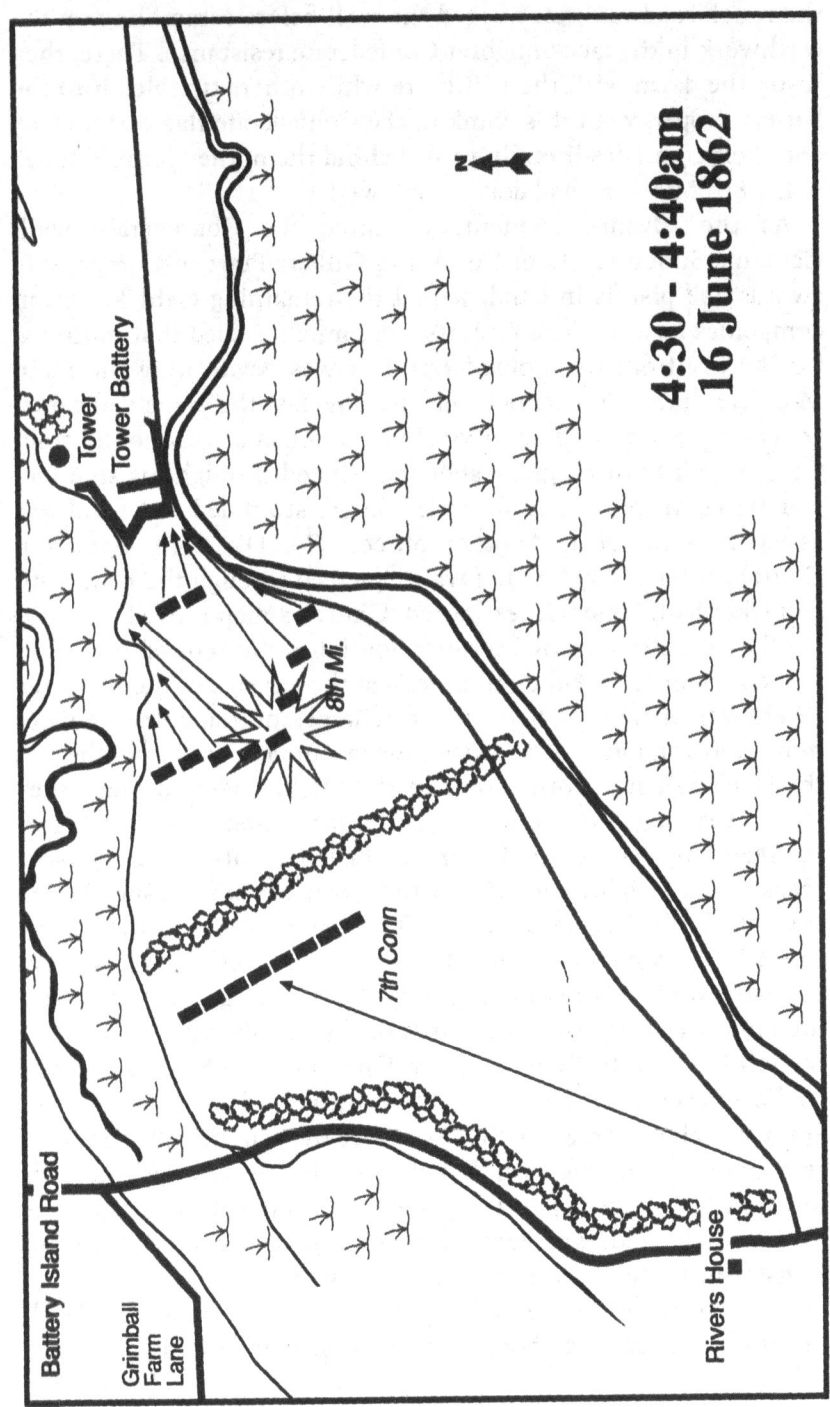

the rough roadway that hugged the wall before scrambling up the earthwork in the face of lighter Confederate resistance. There, they lit up the dawn with their rifle fire while others tumbled into the battery proper. With this chink in the Confederate flank uncovered and their comrades literally yards behind them, the "forlorn hope" of the 8th Michigan had done its job well.[34]

As the advance elements mounted the Confederate wall, Captains Simon Guild of Co. A and Gilbert Pratt of Company B, swords and pistols in hand, willed the remaining eight Michigan companies forward. Their efforts were much needed that morning, for the fire from the Confederate fort was devastating the main Michigan line. "You cannot imagine how fast the grape and canister came," wrote one survivor. Lieutenant James Donohue from Co. B was hit with a grape shot that ripped through his shoulder and exited his back. The wounded officer stumbled away and was assisted to the rear. Another officer, Co. D's Capt. Benjamin Church, collapsed before the wall, "pierced through the head with a musket ball," one witness noted. Church's men moved on, leaving their captain sprawled across a South Carolina cotton row.[35]

Lieutenant G. B. Fuller also recalled the carnage of the morning: "a shower of musket balls and discharges of grape and canister from their cannon...seemed to mow our men down in swaths." In the face of such a storm, some of the Michiganders decided they had had enough. As the center of the formation dissolved before the searching enemy fire, Fuller watched elements of the regiment break "to the right, and left for the cover of some bushes which skirted the field on either side." There they began to fire on the Confederate gunners "or any others that showed their heads above the earthworks." Other Michiganders, however, ignored the sweeping bursts, covered the final yards of the bloody field, and struck the left flank of the Tower Battery. One Michigander remembered soldiers leaping into the protective ditch and struggled up the earthen incline, some "by the assistance of each other," to join the remnants of the "forlorn hope" already on top of the wall. Swarming over the top of the parapet in a pitched frenzy, the surviving Michiganders turned their rifles on the Tower Battery and transformed it into a furnace of deadly combat.[36]

One Michigan man described the bitter fighting as "perfectly horrible...Many of our boys clambered into the fort and died fighting the gunners...No sooner would one get inside than he would charge the gunners, never looking back to see if his comrades were following him." The vicious fights pitted Union infantryman against Confederate artilleryman as the two sides came to grips in the half-light of dawn. Company I's Pvt. William Demond made it over the wall and into the smoking battery, where he took on three Confederates by himself. Emory Curtis of Co. G bayoneted two of the enemy and fought on "with the butt of his musket" before falling to Confederate counterfire. One of his mates, William Tracy, "fought like a little tiger," noted a comrade, and remained miraculously unhurt despite enemy bullets riddling his uniform. The Michiganders carried the battle into the fort's interior, "demanding in imperious but fatal language, the surrender of the place," and wreaking considerable havoc among the stunned defenders.[37]

Some of the Unionists followed the roadway along the fort's left flank and then turned to claw their way up the wall. Here they joined more survivors of the "forlorn hope" companies and blazed away at the Confederate line. With officers fighting like privates, the Unionists quickly blanketed the parapet and fired down into the whirling confusion. Their rifle blasts tore into the Confederate cannoneers, causing nearby crews to fall back before the storm. Some, like Lt. George Newall of Co. A, hugged the side of the wall and endeavored "to put a shot in the face of every rebel who raised his head." Others stood on the wall to take aim at the nearby enemy. The cacophonous pitch of the battle peaked "while the continual discharge of musketry and pistols, the clanking of sidearms, yells of expected victory, groans of wounded and dying" echoed in the morning gloom. The pressure exerted by the 8th Michigan was telling. "(I)n hand to hand fight (we) drove the enemy from the main fort into the wings," wrote one survivor of the shock of those first few minutes. Suddenly, a raking burst of musketry from the rear of the battery cut down some of the more exposed Federals. Swirling into the fort from beyond the low lying magazine came a line of Confederate infantry, loading and firing on the run.

Those Michiganders still in the fort bolted for the wall and safety. For the rest, however, the tables had suddenly turned—the apparent victory of a few moments before was now little more than a fight for survival. As the Unionists sought cover from the fire of

the surging Confederate reinforcements, others looked back across the gutted field and wondered: where were their supports?[38]

*   *   *

As they approached the northern flank of the fort, the stunned remnants of the leftmost companies of the 8th Michigan struggled to form some semblance of a battleline. Benjamin Pease of Co. G found himself on this part of the field, having joined in the race for the fort over the uneven terrain of the cotton field. Fifty feet from the ditch, with minie balls flying "as thick as bees," he remembered, Pease glanced back at the Michigan line. Finding it "tolerably straight, but thin," the panting private made ready to hit the wall. A soldier just ahead cried out for the men to get into the ditch as quickly as possible, and Pease joined others from his company in breaking formation and sprinting for the ditch's protection. Simultaneously, a Confederate ball creased Pease's scalp at the right temple, providing what he later described as "a very peculiar sensation." The stunned private looked about and saw no one within forty feet. Behind him, the field he had just crossed appeared littered with more men than the regiment originally mustered, such was the firepower that had been brought to bear upon the Michiganders. To the north, Pease saw some of his comrades scrambling for the cover of the myrtle bushes and fallen logs that lined the edge of the swamp. The young Northerner, opting for the security of numbers, abandoned the ditch and raced to join this new formation. When he arrived at the swamp line, Pease got his first good look at the battery and guessed the wall to be at least 20 feet high. It was, he wrote, "so steep no one could climb it without help. It would have been impossible for twice the number to have scaled the fort." Pease was right—there would be no Michigan breakthrough in this sector.[39]

Perhaps 15 feet back from Pease's position, "within a few rods of the fort," he recalled, 15 to 20 Michigan men formed behind a fallen pine tree and began blasting away at the nearest Confederate artillery piece. One enemy gunner after another fell until the surviving Confederates found it impossible to serve the gun. Pease, with blood running down the side of his face, moved in among his comrades, where he found his captain, Ephraim Lyon, lying face down among the myrtles. When the private asked his captain if he was wounded, the officer looked up to say "no." Throughout this brief exchange, Lyon remained prone, asking only that Pease keep him appraised of the unfolding action while he kept his own head down. Despite minies coming from every direction, Pease, ever the good soldier, was happy to comply.[40]

* * *

The first Confederate troops to reinforce Lamar were the men of Lt. Col. Alexander D. Smith's 9th South Carolina Battalion. Coming up the rough road from Secessionville, the soldiers from South Carolina's rugged Pee Dee district could easily hear the initial stages of the battle. The sight that greeted their eyes when they rounded the fort's magazine, however, was shocking. In full view of the fort were frantic gun crews working their pieces with desperate speed. Spaced between the artillery positions stood Confederate riflemen, ramming their charges home, aiming, and firing out over the wall. Slumped around the cannon and along the parapet lay other Confederates, shot down at their posts. Most shocking was the sight of the enemy along the left parapet and in the battery itself, shooting at and grappling with those artillerymen still attempting to service their pieces.[41]

Amidst the din Colonel Lamar appeared and ordered Smith's men to move into the breech on the left. In the pause awaiting orders, several Pee Dee's went down before the fire of alert Federal riflemen. Lamar's orders energized the battalion. Smith called out the command and his boys swept around the bombproof and into the battery proper. Small, personal fights broke out along the length of the line, but the Federals were too scattered and too few to last against Smith's ferocious assault. Either they fell before the Pee Dee's onslaught, or they bounded up and over the parapet. The battery had been cleared, but the Federals weren't driven very far. In fact, the enemy still occupied the left flank's outside wall, and the retreat of the Unionists who had fled the fort was arrested by the determination of this line. Suddenly, the battle became a rifle match between soldiers outfitted in varying shades of blue and gray separated by but a few solid feet of dirt.[42]

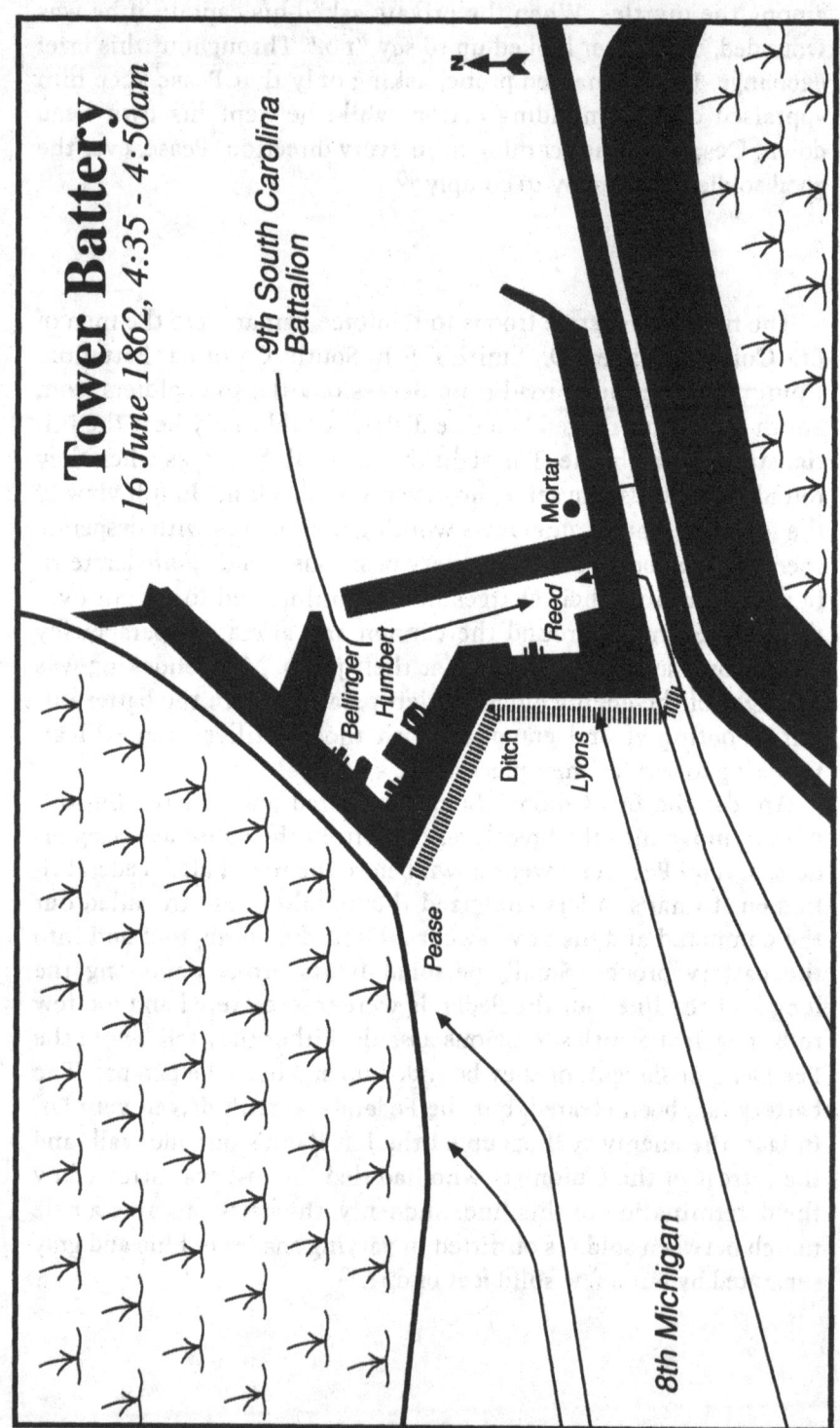

It did not take long for Smith to realize that he faced a potentially devastating problem. Fighting in their first battle, some of his men began to howl that their guns "refused to fire." Watching his men tear into the Federals, Smith knew that this was one problem he needed to solve. For now, he could only shout out encouragement and face down the enemy fire unflinchingly. As ordered, he managed to seal the breech, but the battle continued to rage.[43]

Smith's South Carolinians had arrived in time to blunt the initial Federal thrust, but not before Lamar's two artillery companies had been severely handled. Sergeant Baggott, having fired but one shot from his 24-lb. gun, went down in the first wave of Federal fire. Captain Samuel Reed, moving to bolster Baggott's crew, took a minie ball in the head and died instantly. The Federals mounting the parapet had shot down the Confederate gunners "like beeves," wrote one participant, but the Barnwell men of Co. B kept to their posts, working their pieces with grim determination. The galling fire managed to disperse the crew manning the 24-pounder nearest the Federal breech. Jamieson's people tried to counter the sweeping fire, but they were too few. In the end, the timely arrival of the Pee Dee infantry stanched the bloodletting in the battery, but in the harrowing minutes spent under close musketry fire and slashing bayonets, the defenders of the Tower Battery were decimated. The dead and wounded lay sprawled and bleeding along the line of Lamar's guns.[44]

Defending the parapet on the extreme right, Lt. John Bellinger rammed canister to the muzzles of his guns as the Northern charge pushed up against the base of the wall. His cannon mowed down "scores of Federals," exacting an appalling number of casualties with every blast. But the enemy came on, scrambling for the thin cover of the swamp line. Bellinger turned to his man-servant with orders to find his pistols which, in the rush, had been left in camp. Suddenly a stinging volley erupted from a ragged but potent line of Federals, now ensconced only 25 feet from the wall, and Bellinger's gunners began to go down. Within minutes, the Confederate crew was reduced to only the lieutenant, his brother Vincent, and another private. Bellinger despaired that it was, "a time when all hope fled," but his despair turned to relief when the first elements of the Charleston Battalion rushed up to bolster the nearly invisible force along the Confederate right. Again, reinforcements had appeared in exactly the right place at precisely the right time.[45]

Lieutenant Colonel Peter Gaillard and his Charleston Battalion had followed the Pee Dee Battalion into the rear of the battery, where they found Colonel Lamar firmly in command. Lamar directed Gaillard to take up a position covering the parapet from the center to the right flank of the battery. The sons of Charleston responded as one as Capt. Henry King led his cheering company, the Sumter Guard, up the parapet to support the decimated artillerists. The 43-year-old captain, universally loved by his men, was suffering a debilitating illness but he refused to quit the field, citing a need to uphold his personal honor. Here on a field of honor, exposed at the head of his company, King took a minie ball in his chest and fell badly wounded. With their stricken captain waving them on, more Charlestonians rushed up to brave the Federal fire. Isaac Valentine, a corporal in the Sumter Guard, went down in the same musketry blast that hit King, while his brother Henry was shot through the arm. But the remainder of the Sumter Guard streamed past their fallen comrades and soon lined the wall. Leveling their rifles, they poured what was described as "a deadly volley" into the Federals out in the field.[46]

Confederate Scotsman Lt. James Campbell, of the Union Light Infantry, ran with his company up to the wall and looked frantically around for a weapon. In his haste to reach the front, he had left his rifle behind. With Federal minies buzzing through the air, Campbell found a head log resting along the top of the wall. Observing a Federal storming party preparing to rush his position, he pushed the log over the top and sent it rolling towards the startled Yankees, bowling them over like ten pins. Only then did he find a rifle and begin blasting away at the enemy. In the back of his mind he may well have wondered whether his brother was among the Unionists charging across the field.

Josiah Tennant, a noted marksman with the Sumter Guard, was credited with felling six Federals from the same group. But the attackers gave as well as they got, and Confederates reeled before the fire of the enemy riflemen lining the marsh and the cotton rows. Waiting for his pistols, Lieutenant Bellinger felt a bullet tear through his coat and another rend his pants. His man-servant had just returned with the forgotten firearms only to fall, shot through the legs. Bellinger comforted his stricken friend for a moment before returning to the fight. His brother, Pvt. Vincent Bellinger, took a flesh wound, but the siblings managed to retain their posts, braving the hail of Federal fire as they continued to sweep their front with artillery blasts.

Much of the Federal fire was deadly accurate. An enemy ball drilled Pvt. Thomas Parker of the Calhoun Guards just below his left ear and passed completely through his head, killing him instantly. Private Samuel Edgerton of the Sumter Guard took a minie in his hip and collapsed in agony from the wound. Company mate Pvt. Gustavus Poznanski, Jr. had felt a presentiment of his death for days before the battle, and as fate would have it, his vision came true on the rampart of the Tower Battery. Poznanski and Confederates like him, however, had tipped the balance in their favor. The fight for the Tower Battery had settled into a brutal but even slugging match.[47]

As the Irish Volunteers of the Charleston Battalion moved through the battery towards the parapet, Lt. Col. Thomas Wagner came rushing back, looking to fill a serious vacuum. The Pee Dee Battalion had stabilized the left flank, but Reed's guns along the left front stood silent, their crews hors du combat. When Wagner called for volunteers to man the batteries, Capt. W. H. Ryan and his Irishmen responded eagerly. The bulk of the battalion moved to the right to assist the Bellingers, but Ryan moved his people past the thundering Columbiad to bolster Reed's decimated survivors. Private William Shelton took charge at one piece and fought it with a fury while his comrades manned the other. Soon both cannon were once again belching smoke and raking the cotton field with their flying metal.[48]

Unlike the guns on the left, Lieutenant Humbert's Columbiad had maintained a continual shower of iron into and through the center of the field, leveling practically everyone and everything daring to pause there. Humbert was ably assisted by a number of officers. Lieutenants T. P. Oliver and J. W. Moseley, who had hoped to mount and fight Bonneau's naval guns that day. That proved impossible, so they volunteered as, "cannoneers . . .loading, trailing, and firing the piece." Captain Bonneau and two of his lieutenants—no doubt accompanied by some of their men—also arrived to aid the crews. From their posts, they could see the enemy reeling under the "destructive fire of grape and canister" that neutralized the trailing Federal regiments by either pinning them down in the field's center or pushing them north into the swamp. Captain G. D. Keitt moved coolly from point to point, directing his Orangeburg cannoneers "to maintain the ancient prestige of their district," as the Columbiad and her sisters maintained their fusillade.[49]

Probably fifteen minutes had passed and the Confederates had turned back the Federal thrust with a firing line of determined infantry and barking artillery. Perhaps breathing a little easier despite the pelting rifle fire from the intransigent Federals, the Confederates manning the Secessionville works knew they had beaten off a potentially mortal assault. With the fate of Charleston riding on every shot, the Southern counterpunch had cleared the battery and neutralized the enemy's attempt to support the first wave. Now, determinedly exchanging rifle fire with their stalled opponents, the Confederates waited for the next round. It wouldn't be long in coming.

* * *

When the 8th Michigan jumped off from the first hedge line, Lt. Col. Joseph Hawley worked to get his 7th Connecticut into some semblance of battle order. Directed to support the 8th's left, Hawley moved his regiment through the opening in the heavy hedge, then advanced them piecemeal across the cotton rows of the first field. Companies moved with minimal regard for order as Hawley struggled to align his regiment far enough to the left to properly support the charging Michiganders, now a quarter mile to the front. The units crossed the first field and angled to form behind the second hedge, the first arrivals pausing for the laggards to catch up. One eyewitness was surprised that a comrade "had sufficient wind...to express a verbal wonder whether the sand fort was shoveled by white men or by colored brothers who had not yet contrabanded." The charge had taken the humor from most of the regiment, prompting one soldier to observe, "(T)he men were played out when they got in front of the battery." Just then, the Confederate front exploded with smoke and fire, engulfing the charging Michiganders. Hawley arrived to quickly put his troops into an "excellent" line and started them forward, "clambering over the second hedge." It was there that Hawley finally got his first good look at the Tower Battery.[50]

Despite the smoke from the first cannonade, Hawley could see a small house that appeared to be within the work. Near the house, "clearly distinguishable" in the growing light stood the lookout tower. As his exhausted men moved forward, the colonel also noted how small a front the fort presented, and he looked anxiously to locate the left of the 8th Michigan's line. Suddenly, at a range of some 400 yards, disaster befell the Connecticut Federals. Unaware of the telescoping nature of the peninsula, they pushed left to align with the Michigan charge when their path disappeared, as nearly half the regiment plunged into the bushes lining the swamp north of the fort. Their momentum carried them into the marsh mud beyond. At this, the most critical moment of their attack, the gooey mess thoroughly destroyed regimental cohesion. Simultaneously, a spray of canister and grapeshot "doing still greater execution," noted one who suffered through its effects, doused the regiment's right, first staggering then halting it. "The rifle pits were filled with confederates that fired," remembered one survivor, "and mowed down our men like sheep." As the initial sweep of fire toppled Lieutenant Dempsey with a minie through his shoulder, one survivor reasoned, "(I)t was no wonder that the line became broken and uneven." Amid terrifying confusion, the 7th Connecticut's attack ground to a bloody halt.[51]

As the advance slowed and then halted altogether, the color guard froze near the center of the line. Company G's Capt. Edwin Hitchcock knew that he must keep his men moving or they would die there. With part of his own company and a group from Lt. Atwell's Co. C, Hitchcock drove forward, crossing nearly half the distance to the battery while firing on the run. A Confederate cannon fired and an iron projectile drilled through part of the captain's thigh, but Hitchcock continued on. He ordered his men to hand him loaded rifles, and the wounded officer loosed shot after shot into the Confederates lining the parapet. Cheered by the example of his bravery, the leading elements of these two companies joined the captain firing at the fort. As the bleeding officer continued to lead by example, a Confederate minie slammed into Hitchcock' upper lip and lodged in his head. Four of his men, including Sgt. Haynes and Pvt. J. N. Dexter, tried to carry him away. The latter

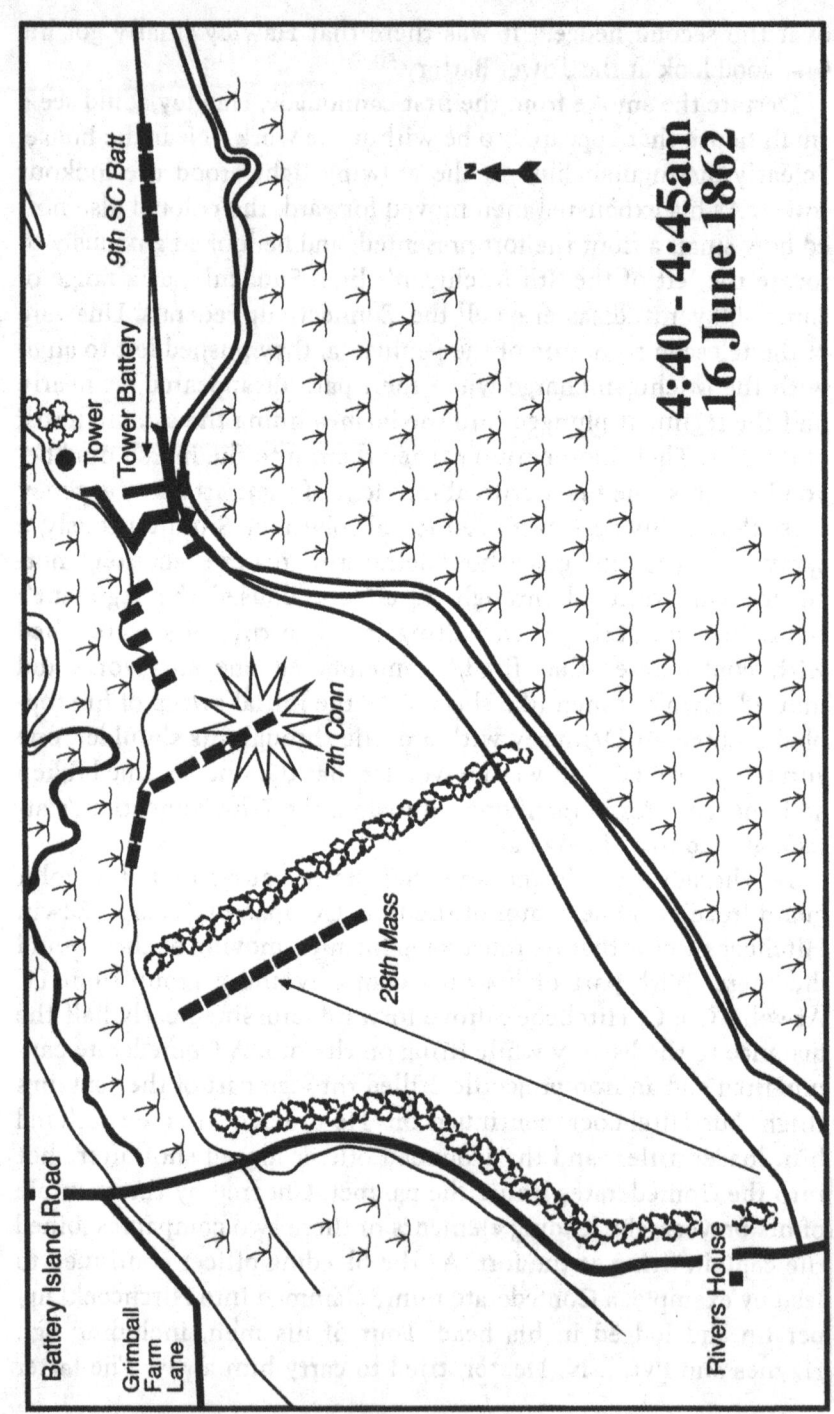

two fell wounded to the storm of metal sweeping the field, and the quartet was forced to abandon their captain in a cotton furrow, "evidently dying when last seen." As one survivor grimly recalled in an obvious understatement, "It was a time of peril."[52]

Back in the swamp, efforts to re-align the muck-stuck companies came undone when elements of the next regiment in line, the 28th Massachusetts, rushed up behind the 7th and plunged into the same mire. The two regiments became hopelessly intermingled in the pluff mud, making it virtually impossible to rescue the situation. All the while, Confederate shot and shell plowed into the mass of milling and confused Northerners.[53]

Hawley and his officers tried as they could to realign the regiment, but the punishing execution of the Confederate artillery made such efforts difficult. While "the shells (were) bursting all about us at the same time," Lieutenant Hooten of Co. D spun around and fell with a projectile lodged deeply in his body. As a detachment carried him rearward, he continued to exhort his men, but within a short time was dead. His death may be unique in the Civil War, for someone bitterly noticed afterward that the Confederate projectile that had killed Hooten was a "junk bottle."

Meanwhile, up and down the line, Confederate fire continued to chew up the disorganized Northerners. Sergeant Upson of Co. F had three fingers severed by a canister shot that went on to gouge his shoulder after removing his digits, felling him in excruciating pain. Private Charles Gilbert reeled as an artillery shot blew his leg off, while George Corbin of Company K was shot through his forehead and died instantly. Another comrade, Andrews Hibbard, went down in a pool of blood with a shattered knee. One lucky soldier named Edward St. Lyon wore his haversack into the battle. When a projectile smashed into his back, he suffered only a bad bruise that lamed him for a couple of days. Had St. Lyon obeyed orders and made the attack without his pack, he would have been killed. One Unionist declared that he looked at nothing "but the place I step(p)ed and watched the flash of the enemys cannon." Here and there, small squads hustled the dead and the wounded back to the safety of the first hedge, but Colonel Hawley knew he and his men had entered the crisis of their existence. Extreme action was demanded if his regiment was to survive the fiasco in which it now found itself.[54]

After judging the situation, Hawley ordered his color bearer to move to the right, where he started forming a line somewhat withdrawn from their point of furthest penetration. Collecting perhaps half of his men and braving fire he later recalled as "constant," Hawley still managed to knead a decent battleline together. As he completed his dispositions, brigade commander William Fenton rode up and ordered Hawley to lead the 7th Connecticut across the field to the right so as to come in behind the 8th Michigan, which was just now fighting for its life on the battery wall. Hawley did what he could and pushed his men south "by fits and starts," parallel to the Confederate wall. Realizing the dangerous position he held in relation to his Michigan allies, Hawley wisely ordered a cease fire to prevent his men from firing into their backs. Luckily, those same Michigan men had silenced some of the Confederate gun crews, so Hawley and his small force were able to cross the fort's front relatively unscathed.

Regimental affairs seemed to take a turn for the better, for Hawley now had his Connecticut men in order with clear instructions as to their objective. But after arriving at a point directly fronting the battery's left flank, their fortunes changed yet again. A sprawling conglomeration of blue-uniformed soldiers moved determinedly for the front and rushed into and through Hawley's re-formed column, throwing the head of it into utter disarray. The charging troop mass moved on, and, once again, Colonel Hawley returned to the work of realigning his disrupted line. As he tried to rectify the damage done by this unfortunate encounter with his division mates, Joseph Hawley must have realized this wasn't to be the 7th Connecticut's day.[55]

* * *

Earlier that morning, Lt. Col. MacLelland Moore led his Irish 28th Massachusetts on the heels the 7th Connecticut through the hedge gap and into the first field. Already the roar of battle swept across the cotton rows and marshlands, but they moved by flank and forward "in column by company," forming just past the hedge on the first company in line. Moore's orders were to support the 7th Connecticut's left, and as his men moved off at the double quick across what one soldier described as "deep furrows...1 1/2 feet deep, 2 1/2 feet wide," they attempted to align on the Connecticut charge unfolding ahead of them. But as they approached the second ditch, a violent blast of Confederate artillery crushed the 28th's right flank. Hiram Nason, one of the color bearers, remembered that "shot and shell mowed down our men in swaths," while the left and center of the line continued manfully on towards the ditch. A private from Co. E, Charles McVey, tried to leap over the five foot wide declivity he later described as "filled with old stumps rocks and stones," but he misjudged his effort and landed heavily, twisting and disabling his leg. Others searched the front for Confederate infantry but were shocked to find that they were assaulting an entrenched position. The continuing barrage forced the rightmost companies to bunch to the center and left of the line, thereby threatening the regiment's cohesion. It was at this point in the action that Lt. Nichols Bannon of Co. H had his sword "smashed to atoms" by a cannonball which also took his thumb and forefinger with it. A bullet through the thigh put Co. C's Michael Campbell out of the battle. The private used his rifle as a crutch and limped all the way back to the 28th's camp on Sol Legare Island.[56]

As the regiment negotiated the second hedge, a terrifying sight nearly froze them in their tracks. Color bearer Nason observed the results of the Confederate barrage—"arms legs heads tore to pieces." The 28th lurched forward again, attempting to align with the 7th Connecticut's flank, but each company seemed to have its own particular difficulties. Predictably, the left wing piled into the marsh-bound Connecticut men and quickly unraveled. Other parts of the 28th became disorganized when elements of the 7th Connecticut blocked their way. Still others, shocked by the carnage and demoralized by the confusion of their first battle, broke for the rear—they had simply had enough fighting for one day. Those that remained found some protection by dropping to the ground and burrowing between the cotton rows. Others remained standing, unwilling to leave the scene. While a Confederate missile blasted the ornamental eagle from one of the color guard's flagstaffs, Hiram Nason watched fellow flag bearer Sgt. John J. McDonald die not an arm's length away. In the midst of the fury, Nason could only wonder why he himself was not yet dead.[57]

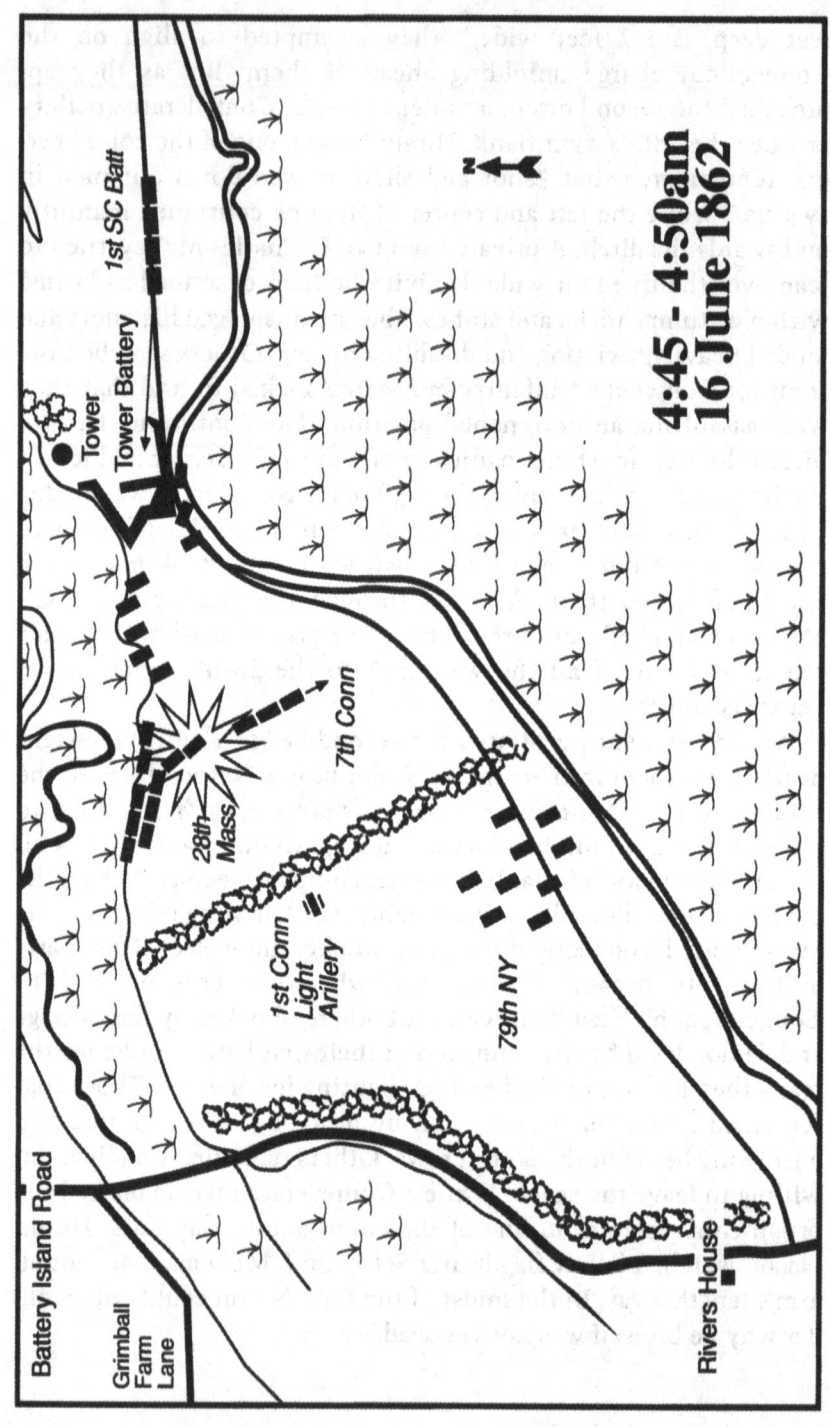

When the 7th Connecticut finally cleared the front, a few disorganized companies from the 28th attempted to press the attack. Major George Cartwright and Cpl. John McDonald led a group that pushed toward the fort, only to find themselves even more exposed to the cannonade than before. Veering left, they came up behind the elements of the 8th Michigan still holding the swamp line. The combination of the swamp's declivity, the myrtle bushes, and some felled trees offered modest protection from the enemy artillery. But poor shooting, perhaps by these men—most certainly by those Irish still embroiled back by the second hedge—discomfited the Michiganders closer to the blazing fort. An officer of the 8th Michigan up near the battery raised and waved his cap to alert the Irishmen to the danger of their friendly fire. He needn't have bothered. While two soldiers from Major Cartwright's group, Pvt. Hugh Gallagher and Sgt. William Kerrigan, went down with bullet wounds, the rest watched as their comrades at the second hedge disintegrated. One eyewitness summed up the 28th Massachusett's performance thusly: "as soon as the enemy discovered and commenced firing on them in earnest, they broke, and as a regiment did not come up again." Except for the few brave souls that hugged the marsh line, the 28th Massachusetts' first battle was over.[58]

For the men of the 8th Michigan, the rush for the Tower Battery had degenerated into a bloody stalemate. On their left among the myrtle bushes, the Michiganders "kept up a fire" on what Confederates they could see. But one Federal groused that the battery's defenders were "only obliged to show their heads when they fired, while we had no cover...Yet our men fired away." If the contest weren't difficult enough, "friendly" rifle fire from some disorganized rear ranks struck down a few Michigan men, prompting Lt. G. B. Fuller to wave his cap and cry out to those in the rear to quit firing so low. Fuller watched in disbelief as renewed Confederate rifle and artillery blasts soon swept away those rear supports. Where two full regiments were supposed to come to the 8th's assistance, only a major, two captains, and nine privates from the 28th Massachusetts made their way to Fuller's position. A few of the privates stayed, but the Irish officers realized quickly that their duty lay back with their broken regiment. In Fuller's words, "They turned back, and again the Eighth was left alone in the field in the fire of the enemy." Off to the south, Fuller could see the end of the

Michigan effort on the other flank, as the few who still stood on the earthwork squeezed off their last rounds—"But the poor fellows—most of them never came away, and those that did, with scarcely an exception, came away with marks that they will carry as long as they live."[59]

Those "poor fellows" still mounted on the battery's left flank had been chopped to pieces by Rebel reinforcements, and the parapet had become a dead zone for the Michiganders. Captain Samuel Guild had stood on the side of the wall blazing away at the enemy with a borrowed rifle when a minie tore into his left side. Three members of Guild's Co. A—Orrin Bump, George Newall, and W. H. Aitken—considered moving him, but they quickly realized that the severity of the wound required that the captain lie still. Another captain, Gilbert Pratt, also fell nearby with a wound so ugly that most who saw it assumed it to be mortal. Company H's Richard Doyle had been seen picking off a Confederate clinging to the lookout tower, but after standing on the parapet to down three enemy gunners, Doyle now lay atop the wall, his arm shattered.

The pressure from the Confederate reinforcements eventually pushed the sullen and stubborn Federal survivors off the bloody wall. Newall and Aitken sadly left their wounded Captain Guild to his fate. Pratt also was left behind, unable to move away from the scene of his wounding. Some of the angry Michiganders fell back to the protection of the swamp line, while others dropped down between the cotton rows and began to rake the fort with a steady fire. For the first time, Union artillery started to answer the enemy guns as shells crashed into the center section of the fort's front wall. Michiganders along the swamp line and between the cotton rows could take little solace from the Northern shellfire. They had come within a minute or two of breaking and taking the Tower Battery. Now, they needed only to view the front and side of the battery's wall to see the bitter harvest their charge had produced. Scattered across the field and on the walls of the fort lay the heart of their officer corps and the muscle of their ranks, broken and bleeding, dying and dead.[60]

CHAPTER EIGHT

"Their Bearing Was Worthy of Veterans."

—Lt. Col. David Morrison, 79th New York Infantry

Fields of Fire

Colonel Clement H. Stevens of the 24th South Carolina had spent a relatively quiet night inspecting his James Island picket posts and searching for signs of enemy activity. As daylight approached, the colonel reined his mount northwesterly towards the New Town Cut to check up on his troops. "On reaching that point I distinctly heard the guns of the enemy in front of Secessionville," he would later write. Wheeling his horse, he hurried back along the Confederate lines. Enroute, a courier dashed up to inform him that a large enemy force was advancing on Lamar's works. Stevens reacted quickly, dispatching two couriers of his own, one to report this intelligence to "Shanks" Evans back at the Lawton House, the other to alert Col. Johnson Hagood, who had spent the damp night in the 1st South Carolina's camp. As the couriers sped off into the growing light, Stevens spurred his mount towards the sound of the firing.[1]

At approximately 4:30 a.m., Stevens' aide tore into the Confederate encampment east of the main defense line and there located Johnson Hagood. After a few rushed words, the colonel moved quickly to gather his command. Hagood found Lt. Col. John

McEnery with his 4th Louisiana Battalion in camp just north of King's Highway and directed him to advance his unit "to the footbridge in rear of Secessionville to the reinforcement of the garrison." Further north was Simonton's Eutaw Battalion and the remainder of Hagood's 1st South Carolina in their camps straddling the Dill's Branch Road. The industrious and far-thinking colonel sent these two units under Simonton's command west towards Artillery Crossroads with orders to advance south from there on the Battery Island Road. With luck, this would concentrate the Confederate forces squarely on the Federal flank. After dispatching his men, Hagood rode for Artillery Crossroads to get any available guns moving south to support his infantry. There he found Lieutenant Jeter from Boyce's Macbeth Artillery commanding a single 6-pounder cannon supported by Co. B of the 47th Georgia Infantry. Hagood commanded Jeter and the infantrymen to advance down the Battery Island road to seek out and engage the enemy. That done, Hagood made for the front.[2]

As Hagood made his rounds, Simonton gathered his Eutaw Battalion "under arms in a very few minutes," and rushed them west on the road towards the Presbyterian Church. The trample of feet blended with the long roll rattling through the camps, assuring the Confederates that serious work lay ahead. Just before Simonton's men reached Artillery Crossroads, he herded them left by file into a field bracketed by a marsh on the left and the Battery Island Road on the right. Moving south through the field "at quick," the men found the landscape opening eastwardly towards a distant marsh. Frantic in their desire to come to grips with the enemy, the Eutaws gave out "a shout (then) rushed on at double quick." They pushed through a shallow creek into an open field where Federal shells were bursting indiscriminately across their front. Ahead of them at the southern edge of the field, the extensive line of felled timber stretched well beyond both their flanks. On their left, in line with the abatis, stood a heavy thicket of trees. Beyond the abatis arose the roar and smoke of battle.[3]

* * *

Just as Simonton had obeyed his orders promptly upon receipt, so had McEnery, who formed his Louisianans immediately and moved west on the King's Highway at the double-quick. After a half-mile trot, as they moved through a crossroads, McEnery became confused—undoubtedly he had never used these roads before and was unfamiliar with this route to Secessionville. The marchers slowed to a halt while the lieutenant colonel and his staff held a spirited discussion as to which direction to take. In the distance, the noise of battle could be heard distinctly, adding extra pressure for a quick decision. "(A)fter a lapse of a few moments," McEnery received assurances as to the right direction, and the 4th Louisiana Battalion was off again, racing south across the front of the Confederate defense line. Straining to reach their comrades, the Louisianans pushed towards the rolling thunder of Lamar's Tower Battery.[4]

* * *

When the first Federal assault fell back from the battery's walls, Lieutenant Colonel Smith of the South Carolina Pee Dee Battalion saw a chance to solve his unit's weaponry problem. He jumped up onto the parapet, crossed the wall, and lowered himself down into the fronting ditch. Rapidly traversing the front and flank, Smith collected as many small arms and ammunition boxes as he could carry and hustled them back into the fort. The arms were distributed among the men, but there was little time for congratulations. Out in the cotton field, a second mass of charging, cheering Federals were bearing down on the fort's left flank.

Southern mouths set, fingers tightened. Round two was about to begin.[5]

* * *

The Highlanders of the 79th New York reached the Rivers Causeway "just as day was breaking," when orders flew down the line to continue their march at the double quick. They covered the intervening distance—estimated to be a mile by one Highlander—and reached the scene of the attack. A deep cheer from the 8th Michigan echoed across the fronting cotton field. As they filed through the hedge opening and into the first field, the lead companies of the 79th New York could see the trail of the 8th Michigan heading well down the peninsula. To their rear, the Highlanders heard the three-gun battery on Sol Legare Island—the same earthwork they had helped build—open on the Confederate fort. Three shots spun through the leaden sky, all of which seemed to land "in or near that work," recalled one blue-uniformed Highlander. The remaining Scotsmen filed through the hedge and into the cotton field, where Lt. Col. David Morrison wrestled with the uneven terrain to work his men into an assault formation. While the New Yorkers struggled to form up, a messenger came charging up from the front to report to General Stevens, who had established his command post near the hedge opening and in full sight of the Highlander line. The courier described the fate of the first wave of the assault and relayed Col. William Fenton's desperate appeal for reinforcements. Upon hearing this, Stevens turned to Colonel Leasure and ordered him to begin his attack immediately. Leasure in turn ordered Morrison to start his advance. The lieutenant colonel had formed only two of his companies when he received Leasure's orders. Nonetheless, he aligned his troops to the right, directly on course with the Michiganders' attack route, and ordered them forward at the double quick "after only a moment's delay," reported a Federal officer. Under the eyes of Isaac Stevens, their former colonel, the Highlanders headed for the fort.[6]

Before the oncoming Scotsmen stretched the scene of battle. Confederate artillery was plastering the center of the field. This same artillery had ripped the 8th Michigan in half and had driven two other regiments onto the ground off to the left. A Federal battery, however, had finally opened on the fort— "a complete storm of shot and shell," as one Federal remembered it—and now Confederate attention seemed drawn to the Union artillerists.

On the right, knots of Unionists had mounted the Confederate fort, but their numbers seemed small, their situation precarious. The succeeding Highlander companies fanned out and swept forward, but the speed of Morrison's advance made alignment difficult if not impossible. Moreover, as the 79th whipped across the field, a confused jumble of Federals milled about just ahead. In the midst of the mob, officers screamed and cajoled in a frantic effort to reform their regiment, while panicky soldiers everywhere clung to the ground. At the second hedge and ditch, the Highlanders were further angered to find elements of the 28th Massachusetts huddled behind their flags and making no effort to support their Michigan mates fighting and dying just ahead. One Scotsman recalled how "many of them stretched out in the cotton furrows, endeavoring to cover themselves with the dirt and litter of the field." Over the cacophony, he recalled hearing a Massachusetts man calling out "Faugh a Ballach, Seventy Ninth! We'll be after yees." Exactly how much of this memory is colored by the natural rivalry between the Scotch and the Irish is hard to say, but many of the Scotsmen evidently took pleasure roughing up these prostrate "Faughs" as they moved toward the Tower Battery.[7]

By this time, the advance of 79th New York had reached the second ditch where, just 500 yards ahead, they could see the 8th Michigan "engaged at close quarters with the enemy." To the New York left was the main body of the dispirited 28th Massachusetts. The Highlanders paused, lying "behind the ditch waiting for orders to advance," trying to get the Irish to join them in the assault. When the men from Massachusetts displayed considerable reluctance to proceed with the assault, the frustrated Highlanders hurled epithets at their cowering brigade-mates. Just then Daniel Leasure and his son rode upon the scene. Failing to get his horse across the ditch, the fiery Leasure dismounted to join the Highlanders on foot.[8]

Confederate artillerists continued to duel with their Federal counterparts, but their fire still had only managed to down but a few of the New Yorkers attempting to cross the first field. When Morrison rang out the order to attack, the Highlanders responded with a vengeance. Up over the hedge, with little regard for formation, the 79th New York tore forward—"Their bearing was worthy of veterans," recalled Morrison in his after-action report—leaving the remnants of the 28th Massachusetts in their left rear. As the charge picked up steam, the Scotsmen encountered part of Hawley's 7th Connecticut—the ill-fated regiment that had finally righted itself. One Highlander recalled, "We hurried past them, pell-mell, in our eagerness to arrive at the fort and assist our storming party."

Leaving Hawley's disrupted troops in their wake, the Scotsmen bore down on the fort while Confederate artillery "bellowed out a

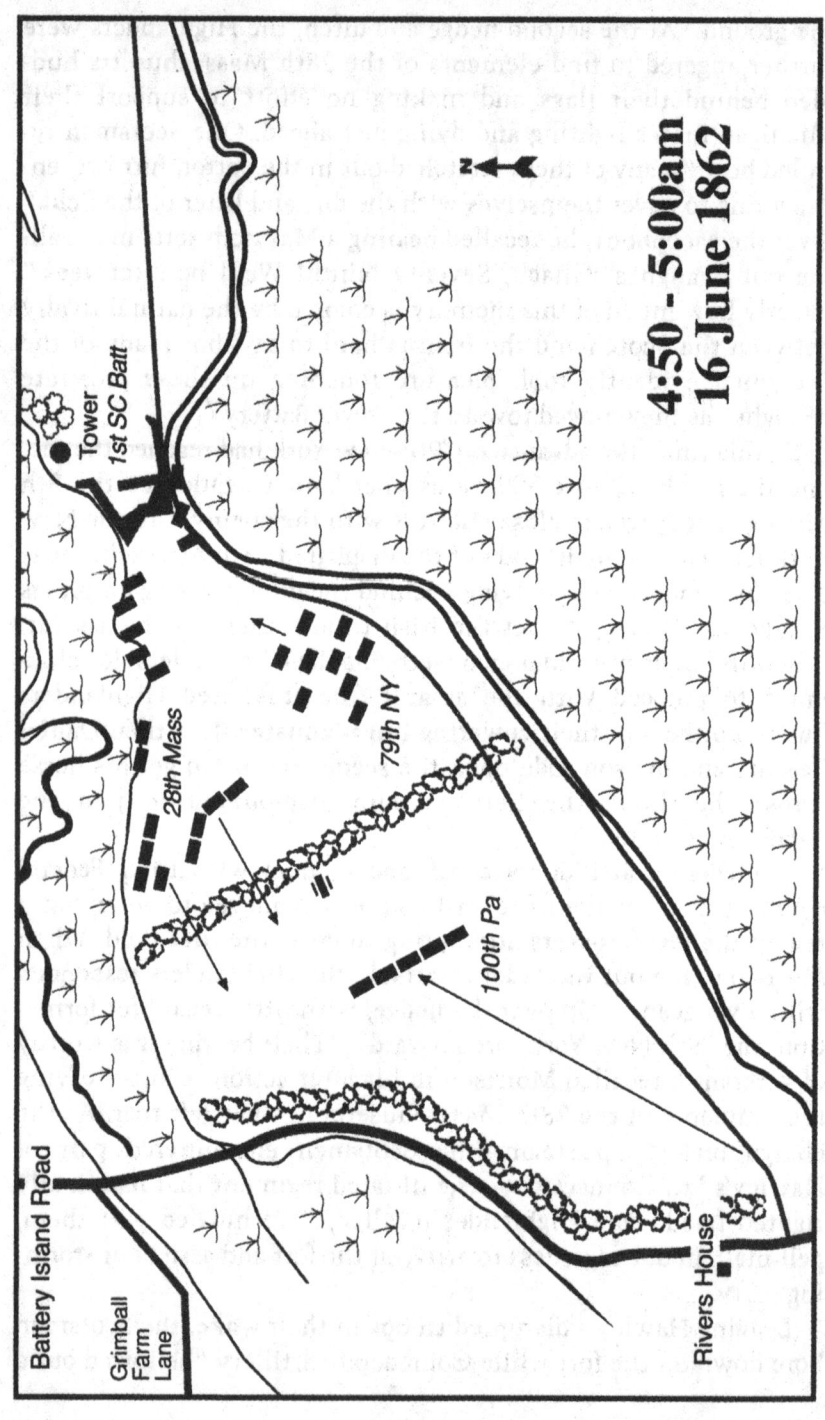

perfect cloud of grapeshot." Wrote one attacker, "The grape tore through our ranks with terrible effect." Another attacker recalled that the "inside of the fort was filled with the rifle men of the enemy, and, as we advanced, would stick up their heads over the parapits, fire, and draw back & reload, in this manner also, quite a number of our men were wounded." The metal spray dropped many to their knees amidst the Michiganders who had blazed the bloody trail. The 8th Michigan's Philip Coleman numbly recalled: "A second charge was made passing by those who were dead and wounded." Ahead, Michiganders were falling back from the battery wall, but the 79th New York's will seemed unshakable as their attack drove home.[9]

The Confederate artillery had forced the leftmost New York companies north towards the right flank of the fort. Colonel Leasure ran with these units, acting for a time more like a spirited captain rather than the acting brigadier that he was. As these elements veered for the protection of the marsh line, leaving stricken comrades in their path, Leasure came to his senses and turned to organize his other two regiments just then forming to support the Highlanders. These left-flank New Yorkers combined with the Michigan men and the few Irish in the area taking potshots at the strengthened Confederate right flank.[10]

As their color guard planted their flags "directly in front of the fort," a Federal proudly reported after the fact, the right front rank of the Highlanders angled towards the same flank of the fort that the 8th Michigan had earlier mounted. Cheering lustily as they reached the ditch fronting the Confederate wall, Lieutenant Colonel Morrison—"cheering and encouraging the men"—and his New Yorkers raced around the flank and along the narrow passageway on the battery's south side. There they were joined by remnants of the 8th Michigan that still wanted back at the Southerners. Curling around the battery, waves of Highlanders began to claw up the littered wall, past the broken bodies of wounded and dead. Morrison gained the parapet first, leaping "without a moment's hesitation," recalled one soldier, to the top of the wall. With a flash of his pistol the melee began. Rifle blast answered rifle blast, and fist answered fist. Morrison emptied his pistol point-blank into Lamar's defenders, as the top of the Tower Battery again became a cauldron of desperation between North and South.[11]

202 SECESSIONVILLE

THE WAR IN SOUTH CAROLINA.—HEROIC CONDUCT OF LIEUT-COL. MORRISON, 79TH NEW YORK HIGHLANDERS, ON THE PARAPET OF THE TOWER BATTERY, JAMES ISLAND.—FROM A SKETCH BY AN OFFICER.

Lt. Col. David Morrison leads the 79th New York over the wall of the Tower Battery.

Harper's Weekly

Some members of the 79th stayed in the ditch and sidled leftward and rightward into positions to fire at Confederate targets on the wall. One of the Scotch color guards—despite his lack of technical understanding of how artillery pieces were fired—reported after the battle that he had witnessed a corporal from Company A shoot an enemy gunner "just as he was about to pull the trigger of one of his guns." This suppressing fire effectively quieted the enemy artillery and helped cover the regiments rushing into the field to the 79th's support. But the New Yorkers that dared to mount the wall ran into a hail of rifle fire that blanketed the entire sector. Unionists on the earthwork began to fall where they stood. Amidst the carnage, one "mere boy," as he was described by a Southern observer, impressed the Confederates when he straightened himself on the parapet and sang out, "here(s) your Little Scotch Man—ainte I brave." In the storm of musketry, he lasted less than a minute.[12]

Many of the Highlanders lay down to hug the outside top of the wall and began to pour rifle fire into the fort's defenders. Morrison directed his troops to keep the Confederate cannoneers off balance, but the Southern artillerists, after some delay, got their pieces roaring, again slamming shot and shell into the Union regiments out in the field. With his supports getting chopped up in the cotton field and cognizant of his regiment's sudden isolation, Morrison determined to order the 79th up and over the wall to carry the works at the bayonet point. The officer called his subalterns together to inform them of his plan, and the officers were soon moving along the wall spreading word of the pending assault into the interior of the cauldron. A few moments passed, then Morrison rose up and called out the command to charge: the Highlanders went over the wall.[13]

The gallant lieutenant colonel leapt to the top of the parapet and almost immediately reeled, stunned by a head-clipping minie fired "by one of the enemy, who was distant only a few feet," wrote a nearby Federal. The officer returned the fire and shot down his assailant, even though "the blood from his wound running over his face almost blinded him." Somehow the officer was able to collect his wits and remain in command, as all around him the Scotsmen mounted the parapet with a bound. Confederate fire burst forth into this new wave of attackers, however, plowing into them with a "withering" strike that tumbled wounded and dying New Yorkers off the wall and into the ditch. The far right wing attempt-

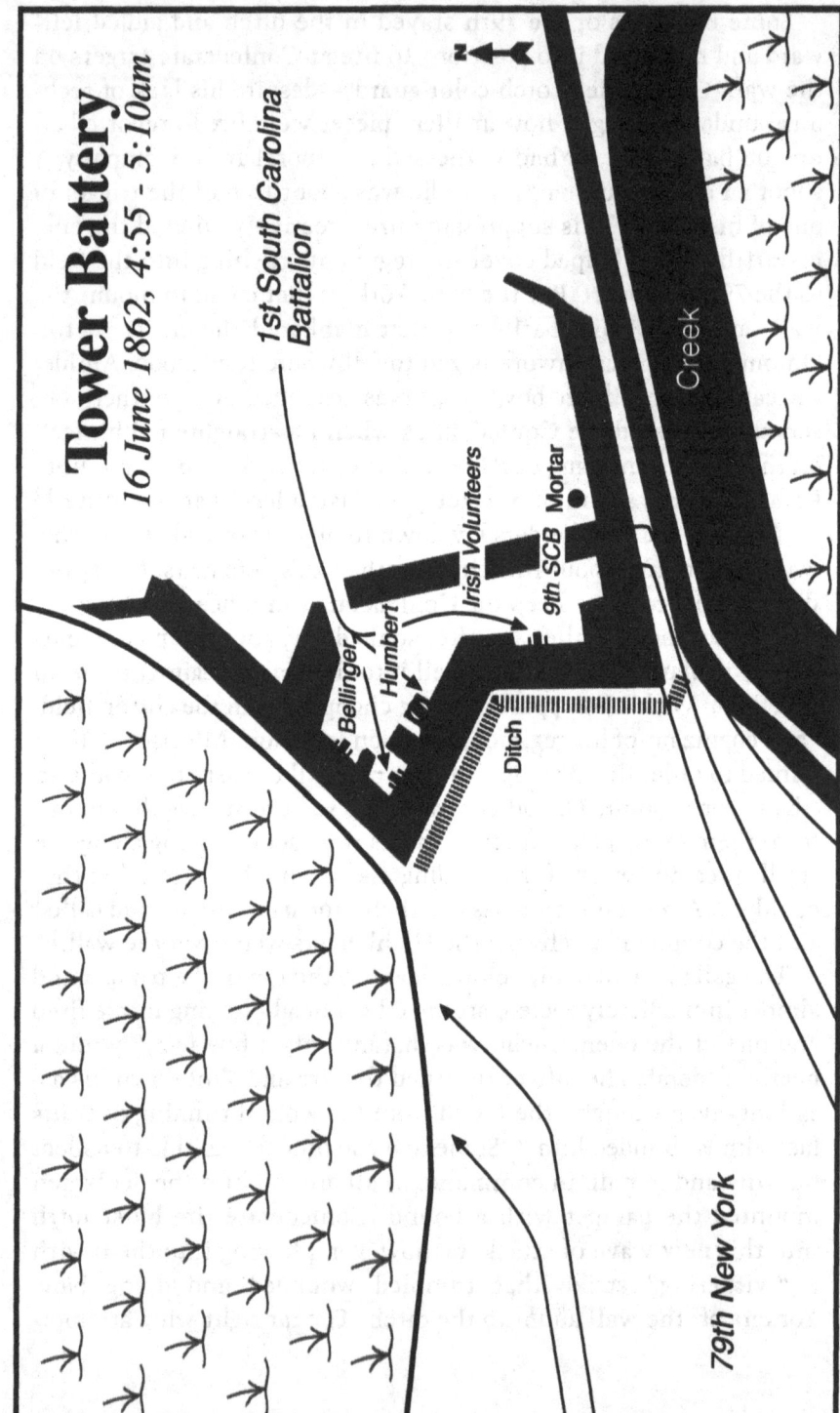

ed to answer with fire of its own and succeeded in checking some of the Confederate response. Wrote one witness of the Highlander efforts, "I never saw our boys fight with such determination." But determination wasn't enough to prevent a bloody repulse of the Union thrust. Lieutenant James Kinnear fell badly wounded before the musketry, as did Lt. Thomas Robertson. One Federal, who described the opposition as "fierce and determined," watched as the gunfire mowed down the New York attack. Discouraged by their inability to effectively combat the "unseen enemies," the surviving Highlanders kept looking back across the cotton field for the promised support. Like the Michiganders before them, they also wondered: where were the reinforcements?[14]

* * *

With Col. Daniel Leasure acting as brigadier, the command of the 100th Pennsylvania had devolved upon Maj. David Leckey. With his numbers reduced by picket duty, Leckey marched from the Sol Legare camps with less than 300 effectives. But by the time the Roundheads reached the Rivers House, about 130 additional Pennsylvanians had rushed up to join their comrades, thus raising Leckey's command to battalion strength. This day, the Roundheads would attack in a weakened state, but their spirit would make up for what their numbers lacked.[15]

Leckey's orders were simple enough: "advance to support the Highlanders." The 100th, slowed only by overshot Confederate artillery shells, maintained a quick pace through the woods as the first four regiments were fed into the attack. Private J. H. Slemmons of Co. G remembered "confederate bombshells cutting the limbs from the tree-tops around us," as the men pushed forward to the sound of battle. Passing the Rivers House and entering the field through the hedge opening, the regiment could see the 79th New York rushing the fort and the mayhem swirling across the intervening fields. Leckey quickly became concerned. The New Yorkers were moving at a furious pace that the jaded Roundheads would have difficulty matching.

"It was extremely difficult to maintain even the semblance of a line," remembered Leckey, "when the men on the left were falling breathless from the great exertions they were obliged to make to get forward into line." Somehow, though, the major managed to cajole his exhausted Roundheads "forward into line," and they pressed ahead in the direction of the enemy fort.[16]

The regiment double-quicked by right flank as they hit the field, uncoiling like a whip as the front companies cut to the right and began the advance. The rear companies strained to catch up on the left, "running and stumbling over the cotton rows to get into line," but they weren't having much success. Private Slemmons remembered that "(the) cotton field was so un-even that we could not get a 'solid" line formed." The second ditch and hedge barely slowed the Pennsylvanians. Dead ahead lay the battery, wreathed in smoke and surrounded by Union troops firing away behind what little shelter they could secure. On the right, Northerners had mounted the parapet and were blazing down into the fort. As they traversed the expanse, the sprinting Roundheads started to feel the squeeze of the peninsula's contour folding their flanks on the center, but the ragged line pressed on.

Just 500 yards from adding their punch to the roaring fray, the 100th Pennsylvania began the final act of their charge.[17]

* * *

Daniel Leasure stood just 30 paces from the fort. Behind him, what was left of the 28th Massachusetts lay in useless disarray. To his right, the Highlanders were reeling—"wilting" as Leasure described them—under small arms fire from the fort. Leasure was stationed with the elements of the left of the 79th New York that had joined those parts of the 8th Michigan near the Confederate's right flank, when he turned to watch his Roundheads "coming up gallantly" across the blood-soaked field.

Suddenly, Confederate artillery exploded, and Leasure's pride turned to horror when "the storm of missiles from the huge guns leaped out with tongues of fire, darkening the air with the projectiles with which they had been crammed to the muzzle." Leasure instinctively hit the dirt, and when he arose, "the ground was strewn with Roundheads dying, dead, and wounded, in all sorts of mangled horrid forms." While the wings of the regiment raggedly pressed on, the center lay decimated by the wave of canister and

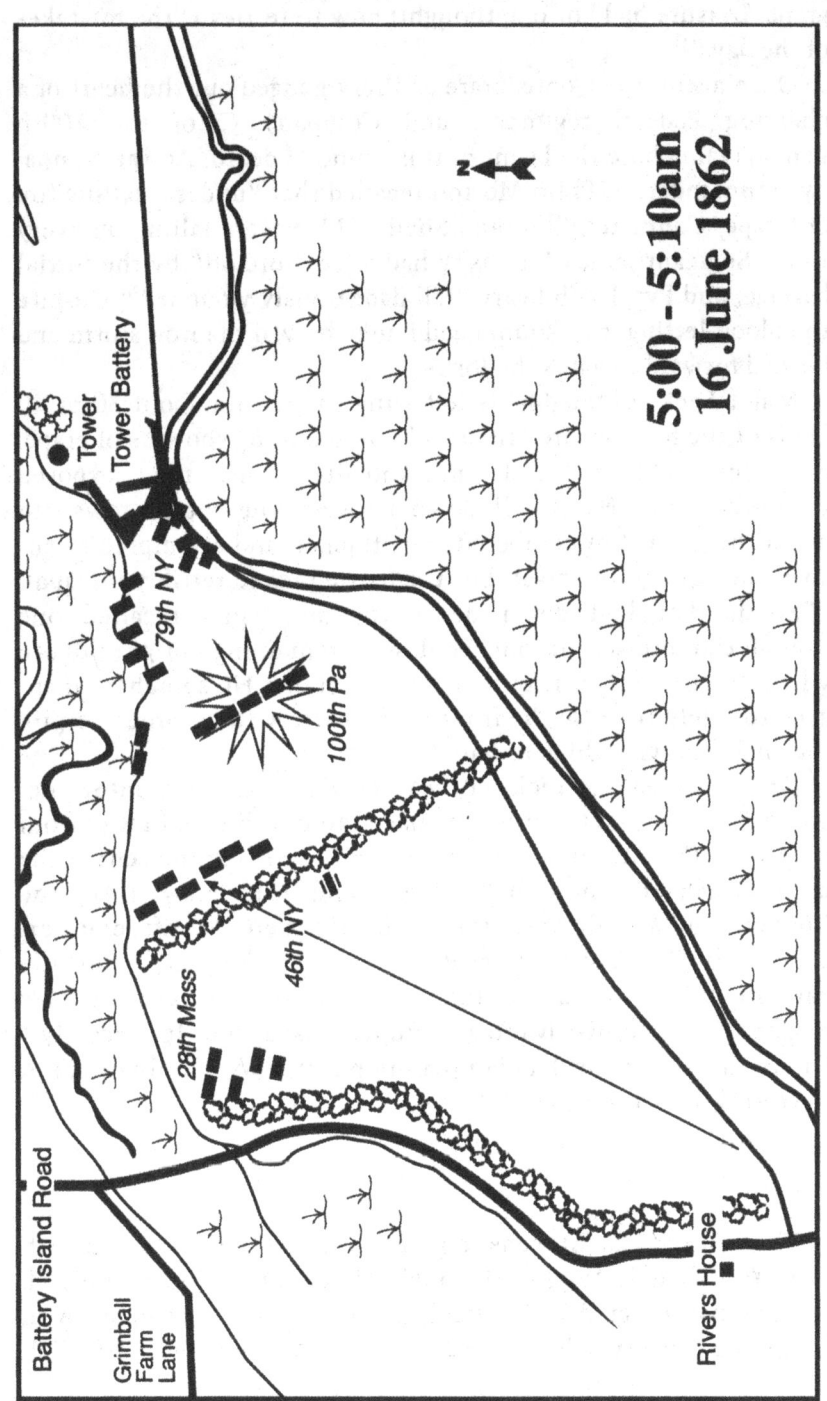

grape. Leasure had but one thought: how to retrieve "the mistakes of the day."[18]

Once again, the Confederate artillery gouged out the heart of a charging Federal regiment, and Company C of the 100th Pennsylvania bore the brunt of this round of death. Acting company commander Lt. Philo Morton recalled that "under a galling fire of Grape, Cannister, Shot and Shell. . .Men were falling on every side." Sergeant James McCasky had a leg "tore off" by the initial barrage, and Pvt. Jacob Leary "fell dangerously wounded." Despite the blood-letting, the Roundhead flanks braved the iron storm and pushed forward towards the fort.[19]

Major Leckey brought his left wing to "within about 30 or 40 yards of the fort" where "the rebels were raining showers of grape, cannister, chains, and musketballs" on the exposed Pennsylvanians. Many fell down between the cotton rows "to avoid the grape," remembered one attacker, and attempted to answer the enemy firepower, but the battle proved terribly unequal. "Several that laid down never got up again" recalled one Roundhead, himself untouched despite remaining upright "to see where it (the cannon fire) was coming from." He somehow managed to safely traverse the front of the battery three times despite the "balls. . .flying thick as hail."

Others weren't so lucky. Private Hugh Wilson had an eye destroyed by a musket ball but managed to pull himself away from the front. Despite such bravery, and in a scene reminiscent of the prior attacks of the 8th Michigan and 79th New York, the Roundheads' assault was stymied by the fierce Confederate artillery. Private Slemmons recalled "how the shot, shell and rifle balls flew. Oh! it was aweful." Another survivor recalled, "We fought with great disadvantages and in consequence lost heavily." Or, as another Pennsylvanian plainly put it, "We could not get in the fort when we got to it."[20]

* * *

The last of Isaac Stevens' regiments, the 474 men of the 46th New York, double-quicked the final 3/4 of a mile to the battlefield. Stevens had ordered Col. Rudolph Rosa to steer his men north along the Battery Island Road to attempt a linkage with Col.

Williams' brigade. Leasure, however, needed the 46th's numbers to support his Roundhead assault, and communicated as much to Stevens. The general acquiesced to Leasure's request and ordered Rosa and his Germans through the hedge opening and into the first field. Rosa shook out a line and began his advance, all the while attempting to align on the 100th Pennsylvania's left. Keeping well to the north, the 46th approached the milling mass of the Irish 28th Massachusetts and those sections of the 7th Connecticut still stymied by both marsh mud and Confederate metal. Unfortunately, when large portions of the latter two regiments finally broke for the rear, some of the 46th's companies broke with them. Other New York companies simply fell apart. Sweeping Confederate canister plowed into the suddenly frozen ranks, and the Germans began to fall. Colonel Rosa fought to keep his men in order, but some in his ranks melted away towards the rear, joining their comrades in flight. However, much of the 46th New York stayed put, incapable of clear firing at the fort and unwilling to run before the Southern gunfire. As they struggled to hold their position, orders arrived from Leasure to begin a general withdrawal. Rosa pulled what was left of his regiment behind the hedge and awaited further orders.[21]

* * *

For the Confederates inside the battery, the maelstrom of the enemy attacks had transmorgrified into a brutal set-to of punching and counterpunching. No sooner had the first enemy rush been broken than a second assault flooded up to the left flank. But this second Federal charge, like the first, had been staggered by blasts of canister from the Columbiad and her sister pieces, sucking much of the spirit—and a significant amount of the blood—from the attackers. The remnants of Jamison's detachment and the Pee Dee Battalion met the enemy head-on. Vicious, close-quarter hand-to-hand fighting raged along the top of the wall in this sector, as rifle butts, bayonets, and fists came into play. Major J. H. Hudson strode among his Pee Dee's and continually realigned them to counter the surging Federal thrusts. Adjutant Miller distributed ammunition to the men and encouraged them "never to surrender to Yankees."

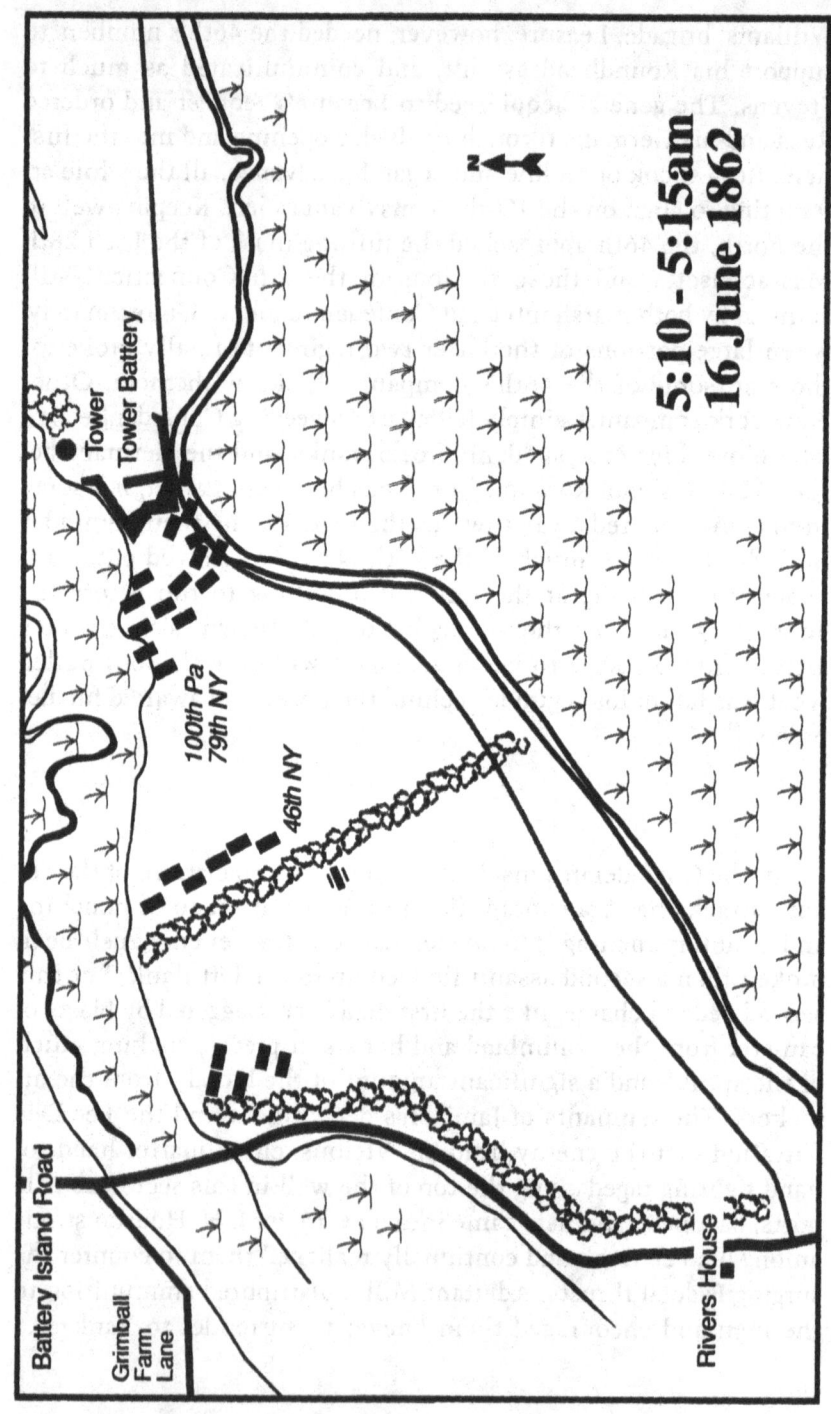

"(I)n the hottest of the battle," Miller kept shouting for the Pee Dee's "to fight until death." Many heeded his orders.[22]

Near the center of the Confederate line, the fighting had been no less intense. Lieutenant Allemong of the Irish Volunteers sprinted between the gun his men were serving and the fort's magazine, transporting ammunition through a pelting fire from the enemy on the wall. Despite completing a number of circuits, he miraculously escaped unhurt. Another Irishman, Pvt. D. Howard, wasn't so fortunate. Howard became engaged near the 24-pounder in what was described as a "desperate hand to hand contest," a deadly encounter from which he did not emerge victorious. Even friendly fire claimed some victims. One of the enormous concussions from the Columbiad's report staggered the gun's commander, Lieutenant Humbert, who found himself too close to the muzzle when a charge went off. Although dazed by the blast, the officer managed to remain at his post.[23]

The battle also had continued unabated on the right flank, where the Charleston Battalion traded musketry with growing numbers of Northerners. Here, Capt. F. T. Miles of the Calhoun Guards had exposed himself while tending to a wounded comrade. Falling under a blast of rifle fire, he paid for his courage with his life. Also lying dead on the field was Sgt. Robert Henery from the Union Light Infantry, one of the many Confederate officers fighting like privates to throw back the Federal assaults. Although the Unionists managed in some cases to reach the wall, none dared to mount the parapet in this sector.[24]

The top two Confederate officers present were no less intent upon fighting at the very point of the Federal attack. Lieutenant Colonel Peter Gaillard was with his fellow Charlestonians on the parapet when Federal metal slammed into his knee. Ignoring the pain and blood, Gaillard remained at his post, unwilling to abandon his men in the midst of battle. The "lionhearted" Thomas Lamar, as he was known by many, was remembered by all as being practically everywhere at once during the battle. He strode along the front as the Federals mounted the left wall. Suddenly, Lamar was jolted as a minie ball severed part of his ear before tumbling along the side and back of his neck. Nonetheless, the colonel righted himself and, despite the dripping blood, continued to urge his men on, animating those around him with his courage. Once the situation had stabilized along the left flank, Lamar coolly directed the artillery at another Federal line then storming across the field. "A third time they came" he later wrote, "but only to meet with a most determined repulse." The Southern artillery, as it had twice before, swept away the center of the assault.[25]

From the firing of Baggott's gun until the collapse of the third Federal charge, no more than 45 minutes had elapsed. But now, the Confederates lining the parapet couldn't help but notice that the Federal pressure, so bitter, so intense, was beginning to subside. Though an enemy battery 500 yards out in the middle of the field was maintaining a pulsing barrage, and individuals and huddled groups kept up a steady rifle fire from the cotton rows and swamp lines out in front of the fort, the Union presence on the left flank—almost continual from the opening moments of the battle—had given way. A slight lull descended upon the Tower Battery.

The parapet was still a dangerous place to be, but the Federal momentum had been blunted and stopped once again.

* * *

The Union battery that continued to pelt the fort was Capt. Alfred P. Rockwell's 1st Connecticut Battery. Lieutenant S. E. Porter had advanced his 12-lb. howitzers from the rear of Col. Fenton's brigade into the first field, aided materially by the engineers of Serrell's Company E, who had enlarged the hedge opening. Despite their efforts, one of the guns spun into the ditch, but quick work righted the piece and the section rattled across the ribbed field towards the front. Arriving at the second ditch, Porter swung his section into battery and opened on the areas of the fort not covered by the Northern infantry. As Porter's men poured what was described as "a galling fire" at the smoking earthwork, "the enemy realized that the Connecticut men knew how to handle their guns."[26]

Captain Rockwell had received Isaac Stevens' orders to advance to protect the division's left flank, so the artillerist sent one gun from the rear of the division north on the Battery Island Road and shifted Lieutenant Seward across the field to Porter's position. After a rough 500 yard ride, Seward drew into action, joining Porter in tossing "a constant fire" at the Rebels. "Shrieking shells" and zinging bullets "tried men's souls," wrote one Federal as the battery went to work. "My God," exclaimed a gunner, "aren't the bullets flying thick?" But with their panoramic view of the scene, perhaps the greatest difficulty that the cannoneers faced was witnessing the bloody results of the Confederate artillery on the infantry ranks. "Great swaths" had been scythed from the blue ranks, and the fields were "strewn with the dead and dying," lamented one, the air filled with "the cries of the wounded, the groans of the dying." "Comrades felt faint" at such sights and sounds, but the Connecticut gunners kept to their duty.[27]

The artillery duel raged ferociously while the three guns did effective work, but slowly, the broken infantry regiments surrounding the fort began retreating steadily back towards the gunners' positions. "It was impossible to contend against such odds" recalled one Connecticut artillerist, probably unaware of the numerical superiority his side held. Confederate rifle fire continued to pick away at the rear ranks, and many Northerners chose to hug the ground near the fort while continually banging away with small arms fire. But the bulk of the Federal attack wave, having braved the close quarters for as long as humanly possible, chose to withdraw and eventually gathered along the hedge in front of the booming Connecticut guns. Porter and Seward continued their barrage.[28]

* * *

Isaac Stevens watched the battle unfold from his position near the hedge entrance to the first field. He had sent a request to Benham for immediate support as he attempted to bring some order to his ruptured columns. Stevens, who possessed a "clear view" of the field, was able to follow the progress of the attacks, but the reports arriving from the front—including those of the wounded Lieutenant Lyons and a number of other stricken officers—closed the case. Seeing the uselessness of continuing the assault with "the attacking force. . .completely scattered and. . .in a manner disappeared," he later reported, Stevens ordered the 28th Massachusetts, 100th Pennsylvania, and the 46th New York to reform at the second hedge, and the brutalized 8th Michigan, 79th New York, and the 7th Connecticut to gather at the first hedge. Hazard Stevens, Isaac's son, bore the orders to the front.[29]

The youthful Stevens raced forward only to come upon a distressing sight. "Not a line, or a semblance of one, could be seen" he later wrote, except Lieutenant Colonel Hawley and perhaps 40 of his men from the 7th Connecticut situated about 100 yards from the Confederate works. Everywhere, dead and wounded Federals covered the cotton rows alongside comrades still attempting to answer the "heavy hail of musketry" blazing from the enemy rifles.

Hazard rode over to Hawley's men and conveyed his father's orders to the officer: "The General wishes you to call the men off." Hawley and two of his officers were grimly trying to keep what remained of their regiment in line, but the searching enemy fire continued to pepper their position. In their desperate search for shelter, some of the Connecticut men lay down between the cotton furrows. Those that remained standing risked the sting of the Confederate rifle fire—two in fact fell within Hazard Stevens' reach. Upon receiving his new orders, Hawley faced his men about by the rear rank and rapidly marched them back to the hedge, with minie balls biting at their backs. Reaching the relative protection of the hedge, the men of the 7th Connecticut were at last relieved from their brutal ordeal before the Tower Battery.[30]

One Connecticut soldier, Pvt. Thomas Elliot, had one more duty to perform before joining the retreat. "(U)nder heavy fire," he returned north to the site of the regiment's first swamp-bound exposure. There he found his gravely wounded comrade, Andrews Hibbard, bleeding from a mangled knee. Elliot managed to lift his stricken friend and muscle him onto his own back. With Confederate shells still bursting about, Elliot carried Andrews Hibbard to safety.[31]

* * *

Word quickly circulated among the Highlanders hugging the earthwork that the attack was over. Some who still clung to their toehold in the fort made for the wall to join the withdrawal. Many were incredulous and still scanned the fields for Horatio Wright's missing brigades, but "not a sound was heard from the direction whence we expected the column to appear," noted one disappointed Scotsman. All felt the retreat was "made necessary by the shameful fact that. . .no support came." Nevertheless, the

Highlanders began to drop off the parapet into the outer ditch and rally upon their colors. As they remembered it, the New Yorkers "succeeded in carrying off about forty of the wounded and six of our killed. As many more—killed or badly wounded—we left behind." One of the last Highlanders in the fort, Pvt. Daniel Lawrence of Co. F, took a minie in his right arm as he crossed the wall. Further along the line, a Confederate, sensing an opportunity for glory, tried to capture Company E's Pvt. Van Horsen. The Scotsman, however, got the better of the scuffle and tugged the unfortunate Confederate by his scalp down from the wall and over to the color guard.

While Van Horsen turned to take another shot at the Southerners, color bearer Alexander Campbell approached the prisoner. No doubt deeply concerned over the fate of his Confederate-clad brother, Campbell asked the Southerner if he knew of the Charleston Battalion's Lt. James Campbell. Wrote one witness to this extraordinary event, "The prisoner replied that he did, and that the Lieut was in the fort. (Alexander's) feelings can be better imagined than described," wrote the Highlander. As one Scotsman stood alone with this thoughts, the rest of the Highlanders, stung by their defeat and angered at their isolation, began a slow and sullen retreat from the flank of the fort.[32]

* * *

Colonel Daniel Leasure stood before the Battery surveying the scene of his brigade's destruction. "(P)anic and disaster were imminent," he later wrote, and he feared a disorderly retreat could lead to even greater peril. He called one of his mounted orderlies to his side and was dictating a message to Isaac Stevens when a cannon ball slammed into the horse's head, spraying blood and gore all over the orderly's face. Leasure calmed the shaken aide and sent him on his way, then turned to rally the few Unionists still remaining in the sector. Another artillery blast dropped the first few men he managed to gather, including one private who was eviscerated by a piece of canister that had first grazed the colonel. The stricken soldier uttered "Goodby Colonel, God bless you, go in," before breathing his last. This was enough for Leasure. Calling out to those men that could hear his voice, the officer directed his charges "to follow me slowly." Pacing the retreat to avoid even the appearance of panic, Leasure began a slow, dogged withdrawal, walking backwards bareheaded with his face to the enemy. His men, singly and in squads, rose up from their cotton rows and marsh lines to join their courageous leader in a methodical retreat under fire.[33]

* * *

As the dawn streaked the cloudy sky and revealed the stark contrasts of the scene, four Union regiments rallied on their colors in full view of their enemy and executed a slow, sure retreat across this field of fire. Men rose from their embattled positions and "hastened to form on either flank of the line." Flags fluttered in the slight breeze as the regiments seemed to materialize out of the blasted ground. "But alas how reduced and scanty were they," recalled Hazard Stevens, these four regiments now challenging the Confederates to fire away. Some intrepid souls, including nearly 100 Michiganders who seemed unwilling to give up the ground they held, remained at the front to continue the fight. Most, however, joined the withdrawal. For 400 yards they strode across the blood-soaked scene of their attacks until they reached the relative safety of the hedge and ditch. Finally, the weary Unionists found an oasis from the violence of the previous hour.[34]

Lieutenant Colonel Joseph Hawley placed what was left of his 7th Connecticut on the right flank. Next in line to the north lay the 79th New York, flattened down behind a slight rise to avoid Confederate missiles, which now included a potpourri of scrap metal and junk. One lucky Scotsman, who had just missed having his legs removed by a cannon blast, sardonically remarked, "A close shave, but a miss is as good as a mile." Many more unamused Scotsmen continued to wonder aloud about the conspicuous absence of Horatio Wright's men. Frank Graves could only rally "a Portion" of the 8th Michigan, for their attack and the subsequent repulse left the 8th badly scattered. On the field fronting the Tower Battery, only one Michigan captain remained unscathed.[35]

Colonel Leasure was fighting to wring some order from the confusion. His two orderlies—quite possibly the only Northerners on the field still mounted—flew across the furrows massaging the shattered units into line. Movement north of the swamp drew

Fields of Fire 217

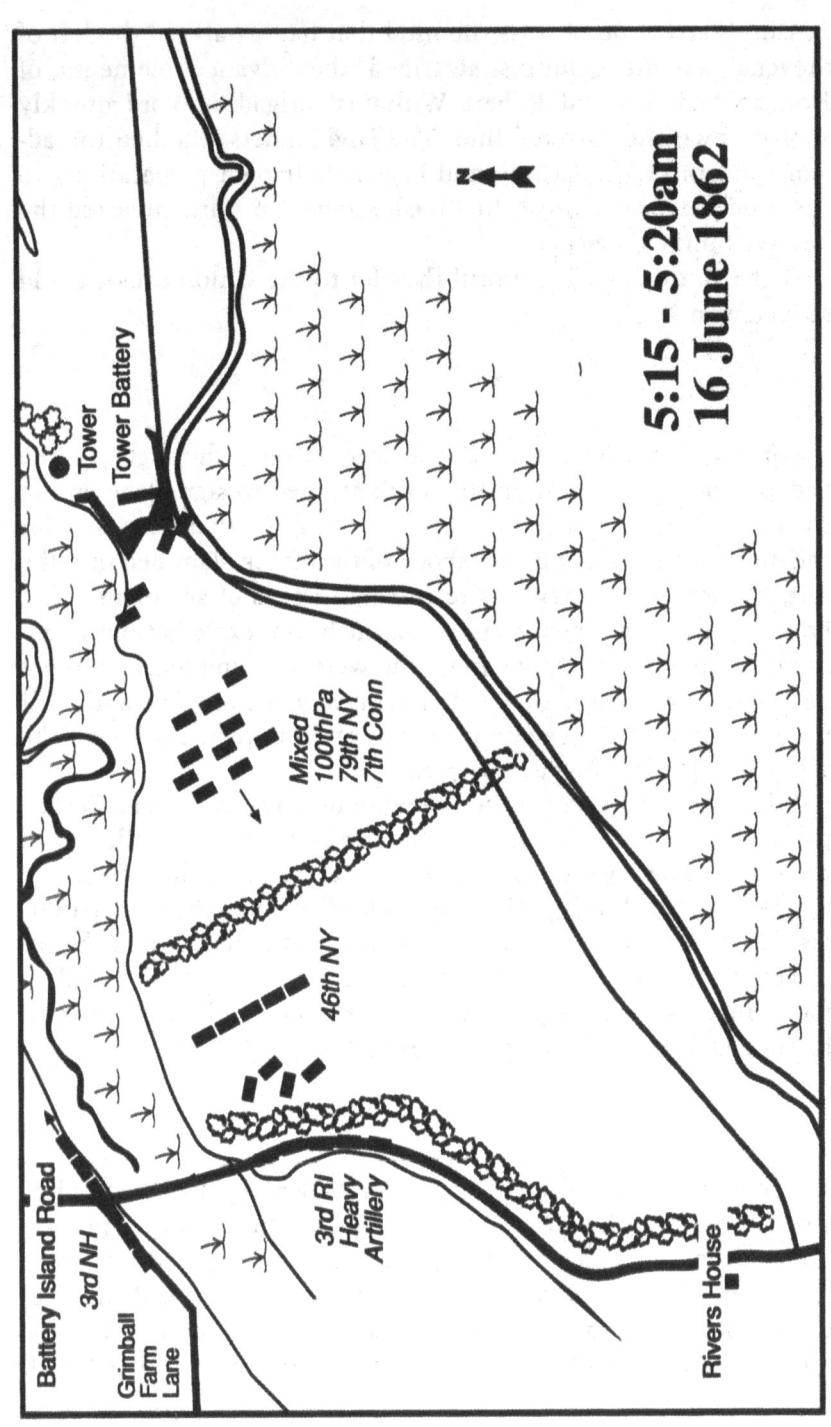

Leasure's attention. Across the mud that had paralyzed the left of Stevens' assault columns swarmed the advance elements of Horatio Wright's and Robert Williams' brigades. Word quickly spread down the battered line. The Highlanders watched the advance north of the swamp and began their own preparations to again take up the contest. In a flash a renewed spirit invested the Federals lining the hedge.

Perhaps, this day, so painful thus far to the Union cause, could still be won.[36]

* * *

For the Confederates in the Tower Battery, the sight of the Federals picking up and pulling back seemed to signal the end of the fight. Despite a handful of still-barking Northern cannon, for the first time since the initial shock of the attack slammed into the fort, the Union infantry was retreating instead of advancing. The brave nature of the enemy's retreat brought out exclamations of admiration from the Confederates, who were savoring their triumph. One Southerner marvelled, "Under a heavy fire of grape and shell from our battery, the enemy retired in perfect order, closing up the gaps caused by our fire as if on parade."

While the artillery kept up the pounding, the grayclad riflemen paused, if only for a moment, perhaps in tribute to the gallantry of their foe. Suddenly one shot, then another, then a volley raked the Charleston Battalion and the gunners serving the right flank batteries. Heads jerked to view, not 125 yards to the right across the intervening marsh, a line of Federal infantry, perfectly formed to flank the Confederate defenses. The battle the Southerners thought had ended in victory had ignited anew.[37]

* * *

According to his original plan, Henry Benham had two objectives in mind for Horatio Wright's columns. In the initial phases, their advance would serve to protect Stevens' exposed left flank from Confederate incursions from the north. Soon after Wright began his advance, however, Benham received Isaac Stevens' request for immediate support, and Benham in turn had ordered Col.

Robert Williams to report to Stevens with his brigade. As Williams' regiments jumped off, the colonel dispatched his aide-de-camp to report to Stevens for orders. With Williams' brigade now added to the assault, the Union reserve committed itself to the battle.[38]

Major Edwin Metcalf started his five companies of the 3rd Rhode Island Heavy Artillery to the east through a piece of woods towards the sound of battle. Leading Williams' brigade into action, Metcalf detached three companies under Major H. T. Sisson to serve as skirmishers. When this detachment burst from the woods at the quickstep, the "full blast," of battle, as one of the Federals explained it, spread out before them. Already, Stevens' first brigade had dashed itself to pieces against the Confederate fort, and the skirmishers pushed forward, knowing "no better than to march toward the enemy." In their advance towards the front, the Rhode Islanders encountered part of a disheveled Union regiment—the 28th Massachusetts—which one witness charitably described as being "in a broken condition." As the Irish Bay Staters passed through the 3rd's line, the skirmishers slowed to allow the last two companies of the regiment to exit the woods and unite with their statesmen near the head of the marsh north of the Secessionville peninsula. Here they prepared for action.[39]

Ahead and to their left, the Rhode Islanders could make out the 3rd New Hampshire's advance, already rolling down the next finger of land to the north. Behind them, Thomas Welsh's and John Chatfield's two undersized brigades formed in support of William's column. A courier rode up to the 3rd Rhode Islander's Major Metcalf and relayed his orders. General Stevens now commanded Williams' brigade and ordered the officer to advance his troops in concert with the Unionists fronting the [Tower] battery. Williams was making haste to comply by ordering Metcalf to support the movement of the 3rd New Hampshire. As the courier departed, the major turned to his men and coolly announced, "Now, we have a job to do." Part of the Battery Island Road ran north along a crude causeway, but Metcalf led the regiment into a vein of the marsh in an attempt to angle off some distance from their route. Unfortunately, the knee-deep mire instead slowed the advance and froze Major Sisson's mount in the mud. "Let the horse go to the dogs," said the major as he dismounted to press his troops through the swamp. When they finally emerged from the clinging pluff mud, Confederate shot and shell seemed to be coming "from all quarters," ringing up the 3rd's first casualties. The men steadied themselves, then advanced in the 3rd New Hampshire's wake.

Ahead and to the right, the Tower Battery seemed alive with busting shell and crashing volleys. More disturbing was the growing rifle fire from a lengthy thicket of felled trees just to the north, a pattering of fire that was already stinging the leftmost companies. The Rhode Islanders knew that the Tower battery was their goal, and, perhaps with just one good push, it would be theirs. And, ahead they pushed.[40]

* * *

As the men of the 3rd New Hampshire waited for orders in the field east of their camps, they heard the sound of musketry drumming out the rhythm of the battle and knew their turn would come soon. Colonel Serrell of the engineers rode by and dryly remarked, "Well boys, there is a hot breakfast waiting for you." The men needed no reminders. First, the 3rd Rhode Island Heavy Artillery had disappeared into the woods, then Confederate artillery began crashing overhead. Wounded men from the front were being shepherded past the waiting Hampshiremen, a sight that did nothing but increase the tension suffered by all. Sergeant Elbridge J. Copp looked down the line and saw he was not alone in his pale terror; many of his comrades shared the same pasty, thin-lipped mien. Just as orders rang out to fall in, a bounding solid shot struck an unfortunate soldier and killed him instantly. Then a succession of orders, issuing from Lt. Col. John Jackson and echoing left and right, drew the men to attention: "Take arms."[41]

By the left flank, left to the front, the 3rd New Hampshire moved rapidly forward, first east on a road through the Federal outworks, then south past a Virginia rail fence into a field, where they were brought to a halt. Off to the right front, the heavy musketry of Stevens' attack could be clearly heard. A drum major came charging up with dispatches but was forced to duck under his horse when a shell burst nearby, much to the braying and teasing of his comrades. This "guying," as it was called, seemed to steady the nerves of many of the Hampshiremen. The order all knew would arrive eventually came, as the 3rd New Hampshire was directed to lend its weight to the advance. It pushed forward in line of battle until the scene of the morning's struggle revealed itself. Federal naval shells, without the ability to distinguish between friend or foe, arched through the clearing sky and landed as often as not among Union troops. To the southeast, the advance of Stevens' second brigade could be seen by the Hampshiremen, one of whom left a vivid description of what he witnessed:

> a wall of steel flashing in the rays of the morning sun, the enemy sending a terrible fire of shell and grape and canister into their ranks; the line is broken and ragged as the men are mowed down with a hail of lead and iron, but closing up and moving on into the very ditch of the fort, some of them onto the works in a hand to hand fight.

The Hampshire men came to a halt near the Battery Island Road, awaiting their turn.[42]

It did not take long. Colonel Jackson rapidly marched his men north up the Battery Island Road, then eastward on a line parallel to Stevens' route of attack. As the men from New England advanced, the marsh separating them from Stevens' brigades gradually widened, but they pressed on with little regard for what lay ahead. Further on, a cluster of wooden slave quarters bordered the swamp line. Two companies broke off and headed for the shanties while the rest of the regiment was brought to a halt. A concerned Jackson assumed that he was supporting an advance, but he could see no Federals to his front. To the north, a Confederate battery boomed, bringing color bearer James Cassidy down with a scalp wound. Some of the Hampshiremen supposed the artillery to be friendly fire, but the continuance of its reports proved otherwise.

Orders now came to resume the advance, so on they trotted until the Tower Battery appeared almost directly south of their line. Another command sounded, "By the right flank, charge bayonets, forward double-quick." The 3rd New Hampshire realigned itself towards the open flank of the Tower Battery and rushed "forward with a cheer and a shout," recalled one of the attackers. Just 150 yards more and the New Hampshire soldiers knew they would be up and over the low walls of the Confederate earthwork. Most

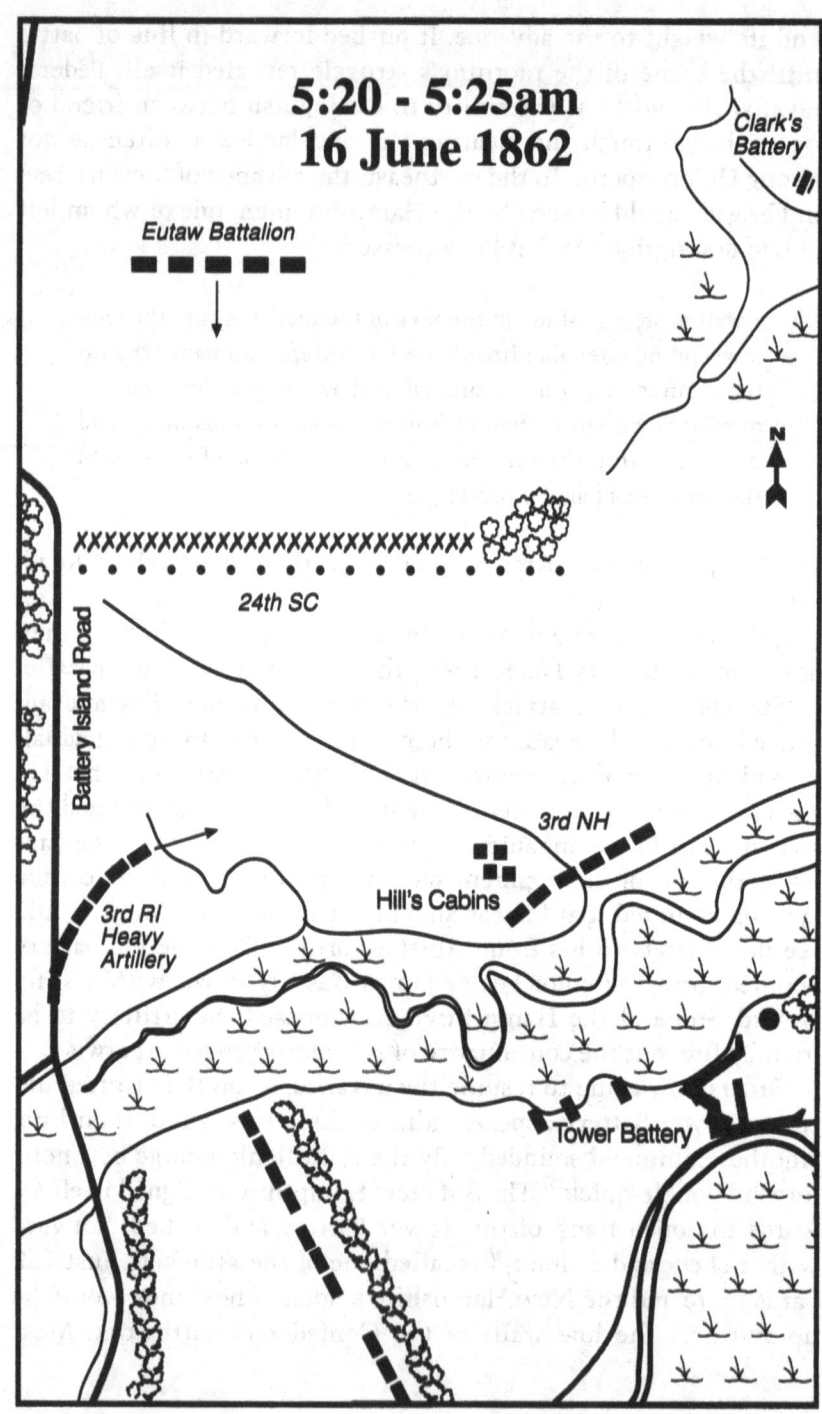

shared one soldier's memory of the moment: "(W)e were determined to come right in and take possession."[43]

The Federals enjoyed their advantageous position for but a few moments. The two companies by the slave shanties made the startling discovery first: the Tower battery—not 150 yards away—was beyond reach. Between the Unionists and their target lay a morass of water and mud, an impassable stretch of marshland that halted the detachment in its tracks. Finding themselves north and west of the fort's flank, the two companies levelled their rifles and blasted a volley into the startled Confederates. Frustrated by the same marshy blockage, Colonel Jackson and the rest of the regiment pulled up further east of the shanties but somewhat closer to and in line with the enemy's flank. "We opened a hot fire on the garrison of the fort, with telling effect," recalled a member of Company K. "The gunners were driven from their guns, and the men could be seen running helter skelter for protection from the leaden hail." Although the Federals in front of the fort had, for the most part, retreated, a Federal battery 500 yards west continued to lay down a battering cover fire. "Our batteries poured in their solid shot and shell, cutting down trees, demolishing barracks, and dismounting guns," remembered one participant, as the 3rd New Hampshire and Stevens' division caught the fort in a pincer movement that was incapable of closing in for the kill.[44]

The officers struggled to form the regiment across the irregular ground, while the jockeying Unionists blasted away at the frustratingly close Confederates. They swept the works with "a deadly fire" that one Federal claimed all but stunned the defenders into silence. Some Southerners rallied by retaking their positions and returning the fire. Concurrently, a masked Confederate battery, 200 yards north and west, began spraying metal into the backs of the Hampshiremen. Sergeant Copp recalled men falling everywhere "sometimes throwing up their arms, with a fearful shriek, pitching forward to the earth, and sometimes dropping to the ground without a groan." Suddenly another Confederate battery, perhaps a mile directly north of the sweating and bleeding Northerners, launched roundshot and shell into the formation, shattering Capt. Ralph Carlton's thigh and hip bones and killing a nearby non-comissioned officer.

Where glory had called not minutes before, a ring of fire began to pressure the fighters of the 3rd New Hampshire. The frustrating pluff mud was claiming another Federal regiment.[45]

* * *

"They then made a flank movement on my right," was Confederate Col. Thomas Lamar's grim recollection of the crisis on his flank. He had held his small force together behind the battered walls of the Tower Battery, but the strain on the defenders was proving to be almost overwhelming. He still had the Charleston Battalion holding the right flank, but the unit was now much reduced by its continuous hour of battle, and the Federal volleys now sweeping over the sector were fierce. One Southerner guessed that at least three enemy regiments had deployed along "a small growth of underbrush" on the marsh line, so heavy was the fire of the enemy. "The gun carriages were perforated and torn by many balls. Many of our men fell at the guns and along the line formed to the rearward of the battery on its right flank," wrote another eyewitness. The Charleston Battalion rallied, but "(t)he contest was very unequal and trying. It raged for some time."[46]

About this time, Thomas Lamar realized that he himself could no longer stand the action. His weakened state impaired his ability to command, and he knew it. Lamar turned the fort over to Lt. Col. Peter Gaillard, and command of the batteries to Lt. Col. Wagner. Lamar claimed, however, that he continued to give orders, while others recalled his being carried away. Whatever version was true, he had already earned the sobriquet "The Hero of Secessionville," for his masterful—and nearly miraculous—defense of the Tower Battery against a full division of determined Federals.[47]

The crisis of the battle had now come to the fort's right flank. The last Confederate reserves had been committed nearly an hour earlier, and now the muscle of the Southern defense lay bleeding at their posts. Those cannoneers still standing faced exhaustion but fought on, using scrap metal and lengths of chain in place of ammunition. Gaillard assumed command but was soon out of action due to his own wounds; Lieutenant Colonel Wagner took over sole command of the Confederate forces.[48]

The Federals north of the marsh sent sheets of rifle fire down the sagging gray lines. By now, little rifle fire answered the riflemen, and the 300 Confederates still standing within the forts battered walls were numb from exhaustion. Although their cannon well to the north still sought out the enemy beyond the marsh, return fire from the battery had slackened as the Confederates expended the last of their ammunition. The Columbiad's crew tried to bring their piece to bear across the marsh against the 3rd New Hampshire, but the carriage wouldn't allow the gun to rotate enough to be effective. Worse, the recently-repulsed enemy throng massed just 500 yards to the west was now showing renewed signs of aggressiveness.

Once again it was the Confederates' turn to look rearward and wonder: where were the supports?[49]

* * *

The 260 men of the 4th Louisiana Battalion had raced at the "double-quick" the half-mile from King's Highway to the Secessionville Causeway, with the roar of battle roiling across the fields and marshes. As the Louisianans lined up single-file to cross the narrow bridge, Lieutenant Colonel McEnery charged ahead to the village, where he learned that the enemy were now advancing "on the right of the battery." It was there his men were needed. McEnery rode back to his command, the head of which was just reaching the Secessionville peninsula, and led them west towards the fight. Crossing the open areas between the village and the fort, past the now deserted camps of the Confederate defenders, McEnery and the Louisianans angled towards the right flank of the Tower Battery, unaware just how desperately they were required.

As they closed with the fort, overshot Federal artillery fire combined with enemy rifle fire to make the final yards a treacherous area to traverse. Guided by Major Hudson of the Pee Dee Battalion, McEnery charged his troops forward to the cries of "Remember Butler!" At the right rear of the fort, the Louisianan halted the breathless soldiers and ordered them to face right before advancing them to the outer edge of the woods along the marsh line. To the north, "about one hundred yards distant," a Federal regiment was still firing across the intervening swamp, but the arrival of the Louisianans was electrifying. "Col. McHenry's [sic] Louisiana Battalion came rushing forward with loud cheers" recounted one defender of the embattled bastion, as the officer paused his line momentarily, a calm before the storm.[50]

The 4th Louisiana Battalion leveled their rifles and loosed a volley that shivered the enemy ranks. One Louisianan recalled the moment: "Our batt[alion] came on the field at a double-quick (and) threw themselves in front of the enemys sharp shooters." Federal fire erupted in return from across the marsh. McEnery later recalled that "(a)t this point...the fire on both sides was indeed terrific." Captain J. H. Walker of the 4th Louisiana's Company F—the Ouchita Rebels—"was shot through the body and dangerously wounded." Private John Reagan of the Franklin Life Guard also went down before Federal fire. The Louisianan's fighting blood was up, however, and they tore at the Federal line with a fierce determination. "It seemed that every man there in defense of the fort felt as though the whole responsibility of holding the fort rested on him," wrote Lea Winnsboro, one of Walker's men, "for it would have been impossible for any force of the same size to have done that."

For a full fifteen minutes the Louisianans and the Northerners waged a stand-up slug fest across a mere one hundred yards of muddy marshland. "(We) poured into the ranks of the vandals volley after volley," colorfully wrote the 4th Louisiana Battalion's adjutant. To the north, a cannon boomed. Further west, another joined in. Shells crashed into the rear of the blue formations as Confederate minie balls slammed into their faces. Catching it from every angle, the Federals began to recoil. The Southern battle arms tightened around them and more Federals fell to the ground. McEnery, whose troops had been exposed to "a terrific fire from the enemy's gunboats, siege batteries, and small arms," described the closing scene: "Finally the enemy wavered, fell back, and then began his precipitate retreat on the right..." Another participant proudly and simply recounted, "(we) drove them from the field." A circle of fire ended the crisis on the right flank of the Tower Battery.[51]

As the threat receded, McEnery moved into the fort and assigned some of his men to the decimated gun crews. Lieutenant Colonel Wagner stepped forward to turn over command of the fort to the Louisianan, who did not hesitate in finishing the action."The gallant Lamar being struck down and being the senior officer present," McEnery later reported, "I caused an incessant volley of grape and canister to be poured into the broken and retreating columns of the enemy until they passed beyond view."

With the pressure on the right flank gone and reinforcements moving to bolster the front line, the revived gunners answered anew, blasting away at the huddling blue mass out in the field.[52]

*   *   *

The stunning artillery barrage that had carpeted the 3rd New Hampshire's formation was but a prelude to even greater difficulties for the Unionists. Colonel Jackson could see a Confederate force moving from the east towards the Tower Battery. He sent word of this development to his brigadier, Colonel Williams, then prepared his men to take on the new arrivals. As the Southerners advanced from left to right across their front, the Hampshiremen opened "with good effect," but the cover provided by the buildings and trees along the Secessionville marsh line allowed the majority of the Confederate force to enter the earthwork and form on the right wing facing north. Jackson admitted, "Their being well covered, their fire on us was very severe."

Men who had been joking about shooting their guns like mortars and wasting ammunition by "firing at the barracks to keep busy" suddenly found themselves fronted by a reinforced, determined and sheltered foe. The Federals ducked as, from the north, Confederate artillery "opened a fresh fire," reported one Federal, and Jackson turned to locate his expected supports. But the 3rd Rhode Island Heavy Artillery had swung north to take on a new Confederate firing line, and the 3rd New Hampshire suddenly stood very much alone against the reinforced Confederate stronghold.[53]

The Southerners that now rimmed the fort's right wing delivered blistering volleys into the struggling Federal ranks. "(W)e could not cope with them to any advantage," wrote Jackson of this new Southern force. Daniel Eldridge of Company K remembered "so hot a fire that there seemed to be no alternative for us except to retire." Some of the Hampshiremen slipped to the water's edge and blasted at the fort while others rammed charge after charge into their rifles, oblivious in the noise and confusion to their muskets' fouling. Ramrods inadvertently left in the pieces flew across the marsh like arrows. A Federal on the north side of the marsh described the re-

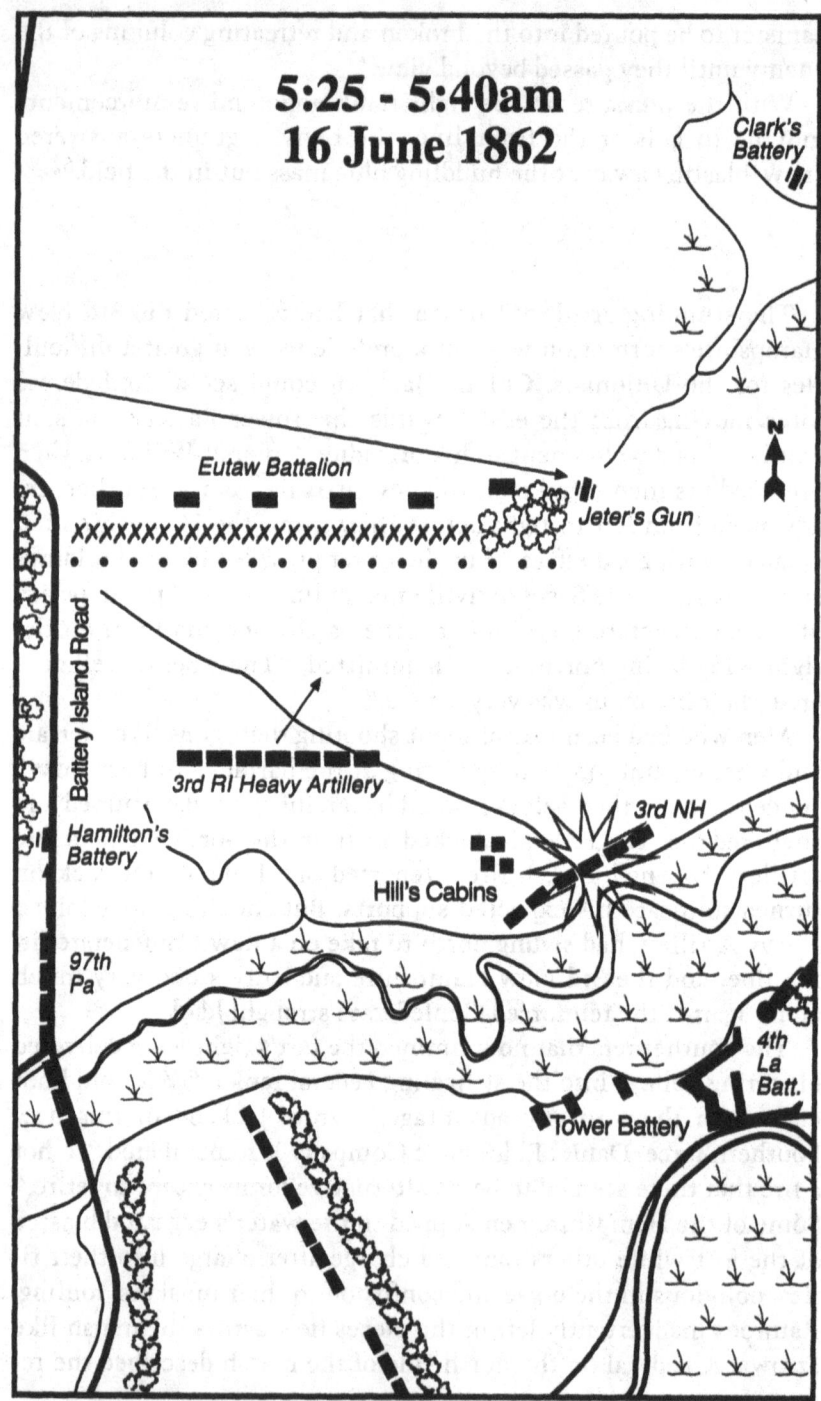

turn fire from the fort, which exacted a terrible price, as "striking the dirt all around us—striking the water in front of us—striking human flesh—boring holes through the trees and men." According to another, "The shrieks of the wounded, the groans of the dying and the mangled dead," combined to form memories too horrible for some survivors to later describe. Efforts to move Captain Carleton proved equally heart-rending. Finally, an old door from one of the slave shanties was pressed into service to cart the gravely-wounded officer away.[54]

New Hampshiremen continued to fall within this ring of Confederate fire. Sergeant Moore of Company F took a minie ball through the cheek that eventually lodged in his throat, nearly drowning him in his own blood. His tent-mate, Sgt. David Wadworth, helped transport his stricken friend off the field. One officer, Captain Robert C. Dow of Company H, was heard to exclaim loudly—and within earshot of his troops—the impossibility of holding such a hot place. As one could imagine, such behavior is not looked for in an officer, and a furious Colonel Jackson mentally noted Dow's unseemly behavior. But for now, Jackson was swamped just keeping his regiment together.[55]

In the midst of this havoc, a lone rider on a dead run pulled up his sweating beast next to Jackson. A few words passed and the colonel turned to his aides and issued orders "to retire (the) regiment and to do it rapidly." The unscathed began to collect the wounded, but there was little time to waste. Quickly, the regiment formed into a ragged procession and retraced its steps west past the slave quarters towards their supports and safety. As the men reached the Battery Island Road and their original jump-off point, Capt. John Hamilton's battery of artillery had drawn up in support of the 3rd Rhode Island Heavy Artillery's attack on the woodland to the north. Shell and grapeshot seemed to deflate any Confederate thoughts of advancing in the wake of the Northern retreat.

Back on the two acres where the 3rd New Hampshire had done its fighting, over 100 of their comrades lay dead or wounded.[56]

* * *

The men of Isaac Stevens' division viewed the contest across the marsh against the Tower Battery's right flank with intense interest.

Wrote one witness, "the roar of musketry was terrific. This was kept up for half an hour." From his position in front of the right flank of the fort, Pvt. Benjamin Pease, the much-beleaguered Michigander, watched Williams' brigade fight north of the swamp. "From where I lay I had a full view of all their maneuvers," he later wrote, and "in fact a much better view than of the movements of our own brigade"—which perhaps explains why Pease hadn't joined his comrades in their retreat to the hedge. "They were also repulsed with great slaughter...you can imagine I felt pretty blue."[57]

* * *

Lieutenant Colonel Ellison Capers had caught up to Col. Clement Stevens and the four picket companies of the 24th South Carolina during their trek toward the fighting. As he helped Stevens locate his troops along the downed trees near the Hill's House, Capers saw Johnson Hagood ride up with elements of Hagood's 1st South Carolina and the Simonton's Eutaw Battalion. As these three units deployed, Capers moved forward through the abatis to get a better view of the fighting then raging to the south. Before him, a Federal regiment that had advanced on his side of the marsh had moved past the Hill's slave quarters and had taken up a post "opposite the Secessionville work, and a little to the rear of its right flank."

With an appreciation of the unfolding tactical situation, Capers returned to the forming Confederate line, where he found Hagood. Both officers seemed to have the same thought at the same time: why wasn't the battery at Clark's House firing? It was perfectly positioned to take just such an enemy movement apart, but for some reason it remained mute. Hagood directed Capers to gallop to the battery and order it to open.[58]

The young officer re-traced his route back to the Artillery Crossroads and headed east, moving as he later described it "with all possible speed." When he reined up to the position, a small work located on a rise just north of the marsh line and west of the Clark House, Capers found some 15 members of Colonel Lamar's regiment, with Lt. J. B. Kitching commanding, doing little more than gaping at the battle raging to the south. Capers demanded an explanation, and Kitching gave the only response that could have possibly mollified Capers: these men had just "come from the country," and knew nothing of loading and firing artillery. Furthermore, they had received no orders but would gladly defer to Capers if he would just show them how the cannon worked.

Capers moved to the right piece with the novices in tow, loaded and sighted it, then fired off the battery's first shot of the battle. The shell roared across the marsh, arched above the Hill plantation, then fell "just in rear of the fence beyond the Hill negro houses with fine effect on the enemy, delighting us all," Capers later reported. Unfortunately, in recoil the piece kicked "off the narrow platform & upset," and was thus disabled. Capers aimed the second piece, "double-shelled," and placed two men with spikes to control the recoil before "let[ting] the rascals have it." Kitching's group took their lessons well. "Kitching and his men worked gallantly," wrote Capers, "and with remarkable aptitude, so much so that I thought it my duty to return to my command." Capers mounted his horse and bade farewell to his students.[59]

He didn't get far. At the Clark House, some 100 yards east of the now roaring battery, Capers ran into two generals, Nathan "Shanks" Evans and William Duncan Smith. "Shanks" had just arrived from the Lawton House, where reports of the battle stirred him to the front. The battle was well developed by the time Evans appeared, but to Capers' disgust, Evans ensconced himself in a second floor window to view the fight from a distance. "Shanks" listened to Capers' report then peremptorily ordered him to return to the battery to oversee the effort there. Capers had little choice but to salute and retrace his route.

Arriving back at the post, Capers dismounted and waded back into the action. "We fired as rapidly as we could load, right into the troops at the Negro houses and the bushes to the east," he would later write. The observers collected at the Clark House watched the battery's fire "piercing" the Federal column eleven times before the enemy began to withdraw. When the Federals disappeared to the west, Capers and his men simply raised their sights and sent more shells screaming into the flank of the Federals massed in front of the Tower Battery. Although the thrust of the Federals onto Hill's plantation had been halted, the enemy remained dangerously posted before the battered earthwork. The 24-pounder continued to bark as Ellison Capers, J. B. Kitching, and their cannoneers from the country tore at the Federal flank.[60]

While Capers was giving artillery lessons, Johnson Hagood continued to prepare his lines for operations. Colonel Stevens had led the van down the Battery Island Road, collecting the 100 men from his own 24th South Carolina which had been on picket duty. By the time he had reached the felled trees north of the Hill plantation, the Federals had already penetrated to the slave quarters in their advance east along the marsh. Stevens posted part of the first company in line, Captain Weaver's Company I, to occupy the abatis east of the Battery Island Road. Stevens rushed portions of three more small companies—something less than 100 men—into "a heavy thicket extending from the abatis to the marsh on the left." Commenting later, Stevens surmised,"(T)his position could only be defensive," but this position would have to do for now. Here the men of the 24th South Carolina nervously watched the Unionists continue their advance on the Tower Battery.[61]

Lieutenant Colonel Charles Simonton and his 220 rifles from the Eutaw Battalion came up as Stevens completed his dispositions. Hagood ordered Simonton into line parallel to and north of the 24th South Carolina's position, with the abatis of felled trees and the heavy thicket dividing the two forces. The Eutaw Battalion was led by Companies A and B, the famed Washington Light Infantry, which trotted eastward and formed "immediately on the edge of the woods." Lieutenant Jeter's 6-pounder was pulled along the length of Simonton's line and deployed on the left flank near the marsh, with Company B of the 47th Georgia Infantry deployed in support. Their orders were simple: open on the Federal advance.

Back on the road, Hagood kept a detachment from the 1st South Carolina as a mobile reserve and extended the rest of it westerly through the woods towards the Stono River. The colonel then alerted Nathan Evans that he would like to silence an enemy field piece that had deployed some distance south on the Battery Island Road, but that he would need supports before launching such an attack. Unfortunately for Johnson Hagood, additional forces were not available to him on this front. Other regiments were moving to the scene, but Hagood had all that he could expect for the moment.[62]

The enemy advance near the slave quarters had opened on the Secessionville earthwork when Jeter's piece and Clark's battery fired off their first blasts, sending their shells crashing into the Federal line. Stevens' skirmishers began to bang away at the

Federals, adding the weight of their musketry. The combination of cannon and rifle fire told immediately on the enemy, but also revealed the Confederate position to the deploying Federal forces. The enemy artillery unit located on the Battery Island Road, not 500 yards south of the gray line, opened on Jeter's position with "a heavy fire...which, from the sheltered position of our troops did little damage," noted one Confederate officer. A Federal projectile did manage to slam into Lt. Benjamin Graham of the 47th Georgia. One comrade grimly noted the damage caused by the shell: "terribly crushing his head, carrying away one-half of it."

Despite their relative safety, Simonton's men had trouble observing the enemy through the abatis and the remaining stand of woods. Colonel Stevens picked his way through the obstructions to warn the Eutaw Battalion that its comrades from the 24th South Carolina stood just to the south of the abatis. The men were warned that care should be given to any shots fired in that direction. Slowly the sounds of battle swelled as a second enemy unit changed direction and began moving toward the 24th's skirmish line. Stevens' men fired furiously as the enemy attack picked up momentum and angled towards Jeter's gun and the left of the Southern line. The 24th South Carolina's position was weak enough without a battalion-sized assault group bearing down on it. As the cheering Federals approached the skirmishers, the left flank of the 24th dissolved into the timber. Elsewhere, Stevens' men struggled to hold firm.[63]

North of the abatis, "The Eutaws were eager for the fight," wrote one, but their officers strove to hold the men's fire in check for fear of hitting Stevens' skirmishers. Lieutenant R. A. Blum of the Washington Light Infantry ordered his Company B "not to shoot," although one member of the unit remembered that "Minie balls were flying all around us." John Sheppard later wrote, "Scarcely had we taken our position and lain down when a shower of Bullets are poured into us." Another member of the same unit, Augustine Smyth, seconded Sheppard's sentiments: "Volley after volley of bullets flew around us cutting off the branches in front of us, & falling behind us & in front of us. It was a trying moment, for we none knew but that the next bullet would finish us, yet the men behaved with the greatest coolness, fixing their bayonets & getting ready for the charge."

Suddenly, three Confederates claiming to be members of Hagood's regiment stumbled out of the thicket to the Eutaw Battalion's front. In Sheppard's words: "(T)hey told us they had been driven in from which we understood that their regiment had been driven in...& the Yankees were close behind." The obstructions were "too thick for us to see clearly into them," but some of the men managed to peer through what openings they could find. The field south of the abatis was crowded with Federals, and the men begged Blum to rescind the order to hold their fire. Blum finally relented, and the two companies of the Washington Light Infantry prepared to volley through the abatis at the enemy. Then, "just as we were about to fire, an order came from Col. Hagood that it was his men, not to fire. This was repeated by our officers, & believing them to be friends, we held back." The delay in opening up would prove costly.[64]

The Washington Light Infantry bore the brunt of the renewed enemy musketry. Lieutenant Richard Greer was instantly killed when a minie ball slammed into his head, while Sgt. Fleetwood Lanneau died with a Federal bullet lodged in his heart. A youngster in the ranks, 17 year-old Thomas Gadsen Jr., dropped to the ground "cut down by the invaders of our soil," recalled a saddened comrade. Other Confederates fell before the flying minies amid shouts of "Don't fire, we are friends, you will kill your own men, etc." Colonel Stevens' warning had come back to haunt the Southern infantrymen, as four or five Northerners pushed through the thickets into full view of the Confederate line. Someone called out if they were friends and one replied that they were. Another asked if they were Confederates, which elicited a quizzical look from the newcomers. Finally asked where they were from, the intruders called out "Rhode Island," at which the Eutaw's line erupted in flame and the Rhode Islanders recoiled. Private Bill Jervey of Company A claimed one kill, and Private S. Van Vector Breese another, "an Irishman," he managed to note.[65]

A Southern officer ran up to Company A and again attempted to restrain the men from firing into their supposed friends. In response, a quick-witted Confederate moved to one of the fresh corpses and held up one of the breast plates, asking whether or not the officer could read the "US" imprint. It was difficult for the officer to argue against such telling evidence, and the line re-opened

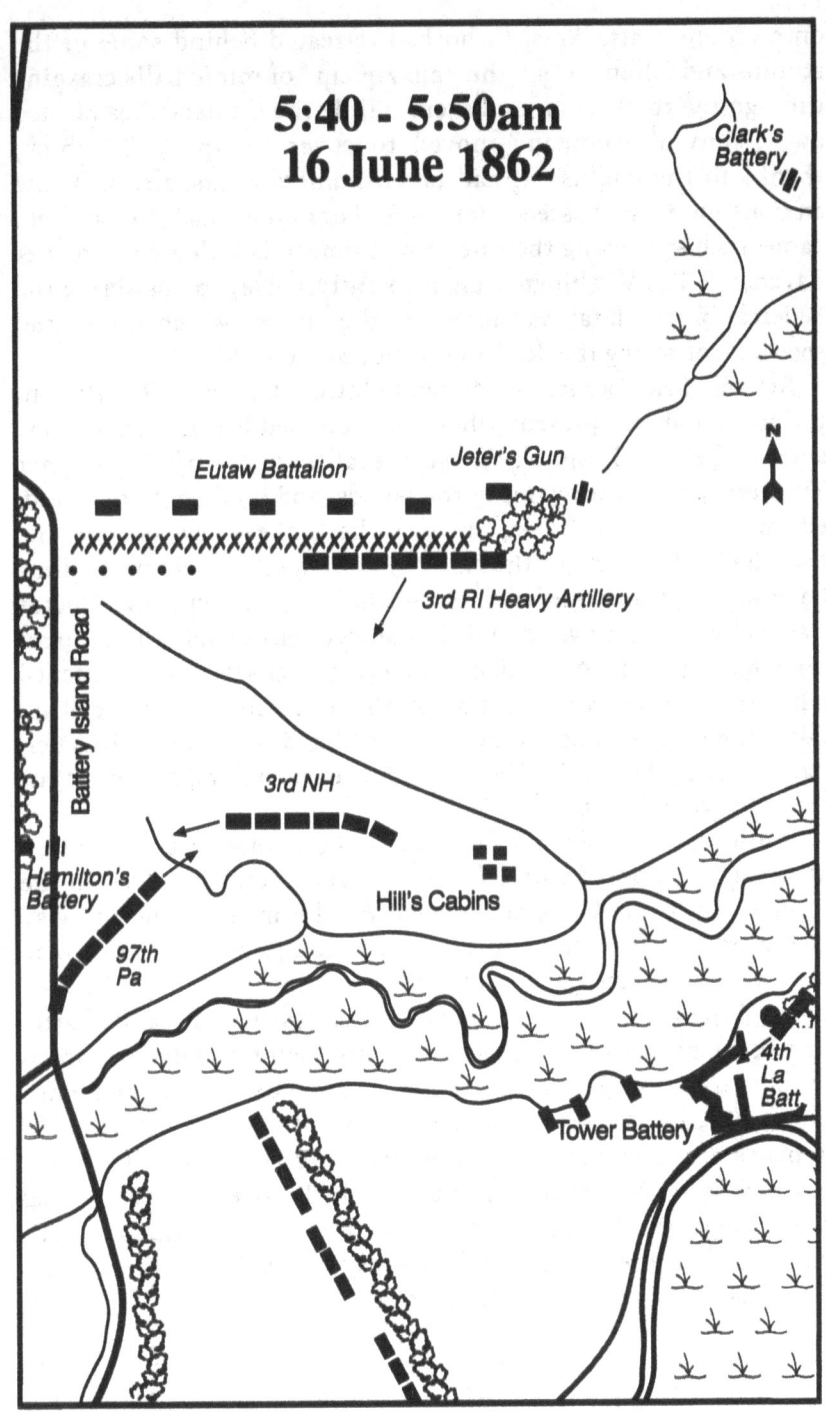

on a group of attackers, "who had retreated behind some of the stumps and fallen trees," the "zip zip zip" of minie balls crashing through the thickets around them. While the Confederates blasted away, Smyth's company moved to cover Company B, which, thanks to the confusion, had taken numerous casualties. A few anxious moments passed before word began to spread: "Soon there came a whisper along the line, 'Sgt. Lanneau is killed, Lt. Greer & Tavener.'" The Washington Light Infantry's delay in answering the Federals proved fatal, as the rest of the Eutaws watched the "sad spectacle of seeing the dead and wounded removed."[66]

Reverend A. Toomer Porter had followed the Eutaw Battalion to the front and was present when the wounded began their procession to the field hospital. He later recalled, "(Y)oung Christopher Trumbo came running out of the woods, and holding up his hand, exclaimed: 'Oh, Mr. Porter, see what the Yankees have done to me; they have shot off my thumb.' 'Thank God,' I exclaimed, 'they have not shot off your head. Go to the rear; you will find Doctor Ravenel waiting for you.'" While a shower of Federal bullets splattered his position, Porter made a sobering discovery. As he watched a line of orderlies carry the dead off the firing line, the young chaplain suddenly realized that four of the dead, Greer, Tavener, Laneau, and Thomas N. Chapman, had been singing psalms in his tent the evening before.[67]

While the Federals and the men of the Eutaw Battalion traded shots on the Confederate left flank, Major Pressley moved to the right to seek out Colonel Stevens. As the major made his way westward, a Federal crouching behind a stump took a poorly aimed shot at the officer that struck the ground near his feet. Pressley pointed the man out to some nearby Eutaws and "after the battle he was found with three or four balls through his body," he noted with satisfaction. In transit, Pressley saw only two Confederates "not acting like heroes." One man was skulking behind a tree only 4 inches in diameter, while another tried to run for the rear but was stopped by no less that Hagood himself. Pressley later surmised that "They probably belonged to some other command. May have been some of the demoralized pickets who had been driven in." The major was positive the skulkers weren't Eutaws.[68]

* * *

Following the trail of the 3rd New Hampshire, Major Metcalf succeeded in moving his 3rd Rhode Island Heavy Artillery to a point where some of his lead elements could actually open fire on the Tower Battery. Unfortunately for Metcalf, uunexpected artillery fire and musketry from the north continued to harass his command. One minie slammed into the major's shoulder and another hit his horse before orders arrived "to capture (the) field battery in (our) rear." Without a so much as a pause, Metcalf reversed his line and faced it towards the woods to the north. Hitting a quick-step, Metcalf roared out, "Boys remember where you are from," and the Rhode Islanders trotted into attack formation.

At two hundred yards, the tangle of felled trees reverberated with rifle fire as the orders to "double-quick" swept across the Rhode Island line. Lieutenant E. S. Bartholomew, the new commander of Company E, went down with a gut shot, but continued "cheering his men in the fight," wrote a Federal witness. Company H's Captain Rogers and Lieutenant Brayton helped carry him off his last field of battle. Lieutenant Isaac Potter of Company B took a ball that shattered his wrist, and he stumbled to the rear to seek succor. The hot Confederate fire was "laying out some of our best men," noted one Rhode Islander, but the others charged on, led by Adjutant Jerry Lanahan's cries of "Let yees yell, Federal men and Irishmen, Let yees yell." One charger recalled that "the men did yell. Right on we dashed." Before them, the thin Confederate skirmish line that fronted the felled trees disappeared into the abatis, just as the 3rd Rhode Island Heavy Artillery plunged into the thickets.[69]

The dense obstructions obliterated the Rhode Islander formation. A group of twenty-five volunteers from Serrell's engineers joined the Rhode Islanders here and tried to remove some of the obstructions on the right flank. Although their effort was great, their numbers were too few to accomplish much. Metcalf attempted to regain control by ordering his men to move west by the left flank, but pockets of the 3rd isolated in the confusing abatis and timber stand never heard the orders. Company B's Sgt. James Batchellor pressed forward through the what he described as an "impassable" thicket, only to come upon a dead comrade sprawled across a lifeless Confederate. As a second Southern line opened on the Federals from somewhere up ahead, the sergeant remembered that, "Here in the woods, many of our men were shot." Batchellor was searching for his unit when a nearby comrade warned that "the rebels are right out there." Suddenly, a voice commanded "Drop that gun, you Federal son of a ____," and the sergeant found himself outnumbered. An officer approached him and confiscated his cartridge-box. Marched away from the battle, Batchellor joined a group of fellow Rhode Islanders, all of whom were coming to realize that their fight, at least for now, was over.[70]

John Mulligan of Company E also became separated from his command but met with some success "scouting and fighting on his own hook" then did many of his comrades. After making his way through the tangled underbrush, Mulligan found himself face to face with a Confederate. Holding the advantage, the Unionist forced his opponent—who "looked like a poor divil that had just buried his grandmother"—to surrender. Another private who earned his spurs that morning was Foster Cook of Company H. Something of a ne'er-do-well, Cook raised himself in Captain Rogers' estimation when, in a hand-to-hand combat, he bayoneted an enemy combatant. Afterwards, the captain was heard to say, "Cook, you have been a very bad man, but this brave conduct of yours atones for a great many sins."[71]

Others were not so lucky. Some groups who broke through the timber found a Confederate line bristling with bayonets. Few, if any, returned from this deep penetration. On the right flank of the assaulting column, however, some Rhode Islanders surprised a quiescent company of the enemy and managed to slam a few volleys into them. A handful of Metcalf's men came within view of the battery that had been punishing the 3rd New Hampshire, but the major made a dangerous discovery as his troops waded through the thickets: behind him, back by the marsh, the 3rd New Hampshire was in full retreat. Unless Metcalf wanted to take on all the Confederates in the vicinity by himself, he had no other choice but to withdraw as well. "I deemed it my duty to order my men to retire."

Word spread along the line and through the abatis as Northerners picked up their wounded and dead and began pulling back from the ground they had captured, "slowly and reluctantly." The 3rd Rhode Island Heavy Artillery exited the felled timber into the field they had entered not 30 minutes before. Angling to the southwest, they began to collect near Union artillery section positioned in the Battery Island Road. [72]

* * *

For the Confederates peering through the obstructions, the action along the abatis seemed terribly brief. With the order to fire, the Eutaw Battalion emptied its rifles into the dense thicket in its front. "Our fire, as well as that of the enemy, was very rapid, but did not last very long," noted one of the battlion members. While it may not have been long, perhaps, it was damaging to many. Private Thomas Simons of Company B had two Federal bullets pass completely through him, but he continued to return fire until some of his comrades bore him to the rear. As the fighting sputtered fitfully to a close, small parties of Confederates probed the fallen timber in search of Federals. Captain Sellars led one such unit into the tangle and soon returned with three prisoners. He also reported that the Federals had departed, leaving some of their wounded and dead behind. Enemy artillery continued to pound their position, keeping the Eutaw Battalion and Stevens' Carolinian detachment on edge. But, for now, the Northern infantry was gone.[73]

* * *

By the time Horatio Wright had reached the field, Isaac Stevens division had fallen back to the hedgeline fronting the Tower Battery, while Williams' brigade was still "hotly engaged and under a cross-fire." Wright saw the Confederate threat to the north and promptly positioned Hamilton's guns to support Williams' beleaguered troops. This battery set up in the roadway with the 47th New York from Chatfield's Brigade positioned on its left. The 97th Pennsylvania, which had separated from William's column and formed in support of the Roundheads' attack on the Tower Battery, plowed through the marsh that had initially slowed the 3rd Rhode Island Heavy Artillery, and aligned on the right of Hamilton's guns. Past these reinforcements trudged the battered survivors of the 3rd New Hampshire and 3rd Rhode Island Heavy Artillery. Soon thereafter, the 97th Pennsylvania fanned out across their line of retreat, taking advantage of an "inequality of the ground" to shield their line. With one flank facing the Rebels near the Hill House and the other covering the downed woods, the 97th lay down "to avoid the shell of both sides." The mere presence of these two regiments and artillery battery seemed to dampen Confederate ardor, for no enemy advance threatened the Northern withdrawal. Such slight success offered little comfort for Williams' soundly defeated troops.[74]

A thread of a story seldom told wound its way through Wright's position about this time. The broken remnants of the 28th Massachusetts had slowly started to reform in the rear under General Wright's observation. The one section of the 28th that had performed well, a mixed unit that Capt. George Cartwright had led up near the fort, rejoined the scattering of its command located somewhere near Battery Island Road. Among them stood Lieutenant Colonel Moore. For reasons lost to history, Wright walked up to the two officers and placed Cartwright "in command of the Regt. . . .in the presence of Col. Moore." Evidently, Wright had seen enough of Moore's performance to risk this remarkable action—the removal of an officer not directly under his command while on a field of battle. While Cartwright moved immediately to bring order to his shaken regiment, Wright turned to view the carnage of the Federal attempt to take the Tower Battery.[75]

CHAPTER NINE

"Oh, God, forgive me, the bitterness engendered by the disappointment of that hour"

—Col. Daniel Leasure, 100th Pennsylvania Infantry

"...A Disturbance to Quell..."

Into the whirlwind entered Brig. Gen. Henry Benham. He joined Horatio Wright at the front near the Battery Island Road and immediately took field command of the division. From his position, Benham could easily observe both Stevens' stalled attack in front of the battery and Williams' disrupted attacks on the left flank. Nearby, Colonels Chatfield and Welsh manuevered their demi-brigades to support Hamilton's guns. Unfortunately for the rattled commander, the signs were ominous: his plans to overwhelm the isolated Confederate post and blast open a route to Charleston had ground to a halt before the staunch Southern defenses. With two of Colonel Williams' regiments limping back from the Hill fields, and Wright's troops moving to shield the army's left flank, Benham was forced to look to Isaac Stevens for victory.[1]

* * *

It was now full morning. The sun had burst forth, dissipating the leaden clouds and shining bright and clear. Stevens remained determined to force the issue and sent orders for Colonels Fenton and Leasure to re-organize their brigades—even at the first hedge if necessary. As these officers hustled to bring order from the chaos, the three Connecticut guns received Stevens' directive to pull back to the roadway. The crews limbered up their cannon and re-crossed the jarring furrows of the cotton field "in good order," noted one, going into battery on, ironically enough, the Battery Island Road. Eager to continue their exchange with the Confederates, one Federal later wrote that the artillerists began to fire "constantly and carefully until the enemy's guns had ceased to answer." With the artillery roaring across the fields, Stevens pushed the 7th Connecticut forward to the first hedge, where it joined the rallying elements of the 8th Michigan. The Westerners had been badly scattered, with terrible losses in men and officers but, slowly, some order began to re-emerge.[2]

The Roundheads of the 100th Pennsylvania were in much the same shape as the rest of the Union regiments. Daniel Leasure could initially muster but two companies after the Roundheads' trial in front of the battery, and those troops that did rally didn't like what they saw. Wrote one stunned sergeant, "I did not go back until the Colonel told me to fall back to the Regiment. And when I looked around I could see only about 20 of our regiment." Sergeant Walter Collins of Company M halted when he found the decorative eagle that had recently graced the 28th Massachusetts' flagstaff lying on the ground. He picked it up, unsure of what to do with it, then moved on. Leasure meanwhile sent two of his aides across the fields to gather up the scattered men. As the formation along the second hedge slowly congealed, Col. Rudolph Rosa's 46th New York advanced and formed on the Leasure's right flank. All the while, the Southern fort kept up a sporadic but deadly fire.[3]

The Highlanders of the 79th New York were also resting along this line when Stevens called them back to the first hedge. Captain Rockwell's Connecticut guns had already initiated a lively barrage from their rearward position just as the New Yorkers "prepared to run the gauntlet of another raking fire," as one Federal recalled. Naval shell fire now joined the Connecticut guns covering the fort. Although the gunboat fire was largely ineffective, the 79th New

A Disturbance To Quell 243

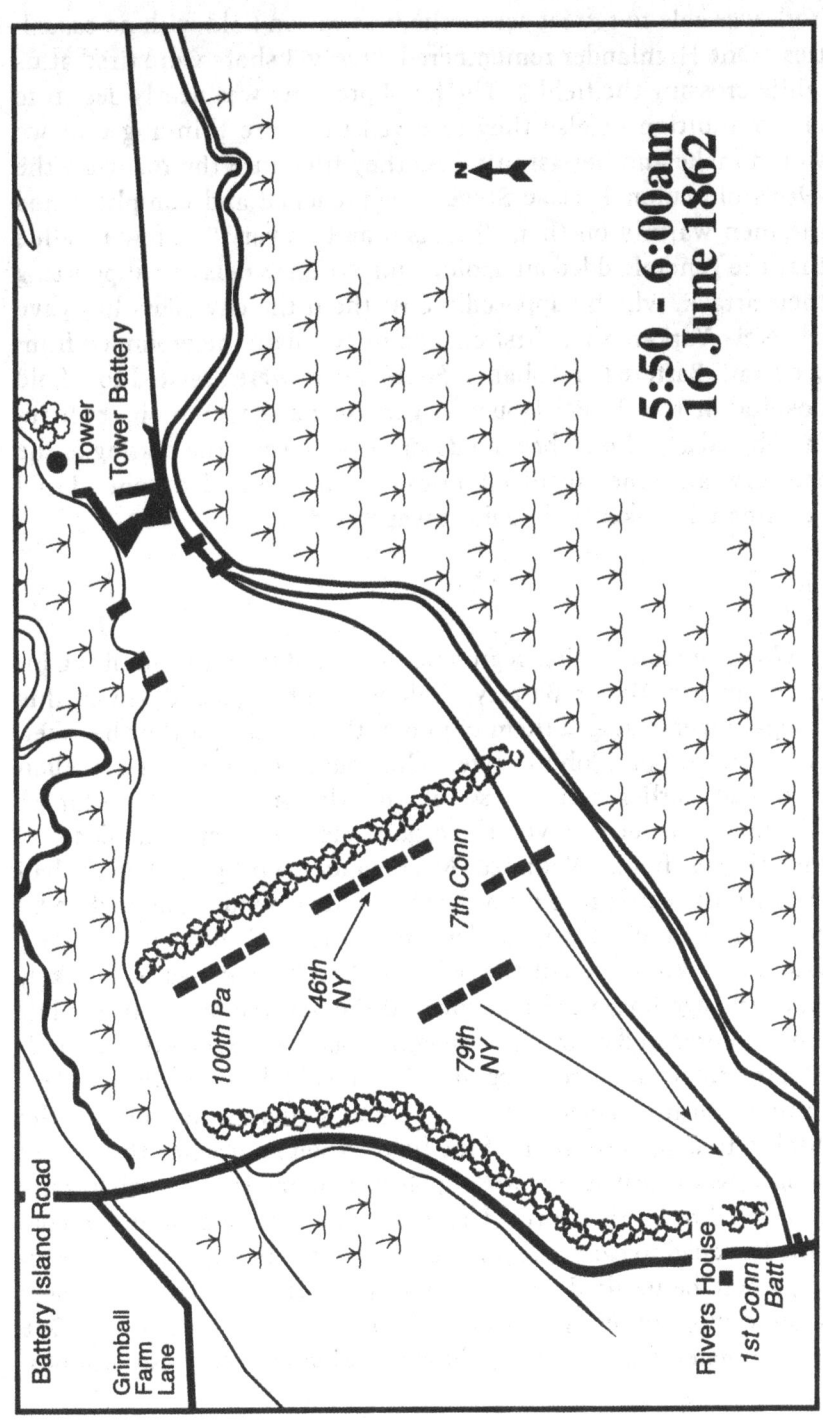

York was able to retreat across the first cotton field with no casualties. One Highlander remembered, "Only 3 shots were fired at us while crossing the field...The fort I presume was nearly destitute of ammunition or else they reserved their fire thinking that we would make another assault." As they filed into the roadway, the 79th's old colonel, Isaac Stevens, approached and complimented the men warmly on their "heroism and bravery." A few recalled that the general added an apology for Wright's delay in supporting their attack, which supposedly cost them the day. This lull gave the New Yorkers their first chance to evacuate the wounded from the front. Battered and shaken Highlanders were assisted to a field hospital at the Rivers House, a gory scene that one observer remembered as "almost beyond description." Amid the roaring of the artillery and the agonized cries of the wounded, one dazed Scotsman mistakenly thought it was 8:30.[4]

* * *

When the four Union regiments retreated from the smoking inclines of the Tower Battery, Colonel Fenton passed among his troops and encouraged them to join in the retreat lest they be taken prisoner. Corporal John Burwell, the young transplanted Canadian who had earlier written so eloquently of "The Day star of Gladness," never received the orders. He, like many, lay dead on the bloody field. Wounded Michigander Philip Coleman had watched the battle rage from the site of his wounding, and when he got wind of the retreat, he determined to pull himself to safety. Wielding a knife, he cut the belts holding his haversack, blanket, and cartridge box, then he squeezed the severed artery in his left arm and prepared to move. Struggling against wounds that included a fractured skull, torn leg muscles, a badly bruised ribcage—not to mention his ravaged arm—Coleman somehow summoned the vitality to drag himself off of the field. When he reached the second hedgerow, the private sat with his legs dangling in the ditch, totally exhausted from his efforts. There, Coleman met a captain who detailed a squad to carry the private to the 8th Michigan's field hospital, where he recalled joining "some 12 to 15 other wounded men, some crying, others groaning and some cursing their fate." One man, noisier than the rest, showed Coleman two flesh wounds, whereupon Coleman announced that he should "break a bone for him so he would have something to cry about." A shamed silence descended upon the premises.[5]

Soon thereafter, an examining surgeon declared, "Coleman, your case is desperate." Feeling a chill—as much perhaps as from the doctor's words as from the morning air—he asked to be moved out into the sun where he might warm up. The surgeon agreed and promised to transport him back to camp in the first available ambulance. Placed on the ground in the yard and surrounded by the cacophony of battle, Coleman rested as best he could.[6]

Another witness to the horrors of the field hospitals was Roundhead chaplain Robert Browne. While ministering to the sufferers from his regiment, the Reverend saw firsthand the destructive power of the Southern artillery. Writing home, he revealed that:

> Many of the poor fellows were dying, many suffering most acutely. Bullets, exploded bomb shells, cannon balls grape and canister had done fearful work even among those who survived. Some were wounded in the head and face, some in the breast and bowells. A discharge of grape with old chains and other miscellaneous missiles of iron, glass, etc. was especially destructive to our men, chiefly shattering their legs. They lay most of them moaning in the hospital.

When Browne wasn't busy "direct(ing) (the wounded) kindly to the Savior," he was praying over hastily dug graves even then beginning to scar the fields around the Rivers House.[7]

* * *

With a numb determination, the Confederate cannoneers fitfully continued to spray a potpourri of canister and scrap metal at the Federal attackers. Union survivors that had doggedly remained up near the fort merely had to lower their heads to avoid the whining projectiles. The only organized Federal resistance remained crouched along the hedgeline, the 46th New York and the 100th Pennsylvania, both wrangled into place by the driven Leasure. A dispatch from Stevens arrived, pressing the colonel to "hold a bold front...artillery and infantry were coming," the colonel later noted. Leasure moved the 46th New York to the left of the Roundheads and awaited the arrival of his reinforcements.

In the meantime, stretcher bearers hustled along the front, evacuating the wounded to the rear. Small knots of the walking wounded staggered over the cotton rows to the hospitals. One injured officer, Lt. Joseph Gilliland of the Roundheads, spent a moment laughing with Daniel Leasure, "insisting he was not hurt much" despite wounds to his leg and face and the bruising effects of a spent cannonball that had slammed into his shoulder. He headed to the hospital balanced between two assisting comrades, leaving the colonel to marvel at his indomitable spirit.[8]

Soon after Stevens' orders arrived, the promised reinforcements made their dramatic appearance onto the field.

* * *

The 1st Connecticut Light Artillery chafed at the length of time it took to reform the infantry at the first hedge, although Joseph Hawley recalled spending only "a few moments" in the rear area. One Highlander succinctly remembered the moment: "Orders were soon received to prepare for another attack." Stevens himself supervised these efforts and evidently attempted to coordinate his assault with Wright's movement to the north of the Tower Battery. Even after witnessing the bloody failure of Benham's ill-fated plans, Stevens was not about to give up the day, at least not yet. When all was in place, he once again ordered his battered columns forward.[9]

The infantry led the way. Lieutenant Colonel Morrison, "pale from loss of blood," remarked a comrade, a handkerchief binding his head wound, refused to be relieved "even at the earnest solicitations of his officers." He rose up before his regiment and called out "Follow me Highlanders." With the sun shining brightly, the remnants of the 79th New York fell into line and began their second crossing of what another described as "those terrible cotton rows."

On the right, Lieutenant Colonel Hawley put what was left of his 7th Connecticut moving into line alongside the New Yorkers, with Captain Rockwell's battery eagerly joining the movement. Isaac Stevens sent the cannoneers on their way, calling out, "'Connecticut boys, go in, and the day is ours!'" With "a wild huzza," the gunners took off. Stevens' division may have been badly bloodied that morning, but the men moved with the same spirit that drove their first thrust to the brink of the Battery's walls. Even after their rough handling earlier that morning, they welcomed another chance at the Confederates.[10]

The gunners in Rockwell's Battery remembered this charge distinctly. Amidst a hail of what one participant described as "chain, glass, railroad iron, and every conceivable missile," the gun sections rattled across the field at breakneck speeds. "How those horses went," wrote Private Griswold, as he grabbed the sighting pin on the muzzle of one of the guns and ran alongside. "It seemed as though every stride I made could have been measured in rods." A few of the artillerists managed to mount the straining horses. Captain Scranton scrambled onto one of the limbers and held on for dear life, later recalling that "we went over those cotton rows in a manner that was trying to the horses as well as the comrades."[11]

When the guns arrived at the second hedge, the Roundhead's right flank drew back somewhat to make room for the cannon. Hawley was already on scene and preparing for the contest's renewal. As the limbers arrived, members of the 7th Connecticut pitched in to locate and place the guns, while the cannoneers "breathlessly" pulled up from their 500 yard sprint. Confederate guns opened upon the area, but Hawley calmly sighted for the gunners and directed their fire. He took it upon himself not only to perform damage assessments but also to warn the gunners when the enemy guns fired. Such timely alerts sent the cannoneers diving behind the embankment, and when the Confederate discharges would pass, the Connecticut men arose to deliver their replies.[12]

Private Griswold recalled it thus: "We worked the guns lively and most of the time in a stooping position, numbers one and two (gunners) seldom getting outside the wheels when the gun was fired. I was number two, and yelled with pain everytime our gun was fired after it got warmed up, as at every discharge it was like a sharp knife through my head from ear to ear." While loading one of the howitzers, Private Lord burned his hands and started "cursing like a pirate," reminisced one fellow battery member. "By G__ ," he exclaimed, "it is so hot it sizzes!" The guns, under the calm eye of Alfred Rockwell, blew through their ammunition, as limbers rushed back and forth to keep the crews supplied. One driver, being somewhat fortified with whiskey, steered his horse to a position behind the right section. When a Confederate cannon fired from the fort directly at him, the rider—Private Holly—jumped off his mount and landed on his head, still clutching the reins. The exploding shell completely destroyed two horses and wounded two more, sending fragments of leather and horseflesh in all directions. One member of the 7th Connecticut 100 feet from the blast was leveled by the flying debris, but the nearby gunners, although rattled, merely picked themselves up and dusted off the dirt and equine entrails. Miraculously, no humans were hurt, and pistol shots quickly put the wounded mounts out of their misery. Curiously, one gunner picked through the mess in an attempt to salvage some scraps of leather. When questioned as to his motives, he calmly replied, "I won't let the damned rebels have a strip of our harnesses." His comrades finally convinced him "to relinquish his useless task." Meanwhile, the inebriated Holly—apparently none the worse for landing on his head in the swan dive off his horse—managed to locate a new mount and rode back to procure replacements for the depleted teams.[13]

When the 79th New York pulled up at Leasure's line, its membered ducked to avoid the Confederate artillery fire. Most New Yorkers assumed that another advance upon the fort would be forthcoming, so they hunkered down behind the hedge to await the assault. Scrap metal and railroad iron from the Confederate guns screamed across their front, moving one wag to observe, "They're firing a whole blacksmith shop at us! Here's the hammer, the anvil will come next!" Another Highlander collapsed after taking a shot to the head. The bullet wound, described as having "ploughed around the bones under the skin," for some reason couldn't crack his skull. He rose with his face covered with blood and doggedly assumed a place in line. Lieutenant Colonel Morrison, meanwhile, picked out some of his best marksmen and ordered them forward. They hopped the hedge, moved out into the field, and began an annoying fire that succeeded in felling many of the Confederate gunners.[14]

Colonel Leasure rode the length of his line, fully satisfied with the new dispositions of his brigade. He knew his men were in good spirits and stood ready to charge the Confederate fort again. While viewing the battery, he at first thought he saw the beginnings of a

A Disturbance To Quell 249

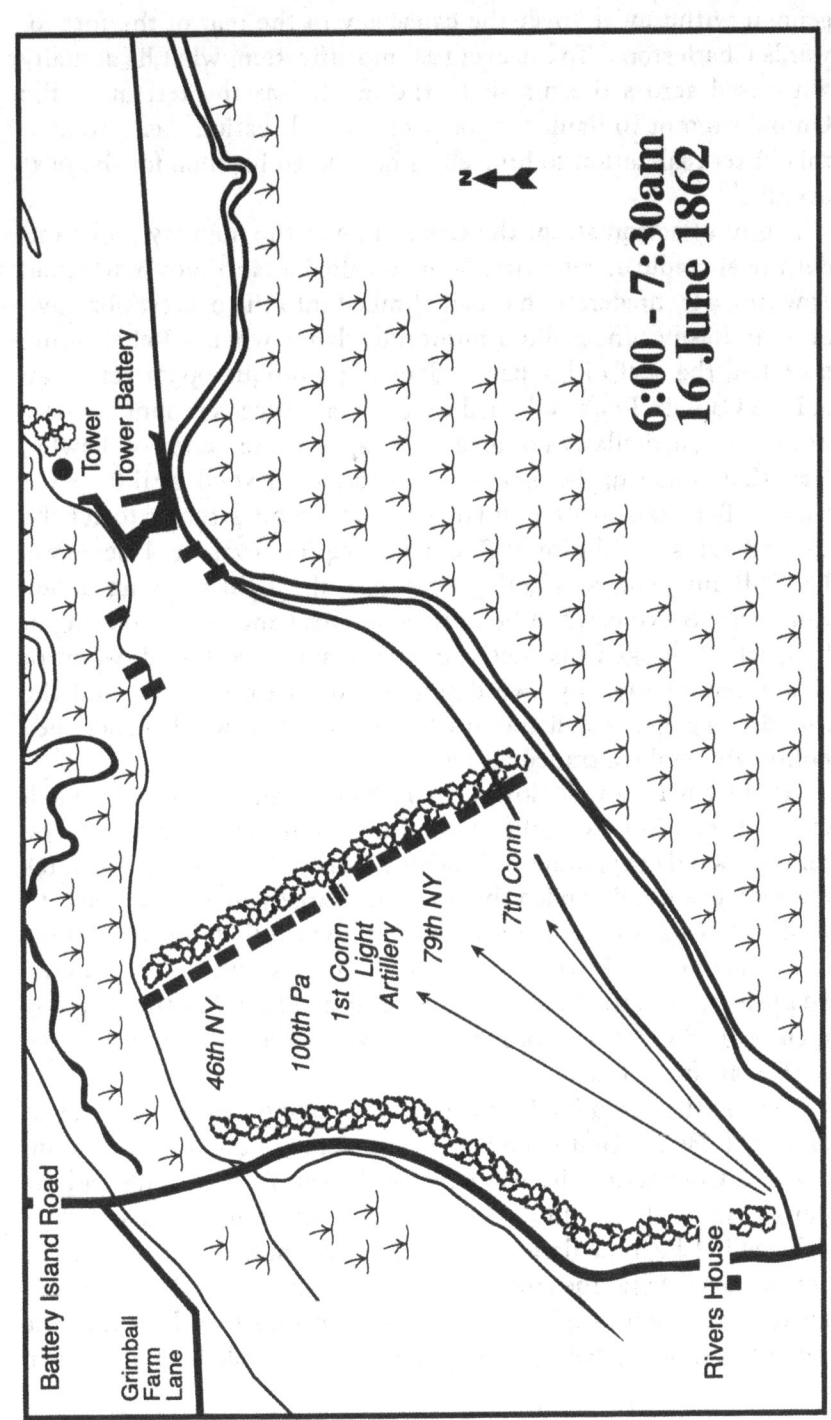

general withdrawal "over the causeway in the rear of the fort towards Charleston." To his eventual mortification, what he actually witnessed across the marsh to the north was the retreat of the Union attempt to flank the fort from that direction. Leasure kept this bitter realization to himself as he readied his men for the next assault.[15]

A blur of action swept the Union line as the men lay prone under the sporadic cannon fire. Some recalled a Northern marksman downing a Confederate that had climbed into the observation tower. One fleshy officer did a humorous dance when a Rebel minie scorched the seat of his pants. Spotting a unique opportunity, an aide to Captain Rockwell tried to lead that officer's mount, an ugly brute, to a particularly hot area. The captain intervened— "Fowler, lead that horse up here, I see an occasional shell striking over there." Thus the crestfallen Fowler failed in his attempt to get the Confederates to rid him of Rockwell's equine eyesore. Elsewhere, Lt. William Lusk was galloping across the field carrying orders from Isaac Stevens when he noticed a sword and scabbard lying in his path. "I looked instinctively at my side, and found, when or how I cannot say, my sword-belt had been torn or cut, and the sword was gone." He dismounted to retrieve his sword, a cherished family gift, and continued on his way.[16]

As the battle ground down, the Federal naval fire caused considerable discomfort along the Union line. Its inaccurate delivery system had shells exploding well behind Leasure's formation. A quick dispatch eventually ended the noisy and largely ineffective barrage. With the cessation of the naval gunfire, the conflict devolved into a duel between Rockwell's guns and Confederate metal. Sharpshooters started popping away at each other, but the infantrymen could do little except nervously await orders to begin the final push against the fort.

Among the assembled officers at the second hedge stood Signal officer Lt. Henry Tafft, who had been ordered to the front to coordinate the Connecticut battery's fire with that of Hamilton's and the navy's. Instead of gunnery direction, Tafft found himself "enveloped in (the) blue flame and sulphurous smoke" that hugged the cotton rows. Amid the smoke and noise, an aide from Isaac Stevens located the "poor artillery subaltern" and informed him that the general wanted to see him immediately. Tafft rode back to find an angry Stevens at his command post near the first hedge. Stevens wanted to communicate with Benham quickly, but heavy woods and foliage had rendered signaling ineffective. The general ordered the lieutenant to find Benham and request "that officer to move up his troops" to support Stevens' renewed attack. Tafft blanched at the thought. The roadway north towards Benham's position ran across what he described as a "narrow causeway. . .enfiladed not only by the artillery, but also by the sharpshooters of the enemy." To reach Benham, Tafft would have to traverse this path. With no choice but to obey, he spurred his horse to the task with "rifleshot and bursting shell filling the air with the song of death."[17]

Tafft negotiated what he described as the "jaws of death" with nary a scratch, but found something even more to his disliking when he reached his destination. According to his candid assessment, Benham was indeed at the front, a "badly frightened officer who was found sitting upon his horse surrounded by his staff, a full half mile away from danger." With the Federal artillery reaching a crescendo, Tafft delivered Stevens' message and stood by in disgust, awaiting a reply.[18]

* * *

Captain Percival Drayton remembered well the naval successes along the Coosaw River back in January 1862. Land-based direction of naval fire had worked masterfully that day, and Drayton hoped to duplicate the operation at Secessionville. A telegraph was run from Benham's forward command post to Drayton's *Pawnee* to direct the barrage against the Confederate works. Unfortunately, Drayton found his telegraphic communication "vague and unintelligible," and, in the end, the *Pawnee* able to toss only a few shells towards the Confederates, some of which "came much nearer our own men than those of the enemy." Seeing "no possible advantage," in continuing the firing, Drayton ordered it ceased.[19]

Things were much the same for the *Ellen* and the *Hale*, the small gunboats that had attempted to support the Stevens' attack from Big Folly Creek. They had pushed up the waterway about 3:30 a.m. and had anchored until the sounds of the battle exploded an hour later. Getting underway, the ships proceeded up the torturous channel until they reached an open point in range of the Tower

Battery. Stevens' troops could be seen huddled well in front of the fort, so the ships fired without fear of hitting their own men. The *Ellen* opened with her Parrott guns, while the *Hale's* Lieutenant Gillis tried to position his vessel to bring her broadsides into play. After fifteen rounds, however, Gillis realized the Confederates were well beyond his range and ceased firing. Frustrated by his inability to maneuver, Gillis requested instructions from Captain Woolsey aboard the *Ellen*. Woolsey responded that they had done all they could do. And so, other than await further developments, they did nothing more.[20]

* * *

As Federal officers began preparing anew for the next assault, Henry Benham stood near the Battery Island Road north of Stevens' position, surveying the disheartening scene. A lone horseman from Stevens' staff had ridden up to deliver a message requesting support for his renewed assault. The messenger assured the commanding general that the regiments before the fort were "reformed and ready." Benham, however, fretted. Not only had Williams' withdrawal served to expose Stevens' left flank, but Williams' troops had taken a real beating and were in no shape to render even the slightest assistance. Benham feared that continued attacks would merely add to the casualty totals and gain little else. Moreover, in his mind he had conveniently changed the scope of the operation and now regarded the entire exercise as a reconnaissance in force. Since Benham now knew how well-entrenched the Confederates were on this part of the field, he could easily argue that the realigned goals of his operation had been accomplished. Thus he arrived at a decision that would come back to haunt him.

Turning to Lieutenant Tafft, Benham "declined the aid demanded, and ordered General Stevens to retreat." The horseman bolted off to relate the orders to Stevens, while other orderlies leapt to their mounts to relay the orders to disengage and withdraw to the camps.[21] Years later, Lt. Henry Tafft, the horseman dispatched by Isaac Stevens, described Benham with one word: coward.[22]

Upon gathering the wounded and the dead, Wright and Williams began the retreat from their positions along the Battery Island Road. With the 97th Pennsylvania covering the withdrawal, the various regiments calmly filed off and returned to the encampments on the Grimball plantation. Gunboats moved closer to shore to shield the returning troops, and the grim soldiers soon began to gather about the camp in small, sullen groups. At the front, as the last elements of Wright's division quit the field, Colonel Guss of the 97th Pennsylvania began his regiment's retreat, pulling back en echelon by division front, as he recalled, "in perfect order and precision." Despite the threat of a Confederate counterattack, "not a gun was fired upon the Regiment after the movement commenced." The Pennsylvanians took up post in the rear of Wright's column, the last Union troops to leave this part of the field.[23]

* * *

The 3rd New Hampshire & 3rd Rhode Island Heavy Artillery's retreat from Hill's peninsula had come as a jolt to Isaac Stevens. Some of the general's equally angry staffers reported that Benham himself had ordered Williams' troops to retire. Off to the north, Confederate cheers all along the line confirmed the extent of the repulse. To Stevens' front, the dogged Confederates, seemingly unshaken and unbowed, kept up their artillery fire from the battered earthwork. Nevertheless, Stevens remained sanguine of the outcome and waited for the reappearance of Federal troops north of the marsh to launch another attack.[24]

Lieutenant Tafft, after retracing his perilous route, reined in next to the general and related Benham's order to withdraw the columns back to the camps. Although deeply angered, Stevens wasn't terribly shocked by the message. He already had but little regard for Benham and had suspected that his ill-considered tactics and poor preparation practically guaranteed the movement's failure from the start. Stevens sent an aide across the field to inform Colonels Leasure and Fenton of Benham's wishes. He then turned to the regiments along the Battery Island Road and began preparations for their withdrawal.[25]

Daniel Leasure paced his line, momentarily expecting an order to renew the fight. Orders to retreat were not what he was expecting, however, and Leasure fairly exploded when he received the news. Unaware that fierce resistance had forced the Federal retreat above the swamp, the colonel assumed that Benham had lost his nerve and, in a snap decision, had ordered everyone off the field. "Oh, God, forgive me, the bitterness engendered by the disappointment of that hour," Leasure would later write. "'Old Benham' without seeing the field at all, relying upon the reports of his frightened young squirts of aides, gave the order to retreat." He assumed that the fort would have fallen within the hour, but the "slaughter" of the morning had now been rendered "useless"—all thanks to the incompetent commander.[26]

As ambulance parties hustled to collect the dead and dying, Rockwell's artillery was the first to depart Leasure's line, pulling back one piece at a time across the furrowed field. As the gun crews reached the roadway, they turned south past the field hospital at the Rivers House. To one man's horror, amputated limbs were being tossed from an open window to a waiting burial party. When the last of the Connecticut guns reached the hospital area, the crews began to deploy in the roadway, but were ordered nearer the Rivers Causeway to cover the retreat. Before quitting the field, however, one battery member witnessed the retreating column of the 46th New York. A German near the tail of the regiment was suddenly struck in his stomach by a minie ball, causing him to somersault onto his head and spin a number of times with his feet in the air. The Connecticut gunners laughed nervously until they realized the soldier was dead. The smoke-grimed, black-faced cannoneers, having expended over 500 rounds during the morning's fight, sheepishly began their retreat to the covering position near Sol Legare Island.[27]

Those Highlanders still hugging the hedge line could only wonder what was taking so long. One Scotsman guessed that they had been under enemy artillery fire for an hour, and he bitterly questioned the wisdom of remaining so exposed if an attack wasn't intended. Another recalled that the Scots were "very much surprised at such an order. . ." Instead, orders circulated to withdraw, and the 79th New York fell in behind the 46th New York in leaving the scene of their bloody struggle. Major Leckey succeeded in gathering the Roundheads together and pulling them away from the hedge "slowly and in good order," noted one, but the mood was dark indeed. One officer recalled, "(Y)ou never saw a lot of men walk so slow, and every little bit they would stop and look back."

Sergeant Collins, still nursing the 28th Massachusetts' decorative eagle, decided to bury it before he pulled out. He later lamented that, "(P)robably some Confederate found it." Next to pull back was the 7th Connecticut, which Lt. Col. Hawley "moved in regular line to the rear, (with) the enemy's rifled cannon and howitzers playing upon us." The scattered elements of the 8th Michigan undoubtedly fell in wherever they could—only a small group rallied once the fight broke off. The 28th Massachusetts, which had reformed and remained in the roadway after their disintegration on the field, joined the retreat under the command of Capt. George Cartwright. The movements of Lieutenant Colonel Moore went largely unnoticed. Slowly, the remains of Stevens' bloodied division limped off the smoldering cotton fields towards their camps.[28]

When Colonel Leasure arrived at the Rivers House, he found the surgeons at work on the broken survivors of the morning attack. The doctors were well aware of the colonel's successful pre-war medical practice and requested that he lend a hand. Within a few minutes, Leasure had taken charge of the field hospital "in relieving, dressing, and amputating." Isaac Stevens paused at the scene and, finding his exhausted colonel thus engaged, emotionally embraced his hand, stating "God bless you, you brave soldier and good man." Stevens left the house weeping. To honor him, the general located Leasure's brigade and marched it to their quarters himself.[29]

As the division slogged down the road for Sol Legare Island and its camps, a strong picket force formed a perimeter around the Rivers House.

* * *

When Stevens' orders to retreat circulated through the troops along the hedge line, Lieutenant Belcher of the 8th Michigan determined to inform the brave men that had remained along to the battery's walls of the division's withdrawal. The officer had gone through most of the battle with a bullet in his shoulder, but that had hardly dimmed his devotion to duty. He picked his way in among the troops still lining the southernmost swamp and spread the unwelcome news. He somehow made his way across the Confederate front to the men still holed up near the northern marsh line. Try as he might, Belcher couldn't get the word out to everyone—not that everyone needed it. Private Benjamin Pease could easily see the game was up, and he struck for the rear on his own. Pausing to inform his still-cowering captain that the army was retreating, the private watched amusedly as the officer "scooted to the rear." Pease himself then took off and veered first for the Northerners still fighting behind some fallen logs. By the time he got there, he saw that most were "already leaving for the rear as fast as their guns were emptied." When a Michigander named Walter Savage squeezed off one last shot, Pease decided to resume his own withdrawal and moved gingerly along the relative safety of the marsh bank. There, a voice called out for help. Pease stopped to find an Irishman from the 28th Massachusetts trying to drag himself from the tangled slashing lining the swamp, but his shattered legs made the task nearly impossible. Pease tried to assist him, but as he struggled to free the Irishman, another retreating Michigander, Adelbert Overton, toppled over with a minie ball to his knee. Benjamin knew his duty lay with his statesman, but he removed enough of the brush so that the Irishman might crawl away. Walter Savage arrived to help Pease pull the bleeding Overton to safety, but Overton grew faint from the loss of blood. Running out of options, Pease sent Savage to obtain a stretcher while he remained with their badly wounded comrade.[30]

To Pease's shock, Confederate parties had already crossed the battery's walls in the wake of the Union retreat to scour the battlefield. He sat with his friend until one such group, led by a sergeant, approached the pair and ordered Pease to come with them. The Michigander asked if he could take Overton with him, but the sergeant said stretcher bearers would soon come for the wounded. Captivity being his reward for loyalty, Pease gave Overton his canteen and haversack and then departed with the Confederate escort for the fort.[31]

Back on Battery Island Road, Private Griswold struggled along in the rear of Rockwell's battery. Riding up slowly from the direction of the battlefield was the 8th Michigan's Col. William Fenton—"crying like a child," remembered the private. Griswold heard the distraught officer utter, "My poor boys! My brave Boys! Where are my boys?" Fenton noticed the private and disconsolately observed that half of his Michigan men had been killed. The crushed colonel then rode on towards the camps. Griswold continued his trek on foot, marveling that no one from his battery had been killed in the hail of heavy fire.[32]

Michigander Philip Coleman somehow endured the jarring torture of the ambulance ride to Sol Legare Island. Arriving at a field hospital near the Stono, Coleman's first attending physician informed him that nothing could be done to help him. By 3:00 p.m., however, Coleman had persuaded the doctor to amputate his arm "which was then black," he recalled. An hour later the doctor returned with four of the strongest members of the 8th Michigan. The surgeon decided that Coleman's weakened state necessitated an operation without chloroform and added muscle would be needed to hold the patient down. After one assistant sat on Coleman and tightly held his good hand, the operation began. It took only a few moments to remove Philip Coleman's arm, and all present agreed that the private barely moved save the moment when the nerve column in the bone was severed. Afterwards, Coleman asked for a mirror to adjudge the doctor's work, then requested a steak and potato dinner—"I was going to have something to eat if I never ate again."[33]

When the surgeons finished their work at the Rivers House and the last of Stevens' division had disappeared down the Battery Island Road, the pickets that had been watching for any Confederate movement pulled back to the roadway. The last of the medical staff were abandoning the now gruesome building, so the pickets went about carrying out the last of Isaac Stevens' orders. Lieutenant Belcher disappeared into the house for a moment before quickly rejoining his squad. Suddenly, flames sprouted from the structure, and smoke began to billow into the air. Still attentive to any enemy movement, Belcher and the Federal infantry sullenly moved off, the last of the blue-uniformed soldiers to quit the field.[34]

* * *

The battered Confederates in the Tower Battery remembered the final phases of the battle through a dim haze punctuated by roaring artillery, snapping musketry, and shouted orders. They ignored the small knots of Federals huddling in the swamps and cotton rows, the closest massed enemy infantry still lay at the second hedge, 500 yards across the field. Although additional infantry and artillery had come up to reinforce the enemy, the Northerners seemed little disposed to renew the contest. Gradually, the battle wound down to a fitful artillery exchange, with the enemy shot and shell either burying itself in the fort's walls or overshooting the parapets. The Confederate cannoneers, for their part, had been loading their guns with anything they could find. Practically anything sufficed, from chain links to blacksmith metal, and it all blew across the field into the Federal positions.

Despite the protection of the earthen walls, the Confederates still took casualties. On the right flank, the Charleston Riflemen's Capt. Julius Blake reeled when a Federal projectile tore through him. When Lt. J. J. Edwards rushed to pull his captain off the wall, another Federal shell exploded nearby. The smoke cleared, and Edwards lay dead, pierced by the flying shrapnel. He would be one of the last Confederate defenders to die inside the fort.[35]

The artillery exchanges continued for some time until the Federal cannon abruptly limbered up and pulled away. Confederate sharpshooters discharged their weapons at the retreating infantry and dropped a number of the Federals pulling back from their forward positions. To the fort's defenders, it seemed that the enemy simply "gave up the contest with the battery and appeared to take up a new line of defense" back by the Rivers House. Even this line was quickly abandoned as the enemy battle flags came down, and, suddenly, the Yankees were gone.[36]

The Confederates were stunned. Captain Bonneau, who had fought at the Columbiad as a volunteer, turned to the gun commander, Lieutenant Humbert, and remarked, "Lt., your gun deserves to be mounted on a golden pivot." Southerners began shaking hands and patting backs. Many prayed. Of course, Lieutenant Colonel McEnery had little time for such celebration. As the ranking officer, he immediately ordered relief parties over the walls to gather up arms and prisoners.

The sights that greeted these units were appalling. Heaped on the outer wall of the left parapet, stretched out between the cotton rows, and strewn along the marsh lines lay the shattered elements of six Federal regiments. Especially gruesome were the torn corpses populating the center of the field, where the three assaults had been broken apart almost entirely by Confederate artillery fire. Southerners ranged across the area, gathering up abandoned rifles and herding wounded and dazed prisoners to the rear. In these moments, the surviving defenders of the Tower Battery began to realize that they had just won, against incredible odds, a tremendous victory of signal importance. The door to Charleston, one of the great ports of this year-old Confederacy, had been slammed shut.[37]

The price of victory, however, was high. McEnery's 4th Louisiana Battalion had numbered about 260 effectives going into the action, and of these, six were killed outright and 22 wounded, including Captain Walker. Spartan Goodlette's 100-man fatigue party from the 22nd South Carolina lost 10 killed and eight wounded. The Pee Dee Battalion, which had rushed to the battery's left flank to throw back the first enemy charge, lost three killed, 23 wounded, and three missing. Among the 100 men of the Charleston Battalion that had rushed to the walls, Capt. Henry King still clung to life, but Lieutenant Edwards and eight enlisted men were dead, 30 additional members were wounded, and two were missing. Finally, Colonel Lamar's two depleted artillery companies suffered 15 men killed, 39 wounded, and one missing. Lamar would eventually estimate that the Confederate effectives in the battery prior to McEnery's arrival amounted to 500 men, which made the proportional losses nearly one in four. Many of the wounded would die as the days passed.[38]

The Southerners never were able to calculate the total Union losses—their guesses ranged from 600 to over 1,000—but they could count the Federal dead laying in the fields and the ever increasing numbers of wounded and captured. These totals alone revealed the terrible cost to the enemy. Lamar reported that 341 Federals were buried on the field, while John McEnery—who commanded the units that performed the burials—reported the internment of 168 of the enemy found in front of the fort. Additionally, the 27 Enfields, 83 rifles, and 62 Springfields collected on the field made a fine cache for the quartermaster department. It was hardly compensation for the losses, but the fact remained that despite steep Confederate casualties, Henry Benham's Unionists had been badly beaten.[39]

* * *

Similar scenes marked the fields north of the marsh. Once the Federals disappeared from that sector, small Confederate parties moved out from the slashing to investigate the ground that the enemy had held. Benjamin Sheppard from the Eutaw Battalion wrote his mother that although the battle was bad, "The scene after the battle is worse than all. . . . I saw men laying in all kinds of postures, some in the very act of shooting off their guns, some loading & some looked as though they were praying after they were wounded and died." Augustine Smyth accompanied a squad that was detailed to gather arms from the Washington Light Infantry's front. "Such a scene I wish never again to witness," he wrote:

> Twenty or thirty men lay stretched out on a small field, wounded, dying, & dead. One must have been in the Act of loading his gun when a grapeshot took out the whole of his back, for he lay dead with his hands raised, just as if he were even then loading. Another one lay close by with his leg entirely shot away, & only a piece of skin connecting his knee & his thigh. Many were in the water, dead, in a small creek between them and Secessionville, one poor fellow, wounded in his back and throat, lay in the water close to the bank, but unable to get out, while tide was up to his shoulders and continually rising. We helped him up and gave him water, & left him on the field for the litters to carry off.[40]

Major Pressley, driven by a professional curiosity to see the effects of the musketry and artillery on the attackers, mounted his horse and moved out beyond the perimeter. Despite the extensive cannon fire during the engagement, Pressley could identify with certainty only two Union soldiers and one horse killed by the artillery. Most of the Federal corpses, he noted, had been shot in the head, "showing that our troops fired too high."[41]

Johnson Hagood would report that 68 arms, mostly Enfields, had been gleaned from the field, with 11 prisoners, including eight wounded, marched off to the rear. Eighteen of the enemy's dead littered the area south of the felled timber, but the retreating Federals had been seen dragging off many others. As for Confederate casualties, Col. Clement Stevens of the 24th South Carolina reported three men dead and seven wounded, including one officer. Two men from his skirmish line were still missing when he filed his report. The Eutaw Battalion had been harder hit—one officer and three men dead, and one officer and 13 men wounded. Most of the casualties came from the Washington Light Infantry. Major Pressley remembered that after the battle, the able-bodied of Company B numbered so few that all hands were needed to evacuate the wounded. Second Lieutenant Benjamin Graham suffered the dubious distinction of being the only member of the 47th Georgia killed at Secessionville, and Johnson Hagood's reserves massed near the roadway—the 47th and 51st Georgia, along with the 1st South Carolina detachment—counted but one wounded. In the end, the abatis had served its protective purpose well. Considering the close quarters, intensity and duration of the fight—and that Colonel Hagood commanded less than 500 men for the entire action—Confederate casualties remained remarkably low.[42]

What remained of the morning and afternoon was spent burying the dead, collecting impedimenta, herding in the prisoners and caring for the Southern casualties. At about noon, Col. Spartan Goodlette arrived with the balance of the 22nd South Carolina, which he filed into the battery. Lieutenant Colonel McEnery passed command of the fort to Goodlette and returned to his Louisianans, who were busily dividing up whatever Federal plunder they could lay their hands on. "(O)ur boys got Federal canteens haversacks oil clothes a few watches and some Federal monney," boasted one of his men.

Crews transported the wounded back to Secessionville, where the houses quickly became rude hospitals. Huddled near the rear of the fort were "50 or 60 Union men, all wounded but 10 or fifteen." Preacher John Girardeau of the 23rd South Carolina had made his way to the battlefield and was moving among the stricken Federals "offering up an earnest and eloquent prayer for their spiritual welfare." Included in this group was Michigander Benjamin Pease, the long-suffering private who earlier had exchanged pleasantries with Colonel Lamar. Examining Pease's head wound, Lamar touched his own ear and remarked, "You had about as close a call as I did." A surprised Pease scrutinized the bullet hole in the Confederate officer's ear and then listened as Lamar addressed the Federal prisoners. The colonel apologized for the limited care he could offer them—no doubt the Confederate medical corps had its hands full just then—but he promised to make the men "as comfortable as possible" by providing "plenty of water." As Lamar departed, Pease and the prisoners sat down to rest in a makeshift corral behind the battered Confederate fort.[43]

Lamar eventually made his way to the Secessionville wharf, where crews were loading the Confederate wounded aboard a small steamer. With reinforcements at hand and a proper complement of officers present, the wounded colonel finally overcame his reluctance to leave his post and decided to proceed to Charleston for medical treatment. Once aboard the tug, Lamar found Capt. T. Y. Simons and some men from the Charleston Battalion guarding a motley group of Federal prisoners headed for the Charleston jail. By noon the boarding was completed and the overloaded tug, its interesting mix of passengers crammed about her decks, made for the pier near Fort Johnson.[44]

John Batchellor, the Rhode Islander captured in the thicket fronting the Eutaw Battalion, was another captured Federal who had his own unique experience with the Confederate brass. He had joined three of his comrades and a number of captured Hampshiremen who were trudging past the Rebel defenses towards Fort Johnson and Charleston Harbor. When they reached the waterline, the group was approached by "Shanks" Evans, who picked Batchellor out for an interrogation. "I knew just then but very little," Batchellor slyly recalled, leaving Evans more than a bit frustrated. After Evans departed, the Unionists sat about until the early afternoon, when a tugboat steaming from the direction of Secessionville pulled up to a nearby wharf. The Northerners were prodded aboard by their guards. Once on board, they were met by an officer identified as Thomas Lamar—"a large man and a rank rebel," claimed one of the captured Federals, "shot in the cheek and a part of his ear gone; and he swore at us, calling us all dear names known to men in our places."

Evidently the boat ride with his wounded comrades had soured Lamar's disposition, so the wounded Confederate had few kind words for the captured Rhode Islanders. Batchellor and the Northerners found some slight space on the crowded deck as the tug shoved off and headed for Charleston.[45]

* * *

Major General John C. Pemberton spent the morning at his headquarters in Charleston, monitoring the battle through dispatches from the field. By noon, he had made his way to Brig. Gen. Gist's headquarters, where "Shanks" Evans joined them. The three officers immediately departed for the front to see firsthand the results of the battle. Crossing the same causeway that had taken the 4th Louisiana Battalion to the peninsula, the trio found the typical post-battle chaos surrounding the houses of Secessionville. Turning west, they rode past a corralled group of Northern prisoners and into the Tower Battery. The ample evidence of the battle's ferocity was everywhere and Evans quickly moved to improve the defenses. Goodlette had already arrived with the 22nd South Carolina, but a concerned Evans could only find 150 men from the fort's garrison ready to stand to their posts. He ordered Colonel Peyton Colquitt's 46th Georgia Infantry to immediately bolster the garrison, and then went on with other pressing duties.[46]

If Pemberton had any doubts as to the battle's intensity, he needed only to view the parade of Confederate wounded filling up the houses in the village. A brief look out over the parapet at the lifeless forms of the enemy would also have confirmed the battle's ferocity. At Secessionville, the doctor of the 1st South Carolina Artillery surgeon, Dr. Robert Lebby, together with his wife, joined John Safford Stoney from Hagood's regiment in attending to the long line of wounded quickly filling the abandoned homes. In front of the fort, perhaps 100 feet from the wall, Confederate burial parties were digging a large pit to serve as a burial ditch for the dead Federals. It would have to be large indeed.[47]

* * *

While the defenders of James Island swelled with pride in their victory, the Federal camps along the Stono filled with rancor and recrimination. The enlisted men, so confident of the righteousness of their cause, so emboldened by their string of victories, exploded in anger at what they regarded as incompetence on the part of their leaders—especially Henry Benham. As the wounded were warehoused "in a large barn or old cotton house near the Stono," as one described their pathetic surroundings, many soldiers began questioning the "poorly managed" affair, wondering why the forces were "put in 'small lots' at intervals," and why the reserves weren't used. Roundhead Private Slemmons placed the blame for the failure of the 100th Pennsylvania's attack on exhaustion: "(T)hey had double quicked us so far that we were tired out before we got up." A Connecticut gunner went so far to wish that "Old Benham should have been the first killed," while another prayed that "our troops will not be led into any more blunders."[48]

While most of the seething Northerners returned to their camps by 11:00 a.m., elements of the 79th New York formed what was described as "a strong picket line with heavy reserves," in case the Confederates showed any aggressiveness. They need not have bothered. The only troops approaching the lines were Federal stragglers. A procession of bedraggled Unionists trudged across the island trying to locate their winnowed commands. Many of the survivors huddled around their campsites to review the disastrous events of the morning, while others simply fell into an exhausted slumber. Tomorrow the letters would be written, the reports would be penned. Today, burial squads placed the dead in a line along the banks of the Stono River.[49]

Isaac Stevens preliminary report reflected the striking toll of the assault. Colonel Rudolph Rosa's 46th New York, 474 strong at the battle's outset, suffered one officer and five men killed, two officers and 16 men wounded, one man taken prisoner, and nine missing, a total of 33 men. The 100th Pennsylvania Roundheads, who numbered about 400 effectives that morning, lost 48, including one officer and eight men dead, two officers and 31 men wounded, one prisoner and six missing. The 79th New York Highlanders suffered significant losses, recording one officer and eight men dead, five officers and 62 men wounded, with 34 captured or missing. The Irish 28th Massachusetts lost eight infantry killed on the field, two officers and 48 men wounded, and one officer and eight men captured, while six privates were missing. The 7th Connecticut lost two officers and seven men dead, with one officer and 68 men wounded, four captured and three missing. Two Massachusetts cavalrymen and one engineer were wounded, while one member of the 3rd Rhode Island Heavy Artillery "detailed for duty at the battery in advance of the First Brigade" was killed.[50]

For the 8th Michigan, June 16, 1862, would be the defining day in the regiment's history. Lieutenant Colonel Frank Graves reported one officer and 35 men missing. Another 34, including Company B's Capt. Gilbert Pratt, had been captured. Eleven had died on the field, while 93 lay wounded. The officer corps was hit particularly hard, with Captains Guild and Church dead and eight others wounded. When the missing and presumed dead were included, 12 of the 8th's 22 officers fell in the line of duty at Secessionville. The 8th Michigan's losses totaled 184 of the 534 who marched out of camp that morning; one in three Michiganders were struck down before the Tower Battery. In later years, in honor of their fallen comrades, the survivors of the 8th Michigan would hold their regimental reunions on the 16th of June.[51]

* * *

A large crowd gathered at the Charleston wharf on the afternoon of the 16th to meet a tugboat bearing news of the morning battle that was waged just five miles away. Making a line from Fort Johnson, the tug docked around 2:00 p.m. Soon, a group of bedraggled Federals filed off the boat, greeted by "shouts and the use of hard names," remembered one. The Confederate guards moved forward to control the rowdy civilians, such was the passion of the moment. One not particularly charitable Charlestonian counted 30 prisoners and noted "Nearly all of them have the appearance of veritable cut-throats, and they are, evidently, the scum of the communities from which they were recruited." Someone recognized one captured Federal as Napoleon Mayo, an entertainer who had appeared in Charleston as a member of "Matt Peel's strolling Negro troupe." With catcalls echoing in their ears, the Northerners marched down East Bay to Broad Street where they entered the Guard House to spend their first night in captivity.[52]

Outside along every street in the city, news of the great victory at Secessionville spread like wildfire, and jubilant citizens celebrated the deliverance of their city from the Federal horde. Rumors tempered the celebrations. With so many neighbors and statesmen serving along the defensive lines on James Island, most civilians soon realized that there would be a price for the victory. For now, they could only wait and hope; the casualty lists would follow.

Back at the fort, Union prisoners made the best of their new surroundings. Benjamin Pease remained with the captured Federals until the evening. As darkness approached, the Michigander helped carry some of his wounded comrades back to the hamlet of Secessionville, where they were lodged in one of the abandoned mansions. Despite the "almost universally" kind treatment afforded the wounded Federals, "(Q)uite a number of them died during the night and some of them during the following night," The Secessionville battle would continue to claim its victims long after the guns fell silent.[53]

* * *

Most of the Union troops were too spent to record their thoughts immediately, but within a few hours, one Northerner fought off his exhaustion to write a letter to his wife. The Highlanders' flag bearer, Alexander Campbell, began, "I am all safe...we are very tired," then went on to describe in some detail his role in the battle. In mid-letter he revealed a startling bit of news: "Brither James was in the fort." Campbell spoke of a wounded Confederate who told him that his brother was a lieutenant in the Union Light Infantry of the Charleston Battalion, a unit that had fought on the fort's right flank. Campbell concluded, "(P)erhaps he is Killed for our guns shelled them terrebly," but he determined to find out his brother's fate. Another member of the Highlander color guard, William Todd, took time to write a lengthy description of the battle to his parents. In the midst of his surprisingly accurate narrative, he tellingly revealed a rumor circulating thoughout the Federal camps, that "there was much talk of disability displayed by (Benham) all through the action."[54]

Before long, the officers whose duty demanded an official explanation began to write their reports. Colonels Chatfield and Welsh outlined their respective brigades' movements. Joseph Hawley described the 7th Connecticut's trials, and Frank Graves wrote of the 8th Michigan's actions.

Somewhere near Grimball's, Henry Benham sat down to try to make some sense out of his badly mangled plans. In words obviously intended to mask the appalling extent of his losses, Benham reminded General Hunter that the Confederate battery before

Secessionville had daily threatened the security of the Federal camps and needed to be silenced. Therefore, he had ordered a reconnaissance with the hopes of taking the fort, if possible. After the initial assaults ground down before the Confederate musketry and artillery, he explained, and the infantry ceased to make any "marked impression on the fort," Benham had ordered the withdrawal to avoid "a useless sacrifice of life." It was a creative bit of reporting. Nonetheless, he believed that "the main object of the reconnaissance was accomplished in ascertaining the nature of the fort" and the surrounding area. He highly complimented his commanders, both Wright and Williams, and noted the "cool courage" of Isaac Stevens—but was forced to admit that the casualties "are quite serious as to number and character." Benham cast those figures in a decidedly favorable light by writing that he expected half of the 150 missing to return to camp.

It was quite a performance. In nine paragraphs he managed to blur both the scale of Monday's action and the extent of his losses—to say nothing of the crushed morale of his command. Perhaps he thought that this would end the affair, these few, short paragraphs. Perhaps Hunter would return, the siege would continue, and the Battle of Secessionville would be soon forgotten. Whether Benham would be permitted to avoid the consequences of his actions would be another matter.[55]

As for Isaac Stevens, word spread that night that he "cryed like a child."[56]

CHAPTER TEN

"General Benham...calls it a reconnaissance in force: but if it was a reconnaissance, I would like to know what a battle is."

—Private 7th Connecticut Infantry

After Action

Tuesday
June 17, 1862

The dawn was barely able to light the stormy sky. Rain fell fitfully. Federal pickets manning the outposts near the Rivers Causeway squinted at the murky outlines of the distant Rebel defenses. Further west, pacing sentries shuffled through muddy camp streets where men gathered around smoky fires to brew coffee and munch hardtack. Some watched as their officers picked through piles of personal belongings now neither claimed nor needed. Others cleaned their guns and inspected their gear while burial parties and medical details trudged past in pursuit of their unfinished duties. Orderlies bore the wounded from rude shelters onto the waiting transports lying in the Stono River.

Everywhere along the tent rows, the Federals attempted to make sense of Monday's debacle. Some were simply grief-stricken, like the chaplain of the 3rd New Hampshire who wrote, "The day has been spent in caring for the wounded and dying. I have done all I could. My heart is sick. The day has been stormy and sad." For the most part, however, anger ruled the hour, especially among the ranks of the 8th Michigan. Having lost one in three comrades for no apparent reason, they lashed out at the brass that had ordered the assault. Wrote one Michigander,

> We are before a Gibraltar underground, a Manassas, inaccessible, unassailable, except at the point of one hundred thousand bayonets, and the expense of fifty thousand lives. Yet General Benham ordered these batteries to be taken at the point of the bayonet!"....But woe unto us. Look! Where is the nine hundred now? Five or six hundred are crippled or sleep beneath the soil of the South...Three hundred are left to be sacrificed on the altar of our country.

Company A's Lt. George Turner feared that "The Michigan Eighth may be said to be no more." One Connecticut survivor perceptively wondered why "Benham did not ascertain their (the Confederate's) strength first and if finding a weak spot did not use some stratagem." Angrily, he concluded that the Northerners did "just what they (Sesesh) wanted." Others composed letters out of a deeper sense of duty. Private Elmer Packard of the 8th Michigan had promised his comrade from Company C, Pvt. Clarkson Burgess, that he would contact Burgess' parents if anything happened to their son. While nursing a foot wound, Packard took up the pen and wrote to his friend's father: "Dear sir as it seems to be my fortune to write to you of the fate of your Clarkson ... about two rod from the fort they poured a most terribel shower of grape and canister and rifle balls a great many of the boys fell Clarkson with the best..."[1]

The weather matched the mood in camp. One Roundhead wrote, "It has rained all day & everything is mudy and very disagreeable." And while one New Yorker decried the "horrible conditions" of camp life, another looked angrily past the rain and the mud. Lieutenant William Lusk of Isaac Stevens' staff composed a letter to his mother that stated in no uncertain terms his feelings about Monday's events. He began, "Yesterday was a hard, cruel, memorable day, memorable for its folly and wickedness, memorable for the wanton sacrifice of human life to gratify the silly vanity of a man..." He characterized Henry Benham's orders to advance a "direct defiance of his subordinate Generals' opinion," an attack conceived "in utter folly." Lusk ripped Benham, claiming that the general had sacrificed the men's lives not for some strategic good, but in hopes of becoming a major general. ". . .W]hen I see their pale fingers stiffened, their poor speechless wounds bleeding, do you wonder at the indignation that refuses to be smothered. . .that the country which our soldiers love so well, loves them so little as to leave them to the mercies of a man of blasted reputation, to a weak, vacillating cowardly infamous knave." He signed the harsh letter before going about his business of collecting documentation for Isaac Stevens' official report.[2]

Stevens himself was preoccupied with the fallout from Monday's loss. Of primary concern were the Federal dead abandoned on the battlefield, so Stevens arranged for a flag of truce to enable his men to complete the burials. He assigned Lieutenant Holbrook of his staff to oversee this effort, and soon the Northerners were working within hailing distance of the enemy. Although things went smoothly, shock could still visit the battlefield. In the course of handling one Confederate corpse, some Hampshiremen recoiled when the "corpse came to life." Despite his terrible wound, the Southerner was transferred to the Federal hospital on the Stono.[3]

* * *

The mood was an altogether different one across the harbor, where the *Charleston Mercury* trumpeted the glory of the victory at Secessionville:

> (T)he ancient fame of Carolina (is) once more vindicated on a bloody field. . .It was the old story of patrician against proletarian. . .And once more, blood had told, and the insolent invader has been scourged back, beaten and crowding, under the aegis of his protecting floating batteries.[4]

Surprisingly, the reporter went on to admit that, "The foe, it is true, displayed admirable courage," and cited "the famous Highland Regiment, the 79th New York," for its role in the charge. Between the *Mercury* and the *Courier*, the details of the battle began to emerge, although these early reports suffered from myriad inaccuracies. One rumor claimed that the "Scotchmen. . .[were]

[m]adly intoxicated. They had poured out whiskey for them like water." But the casualty lists revealed the true intensity of the fight better than any reporter's loftily-turned phrases. Throughout the day, the *Fort Clinch* and the *Etiwan* ferried Confederate wounded from the front to the Charleston wharf. Elation turned to grief as the citizens of the city began to feel directly the sting of war's hard hand.5

One man who seemed oddly removed from the battle's aftermath was John Pemberton. The commander of Charleston issued a short communiqué congratulating all "whose happy fortune it was to participate in the glorious work of Monday. . ." Both Lamar and "the noble dead" came in for special thanks, but, considering the circumstances, the document was downright paltry. Pemberton's strategy had proved prescient, and the defensive works he helped design stood the test—although ultimate credit for the Tower Battery's success certainly rested with Col. Lewis Hatch. After all the internecine squabbling, this was Pemberton's chance to gloat, but for now he decided to hold his hand.6

On this day, some of the wounded defenders of the Tower Battery managed to get word to their worried families. From a Charleston hospital, Edward Smith Tennent of the Charleston Battalion's Company C wrote his wife, "On Monday morning early they attempted to take our battery by storm, when we repulsed them with great slaughter, three times they rushed upon us, and at one time actually made a lodgment in our battery but we drove him back at the point of the bayonet."7

Lieutenant Colonel Ellison Capers wrote his wife a detailing of the fight, but much of his commentary concerned the behavior of his commander. He acidly noted, "Genl. Evans is a coward with a reputation for bravery which he has earned by sending his men and officers where he never dreams of going. He keeps himself out of range and gets away from fire whenever by chance he gets in it. He is reckless, without any judgement & terribly pompose & drinks to excess." Both Pemberton and William Duncan Smith came in for tough words as well, although States Rights Gist escaped with a begrudging compliment. The victory had failed badly to assuage Capers' growing disgust with his superiors.8

There was no time out on the front lines for such thinking. A soldier might share some prideful moments with his comrades, but vigilance was still required as the Eutaw Battalion drew picket duty. One roving unit pushed down the Battery Island Road to find the charred ruins of the Rivers House. Here, the Confederates came upon a gruesome scene, described by one Southerner as "many of the enemy's unseplechured dead." Burying these unfortunates kept these Confederates busy, but one member of the battalion rejoiced, "The enemy were perfectly quiet all day."[9]

* * *

Private Benjamin Pease returned with a Confederate officer to the Secessionville mansion-turned-hospital to identify those members of the 8th Michigan that had died there during the night. Entering the first room, Pease found Pvt. Edward Dart, one of the wounded Michiganders he had helped relocate the night before. "His leg had just been amputated," Pease recalled, and "He lay on the floor with nothing but a blanket under him and a pile of legs and arms in the corner of the room opposite him. His face looked very pale and haggard. . . ." Moving on, Pease found many more of his comrades in similar straits.[10]

Early that rainy afternoon, Pease joined a group of prisoners that left Secessionville to march off for Charleston and captivity. Sometime after midnight, he and his comrades crowded into a cell in the Charleston police station. For now, their war was over.[11]

* * *

Most of the after-action reports had arrived at Isaac Stevens' headquarters by day's end. In completing his, Col. William Fenton of the 8th Michigan made a special effort to be kind to Lt. Col. McLelland Moore and his 28th Massachusetts. The Irish officer had been reinstated to command of the regiment, much to George Cartwright's disgust, and he could only manage a one paragraph-three sentence description of his role in the fight. Not surprisingly, Horatio Wright's relief of Moore in mid-battle didn't find its way into Moore's report. In fact, Moore's skimpy paragraphs covered very little of his regiment's fiery trial. On the other hand, Col. Daniel Leasure furnished an extensive brigade report based on both his subordinates' detailings and the colonel's own experiences before the walls of the Tower Battery.

By that evening, with his subordinates' papers in hand, Isaac Stevens readied his official return on the Battle of Secessionville, little realizing that as one fight ended, another was about to begin.[12]

* * *

In the makeshift Federal hospital, the 7th Connecticut's Andrews Hibbard, the soldier borne from the battlefield on the back of Thomas Elliot, bled to death.[13]

* * *

In one of Charleston's crowded hospitals, Capt. Henry King of the Charleston Battalion's Sumter Guard died of his wounds.[14]

Wednesday
June 18, 1862

Almost out of habit, John Pemberton busied himself with another high level reorganization of the forces on James Island. He placed William Duncan Smith in overall command of the island, while States Rights Gist was placed in charge of the lines southeast of James Island Creek, and Col. Johnson Hagood in command of those defensive positions to the northwest. Worried as he was over a renewed enemy offensive, Pemberton also dispatched a request to Richmond for more artillerists to replace those lost in Monday's battle. But the rainy weather seemed to dampen any Federal martial ardor. Only one slight confrontation between the opposing pickets marred an otherwise quiet day in no-man's-land.[15]

* * *

Brigadier General Henry Benham's request for a truce to exchange prisoner lists and complete the burying of the dead was granted by the Southern command. Federal burial parties cautiously advanced past their perimeter and soon made contact with their Southern counterparts. Suddenly, if only for a few short moments, the bitter enemies became fast friends. The Federals probably learned here that the Rebels had buried a large number of Northerners in a common trench somewhere near the front of the fort. In the course of the fraternizing, one Confederate passed a letter to a Unionist to deliver to the flag bearer of the 79th New York. The Unionist agreed and continued on with his work. Suddenly, a deep report echoed across the island, followed by a screaming naval shell that buried itself near the Confederate pickets. A furious Col. Spartan Goodlett, who was supervising the truce, boldly rode up to the Union pickets and demanded an explanation. Within seconds, a chastened Federal aide arrived to explain to the fuming Goodlett that the navy had been unaware of the truce. Apologies were accepted, and Goodlett returned to his men.

The burials continued.[16]

* * *

Later that day, Highlander Alexander Campbell was handed the note which had crossed the picket lines during the truce. Campbell opened the letter. The handwriting belonged to Alexander's brother James. "I was astonished to hear from the prisoners that you was the color Bearer of the Regmt that assaulted the Battery at this point the other day," wrote the Confederate Campbell. He spoke of searching for his brother on the battlefield after the fight, and noted that, "I was in the Brest work during the whole engagement doing my Best to Beat you, but I hope that You and I will never again meet face to face Bitter enemies in the battlefield." But realizing that was still a possibility, however remote, James Campbell went on to explain that if they should meet, "You have but to discharge your deauty to your caus for I can assure you I will strive to discharge my deauty to my country & My cause." James commiserated with his brother on "the slaughter terrable," but assured him that most of the wounded Federals were getting along fine. "(P)lease Let Sister Ann know that I am still alive," he asked, and finished by signing the note, 'I am Your Brother James Campbell." By the time Alexander received and read his brother's letter, the flag of truce had expired, making further communication impossible. Instead, Alexander was left with James' handwriting on a piece of paper that spoke volumes on the "brothers' war."[17]

* * *

The following day, a Federal steamer left the Stono bound for Hilton Head. Included on board was a packet containing Henry Benham's report on what he described as Monday's "reconnaissance." From all accounts, he seemed fearless of the consequences of his actions and remained unaware that repercussions must surely follow. Meanwhile, he made Col. Edward Serrell chief engineer of the James Island operation, then took a moment to publish a congratulatory order for his troops, a somewhat ludicrous attempt to bolster the stricken morale of his brigades. Not to rival "Veni, Vidi, Vici," Benham announced, "We need only to say in conclusion what we all feel: We have met, we have examined the works of the enemy, and they shall be ours."

To assume that Benham truly believed that his launching of 6,000 troops at fortified earthworks constituted a reconnaissance-in-force strains credulity. Whatever his thinking, his report, like a torched fuse crackling towards a powder keg, snaked towards army headquarters at Hilton Head.[18]

Meanwhile, Horatio Wright completed his report of Monday's action and submitted it to Benham. Wright's casualties were not as heavy as Isaac Stevens', but the numbers were still notable. In its brief stay north of the battery, the 3rd New Hampshire lost 104 men—one officer and eight enlisted men killed, five officers and 88 men wounded, and two men captured. The 3rd Rhode Island Heavy Artillery lost 45 of its number: one officer and seven men killed, one officer and 28 men wounded, and eight men captured. The 97th Pennsylvania reported lighter losses, just two men wounded with one man captured, while the 45th Pennsylvania tallied but one man wounded. While Wright concluded the grim mathematics, the *Ben Deford* continued to rest in the Stono. Federal medical orderlies had spent most of the day gingerly loading the wounded aboard for transfer to the hospitals at Hilton Head. By dusk over 200 wounded soldiers had been placed on her decks and in her holds, but she was held overnight waiting for more.[19]

* * *

General David Hunter left James Island on June 12 and had remained at Hilton Head since. There was some risk of impropriety with his headquartering so far from the scene of action, but his orders to Benham had been unequivocal. He could naturally assume that nothing untoward would occur in his absence. Unfortunately, Hunter's wife happened to be visiting Hilton Head at the same time, and whispers dogged Hunter's extended visit. On the evening of the 15th—the same evening Benham ordered up the James Island divisions for battle—the general and Mrs. Hunter joined Flag Officer Du Pont for a showy dinner aboard the *Wabash*, replete with sideboys and a choir. Du Pont found the couple "highly interested and gratified," but he also saw a puzzling side to Hunter. The festivities were interrupted when a message from Washington ordered Hunter to detach the 1st Massachusetts Cavalry and an unnamed infantry regiment for service in Virginia. Watching Hunter's reaction, Du Pont noted that "The General was much put out and said he would withdraw all the troops from James Island." Although the orders were quickly countermanded, Du Pont duly noted the variability of Hunter's "military course."[20]

On June 17—the day after Henry Benham's "reconnaissance" at Secessionville—Hunter dispatched a testy message to Secretary of War Edwin Stanton. First, Hunter complained that his expedition had been hamstrung by lack of "marine transportation," which prevented ready access to all his scattered posts. Second, he ruminated over the lack of attention to his requests "for straw or light felt hats," and fresh tenting, which had left his command gutted by health problems.

The general had also sent another undated letter that supposedly reached Washington on the 17th, a dispatch prescient in its fears and ominous in tone. Hunter flatly claimed that he would have occupied Charleston already had he been properly supported and added the following disclaimer: "I deem it a duty I owe to frankly state. . .that reverses may not be attributable to me." It was almost as though Hunter had foreseen the disaster at Secessionville and was now craftily covering his tracks—an ability he would sharpen during the course of the war. He ended the letter by disingenuously requesting more troops for his final push on Charleston, evidently unaware that the setback had already occurred.[21]

Benham's report on the Battle of Secessionville arrived on a transport the evening of June 18, and was immediately delivered to Hunter.[22]

Thursday
June 19, 1862

Hunter spent the night mulling over his limited options, then awoke on the 19th to write up his directives. He gave a packet containing his orders to his nephew, Samuel Stockton, to deliver in person. Before departing, the young man proved talkative, and soon the news of the defeat on James Island had spread among the naval personnel and quickly reached the ears of Flag Officer Du Pont. He, in turn, summed up most of what he had heard for his wife: "It seems General Benham, with his usual chaotic way of doing things, ordered an advance of about 7000 men on Secessionville." Du Pont revealed some of the details of the battle, in particular the bravery of the 8th Michigan and the Highlanders, "a lawless set but plucky," and although their attacks were repulsed, their losses were evidently not great—only in retreat did the bulk of the casualties supposedly occur. Du Pont then revealed that "Hunter is indignant, has recalled Benham to this place, and I trust will send him home. I hear the other Generals blame him, particularly for ordering a retreat." He went on to add that, "A Massachusetts Irish regiment behaved badly." How much of his information was scuttlebutt and how much reflected official opinion is easy to estimate, for Hunter would do and say as much in the next few days. What was obvious amid all the talking was simple—the Battle of Secessionville had yet to end.[23]

The nephew and the packet steamed north to the Stono River.

* * *

Back on James Island, Major Pressley and the Eutaw Battalion stood picket duty that day and observed that "The enemy were perfectly quiet all day and night. Their drums, bands, and trumpets were distinctly heard." By nightfall, another "terrific" thunderstorm had doused the island, triggering a new wave of blood-thirsty mosquitoes. From all appearances, the Federals had lost, at least temporarily, all interest in capturing Charleston, but the Confederates labored to improve their earthworks—just in case the Federals changed their minds.[24]

* * *

Across the way, Union troops continued to wrestle with the aftermath of Monday's battle. Captain Ralph Ely tended to the 8th Michigan's casualties while "preparing to send them to Hilton Head Hospital." As he helped load his wounded comrades aboard the *Ben Deford*, Ely made "inventories of the effects of the dead and description lists of the wounded." Several Michiganders died during the loading process, but Ely still considered himself lucky, having suffered only two wounds, "one in the mouth and one on the leg, but slight." Most of his brother officers were either badly hurt, maimed, or dead. Nearby, Lt. Col. MacLelland Moore of the 28th Massachusetts wrote his state's adjutant general requesting 100 recruits to bolster his regiment's thinned ranks. "Please keep this communication as private as possible," the officer fretted, "as the General (Benham) does not wish it known we were defeated so badly."

Moore needn't have bothered. One of his own privates was just then describing Secessionville to the editor of the *Boston Herald* as a battle where "the rebels had nothing to do but shoot us down like dogs...." The reporter promptly published the Irishman's letter on the front page of his paper. Elsewhere, a member of the 7th Connecticut wrote to a friend, "We have just been gloriously repulsed...The Secesh threw everything from a 13 inch shell to a junk bottle. The way the bottles flew you would think they were going to treat you to champagne." He closed by wondering, "General Benham...calls it a reconnaissance in force: but if it was a reconnaissance, I would like to know what a battle is."[25]

* * *

The *Ben Deford* left for Hilton Head with 300 wounded "crowded above and between decks, where they were laid on their blankets on hay with their knapsacks under their heads," remembered one who traveled on the misery ship. Many, like the 8th Michigan's Philip Coleman, still remained in the large barn on the Stono—they would need to recuperate further before they could be moved. Somewhere in the Atlantic, as the *Ben Deford* plowed south through yet another summer storm, she passed the Federal vessel bearing Hunter's commands heading for the Stono River.26

* * *

Henry Benham spent much of the day shoring up his defenses. He ordered Horatio Wright to submit plans for improving the lines around Grimball's, and circulated an order prohibiting pickets from clearing their gun tubes by firing into the Stono. Wright quickly submitted a short overview prepared by engineering officer Colonel Serrell for combining the defenses of the two Federal camps, and he promised to review the Sol Legare lines to further coordinate the effort. Wright seemed prepared to fight it out on the James Island line, as he closed his report with a reference to "future operations in the reduction of the enemy's lines and batteries."27

An eerie quiet had descended on the camps, disturbed only by rumors that the troops would be stationed on James Island for quite a while. Wrote one Roundhead, "There will not likely be another advance made till the Fort is reduced by our gunboats and Seage Guns; which should (we think) have been done before we were cut up so." The assignment of Serrell as the new ordnance officer and the increased engineering activity served to support the camp talk, but, for the third day in a row, very little fighting occurred.28

Sometime that afternoon, a steamer arrived from Hilton Head, and "young" Stockton, as he was described, disembarked and sought out Henry Benham. Hunter's aide handed the general the packet containing Hunter's directives, and a stunned Benham soon learned that he had been relieved of his command for disobedience of "positive orders and clear instructions." He immediately ordered his assistant adjutant general, Capt. Alfred Ely, to make arrangements for both men to repair to Hilton Head. Meanwhile Stockton located Horatio Wright to inform him that he was now in command of the James Island forces. Chief among Hunter's directives for the new commander was this caution: "You will not attempt to advance toward Charleston or Fort Johnson." Soon, Wright was wrestling with his new duties, and Benham was heading south to attempt to repair damage already inflicted.[29]

Benham reached Hunter's headquarters that evening and quickly presented himself to his superior. The aggrieved commander spoke first. He made a verbal report of Monday's action, emphasizing that the movement had been a reconnaissance-in-force. David Hunter calmly looked on. When Benham finished, Hunter called for Benham's order book and read aloud the June 10 directive forbidding any attack on Charleston or Fort Johnson. Then Hunter applied the coup de grace, "General, I put you under arrest." Benham left the room crushed, his short career as an army commander in shambles.[30]

One of Horatio Wright's first actions as the new commander of the United States forces on James Island was the receipt of Isaac Stevens' official report of the Battle of Secessionville. After an extensive detailing of his brigades' movements and an equally generous distribution of praise, Stevens closed his report with a startling revelation:

> I desire in this official report to place on record my objections to these early morning attacks. They are justifiable, in my humble judgement, only under extraordinary circumstances... An attack at a more advanced period of the day I considered vastly preferable. These views I presented with all possible cogency and earnestness to General Benham on the evening of the 15th in stating my objections to his proposed attack. I must confess that the coolness and mobility of all the troops engaged on the 16th instant surprised me, and I cannot but believe, had proper use been made of the artillery guns from the Navy, and our own batteries, fixed and field; had the position been gradually approached and carefully examined and the attack made much later in the day, when our batteries had had their full effect—all of which you will recollect were strongly urged by me upon General Benham the evening of the conference—the result might have been very different.

Neither then nor anytime afterwards did Horatio Wright disagree with a single point in Isaac Stevens' report on the battle.[31]

Friday
June 20, 1862

Captain Alfred Ely boarded the *Wabash* early that morning and had a long meeting with Captain John Rodgers. No doubt coached by Benham, Ely attempted to implement his commander's strategy to assuage Hunter. He began by repeating Benham's argument that Monday's operation had been a reconnaissance but swiftly changed his tack. He cowardly impugned the courage of the men who made the assault, insinuating that the operation would have been a success had brave men stormed the Rebel works. Ely also listed a number of other reasons why the assaults failed: Stevens' attack was late; the rifles should have been loaded; Stevens' assault formations were faulty; Williams took the wrong road; and, Wright's troops fought with "no vigor, no dash."

Rodgers listened but offered the officer little real hope of assistance. He, like most naval officers, remembered his own difficulties with the petulant general and privately admitted that he would do nothing for the man. Rodgers did relent on one point. Having known Benham for several years, Rodgers agreed to meet with him, because Ely candidly admitted that protraction of this quarrel—especially after Benham's trouble with Rosecrans in western Virginia—could lead to the general's professional demise.[32]

Word of the Rodgers-Ely meeting reached Francis Du Pont. The extent to which Ely succeeded in making his case may be seen in Du Pont's letter to his wife, dated June 20. Du Pont recalled departed Brig. Gen. Thomas Sherman's observation that the Federals on James Island were "men that won't fight." He quoted Drayton's report—"the rebels were few in number"—and concluded that Ely's estimation of the Federal forces' fighting ability was correct. Du Pont further stated that Benham's subordinates didn't like the assault plans and "did not care to earn laurels for a man they do not like." Of course, the arrival of the 300 wounded may have given the Flag Officer some pause, for he confided to his wife that Hunter shouldn't be in charge, and that "These are times that make Sherman loom up...yet he had many faults too."[33]

On Hilton Head, Benham spent the morning composing an addendum describing his meeting with Hunter. He asserted that Hunter had approved his intention to "have and hold" the

Secessionville works in their final meeting on June 11, in order to ensure the security of the Federal camps. Why else would Hunter approve the construction of the battery at the eastern tip of Sol Legare Island? Benham viewed the Tower Battery as a clear danger to the Stono camps and regarded its capture a vital necessity. Then Benham lit a bonfire: "The orders of General Hunter I may say were made known to General Stevens and General Wright, and neither of them ever intimated or appeared to think that the reconnaissance upon the fort upon the 16th would be contrary to those orders." Benham ended by citing the weakness of the enemy works—"The fort was only a common earthwork"—and by reiterating the necessity of the attack. The implication of his final point—"I did not doubt that 2,000 men would have amply sufficed" for the attack—was clear: had brave men assaulted the Tower Battery on the morning of June 16, success would have been assured.[34]

Later that day, Captain Rodgers went ashore to meet with his old acquaintance. He found him "crushed but calm." Benham worried about his previous quarrel with Du Pont, but Rodgers assured him that the commodore sympathized with him in his misfortune. That was the extent of what the navy was willing to offer.[35]

* * *

On Sol Legare Island, Col. William Fenton, commander of Isaac Stevens' 1st Brigade, petitioned Stevens to relieve him of brigade duty and allow him to return to his Michigan men, for he intended to resign from active duty. His reasons were simple: "The iron constitution I was blessed with up to our arrival at Hilton Head has given way, and for many months the duties I have done have been performed in violation of the laws of health." Of the 8th Michigan's recent ordeal, Fenton wrote almost tenderly, "I greatly fear as a Regt it can not again do itself justice in battle, for the gallant officers and men slain and disabled on the battlefield were of its truest and best." If Henry Benham had visited the 8th Michigan's camp this day, he would have found only 300 Michiganders answering roll call.[36]

The 79th New York received some welcome news this day. Their camp was to be relocated to Grimball's with access to dry ground and good water. Some of the Scotsmen visited a newly constructed, 120-foot high observatory, from which Charleston's famous church spires could be easily seen, as one climber noted "so near yet so far." But in yet another reminder of Monday's fight, James Kinnear, the 79th's badly wounded lieutenant, succumbed to his injuries and was buried "with military honors" in James Island's rapidly-expanding cemetery. Meanwhile, all was quiet along the lines.[37]

Horatio Wright acknowledged Hunter's orders and firmly stated his confidence in the army's ability to maintain itself south of Charleston, announcing that "We can hold on for a long time." Hunter had admonished the new commander to strongly fortify his positions, but he also warned Wright to "make all the necessary dispositions for abandoning James Island and John's Island" should all else fail. Wright desired to stay put, fearing that withdrawal would "be deemed by the enemy an indication of weakness on our part." But he did request that Hunter come to inspect the camps, perhaps hedging his bets against the very real possibility of a general withdrawal. Wright forwarded the orders announcing Hunter's changes to Isaac Stevens.[38]

When Stevens heard of the change in command, he immediately wrote his wife, "This is a great improvement. Benham not only ought to be arrested, but he ought to be struck from the. . .army for that affair."[39]

* * *

Across the bay, a newsman from the *Richmond Dispatch* spent the day filing a report on the operations around Charleston, a document betraying the widespread dissatisfaction with Pemberton's performance. The writer described Monday's battle as having little direction from the commanding general—"(T)he enemy's attack was a surprise to our troops. Had a competent Confederate General been on the field. . .the whole of the enemy's attacking force might have been cut off." Wishful thinking, perhaps, but the reporter was very near the mark when he wrote, "There is much dissatisfaction here with the military authorities of the department, and a strong wish expressed for a change." Despite this recounting of the petulant sniping between the civilian authorities and the army brass, the reporter gave due credit to the people who deserved it the most: "To the rank and file, then, be the glory given. . ."[40]

Saturday
June 21, 1862

From the pages of the *Charleston Mercury*, a voice describing himself as "A Son of the Soil" reminded Charleston of Col. Lewis Hatch's contribution to the victory at Secessionville:

> Whilst we are indulging in congratulations on the victory of Secessionville, it should not be forgotten that the erection of the work, which alone saved this important position, is due to Col. L. M. Hatch. Months ago, before anyone dreamed that the enemy could be allowed to come this far, he labored in putting up this battery. In spite of the ill-conceived sneers of many, and against the opinions of nearly everyone, he persevered and completed the work. It has cost him his regiment. It should obtain for him the gratitude of the state.[41]

A mid-1865 photo of the Secessionville peninsula taken from on top of the earthwork near the Secessionville wharf. The structures in the immediate foreground are either slave quarters or soldier's huts. Visible to the left is one of the remaining mansions of the original village. National Archives.

CHAPTER ELEVEN

"(We) behaved as well as could be expected under the circumstances."

—Officer, 28th Massachusetts Infantry

Exit

For the Federal soldiers assembled on James Island, the last days of June slipped by drearily. To pass the time, some of the engineers took to collecting and analyzing Confederate artillery projectiles, but most of the infantry simply sat and waited for something to happen. One rare exception to the drudgery occurred on Sunday June 22, when the Highlanders bestowed a gift sword upon an emotional Isaac Stevens. The general responded warmly that his ties to his former regiment would never be broken. During the same time, the 8th Michigan continued its slow recovery, and it wasn't until the 24th of the month, after a full day on the picket lines, that Capt. Ralph Ely could note that "the men are beginning to feel better." But the passing time couldn't heal all wounds. On the last day of the month, while making out the rolls, Ely tallied only 275 Michiganders present for duty, prompting him to write, "The Regiment looks very small."[1]

Since he now expected to remain on the island for some time, Horatio Wright went to work with great energy strengthening the defenses. A witness to the buildup counted emplacements for 27 guns along the lines with 13 cannon of various caliber already mounted. One detached work named Battery Wright covered the

Rivers Causeway from the nearby Grimball fields. Engineering officer Edward Serrell designed it to house nine heavy guns, including four 10-inch Columbiads. Overlooking the Rivers Causeway from Sol Legare Island was Battery Williams, an enclosed work designed for four guns. The earthwork built by the Highlanders near the eastern tip of Sol Legare Island had been materially strengthened with new platforms, extensive revetting, and the construction of a pivot gun. In honor of the division commander, the work was christened Battery Stevens. Mortar emplacements flanked both Battery Wright and Williams, and construction of an infantry parapet linking these batteries with the Grimball works had begun. This massive buildup hardly went unnoticed. Reacting to the Federal expansion, a strengthened Tower Battery broke the ten day calm with a bombardment on June 27, with the Confederates' first shot killing a member of a Highlander work party. The picket fire increased in the wake of the renewed artillery fire, and both sides began to take casualties. Neither Federal nor Confederate realized that these exchanges would mark the end of the James Island campaign.[2]

Despite his earlier bravado, David Hunter had warned the War Department about the possible failure of the James Island campaign. He had begun to claim that his command was too small to successfully attack Charleston, and he questioned Benham's eagerness to launch the assault. Having laid this groundwork, Hunter informed Washington of the June 16 battle and Benham's subsequent removal in a report dated June 23. In the report, he meekly voiced hope that reinforcements could be sent to help bolster his Stono River operations. The War Department was preoccupied with McClellan's daunting troubles before Richmond, and word came that no reinforcements would be available for the Southern Expedition. This information provided Hunter his out. He distributed general orders on the 27th, announcing that James Island would be abandoned and the forces there would return to Hilton Head, Port Royal or Edisto Island. Hunter cautioned Wright to take sufficient time to retrieve all stores and equipage. On the 29th, Wright replied that the evacuation would begin immediately.[3]

The naval officers that had worked so diligently to make the army's invasion of James Island a success exploded in rage at word of the withdrawal. Although Du Pont refrained from being openly critical of Hunter's decision, Captains John Rodgers and Percival

Drayton did little to mask their own disappointment. Rodgers reported to Du Pont that the now hopeful Drayton was "in a state of loud disgust at the abandonment of James Island," and felt compelled to ask the generals "when Pulaski or Fernandina are to be given up!" Du Pont would only observe that the James Island invasion was "the finest operation...in its promise of results" since the flag officer himself had taken Port Royal. Now, the navy's only interest was to save face—hardly a concern that could have been foreseen but a month before.[4]

Federal army officers were barely less angry than their naval counterparts. Edward Serrell's outworks were literally hours from completion when the abandonment of James Island was ordered. Serrell complained, "It is to be regretted...that these works could not have been completed. We should within two or three days have had from four to five times the weight of metal in position that was possessed by the enemy opposed to us." Isaac Stevens was so vehement in his protestations that his outburst was noted by Commodore Du Pont all the way down at Hilton Head. Robert Gould Shaw, a young Federal officer stationed in Virginia with the 2nd Massachusetts, received a letter from a Secessionville veteran "boiling with rage at having to retire from before Charleston." To the writer, the problem was simple enough: "Benham, after having got himself foolishly into a scrape, didn't have courage enough to carry the thing through." Shaw's friend concluded with an indictment of all the West Pointers on James Island: "We are dying of the regular army."[5]

Of course, the Confederates had no way of knowing Hunter's decision. For them, the arrival of Federal transports on June 29 simply meant that enemy reinforcements were arriving. Most of the Island's defenders agreed with Sgt. S. M. Crawford of the 22nd South Carolina: "we are expecting a fite every day here but I cant tell when it will be attall we have a strong brest work to fite from." One Louisianan wandered over the fields around the Tower Battery and found still-fresh scars of the battle: "Houses were riddled trees were cut to pieces and the ground tore up in all directions." But even with the policing efforts both sides made after the Secessionville fight, the battlefield could still be a shocking place, as Lt. Col. Charles Simonton and Rev. A. Toomer Porter discovered for themselves. On the 26th, in the underbrush fronting the Eutaw

Battalion's position, they found "4 or 5" Federal corpses, and one in particular was sadly memorable:

> One poor fellow who had evidently been wounded, had crawled to the edge of the bushes, & there taken off his clothes, viz: pants, coat & shoes, & laid them by his side, then folded his hands across his breast & died. Poor fellow, had he been attended to & had food, he might have lived. He must have heard horrible stories of having his clothes torn off him after death, & wished not to have his body disturbed.——Awful![6]

* * *

Though the Southerners continued to stand to, the Unionists spent the last days of June shipping out the cavalry and the remaining wounded. By July 1, Northern troops began embarking on transports that would take them away from the scene of their defeat. Not everything went smoothly, and Horatio Wright was "very much embarrassed" by his woeful lack of transportation. Many of the transports were still at Hilton Head, and rough weather precluded the use of the massive *Vanderbilt*. Worse yet, a number of his available smaller vessels had broken down under their increased loads. Nevertheless, Wright diligently went ahead with the operation. The 3rd New Hampshire boarded the *Cosmopolitan* and steamed away on July 2, arriving at Hilton Head before dark. The bulk of Wright's old division soon followed, and by the 3rd, quaker guns (shaped and painted tree trunks made to look like artillery) fronted the abandoned camps at Grimball's plantation.

Stevens' troops started their evacuation on July 4, accompanied by the firing of national salutes by Hamilton's artillery. The rain poured down, but the assembled flotilla broke out the pennants and the flags, moving one New Yorker to note,"(E)verything had the appearance of a gala day." The men of the 100th Pennsylvania and the 79th New York "tried hard to feel patriotic," but couldn't seem to summon the energy. One Highlander was particularly downcast. Alexander Campbell had just received word that his Confederate brother James had crossed no-man's-land the previous afternoon to inquire about Alexander's health—rumor had it that the 79th's flag bearer had been wounded in the battle on the 16th.

Unfortunately for both brothers, the Roundheads were on picket duty at the time, so Alexander didn't get word of the contact until it was too late. Once again, the war that had conspired to bring the brothers so close together also continued to keep them apart. With the 4th of July salutes echoing down the banks of the Stono, Alexander Campbell and the rest of the Highlanders rested aboard the *Delaware* while their band struck up "the popular air—'Ain't I glad to get out of the Wilderness.'"[7]

The 8th Michigan covered the withdrawal from Sol Legare Island and at 10:00 p.m. on the the nation's independence day started to pull their lines back towards the Stono, followed as one remembered, "within speaking distance" by the Southern pickets. "I conversed with them considerable during the day" recalled Capt. Ralph Ely, for "they were willing to talk." At 7:00 a.m. the next morning, the Michiganders joined the 46th New York and "four pieces of artillery"—probably Hamilton's Battery—aboard the *Cosmopolitan*. "(T)he weather very warm and the ship crowded and the sea rough," recorded one wind-tossed infantryman as the transports departed for Port Royal. On July 6, the *Ben Deford* carried the 28th Massachusetts and the bulk of the stores to Hilton Head, while Wright held the small beachhead on Battery Island with a skeleton force. Little was left to do. Wright ordered his remaining regiments, the 6th and 7th Connecticut, the 97th Pennsylvania, and at least one company of the 100th Pennsylvania, to destroy the Confederate fort on Battery Island. Then he herded them onto the waiting transports and directed the squadron south. By July 7, the Federals were gone from James Island.[8]

* * *

Despite the booming reports of the Federal artillery, the Southerners on James Island celebrated the 4th of July as a day of joy. For the previous few days, the Unionists had been abandoning their camps at Grimball's and disappearing onto the transports in the Stono River. Now, with the big Confederate guns blasting off their own salutes to Independence Day, the enemy front constricted, and the Confederates moved in as quickly as their enemy moved off. Occasionally the pickets from both sides conversed and laughed, with some Northerners actually bowing farewell to their opponents. A Federal cordon still protected Battery Island, but the 14 vessels lying in the Stono were obviously effecting an evacuation which was now nearly complete. One Confederate considered the irony of both sides celebrating "the glorous fourth of '76 when the North and the South stood as one. . .it is far different now. . ." But others had no use for such sentiment, with one Southern soldier sarcastically calling out after the departing Federals, "Joy be with them."[9]

On the following day, July 5, Confederate parties gingerly approached the abandoned enemy camps surrounding Grimball's. One group, led by Maj. William Duncan of the 1st South Carolina, narrowly missed being captured when they were surprised near the Rivers Causeway by a Federal patrol. Another group entered the camp perimeter and nosed curiously through the Federal refuse. Posted next to the road northeast of Grimball's were two signboards, one reading "7 1/2 miles to Charleston," and the other —"2 miles to Hell." A nearby gouge in the earth marked the former grave of 47th Georgia's Captain Williams, the officer who was killed in the June 10 fight and whose corpse was returned to his regiment two days later. In a now-abandoned earthwork, the Southerners found a signboard conveying a brave warning: "Farewell Secesh! We go but will soon come again."[10]

On July 8, Federal intentions were clear enough for one Southerner to write, "Enemy known to have altogether abandoned James Island, and our city to be safe for the present." By the following day, knots of soldiers from the Eutaw Battalion had pushed completely across Sol Legare Island. Meeting no enemy resistance, they established a forward post on Battery Island where, as they peered across the Stono River, they fully understood the import of the scene—the Federal advance on Charleston was indeed over.[11]

* * *

When Brig. Gen. Henry Benham boarded the *Ericsson* to steam north, he had little idea of the forces that were then arraying against him, but he would soon discover the depth of his former subordinates' resentment for his actions on James Island. David Hunter forwarded Benham's June 20 addendum to both Horatio Wright and Isaac Stevens for comment, and he didn't have to wait long for their reply. On June 22, Stevens erupted: "I repudiate the use he (Benham) attempts to make of my name... .I was utterly opposed to the attack on Secessionville on the morning of the 16th and so expressed myself unequivocally in conference. I also understood unequivocally that General Wright and Colonel Williams were opposed to it." Wright replied the same day in the same vein: "I fully endorse all that is said by General Stevens in his letter, and I repudiate as emphatically as he has done for himself any attempt to use my name as favoring the operations of the 16th instant."[12]

Hunter forwarded Benham's addendum, Hunter's own June 10 directives, and the Stevens/Wright memoranda to Washington on June 27. Rather transparently, Hunter added a request that the documents might be published, in order to set "this department right before the country," he explained. Although the evacuation of James Island dominated his efforts well into July, by the time his camps were reassembled near Beaufort and on Hilton Head, Stevens felt ready to continue the skirmish. He began by preparing a detailed report of Benham's June 15 council of war and submitted it as his official record of the proceedings.

According to Stevens, Benham began the meeting by requesting his subordinates' views on the advisability of an attack on the Tower Battery. General Wright proposed a series of questions to Stevens to better shape his own position. Wright first asked whether the Federal artillery bombardment had impaired the Confederate battery, to which Stevens answered, "Not in the least." Wright then wondered whether volunteer troops had ever successfully assaulted works as strong as those fronting Secessionville. Stevens replied, "I know of no such instance." In his final query, Wright asked whether anyone could expect a different result "from what it has invariably been heretofore?" Stevens' reply was to the point: "I have no reason to expect a different result," he answered firmly, for "(i)t is simply a bare possibility to take the work."

According to Stevens recollection, all three of Benham's subordinates, Colonel Williams included, agreed with this assessment. Stevens went on to describe his own plan for the attack: if one had to be made, it should occur later in the day so that the artillery might pulverize the position while the engineers survey the proper approaches. At this point, Wright interjected "that his (Benham's) orders were in fact orders to fight a battle," an unspoken inference to Hunter's orders forbidding an attack. Despite the unanimous opposition, Benham claimed Stevens, "overruled the objections and peremptorily ordered the attack to be made." His subordinates promised full cooperation, then the council broke up.[13]

Stevens addressed two additional points of contention. First, he updated the timetable of the assault, and thus his division formed at 2:00 a.m., reached the outer pickets at 3:30 a.m., launched the attack at 4:00 a.m. ("It was so dark that one man could not follow another except at very short intervals.") His division reached the fort at 4:30 a.m., and began reforming at the second hedge one-half hour later. These calculations changed the time of the arrival at the fort to one half hour earlier than the figure Stevens used in his original report.

His second contention was in response to statements that his regiments were not in supporting distance of each other. Stevens countered this criticism by simply describing the battle. If six regiments could form, press an attack, and reform while losing 500 men in 25 minutes, "there can be no doubt but they followed each other closely," he cogently argued. In fact, "So rapid and prompt were the operations of my division that I was hard at work reforming my troops before Williams' advance came in sight." He concluded his addendum with a telling jab at Henry Benham: "The fault is not in my orders or arrangements, but in having a fight there at all under the circumstances."[14]

Newspapers of the day routinely published official reports of the engagements then dominating the news. Inasmuch as these reports often contained the first relatively accurate descriptions of the battles, they were given great scrutiny by the civilian population. Up to this point, daily shifts of editorial opinion concerning the issue of Benham's culpability in the Secessionville Campaign were commonplace. One day a paper might exonerate him of all wrongdoing, while, on the next, another would find further fault with his conduct. Add to this the participation of a local regiment—the 79th New York—and suddenly New Yorkers found the Battle of Secessionville particularly fascinating.

Into this heated atmosphere the *New York Times* dropped the bombshell of Isaac Stevens' addendum. Unfortunately, as is often the case when the media imposes itself upon a story, the *Times* added a word to the report—an act of commission that tended to confuse the issue. Stevens had quoted Wright as telling Benham that his Secessionville orders "were, in fact, orders to fight a battle." The *Times* reported Wright's words as ". . .orders not to fight a battle," thereby implying that Hunter's instructions forbidding an attack had come up officially during the council. Suddenly it seemed as though Horatio Wright had reminded Benham that Hunter had specifically ordered that no fighting take place while he was at Hilton Head.[15]

It so happened that Benham was in New York badgering the assistant adjutant general of the army with requests for either a court of inquiry or a court-martial, when the *Times* published Stevens' addendum. When he read Stevens' version of events, Benham exploded with anger. He responded quickly with a letter to the newspaper dated July 16, in which he launched a heated defense of his actions in South Carolina. In Benham's mind, there was no council of war, merely a meeting to ensure what he labled a proper "concert of the action," for the decision to attack had already been made. As for the necessity of the attack, he first reiterated the security needs of the camps, then went on to state that the action was "fully sanctioned" by Hunter three times in writing. As for Stevens' actions on June 16, he would have been immediately arrested for disobedience of orders "but for my kindness."

Benham also dragged the navy into the drama by quoting Percival Drayton as remembering that none of the army officers present voiced disfavor of the proposed movement. Benham concluded his commentary by turning Wright's questions and Stevens' answers into support for his own position—that a night assault held the only possibility for success. Alluding to the *Times'* insertion of the offending word "not," Benham simply denied that Wright discussed Hunter's previous objections to the movement.[16]

Benham, despite having vented his anger in several different directions, was hardly finished. He next challenged Stevens' revised chronology, pinning the failure of the battle on Stevens' delay in launching the attack. Benham claimed that he had ordered the attack to begin 4:00 a.m., but that Stevens attacked at 5:00 a.m.— "Stevens' watch, if he looked at it, proved that to him," Benham sneeringly penned. He further buttressed his case, or so he believed, by selectively quoting from statements made by two other officers: the 79th New York's Lt. Col. David Morrison, who said that he needed but "40 more men" to take the position, and Capt. Richard Doyle of the 8th Michigan, who mentioned having "good light to aim."

Of course, Stevens couldn't have known what was happening at the front, for he was never "nearer than the second hedge, or over 800 yards from the fort," Benham wrote, perhaps insinuating something even worse than incompetence in the eyes of a soldier. Benham went on to quote Stevens' battlefield note that "the supports did not follow closely enough," to undermine Stevens' tactics in the assault. For Henry Benham, Isaac Stevens remained "the only person responsible for the slaughter there, and the loss of the key to the eventual attack on Charleston." With his case made, Benham entrusted the facts to what he called the "intelligent public" to decide who was in the right.[17]

Not surprisingly, Isaac Stevens felt compelled to reply, although his volley was somewhat subdued in light of the vehemence of his addendum and Benham's phony allegations. There were good reasons for the tenor of his response. His old mentor at the Coast Survey, Alexander Bache, had learned that the Lincoln Administration was aligning itself with Stevens on the issue, and Bache was privately advising Stevens to ignore Benham's fulminations. Furthermore, Horatio Wright had weighed in, assuring Stevens that both he and Col. Robert Williams "shall be ready to do justice to you." President Lincoln had decided to move some of Hunter's troops north, so a calm Isaac Stevens responded to Benham from Newport News, Virginia, where his division had transferred into Ambrose Burnside's Expedition—the future IX Corps.

Stevens began his reply by begging that the mistaken word "not" be removed from the earlier report. For the rest, he plainly stated that he could prove everything in both reports, and then quoted Benham's glowing tribute of his own ability and courage on June 16. The latter was his last official statement concerning the Secessionville controversy.[18]

Henry Benham went on to mount an extensive campaign to refute the various charges, but Lincoln, after reading Hunter's charges and meeting with Benham, was aleady convinced of who was at fault for the June 16 bloodletting. On August 7, 1862, upon the recommendations of newly-installed General-in-Chief Henry Halleck and Secretary of War Edwin Stanton, the president decided to revoke Benham's earlier promotion to brigadier general. An angry Lincoln went so far as to accuse Benham of lying to him about Halleck's role in the matter. Benham, however, was nothing if not persistent, and over the next six months the aggrieved officer repeated his version of the Secessionville assault to anyone who would listen—always stressing the points that Stevens was late and Williams was misdirected. Benham continued to infer a lack of courage on Stevens' part, a vicious tactic he quickly dropped when Isaac Stevens died—just after the crushing Federal defeat at Second Manassas and while at the head of his troops at Chantilly, VA—on September 2, 1862.

Eventually, however, it was Benham's political influence that salvaged his reputation. On January 26, 1863, after the intercession of four Northern governors, Judge Advocate General Holt ruled that Benham's attack on the Confederate earthwork was justified and that nothing in Hunter's June 10 directives prohibited it. Of course, with his primary accuser dead, Benham's restoration to the army became that much easier. On February 6, 1863, Lincoln reinstated Benham as a lieutenant colonel of engineers. In the coming months he rose to command the Engineering Brigade of the Army of the Potomac, and finished the war as a brevet brigadier general. Never again would the War Department entrust Henry Benham with a field command.[19]

In later years, Benham continued to blame Isaac Stevens for what he called "the only military movement ordered by me, not perfectly successful." In Benham's view, Stevens simply waited for daylight to assault the Tower Battery, "opposed as he was to a night attack," and thus ensured the failure of the operation by his delay. This spin accompanied other spurious assertions that Benham used to inflate his wartime accomplishments. He repeated the fatuous claim that he was "in personal command of all the troops engaged in the bombardment and capture of Fort Pulaski," brushing aside the efforts of Capt. Quincy Gillmore, the officer who had devised, designed and oversaw the operation. Benham also lied when he claimed that he was present in the trenches "as much or more so than Capt. Gillmore (the chief Engineer) himself." Indeed, so conspicuous was his supposed presence on Tybee

Island during the Federal bombardment that the Confederate gunners made him "the repeated object of their fire."[20]

Few soldiers who served with Henry Benham shared such a lofty opinion of the man. Stephen M. Weld served on Benham's staff during the Chancellorsville Campaign and remembered the engineer somewhat differently. When Benham was ordered by Maj. Gen. John Sedgwick to lay pontoon bridges across the Rappahannock River early in that campaign, Weld recalled that Benham became so drunk that he fell off his horse, "forming a disgusting sight altogether." Weld added, "General Benham's being drunk delayed the laying of the bridges for four hours; his mismanagement all but ruined the whole plan." The staff's mortification deepened when the drunk engineer, bleeding from a facial gash caused by his fall, accosted another general, John Reynolds. As expected, Benham remembered that night somewhat differently: "...not a life was lost, though some of the men were wounded, and my own horse was shot under me."

Despite his many shortcomings, Henry Benham survived the war and led the Engineering Brigade of the Army of the Potomac down Pennsylvania Avenue in the Grand Review—almost three years after he mishandled his troops on James Island.[21]

* * *

When they arrived at Newport News, Isaac Stevens' men were hooted as "the force that got licked down on James Island." The cat-calling ended six weeks later when Isaac Stevens was killed leading the Highlanders against Thomas J. "Stonewall" Jackson's Corps at Chantilly, Virginia. As a vicious summer storm broke over the battlefield, he had grasped the regimental colors and called "upon his old regiment: 'Highlanders! My Highlanders! Follow your General!'" Amid the pouring rain and blinding thunderclaps, the general willed the Scotsmen forward until a Confederate bullet ended Isaac Stevens' remarkable life. He had said that the war would bring him either glory or death, and despite Benham's efforts to sully his reputation, Stevens died widely respected. Lincoln certainly recognized his leadership qualities, and was considering placing him in command of the Federal Army of Virginia when word came of his death. The officers who served with him also held the general in high esteem. The Roundheads' colonel, Daniel Leasure, wrote of Isaac Stevens almost 25 years later, "General Stevens and I had not been very good friends till after the battle on James Island, after which I never had a more ardent friend, nor one whose ability I had more implicit confidence. He was a man of many resources. . .and of indomitable personal courage." General Philip Kearny, the one-armed dynamo who also fell at Chantilly with Stevens, may have put it best: "By——! I'll support Stevens anywhere!"[22]

But the men who had fought under Stevens seemed to capture best the nature of the respect that the diminutive leader generated. For three years, David Morrison watched the rigors of war turn the Highlander colors into "but a rag." In September of 1864, when the majority of the men of the 79th New York mustered out of the regiment, Morrison and the Highlanders encased the tattered flag that Isaac Stevens bore in his final moments—the same flag that had led their rush at Secessionville—and sent it to his widow in Newport, Rhode Island.[23]

* * *

"(We) behaved as well as could be expected under the circumstances." With those loaded words, one officer of the 28th Massachusetts would dismiss the Battle of Secessionville. But within a few months, almost all of the fighting men present—even the Scotsmen of the 79th New York—commented on the Irish fighting prowess at Chantilly, in sharp relief to their baptism of fire down in South Carolina. And, although he nearly died at Second Manassas, George Cartwright would return to help mold the regiment into a tough, fighting force. Eventually the Irishmen would leave the IX Corps for their proper place with the Irish Brigade, and after Antietam, Fredericksburg, Gettysburg, and the Overland Campaign, no one doubted the 28th Massachusetts' courage or fighting ability. Indeed, at the expiration of the term of their enlistment, only Cartwright and twenty-one enlistees remained from the 1,703 aggregate that had served in the unit. Secessionville had been a poor start, but the 28th Massachusetts eventually compiled a service record equal to that of any of the Civil War's finest regiments.[24]

Unlike the troops of Stevens' division, many of the Federal regiments that served on James Island remained in the Department of the South for some time, among them the 3rd New Hampshire, the 6th Connecticut, and the 76th Pennsylvania. A year after Secessionville, in an action eerily reminiscent of the charge on the Tower Battery, they all would participate in an assault on another South Carolina earthwork not far from James Island: Battery Wagner. Hampshire officer John Jackson would be wounded in the attack, but he would survive the war and live into his seventies. Later in the war, in another state and in another year, the Hampshiremen joined Col. Joseph Hawley's 7th Connecticut in an attack on the Confederate lines in Virginia at Bermuda Hundred, lines that included remnants of the Charleston and Pee Dee Battalions, and the 21st and 25th South Carolina, all serving in Johnson Hagood's Brigade.25

Following the James Island campaign, the Roundheads of the 100th Pennsylvania, the 79th New York, and the 8th Michigan left South Carolina to begin a trek that took them from the Potomac River to the Mississippi River and back again. As part of the IX Corps, they fought at Second Manassas, South Mountain and Antietam. Transferring west with the corps, they encountered Lt. Gen. John Pemberton yet again, this time at Vicksburg. They also came head-to-head with Nathan "Shanks" Evans in a sharp little action at Jackson, Mississippi, where troops from the 22nd South Carolina and the Pee Dee Battalion again blocked their way. But wherever they marched, Secessionville wasn't far from their minds. In December of 1863, while they waited in the fortifications surrounding Knoxville for a Confederate attack to be launched against them, they passed the word, "Remember James Island."

In 1864, all three regiments returned east to participate in Grant's Overland Campaign, but after Spotsylvania and what can only be described as a varied and proud military career, most of the Highlanders mustered out when their terms expired. Still, two companies reenlisted and returned to the front to join those Roundheads and the Michiganders who had volunteered for the remainder of the war. Years later, a Michigan veteran remembered the Michigander's debt to their Highland comrades: "(At Secessionville) The 79th New York. . .followed and saved us from annihilation or. . .capture. . .That morning was the moment of true reconciliation between these two commands and the ties became stronger than those of bloody brotherhood."²⁶

Those Federal army officers who held command on James Island enjoyed equally varied careers after Secessionville. David Hunter eventually left the Department of the South and is now best remembered as the first man to torch the Shenandoah Valley, burning areas around Lexington and Lynchburg in May of 1864. His actions earned such intense enmity in the South that he was threatened with immediate execution should he be captured. Despite such animus, Hunter escaped the war with his few victories and served as the president of the committee that tried the Lincoln conspirators. His own death came just a year after the war ended.

Horatio Wright eventually rose to corps command, taking over the VI Corps in May 1864 when John Sedgwick fell at Spotsylvania. Wright went on to fight under Phil Sheridan in the Shenandoah Valley, and took part in the siege of Petersburg and the pursuit of Lee to Appomattox Court House. When he died in 1899, a brigadier general of the engineers, Wright was buried in front of Robert E. Lee's former mansion at Arlington across the Potomac River from Washington, D.C.

Joseph Hawley became a brigadier in the X Corps and fought at the Battle of Olustee in Florida before transferring to Virginia, where he spent the last year of the war. Hawley would eventually represent Connecticut in both houses of Congress and served as his state's governor.

All was not glory for the veterans of Secessionville, however. William Fenton's health continued to decline, and he finally left his beloved 8th Michigan in March 1863. Daniel Leasure went on to command the brigade that included his Roundheads. He remained with them until numerous woundings, IX Corps politics, and the death of his son, George, at the Battle of the Crater near Petersburg, left Leasure a dispirited man. Having seen enough of the war, Leasure resigned at the end of his enlistment in August of 1864.²⁷

Flag Officer Samuel F. Du Pont remained in command of the Southeast Atlantic Blockading Squadron, and although he served effectively, he eventually departed the scene of his early triumphs a beaten man. Political pressures forced him, against his better judgment, to make an assault on Fort Sumter with a collection of ironclad monitors. When his attack on April 7, 1863, failed badly, he asked to be relieved of command. Secretary of the Navy Gideon Welles quickly accepted the offer, and Du Pont left the theater for good. He was never given a new command, and already in failing health, Samuel F. Du Pont barely survived the war, dying in Philadelphia on June 23, 1865.[28]

* * *

For the Confederacy in general and Charleston in particular, the victory at Secessionville represented part of a general resurgence of Southern hopes in the summer of 1862. Although the Confederate success in South Carolina would soon be overshadowed by Stonewall Jackson's Valley campaign and Robert E. Lee's stunning repulse of George McClellan's forces during the Seven Days Battles, the participants in the James Island fight still jockeyed mightily for the limelight. After all, a Northern horde of invaders had been pushed back from the very gates of one of the South's most important and influential cities.

Nathan "Shanks" Evans published a short note in the June 23 *Charleston Mercury* which included the line, "I commanded in person the engagement on the morning of the 16th of June." The following day, the *Mercury* published an "Eyewitness" account from inside the Tower Battery which directly addressed Evans' contention with these pointed words: "I shall not pretend to give an account of the conduct of the forces under the immediate command of Gen. Evans, as they were some distance from us, and I did not, therefore, witness their operations."

Years later, Evans' words still rankled Johnson Hagood. The South Carolinian refuted Shanks' various claims and credited Col. William Duncan Smith for the dispositions that repelled the Federal attack that Monday morning. Fortunately for all, "Shanks" would leave for Virginia in July 1862, taking Col. Spartan Goodlett's 22nd South Carolina and Smith's Pee Dee Battalion with him. Eventually, an alcoholic Nathan Evans spiraled into the backwater of Confederate command, but not before preferring charges against Goodlette for leaving his post in the face of the enemy. Despite the turmoil, the regiment would serve honorably from Mississippi to Virginia, and at the end of the war, only 88 effectives from the 22nd South Carolina were still in the ranks to surrender at Appomattox.[29]

John Clifford Pemberton seemed genuinely energized by the Secessionville victory. In his official report, Pemberton finally claimed credit for the triumph of his defense in depth—a strategy that had forced the Federals to fight a battle beyond the cover of their sheltering naval gunfire. Despite the rumblings of Roswell Ripley and assorted South Carolinian politicians, the outcome of the James Island campaign had proven Pemberton correct. After the battle, he was visible everywhere on James Island, superintending improvements and generally making his presence felt. During this period, the *Courier* editorialized, "Be assured, he will do all he can for Charleston." But his feud with South Carolina's politicians and friction with his own officers continued, and on August 29, 1862, Pemberton was replaced by Gen. Pierre Gustave Toutant Beauregard, the hero of Fort Sumter and First Manassas. Soon the ill-fated commander was on his way to Vicksburg—and a rendezvous with Ulysses S. Grant.[30]

William Duncan Smith, the man Pemberton felt was most responsible for the victory at Secessionville, reassumed command of James Island two days after the battle on June 18, and eventually rose to command the state's 1st Military District. Unfortunately, yellow fever struck Smith down on October 4, 1862, thus cutting short a promising military career.

Like many others, States Rights Gist also went west, leading a brigade in the ill-starred Army of Tennessee. He was killed in action on November 30, 1864, at the head of his troops just south of Franklin, Tennessee, charging a blazing set of staunchly-defended earthworks.

Ellison Capers served much of the war under Gist and was wounded in the same engagement in which Gist and over half of his own 24th South Carolina were struck down. Returning home to Charleston to recuperate, Capers later joined forces opposing William T. Sherman's 1865 march through his state. After Appomattox, Capers turned his back on the horrors of war and became a respected Episcopal bishop, even serving for a time as the chancellor of the University of the South. But he always kept a memento of the James Island campaign with him, a rifle taken from a captured Federal named Milton Woodford. In 1904, the Bishop went to great pains to locate Woodford's widow. When he finally did locate the woman, Capers returned her late husband's rifle and wrote with deep emotion, "I trust that one reunited country may grow stronger and greater in those nobler bonds of union which bind her people to each other." It is no wonder that much of the Union mourned when Bishop Capers died in Columbia, South Carolina, on April 22, 1908, almost forty-six years after he taught those "country" boys near Clark's House how to fire a cannon.[31]

Another unit that went west was the 4th Lousiana Battalion, which served in a number of brigades in the Army of Tennessee. In April of 1865, some of the Louisianans surrendered at Mobile, Alabama, but the remnants were reorganized as two companies of the Pelican Regiment, the organization in which they would surrender a month later. Lieutenant Colonel John McEnery, who had remained at their head, entered politics after the war and served as one of two concurrent governors during one of the more interesting periods in Louisiana politics. Rarely in his later years did he comment on the bravery of his unit at Secessionville.[32]

The Eutaw Battalion became the 25th South Carolina in July 1862, and remained on James and Morris islands until joining Johnson Hagood's Brigade in September 1863. Bloodied in various battles around Petersburg, the 25th South Carolina made its final stand as the last reinforcements to enter Fort Fisher near Wilmington, North Carolina in January 1865. All the men who made it into the fort surrendered under the weight of a Federal onslaught that included old foes like the 7th Connecticut, the 3rd New Hampshire, and the 76th and the 97th Pennsylvania.

Another group of Secessionville veterans, Alexander Smith's Pee Dee Battalion, was merged into the 26th South Carolina. When the Carolinians completed their service under "Shanks" Evans in Mississippi, they returned to Charleston for but a brief stay. Once again Richmond needed troops, so the regiment left Charleston for Virginia, where it joined Robert E. Lee and the Army of Northern Virginia in defending another important Southern city—Petersburg. The men from South Carolina remained there through the end of the war. After three years of service, the Pee Dee Battalion stood with Lee at Appomattox.[33]

The Charleston Battalion remained in the theater to defend the city whose name it bore. A year after the stirring repulse of the

Federals at Secessionville, Lt. Col. Peter Gaillard and his men faced a new Federal attempt to take their city. The battalion was stationed in a large Confederate battery on Morris Island named after Thomas Wagner, the officer who had commanded the Tower Battery after Colonel Lamar and Gaillard went down. In a bloody Federal assault on the position on the evening of July 18, 1863, David Ramsay, who had taken command of the Charleston Battalion when Gaillard fell at the Tower Battery, died before the Federal guns. The Confederates beat back the desperate assault, but Gaillard lost his hand to a Federal shell during the subsequent siege and was forced to retire from active service. In September of 1863, the Charleston Battalion became part of the 27th South Carolina and served in Hagood's Brigade until the end of the war. Once more would they, the Pee Dee's and the 22nd South Carolina, meet their old adversaries—the 100th Pennsylvania, the 8th Michigan, and the 46th NY—this time amidst the horrors of the Crater before Petersburg. Eventually the battalion would surrender with the Army of Tennessee in North Carolina, but the sons of Charleston could always point proudly to the heroic defense of their beloved city.[34]

Johnson Hagood and his brigade left South Carolina in May of 1864 to serve under both Lee in Virginia and Joe Johnston in North Carolina. At war's end, Hagood returned to run his plantation but soon moved into politics under the Democratic banner of cavalryman Wade Hampton. In 1880, Hagood carved out another distinguished record, this time on a political battlefield as South Carolina's 51st governor. He died peacefully eighteen years later in 1898. His passing prompted one writer to comment, "Out of the thinning line falls one more man in gray."[35]

After Secessionville, Colonel Lamar's Artillery was redesignated the 2nd South Carolina Artillery and served in the department until it was converted into an infantry regiment during the waning days of the war. Unfortunately, when the unit finally surrendered to William T. Sherman, Lamar wasn't with it. He had continued to serve on James Island and was eventually accorded a unique honor. In thanks for his heroic exploits commanding the earthwork on the Secessionville peninsula, the Confederate high command gave the Tower Battery a new name—Fort Lamar—and Thomas Lamar became the acknowledged "Hero of Secessionville." In early October, members of Lamar's district placed his name as a candidate for the legislative seat. Lamar heard of their action and quickly begged off: "I can much better serve my country in the field, and as long as the war lasts and I keep my health, I prefer to continue in the military service." Ironically, just one week after he penned these words, the same wave of malaria and fever that killed Duncan Smith claimed Lamar. When stricken, he was taken to the Charleston Hotel where he lingered for a week. Finally, at 5:00 a.m. on the 18th of October, 1862, he succumbed to the fever. Peyton Colquitt's 46th Georgia and Peter Gaillard's Charleston Battalion rushed from their camps on James Island to form an escort for his body. Later that day, a somber procession wound through the streets of Charleston, from the hotel to the railroad station, for the transportation of his remains to his native Edgefield. There, his wife Sarah and their grieving children lay Thomas Gresham Lamar—the Hero of Secessionville—to rest.[36]

* * *

The earthwork that bore Lamar's name became part of an extensive defense line that eventually collared the entire Secessionville peninsula east of the neck. Many more guns were mounted in the works and the bombproof was redesigned, as the importance of the position needed little reminder after June 16, 1862. The causeway that had enabled the 4th Louisiana Battalion to come to the fort's relief was reconstructed further to the west.

In another tribute to Charleston's defenders, the emplacement near the Clark House was renamed Battery Reed, in honor of fallen Capt. Samuel Reed, Lamar's trusted leader of the Barnwell boys. These works stood firm for nearly three more years of war, but the James Island defenses could do little to stop Gen. William T. Sherman's juggernaut. In early 1865, when Sherman flanked Charleston from the rear, Southern forces abandoned James Island and Charleston finally fell, its seaside defenses holding until the last.

Since then, the forts and trenches of James Island have stood as mute reminders honoring the tenacity of the Confederate defense of Charleston. Today, the campsites at the Grimball Plantation still look much the same as they did when the Federal gunboats first

The Tower Battery: "Fort Lamar, the most easterly of the line of Confederate works on James Island. As it appeared in 1895. Estimate the height from the horse and wagon." Division of Rare and Manuscript Collections, Carl A. Kroch Library, Cornell University, Ithaca, NY.

entered the Stono River, but elsewhere James Island little resembles her Civil War appearance. Fort Pemberton now serves as a lot line for a beautiful home overlooking the Stono. Sol Legare Island has become a neighborhood of older, modest homes, and newer upscale residences. Traffic roars by the graveyard of the James Island Presbyterian Church, where a large headstone recalls the Battle of Secessionville for the interested onlooker. East of the church is a quiet intersection that was once called the Artillery Crossroads, and beyond that, among the homes and schools, the gas stations and stores, stretch the remnants of the Island's first defensive line.

Along a quiet marshline that borders a residential neighborhood, a small plaque hidden by low-lying bushes commemorates Ellison

Capers' efforts at the Clark House battery. To the south lies a housing development overlooking the marsh where the 3rd New Hampshire was trapped in the stinging Confederate crossfire. North of these buildings sits a well-preserved earthwork from a later defensive line, and an overgrown field, where the 24th South Carolina, the Eutaw Battalion, and the 3rd Rhode Island Heavy Artillery, fought with great courage.

To the south, across the intervening swamp, may be found tracts of modest homes, streets named after things military, and a real estate development named after a long-dead Confederate colonel. Houses cover the field where the 28th Massachusetts received their baptism of fire, where Joseph Hawley worked to keep the 7th Connecticut from disintegrating, and where David Leckey drove his Roundheads into the Confederate guns.

To the east, the peninsula narrows to a neck where a telephone pole rises from thick overgrowth. One must search for a moment or two, but eventually the outline of the northern parapet of Fort Lamar becomes evident. A modern road gouges the right front wall of the earthwork, the location of Bellinger's guns and the Charleston Battalion's rush to man the smoking walls. The telephone pole stands very near where Lamar sighted the Columbiad and sent his first roaring response to the Federal attack. Beyond that, heavy vegetation obscures the left front where the 8th Michigan and the 79th New York came to grips with Goodlett's detachment, Lamar's artillerists, and Smith's Pee Dee Battalion. The enlarged bombproof looms up just a few yards to the rear. Further east, the fields where soldiers once camped now bear witness to the sad expansion of civilization, as it stretches out to the few remaining buildings of the planter village of Secessionville.

But back at the neck, Fort Lamar grimly continues to resist the march of man and the years of wind and rain. The walls are rounded now and much lower, and the marshes on both flanks still fill with the tides, girding this haunted remnant of American history, this haunted scene of American courage.

Epilogue

The Federal steamers that departed James Island that early July of 1862, carried away more than the battered remnants of Hunter's Army from the swamps and sand hills of South Carolina. With these troops went the North's last best chance to capture the city of Charleston. The Southern Expedition had generated slow but sure momentum from the fall of Port Royal to the invasion of James Island. A seemingly unstoppable strategy had gobbled up large chunks of Confederate real estate with little Federal loss. An army had landed within sight of one of the South's great harbors and seemed poised to simply walk in and take it. But in three bloody hours, the Southern Expedition's string of successes came to an abrupt end on the walls of the Tower Battery. The Federal tide was stopped cold one half mile from the planter village of Secessionville, and the pendulum would now swing dramatically in the South's favor.

What would have been the results had Benham's forces ruptured the Confederate lines that dreary Monday? While we will never know for certain, reasonable speculation is possible. In the same way that New Orleans' capitulation created innumerable possibilities for the Union armies operating on the Mississippi, a Federally-controlled Charleston could have provided the Northerners with an unparalleled staging area for strikes into the South's heartland. A wide arc of potential targets well within Charleston's range presented themselves. Working south, a Unionist army could have moved with impunity along the Charleston-Savannah Railroad to threaten the Georgia river bastion at Savannah. Upland, South Carolina's capital city of Columbia, considered by many Northerners as the "Cradle of the Confederacy," would have been easy prey for a Federal thrust. Her fall would have provided the North a moral victory almost equal to that of Charleston's surrender. Perhaps most importantly, a Federal force moving north along the Atlantic coast would have endangered one of the South's last major harbors, Wilmington, North Carolina, from the rear. Had any of these three cities fallen in the summer of 1862, the complexion of the fall campaigns, especially in the West, would have changed dramatically. Had all three cities fallen, the Southern war effort would have been fatally constricted, her vital international trade practically destroyed, and her moral authority to claim nationhood compromised.

On the Union side, David Hunter certainly proved himself the wrong man for the job. Despite his early bluster, he never came near summoning the energy to test the Confederate defenses. Instead he spent much of his time either inventing excuses for the campaign's failure or entertaining his wife on Hilton Head. Worse, he ceded the operation to a subordinate mistrusted by all. In the last analysis, Hunter floats through the James Island Campaign like a detached phantom, nominally in charge of the Union effort but exerting little, if any, influence.

One can only surmise what an Isaac Stevens or Horatio Wright might have done with command of the Federal brigades camped along the Stono River. We will never know, because it was Henry Benham who guided the Federal force on James Island with his unique combination of poor management, faulty tactics, and blind ambition. By the time the Federals had solidified their beachhead on James Island, Benham's blustering command style had angered and isolated most of his subordinates. Although students of the campaign could pick any number of instances illuminating Benham's shortcomings, his June 15 council of war remains the prime example of his poor command technique and muddled priorities.

First of all, the results of the council contradicted Hunter's direct orders prohibiting any kind of assault on the Confederates. Benham, however, convinced himself that an attack upon the

Tower Battery was not only within the spirit of Hunter's orders but also demanded by them. Obviously, an attack farther north along the Confederate line would have held greater chance for success, but Benham couldn't possibly have justified such a move on the grounds of providing for camp security. He desperately wanted to have at the Confederates—especially with Hunter gone—but the only point he could logically assail while supposedly staying within his chief's orders was the Tower Battery, which happened to be the strongest Confederate position on the entire James Island line. Even then, Benham's failure to properly reconnoiter the area was a baffling oversight—witness the 3rd New Hampshire's surprise when its members stumbled onto the swamp that halted their attack within sight of their objective. Instead, Benham peremptorily launched six regiments down a chute of land telescoping towards an artillery position flanked by impassable swamps—against all advice and orders. When the assault failed, Benham covered his own flanks by recasting the operation as a "reconnaissance in force," but his subordinates refused to join the subterfuge. He then turned on his brigadiers and his troops, but the case he tried to build against them—especially Isaac Stevens—was transparently self-serving. This is what marks Benham forever, his inability to accept responsibility for his mishandling of the affair. When he and his staff attempted to spread the canard that his troops were somehow lacking in courage, Benham forfeited the moral authority to lead men in battle. Unfortunately, even modern writers, Rowena Reed for example, accept Benham's slanderous estimation of his troops' abilities.

But the story of the war is written in the blood of regiments like the 8th Michigan and the 79th New York, the 7th Connecticut and the 3rd New Hampshire, the 28th Massachusetts and the Roundheads of the 100th Pennsylvania. Henry Benham wasted these regiments in the service of his overreaching ambition. The War Department in Washington seemed to concur in this assessment, for Benham never again held a field command.

Ironically, many of the command problems that plagued the Federal forces on James Island were mirrored on the Southern side. From the time he rose to theater command until he left South Carolina for service elsewhere, John C. Pemberton fought a constant battle with the politicos of South Carolina and the officers of his own command in an attempt to force his will upon the campaign. Unfortunately, his problems seemed more a product of personality than substance. When he first took command of the theater, he simply enlarged upon the defensive concepts begun by Robert E. Lee during that officer's earlier sojourn on the Atlantic coast. But what worked for a diplomatic Virginian didn't for the brusque Pennsylvanian. Everywhere from the highest state offices to the streets of Charleston, people found Pemberton exasperating, and in some minds, he was a traitor. He could barely make a move without some scion of South Carolina society calling for his replacement. Of course, his constant shuffling of subordinates and his public feuding did little to inspire confidence. But, the Battle of Secessionville was fought and won under his leadership, and his enlargement of Lee's defensive scheme contributed greatly to the victory. Granted, Pemberton didn't take the field during the June 16 battle, and his local commanders rose to the challenge while he watched from the rear. But as a result of the success, he enjoyed a brief honeymoon with his detractors. Unfortunately for the Pennsylvania Confederate, the truce wouldn't last long. Again his old problems would rise to the surface, and he would soon leave Charleston amidst rancor and recrimination, proving that he was simply the wrong man, in the wrong place, at the wrong time.

Luckily for the Confederate cause, the defenders of James Island were able to surmount the shortcomings of their commander. William Duncan Smith's implementation and use of the Advanced Forces and Grand Guards created a strategic framework that would allow swift mobilization of the limited Southern resources at the point of attack. While the Tower Battery withstood the Federal frontal attacks, Hagood's forces repulsed the enemy's flanking movement and shattered Benham's nerve in the process. The Lee-Pemberton concept of interior defense may well have pulled the Union infantry away from their naval guns, but it was Smith's strategy that flanked the Federal left and made possible the Confederate victory at Secessionville.

Duncan Smith's plan was carried out by an superb supporting cast. Thomas Lamar, Peter Gaillard, Alexander Smith and Johnson Hagood were but a few of the many fine leaders on hand. But as is true in virtually every military engagement, ultimate credit for the victory at Secessionville must go to the rank and file. The

Confederate defenders of the Tower Battery exemplified the indomitable spirit of men who simply refused to be defeated. Supported by well-placed artillery in a position of great advantage, the men lining the parapet of the Tower Battery threw back six times their numbers in an incredible display of tenacity and grit. They could laugh later that they had to win the fight for James Island for fear of facing the angry female population of Charleston. But in the end, it was the bravery of the defenders that enabled Charleston to withstand the Union assault.

From 1860 to 1865, Charleston embodied Southern flaunting of Federal authority. For nearly the entire length of the national conflagration, she remained the site of the war's first shot and the cultural center of plantation society. A reporter for the *New York Times* captured the Northern attitude best in a piece written just two days after the Battle of Secessionville, before the details of the Union loss became public:

> When the time comes for the assault on Charleston, we trust that it will not be by any back door passage...We trust it will pass up directly under Fort Sumter—if need be, laying it in ruins, and, at whatever cost, restoring the Stars and Stripes over the citadel where first they were lowered to traitors fifteen months before. Not till these acts of justice have been performed, would we have the naval and military force of the Union pass up to take possession of that wretched and half-ruined town...The instinct of the people demands that the capture of Charleston shall be as conspicuous as its enormous crime.

To the great displeasure of the *New York Times'* reporter and the North in general, the time for the assault on Charleston came and went. The Federal effort ended in defeat, and the James Island campaign would be all but forgotten, overshadowed by both other campaigns in other theaters of the war, and later efforts to reduce Fort Sumter and capture Charleston Harbor. Despite the capricious tides of history, what remains conspicuous, however, is the bravery of those Americans that faced each other on June 16, 1862, across the swamps and fields of James Island, Charleston, South Carolina.

Order Of Battle
June 16, 1862

Federal Forces: Department of the South
Major General David Hunter

Commander, Northern District: Brigadier General Henry Benham

Left Column
Williams' Brigade

Col. Robert Williams (1st Massachusetts Cavalry)
3rd Rhode Island Heavy Artillery (5 Co's.): Major Edwin Metcalf
3rd New Hampshire: Lt. Col. John Jackson
97th Pennsylvania (detached from Chatfield's Brigade):
Col. Henry Guss
3rd US Artillery (1 section, detached from Welsh's Brigade):
Capt. Ransom

First Division
Brigadier General Horatio Wright

First Brigade
Col. John Chatfield (6th Connecticut)
6th Connecticut (2 Co's.)
47th New York: Maj. P. C. Kane

Second Brigade
Col. Thomas Welsh (45th Pennsylvania)
45th Pennsylvania (6 Co's.)
76th Pennsylvania (8 Co's., detached as camp guard): Col. J. M. Power
1st New York Engineers (5 Co's.): Maj. Butts
3rd US Artillery (2 sections)
1st Massachusetts Cavalry (2 squadrons)

Right Column, Second Division
Brigadier General Isaac Stevens

First Brigade
Col. William Fenton (8th Michigan)
8th Michigan: Lt. Col. Frank Graves
7th Connecticut: Lt. Col. Joseph Hawley
28th Massachusetts: Lt. Col. McLelland Moore

1st Connecticut Light Artillery (4 guns): Capt Alfred Rockwell

Second Brigade
Col. Daniel Leasure (100th Pennsylvania)
79th New York: Lt. Col. David Morrison
100th Pennsylvania: Maj David Leckey
46th New York: Col. Rudolph Rosa

1st New York Engineers (1 Co.): Capt. Alfred Sears
1st Massachusetts Cavalry (1 C0.): Capt. Lucius Sargent

* * *

Confederate Forces: Department of South Carolina and Georgia

Major General John Pemberton

First Military District of South Carolina:
Brigadier General Nathan Evans

James Island
Brigadier General William Duncan Smith
Brigadier General States Rights Gist

Tower Battery
Col. Thomas Lamar (1st South Carolina Artillery)
1st South Carolina Artillery (2 Co's.)

22nd South Carolina (100-man detachment): Capt. Joshua Jamison
9th South Carolina Battalion (Pee Dee Battalion):
Lt. Col. Alexander D. Smith
1st South Carolina (Charleston) Battalion: Lt. Col. Peter Gaillard
4th Louisiana Battalion: Lt. Col. John McEnery

Advanced Forces
Col. Johnson Hagood (1st South Carolina)
24th South Carolina (detachments from 4 Co's.): Col. Clement Stevens
1st South Carolina (detachments from 4 Co's.): Col. Johnson Hagood
Eutaw Battalion: Lt. Col. Charles Simonton

Boyce's Light Battery (MacBeth Light Artillery) 1 gun: Lt. B. A. Jeter

47th Georgia: Col. Gilbert Williams
51st Georgia: Col. William Slaughter

Battery at Clark's Point
24th South Carolina: Lt. Col. Ellison Capers
1st South Carolina Artillery (1 Co.): Lt. J. B. Kitching

Notes

Chapter One
A Change in the Weather

1. Burwell, John Rice, letter home, May 22, 1862, Mary Jo Verran Collection, for "May the time. . ."; Henry Applegate to Mr. Lewis Hay, March 7, 1862; *Civil War Times Illustrated* (hereafter *CWTI*) Collection, United States Army Military History Institute (hereafter USAMHI), for "(we) will. . ."

2. Richards, Kent, *Isaac I. Stevens: Young Man In A Hurry* (Provo, 1978), p. 366, for Stevens' early views concerning Savannah. Stevens, Hazard, *The Life of Isaac Ingalls Stevens* (Boston, 1900), pp. 376-380, for the evolution of Isaac Stevens' plans. Attacking Charleston via Church Flats was discussed in navy circles as early as November 1861. Davis, C. H., *Life of Charles Henry Davis, Rear Admiral, 1807-1877* (Boston, 1899), p. 174; Stevens, *Life of*, p. 380, for "enemy. . ."

3. Ibid., p. 379, for Thomas Sherman–Isaac Stevens meetings and Samuel Du Pont's support of plan. In a mirror image of Stevens' plan, Sherman originally wanted to sever the railroad near Hardeeville and attack Savannah from the north. These early attempts to take Savannah collapsed amidst miscommunication and lack of cooperation, with the army and navy simultaneously blaming each other for the failures. Sherman offered his own opinion of what went wrong soon after he was relieved: "The great trouble was that there was no one there responsible for the whole command. If Commodore Du Pont or myself had had sole command I thing we would have accomplished a great deal more." Report of the Joint Committee on the Conduct of the War, vol. 3, p. 306, for "The great trouble. . .", and p. 298, for Sherman's Savannah assault schemes; ibid., p. 300, for Du Pont's evident reluctance to support the army's operation. On the other hand, see Daniel Ammen, *The Old Navy and the New* (Philadelphia, 1891), p. 359, for Sherman's supposed reluctance to attack Savannah via Skull Creek; Isaac I. Stevens Papers, University of Washington, Seattle Washington (hearafter ISP), Stevens to "My Dear Wife," February 16, 1862, for "I am. . ."

4. Richards, *Isaac Stevens*, p. 369, and Stevens, *Life of*, p. 385 for confirmation problems. Stevens had something of a reputation as a spirited imbiber, but there is no evidence that he brought a drinking problem to Port Royal. Richards, *Isaac Stevens*, p. 377, describes the basis for the Benham-

Stevens friction. In 1853, Benham took Stevens' place as a member of the Coast Survey and claimed he had to "clean up the mess Stevens left behind." The two also argued about the proper methods to raise the status of the Engineering Corps in Congress.

5. ISP, Meg Stevens to Bache ("My Dear Proff"), April 8, 1862, for "in high. . .", Stevens, *Life of*, p. 383, for "untimely. . .," "enfants. . .", p. 387, for "dense," "rejected. . .," and "to any suggestions. . ."

6. Details of Benham's career are culled from Sifakis, Stewart, *Who Was Who in the Civil War* (New York: Facts On File, 1988), pp. 49-50; Boatner, Mark M.; *The Civil War Dictionary* (New York: McKay, 1959), pp. 58-59; *Biographical Register of the Officers and Graduates of the U.S. Military Academy 1802-1867* (Boston & New York: Houghton Mifflin & Co., 1891), vol. 1, covers both Benham and Stevens. See ibid., pp. 660-662 for Benham, and pp. 729-733 for Stevens.

7. Fleming, "The Northwestern Virginia Campaign of 1861," *Blue and Gray Magazine*, Vol. X, Issue 6, pp. 59-60, for Corrick's Ford.

8. Stevens, *Life of*, p. 383, for "claiming. . ."; Henry Benham file, National Archives, for official correspondence from western Virginia; Lusk, *William Thompson: War Letters of William Thompson Lusk* (New York: Privately Published, 1911), p. 152, for one officer's view of Benham/Rosecrans feud.

9. Sifakis, *Who was Who*, p. 622, and Faust, Patricia (ed.), *Historical Times Illustrated Encyclopedia of the Civil War* (New York: Harper & Row, 1986), pp. 717-718, for thumbnail sketches of Isaac Stevens' life; Kent Richards' *Isaac Stevens*, the definitive biography of Isaac Stevens, includes a succinct physical description of the man—a "large head on a slight body" (p. 30). Also see Sears, Stephen W., *George B. McClellan, The Young Napoleon* (New York: Ticknor & Fields, 1988), pp. 39-41, and Stevens, *Life of*, pp. 339-341, for the McClellan-Stevens feud; Leasure, Daniel; "Address By Col. Daniel Leasure." MOLLUS, Minnesota Commandery, "Glimpses of a Nation's Struggle," (St. Paul, MN., 1887), pp. 141-142, for "a small. . ."; Thompson & Means (eds.), *Confidential Correspondence of Gustavus V. Fox* (New York: Naval Institute Society-De Vinne Press, 1918), p. 72, for "Stevens is. . ."; ISP, Stevens to James Nesmith ("My dear Sir"), May 13, 1862, for "I rely. . ." While both interesting and important, Hunter's treatment of the freed slaves, which included the unofficial mustering of an all-black regiment, as well as the actions of cotton speculators and New England missionaries in the Department of the South are beyond the scope of this book.

10. Ballard, Michael B.; *Pemberton, A Biography* (Jackson, Mississippi: University Press of Mississippi, 1991), pp. 83-95, for Pemberton's experiences in South Carolina up to the fall of Fort Pulaski. Ballard's biography of the general is the most balanced treatment of the Pennsylvania Confederate.

11. *Southern Historical Society Papers*, 52 Volumes (Richmond, Virginia: Southern Historical Society, 1876-1959), vol. 1, pp. 103-107 (hereafter *SHSP*), for a short overview of Lee's defensive strategy to offset

Federal naval power. U.S. War Department. *The War of the Rebellion: A Compilation of the Official Records of the Union and Confederate Armies*, 128 vols. (Washington, D.C.: U.S. Government Printing Office, 1880-1901), Series I, vol. 6, pp. 417-418 (hereafter cited as *OR*. All citations are to Series I unless otherwise noted), for Arthur Manigault's orders; ibid., p. 420, for report of Roswell Ripley's orders; ibid., pp. 423-424, for Governor Pickens' reaction to the abandonment of Coles Island; ibid., pp. 424-425, for Lee's advice; ibid., p. 425, for Manigault's report.

12. Ibid., p. 427, for Pemberton's accession on Coles; ibid., pp. 429-430, for Pemberton's calming of Lee.

13. Ibid., p. 432, for Donelson's transfer orders and Pemberton's response. Donelson, the locater and namesake of Fort Donelson in Tennessee, had served under Robert E. Lee in western Virginia. He and his men were transferred to South Carolina in December of 1861. Sifakis, *Who was Who*, pp. 186-187; *OR* 6, p. 434, for Governor Pickens' response and "two raw . . ."; ibid, p. 433, for Ripley's orders; *OR* 11, p. 476, for Pemberton's relenting on Graham's troops; ibid., 6, p. 435, for Gregg's orders.

14. Nathan "Shanks" Evans is covered in Sifakis, *Who was Who*, p. 208; Faust, *Encyclopedia*, p. 248; and Davis, William C. (ed.), *The Confederate General*, 6 vols.(Harrisburg, PA: National Historical Society, 1991), 2, p. 107. The arrival of Evans and Pemberton in the theater is covered in Ballard, *Pemberton*, pp. 83-90; *OR* 14, p. 434 for Evans' orders regarding Willstown; ibid., pp. 470-471, for Evans' defense of his Adam's Run position; ibid., p. 474, for Pemberton's response.

15. Ibid., p. 480, for both the Lee and Davis directives; ibid., pp. 480-481, for Pemberton's wrestling with the rifle problem; ibid., p. 481, for Gregg's orders; ibid., p. 482, for Pemberton's shuffling of his available forces.

16. Ibid., p. 484, for the Ripley memo.

17. Ibid., pp. 485-486, for "Sink. . ."

18. Hagood, Johnson, *Memoirs of the War of Secession* (Columbia, SC: State Company, 1910), p. 60, for the flip-flop and "outside pressure. . ." Côté, Richard N., *Rice and Ruin: The William Bull Pringles and the Death of the South Carolina Rice Culture, 1800-1884* (Privately Published, Revised 1994), p. 397, places Lucas' Battery on Battery Island on July 10, 1861, and on Coles Island soon thereafter. Abstracts of Troops Strengths, South Carolina State Archives, lists Lucas' three companies thusly: "95+11 A; 92 B; 84+11 C."

19. Johnson Hagood's early life is covered by Sifakis, *Who was Who*, p. 273; Faust, *Encyclopedia*, p. 331; Davis, *Confederate General*, 3, pp. 48-49; and Hagood, *Memoirs*, pp. 16-22.

20. Ibid., pp. 27-60, for the raising of Hagood's 1st South Carolina and life on Coles Island; Mixson, Frank M., *Reminiscences of a Private* (Columbia, SC: The State Company, 1910), pp. 17-20, for a further look at the 1st South Carolina; John G. Pressley, "The Wee Nee Volunteers of Williamsburg District, South Carolina, in the First (Hagood's) Regiment,"

SHSP, 16, pp. 116-133, for the Wee Nee's experiences as part of Hagood's Regiment; Izlar, William Valmore, *A Sketch of the War Record of the Edisto Rifles, 1861-1865* (Columbia, SC, The State Company, 1914), pp. 17-33, for the Rifles' experiences in Hagood's Regiment; *South Carolina Troops in the Confederate Service*, vol. 1, pt. 2, pp. 429-720, for a roster of Hagood's regiment; Cauthen, Charles Edward, *South Carolina Goes To War 1860-65* (Chapel Hill: UNC Press, 1950), pp. 110-151, for a good study of South Carolina's mobilization.

21. Davis, *Confederate General*, 6, pp. 4-5; Faust (ed.), p. 717; and Sikfakis, *Who Was Who*, p. 622 for the life of Clement. H. Stevens and the raising of the 24th South Carolina.

22. Davis, *Confederate General*, 1, pp. 162-3; Faust, *Encyclopedia*, pp. 112-13; Sikfakis, Who Was Who, *Who was Who*, p. 105, for short accounts of Ellison Capers. A fuller treatment of Capers can be found in a work by his son, Walter Capers, *The Soldier-Bishop Ellison Capers* (New York: The Neale Publishing Company, 1912).

23. Hagood, *Memoirs*, p. 60, for the 24th South Carolina's arrival on Coles; ibid., p. 66, for Stevens' orders to advance to Coles.

24. Kevin C. Ruffner, "Before the Seven Days: The Reorganization of the Confederate Army in the Spring of 1862," in Miller, William J., ed., *The Peninsula Campaign of 1862: Yorktown to the Seven Days*, 3 vols. (Campbell, CA: Savas Publishing Company, 1994), 1, p. 48, for "unprecedented. . .", and p. 61, for "to reorganize. . ."; Hagood, *Memoirs*, pp. 62-6, for Hagood's view of the reorganization. Izlar, *Edisto Rifles*, p. 33, and Pressley, "Wee Nee Volunteers," pp. 132-33, for company-eye views of the process. Hagood, *Memoirs*, p. 65, for the additions to Lamar's command. Stewart Sifakis,*Compendium of the Confederate Armies, South Carolina and Georgia* (NY: Facts On File, Inc., 1995), p. 83, states that the Eutaw Battalion was officially designated the 11th South Carolina Battalion, although it was rarely referred to by this designation.

25. Ibid., pp. 65-7, for the subsequent reorganization of Hagood's Regiment.

26. *OR* 14, pp. 486-92, for the establishment of martial law in South Carolina; Ballard, *Pemberton*, pp. 95-7, for Pemberton and martial law. Hagood, *Memoirs*, pp. 69-81, for Hagood's take on martial law; ibid., pp. 70-1, for the `warning'; ibid., pp. 80-1, for the 1st South Carolina's experience as provost guard; Stoney, John, "Recollections of John Stafford Stoney, Confederate Surgeon," *South Carolina Historical Magazine*, vol. 60, p. 216, for the regiment's campground.

27. Crute, Joseph H. Jr., *Units of the Confederate States Army* (Midlothian, VA: Derwent Books, 1987), pp. 246-7, for a brief sketch of the Charleston Battalion; Capers, Ellison, ed., *Confederate Military History*, 19 vols. (Wilmington, N.C, Broadfoot, Extended Edition, 1987), 6, *South Carolina*, p. 585, for capsule history of Gaillard's life; *The Irish Volunteers* (Charleston, SC., The News and Courier Book and Job Presses, 1878), pp. 3-39, for a history of the unit.

28. *OR* 14, pp. 336 and 338 for April 30, 1862, returns for Hunter's de-

partment. Two companies of the 45th Pennsylvania garrisoned Fenwick Island and one company manned Raccoon Island, ibid., p. 336.

29. Sikfakis, *Who Was Who*, p. 327, and Faust, *Encyclopedia*, p. 376, for David Hunter's career. In her book, *Combined Operations in the Civil War* (Annapolis, Md.: Naval Institute Press, 1978), Rowena Reed makes several observations concerning the quality of the troops in the Southern Expedition. On p. 45, she claims that the Federal troops "were useless for any military movements" until several executions helped reassert discipline. Her source for this information never mentions these executions but does claim that Isaac Stevens "put his command through a severe course of drill, discipline, and picket duty." On the same page, she claims that the opportunities "to loot and destroy" were just too much for the inexperienced troops from the "'slums' of Boston and New York" to ignore. Oddly enough, there were no troops from Massachusetts present in the theater at this time, and the "slum dwellers" of 79th New York were the only troops accompanying the expedition with any real combat experience. The 79th spent most of its time early in the operation isolated on Bay Point. If anyone should be blamed for the inexperience of the troops in the Southern Expedition, it should be George McClellan, who resisted assigning any experienced regiments—even the 79th New York—to Sherman. Reed also selectively quotes Commodore Samuel Du Pont to buttress her theory: "I have one misgiving—our army here are depradators and freebooters—they are robbing...in all directions...," ibid., p. 51 (see Thompson & Means eds., *Gustavus V. Fox*, p. 70, for the full quote).

Du Pont's opinions came one week after the army landed on Hilton Head and could hardly have been the result of a lengthy, even-tempered observation. There is much evidence regarding the understandably rough command relations between the two arms early in the Southern Expedition, so any evaluation of either army or navy effectiveness cannot rely strictly on one side's opinion of the other. Crowinshield, Benjamin W., *A History of the First Regiment of Massachusetts Cavalry Volunteers* (Boston and New York: Houghton, Mifflin and Company, 1891), pp. 51-4, for transfer of the unit to Hilton Head; Conyngham, D. P., *The Irish Brigade and Its Campaigns* (New York: William McSorely & Co., 1867), p. 576, for the 28th Massachusetts' transfer to Hilton Head; OR 14, p. 338, for "may be..."; ibid., 14, p. 337, for "A profound..." and "Why they...," and Hunter's analysis of his troop strength.

30. Pease, Benjamin, *Civil War Memoirs of Benjamin F. Pease* (Courtesy of Bill Compton, Oakland, California), p. 29, for "The whole...," and "(w)e thought..."

31. Hagood, *Memoirs*, p. 87, for the "new bridge" sources.

32. OR 14, p. 493, for orders announcing the abandonment of Coles and the dispositions for the guns; Grayson, William, *The Confederate Diary of William John Grayson* (SCHM, LXIII), p. 139, for "This is..."; see OR 14, pp. 499-500, for further dispositions of the guns.

33. Côté, *Rice and Ruin*, p. 397, for Lucas' departure; OR 14, pp. 502-3, and *A Compilation of the Official Records of the Union and Confederate*

Navies in the War of the Rebellion, 31 vols. (Washington, D.C.: U.S. Government Printing Office, 1894-1927), vol. 12, p. 825 (hereafter cited as *ORN*) for description of the transported guns; Burton, E. Milby, *The Siege of Charleston* (Columbia, SC: University of South Carolina Press, 1970), p. 94, for the *Planter* at Coles. A comparison of the arms on Coles Island, in Hagood, *Memoirs,* p. 58, and the weapons aboard the *Planter,* ORN 12, p. 825, supports Burton's contention that the *Planter* was at Coles on the 12th. OR 14, p. 500, for sighting of the *Planter* from Coles.

34. Hagood, *Memoirs,* p. 77, for make-up of the crew and armament. A number of sources describe the ship's guns, *ORN* 12, p. 821; ibid., p. 825; Uya, Okon Edet, *From Slavery To Public Service—Robert Smalls 1839-1915* (New York: Oxford University Press, 1971), p. 14, for the amount of ammunition. Cowley, Charles, *The Career of Gen. Robert Smalls, Individual Biography* (Lowell, MA., 1882), for the *Planter's* various uses and the amount of wood. Cowley was the judge advocate of the South Atlantic Blockading Squadron. *ORN* 12, p. 825, gives the names of the white crew as "C. J. Relyea as master, Samuel Smith. . .being mate, and Zerich Pitcher, engineer. . ." Also listed here are the types and calibers of the dismounted guns aboard the vessel: ". . .a banded rifle 42, one 8-inch Columbiad, one 8-inch seacoast howitzer, and one 32-pounder."

35. The particulars of the *Planter's* flight were culled from a number of sources. Uya, *From Slavery,* pp. 13-15, for the hatching of the plot and the flags, and for Smalls' prayer and the signal at Fort Sumter. Ammen, *The Old Navy,* p. 65, and Uya, *From Slavery,* p. 14, for the number of women and children (Uya gives the crew's names as Robert Smalls, John Smalls (no relation) Alfred Gradine, Abraham Jackson, Gabriel Turno, William Morrison, Samuel Chisholm, Abraham Alston, and David Jones). Cowley, *Robert Smalls,* who also mentioned the presence of the *Etiwan,* claims the *Planter* moored at the "South Commercial Wharf" while Uya terms it the "Southern Wharf" (p. 14). See also *ORN* 12, p. 826, for the unsuspecting sentinel (". . .she [the ship] was but pursuing her usual business."); Du Pont, Samuel Francis, Hayes, John D., ed., *A Selection From His Civil War Letters,* 2 vols. (Ithaca, New York: Cornell, 1969), 2, pp. 50-1, for Smalls' story; *ORN* 12, pp. 820-21, for Du Pont's report; *New York Tribune,* June 17, 1862, for Smalls' log.

36. *ORN* 12, p. 822, for Nickels report; ibid., pp. 822-25, for the official appraisement of the captured material, and pp. 825-6, for Confederate official report.

37. Du Pont, *Letters,* pp. 50-2, for the startling revelations of Smalls' intelligence.

Chapter Two
The Island and the Railroad

1. Army College staff ride, Charleston, SC, January 1993, for "land to water..."concept. My apologies for mislocating the captain's name. The best maps of James Island are available from U.S. Department of the Interior Geological Survey, 1959. Also see Davis, G. B., *The Official Military Atlas of the Civil War* (Arno Press: NY, 1978), Plate XXIII, maps 6 and 7.
2. Preservation Consultants Inc., James Island and Johns Island Historical and Architectural Inventory, pp. 4-39, provides a good history of James Island. For material on this paragraph, see pp. 4-8.
3. Ibid., pp. 8-14.
4. Ibid., pp. 16-18, for a brief view of Charleston during the Revolutionary War. Middlekauf, *The Glorious Cause*, pp. 438-450, for a detailed look at the British siege of Charleston.
5. Preservation Consultants Inc., pp. 18-21.
6. Ibid., p. 21-3, for a discussion of James Island's summer villages. Chambers, *Art and Artists of the South*, p. 25, offers another spin on the origin of Secessionville's name; *Charleston Courier*, May 6, 1862, published a letter from "Camp Yeadon, Secessionville" that covers the renaming of the village and includes "from the abortive...," "refreshing...," and "cool...," The letter contains a wealth of information about the village. The writer interviewed one of the residents, Edward Freer, who claimed that his move to Secessionville and subsequent exposure to the sea breezes had given him a lifetime of "unbroken and perfect health." The writer also lists the seven owners of the houses there—"1. Estate of Washington Hill; 2. Thomas H. Grimball; 3. Edward H. Freer; 4. Horace Rivers; 5. Edward Freer; 6. William B. Seabrook; and, 7. James W. Holmes." Dick Côté's "Jewel of The Cotton Fields," an exhaustive study of the summer homes of Secessionville, also makes a strong argument for the political origins of the village's renaming (pp. 61-4), but claims that the secession crisis of 1860 was the motivation. A Georgia sergeant, William H. Andrews, in his memoir *Footprints of a Regiment* (Longstreet Press, 1992), p. 146, later claimed that Secessionville was "where the first secession flag was raised"—an interesting observation since the peninsula is in sight of Fort Sumter.
7. *Charleston Courier*, May 6, 1862, describes the Confederate engineers' source of labor: "Wm. Mazyck Porcher...with a number of his negroes, and of those of his neighbors, of St. John's, Berkley and St. Steven's Parishes..." The letter's author climbed the observation tower on the 29th of April and reported that the "vista...gives a full view of Gen. Ripley's Headquarters, in Charleston, so as to admit of communication, between Headquarters and the Observatory, by means of telegraphic signals."

Col. Lewis Hatch is one of the many unknowns of the James Island campaign. Krick, *Lee's Colonels*, p. 187, provides what little detail we know of this officer, but his name surfaces repeatedly in the various reports and records; *OR* 14, p. 596, for one of many creditings of Hatch for the Secessionville works. See Pressley, "The Wee Nee Volunteers," pp. 135-6, and *OR* 14, p. 595, for good descriptions of the James Island line; the *Charleston Mercury*, June 21, 1862, describes the "ill-concealed sneers" that greeted Hatch's positioning of the Tower Battery; Pemberton's April 1862 returns located in *OR* 14, p. 487, places Hatch in charge of a unit called the Coast Rangers, on nearby Morris Island. In mid-May, Hatch organized a corps of signal men to link Morris, Fort Sumter and Fort Moultrie. Evidently, he remained in the Charleston area for the duration of the war. One surprising note is a single line from a copy of a Roswell Ripley's April 17 directive, Pemberton Order Book, Author's Collection, that placed Hatch in command of the 24th South Carolina. However, no other evidence supports this find.

8. Davis, *Atlas*, plate XXIII, maps 6 and 7 for the James Island roadways.

9. *OR* 14, p. 493, for Ripley's intended distribution of the Coles Island armament.

10. Cisco, *States Rights Gist*, pp. 1-76, for a history of Gist's life up to the James Island campaign.

11. *OR* 14, pp. 499-500, for Gist's report on the evolving James Island defenses.

12. Pressley, "The Wee Nee Volunteers," p. 134 for the Eutaw Battalion at Secessionville; Izlar, *Edisto Rifes*, pp. 34-5 for "a most..."

13. Hagood, *Memoirs*, p. 87, and *OR* 14, pp. 16-7 for observations of the Federal naval maneuvers from Coles Island.

14. *ORN* 13, pp. 5-7, for Du Pont's orders for a Stono reconnaissance and for Marchand's corresponding commands; Hagood, *Memoirs*, p. 87, and Du Pont, *Letters*, p. 60, for different views of the Federal frustrations on May 19.

15. *ORN* 13, p. 16, for Boutelle's report on the May 20 Stono reconnaissance; ibid., p. 15 for Marchand's brief report, and pp. 17-18 for Confederate reactions. On the 19th, Marchand developed a workable plan to take James Island with a quick rush on Fort Johnson, ibid., pp. 13-14. Coincidentally, Du Pont was then steaming on an inspection tour from Georgetown to St. Simons and could see the smoke of the burning forts as he passed the Stono Inlet. Du Pont, *Letters*, p. 61.

16. Hagood, *Memoirs*, p. 87 for a short account of Capers' retreat; *OR* 14, p. 16 for "shelling...," and Gist's view from the Battery Island environs. Hagood, *Memoirs*, p. 87 for the dumping of the carronade; Carlos Tracy, "A Real Soldier's Diary," in Frank Moore, *Rebellion Record* 12 vols. (New York: G. P. Putnam, 1862-1869), vol. 5, p. 279 (hereafter cited as Tracy, "Rebel Diary"), for "Our men..."

17. *OR* 14, p. 18.

18. Ibid., p. 18, for Stevens' report on the "affair" and "completely..."

19. Ibid., p. 18.

20. *ORN* 13, pp. 16-17, for Boutelle's report of the "affair."

21. Ibid., p. 17, for Bradford's report.

22. Ibid., pp. 16-17.

23. *OR* 14, p. 983-986, for Benham's reported plans; ISP, Benham to Stevens, May 18, 1862, gives a somewhat different take on his concepts which included a plan to take Morris Island "for the breaching positions of Sumpter." *OR* 14, p. 344-346, for Benham's transportation concerns; *ORN* 13, pp. 12-15, for the "sniping" between Du Pont and Benham, and for Rodgers' requests from Benham.

24. Ibid., p. 14, pp. 23-24, for "This of course...," "very courteous phrase," "a little...," and "difficult..." Luckily, Rodgers' report reiterates Benham's concerns, since Benham's original hasn't survived.

25. *ORN* 13, pp. 25-6, for Rodgers' countering positions; H. Benham to John L. Goldsborough, May 23, 1862; Author's Collection, for "you can."

26. Goldsborough to "My Dearest Wife," Author's Collection, May 24, 1862, sets forth the captain's efforts. "I have sent the Sumpter up the Wilmington River...At the same time two light draught steamers will go up the Savannah to make a reconnaissance...Likewise a balloon is being sent up to make believe that Savannah is our object. So that before long I hope will hear that Charleston is ours." Goldsborough also included Benham's letter of the 23rd, see note 25, supra, so that his wife "may better understand his (Benham's) wishes." *ORN* 13, pp. 27-8, for Du Pont's letter to Hunter; Du Pont, *Letters*, p. 81, for "calm...," "(C)oarse...," and "I think..."

27. Denison, Frederick, *Shot and Shell: The Third Rhode Island Heavy Artillery In The War of The Rebellion* (Providence: JA and RA Reid, 1879), pp. 86-86 for the 3rd's transfer to Edisto; ibid., pp. 59-62 for Company I's duty on Otter Island; ibid., p. 87 for drilling on Edisto.

28. Crowinshield, *First Regiment of Massachusetts Cavalry*, p. 46, for "a man...," and p. 63, for "Dreary..." Crowinshield provides a basic history of the 1st Massachusetts Cavalry.

29. Sifakis, *Who was Who*, p. 676, and Du Pont, *Letters*, pp. 64, 101, for Viele's departure to Norfolk. Especially interesting is Du Pont's characterization of Viele as "a prince of donkeys," p. 101. Darling, Roger, *A Sad and Terrible Blunder* (Vienna, VA: Potomac Western, 1990), pp. 79-85, for a recent account of Alfred Terry's service in the theater. Walkley, Stephen W., Jr., *History of the Seventh Connecticut Volunteer Infantry, Hawley's Brigade, Terry's Division, Tenth Army Corps, 1861-1865* (Hartford, CT., 1905), pp. 7-47, for Terry as colonel of the 7th; Cadwell, Charles K. *The Old Sixth Regiment* (New Haven: Tuttle, Morehouse & Taylor, 1875), pp. 38-9, for the 6th Connecticut's transfer to Edisto; Nichols, *Perry's Saints*, p. 105, for the 28th Massachusetts' departure; Palmer, Abraham J., *The History of the Forty-Eighth Regiment New York State Volunteers* (Brooklyn and New York: Dillingham, 1885), p. 40, for "greatly..." Named "Perry's Saints" for their preacher-turned-colonel James Perry, the 48th hated their assignment to Fort Pulaski.

30. Stevens, *Life of*, p. 388, for "took this..."

31. Ibid., pp. 388-9, for the Benham–Stevens friction; *OR* 14, p. 20 for Stevens' official descriptions of Benham's fluctuations.

32. Ibid., pp. 20-1 for Stevens' report, and pp. 22-4 for Christ's. Beecher, *History of the First Light Battery Connecticut Volunteers*, p. 118 for more on the delay.
33. *OR* 14, pp. 22-4.
34. Ibid., pp. 22-4.
35. Ibid., p. 22-4. See also p. 22 for Christ's dispatches to Stevens from the Pocotaligo front; *Charleston Mercury*, June 26, 1862, for the Federals' unique crossing method; *OR* 14, p. 21 for Cannon's excuses as told to Isaac Stevens.
36. Ibid., p. 21 for "abundant caution" and Stevens at the Ferry.
37. Ibid., p. 23 for the scattered Confederate pickets' delaying tactics. Unfortunately, no Confederate accounts of the battle identity them; *Charleston Mercury*, June 3, 1862, for a detailed account of Morgan's actions that morning, including the various troop dispositions; *OR* 14, p. 525 for Pemberton's responses to the enemy movement.
38. Ibid., p. 25 for reference to "Screven's Canal"; *Charleston Mercury*, June 2, 1862, for "old oaks"; *OR* 14, p. 25, for the troop numbers and "with. . ."; *Charleston Mercury*, June 3, 1862, for "Soon. . ., " and gun types. *Times* for the battle range from "at least an hour and a half," *Mercury*, June 3; to three hours, *OR* 14, p. 25. Walker's arrival is generally accepted as near 10:30. A trooper stopped the train Walker was on to inform the colonel of the enemy advance.
39. *OR* 14, p. 25 for the Rutledge retreat. Walker claimed that he ordered the general retreat because of the enemy flanking party, although he admits that ammunition had been summoned. *OR* 14, p. 25. While describing Walker's dispositions, the *Charleston Mercury*, June 3, 1862, noted that a "want of ammunition" contributed to the withdrawal; *OR* 14, p. 25 for "upon. . ."
40. *Charleston Mercury*, June 2, 1862, for location of the "Lincolnites" furthest penetration; *OR* 14, p. 25 for Elliot's arrival and "difficult."
41. Ibid., p. 25-6 for the firing at Gardens Corner and Walker's decision to halt; Krick, *Lee's Colonels*, p. 268 for some detail on Means and *OR* 14, p. 25 for Means' numbers; *Charleston Mercury*, June 2, 1862, for "after. . ."; ibid., June 3, 1862, for identity of Rutledge and Stokes; *OR* 14, p. 26 for Walker's orders to Phillips and his plans for the morning.
42. *Charleston Mercury*, June 2, 1862, for details of this incident.
43. Beecher, *Connecticut First Light Battery*, pp. 118-25, for the Connecticut guns at Pocotaligo, and p. 120 for "thick. . ."
44. Todd, William, *The 79th Highlanders, New York Volunteers in the War of the Rebellion* (Albany, 1886), pp. 129-32, for the Highlanders' movements, and p. 131 for Christ's orders to clear the ferry and the timings of the crossings *OR* 14, p. 24 for 3:00 am clearance; Andrew Fitch to "Dear Father," June 10, 1862, for "The attempt. . ."; Stevens, *Life of*, p. 389, and *OR* 14, p. 21, for Stevens' reaction to the operation.
45. *Charleston Mercury*, June 3, 1862, for "a brisk. . ."
46. *OR* 14, p. 26 and *Charleston Mercury*, June 3, 1862, for the May 30 pursuit and return to Pocotaligo.

Chapter Three
Yankees Come To James Island

1. *OR* 14, pp. 501-2, and p. 502, for Pemberton's sparring with Ripley and Taylor; ibid., pp. 503-4 for Lee's reactions to Pickens, et. al.; ibid., p. 505 for Lee's "request"; ibid. p. 507 for Ripley's nonchalance; ibid., p. 508 for Chesnut's concerns and the obstruction layers' frustrations; ibid., p. 510 for the council's resolve; ibid., pp. 509-10 for Pemberton's contrary defensive views.
2. Ibid., p. 511 for Evans' withdrawal, and ibid., pp. 509 and 511 for Pemberton's concerns; ibid., p. 514 for the possible attack.
3. Ibid., pp. 515-16 for Governor Pickens' letter to Lee, and p. 516 for "we want. . ."; ibid., pp. 517-18 for Pemberton's response to Chesnut. Grayson, *Diary of William Grayson,* p. 139 for "The provost. . . ," and p. 140 for "The domestic. . ."
4. *OR* 14, p. 518 for Lee's request; ibid., pp. 519-20 for Pemberton's orders for the Ripley transfer and replacements.
5. Ibid., p. 520 for official plans for the attack and "the battery. . ."; Augustine Smyth to Aunt Janey, May 29, 1862, Augustine Smyth Papers, Charleston Historical Society, for the siege train. Smyth was one of the sharpshooters assigned to the operation and remembered that the *Chesterfield* was to be towed into the Stono to "cut off their (the Federal gunboat's) retreat." Ibid.
6. *ORN* 13, p. 37 for Collins' report and p. 36 for "tight place."
7. Ibid., pp. 37-8 for Gist's report and Hagood, *Memoirs,* p. 87 for another view of this action. Not all of the Confederates were happy with this operation. Augustine Smyth thought that the "plan was spoiled by the enemy seeing the *Chesterfield,*" thus preventing the siege train from rushing Battery Island and cutting off the gunship. In an interesting sidelight, Smyth wrote, " . .as we were just between them, about 300 yards from the gun boat, we had full benefit of their shells which whizzed over our heads in fine style." Smyth to Aunt Janey, Augustine Smyth Papers, Charleston Historical Society, May 29, 1862.
8. *OR* 14, p. 521 for Mercer's arrival.
9. Ibid., p. 522 for the completion of the obstructions, and p. 523 for the new district alignments.
10. Ibid., p. 530 for James Island force; Hagood, *Memoirs,* p. 88 for Secessionville forces. Brown's and Lamar's Battalions eventually united as the 2nd South Carolina Artillery. Crute, *Confederate Units,* p. 249.
11. *OR* 14, p. 523 for "to the. . ."; ibid., p. 524 for Lee's letter to Pickens; Ballard, *Pemberton,* p. 104 for "astonished."
12. Ballard's *Pemberton,* Chapter 6, deals with Pemberton's problems with Pickens. See ibid., p. 104 for "confused. . ."; Grayson, *Diary of William Grayson,* p. 141, for "(throwing) up. . ."; *OR* 14, p. 526 for the channel obstructions and Pemberton's non-response to troop requests; ibid., p. 526 for the talkative Federal.

13. Ibid., p. 528 for Lee's advice.

14. Ely, *Ralph, The Diary of Captain Ralph Ely of the Eighth Michigan Infantry* (Mount Pleasant, MI.: Central Michigan University Press, 1965), p. 35; Pease, *Memoirs*, p. 31 for the shark shoot.

15. Adjutant General's Office-Michigan, *Record of Service of Michigan Volunteers in the Civil War*, (Kalamazoo, Mi., 1907), 8, pp. 149-50.

16. Todd, *The 79th Highlanders*, p. 91 for "unsophisticated" remark. See Pease, *Memoirs*, p. 14, for a more realistic rendering of the two regiments' early relationship; OR 6, pp. 47-54 for Isaac Stevens' and Col. William Fenton's reports on the battle at Port Royal Ferry, and ibid., OR 14, pp. 8-9 for Fenton's report on Whitmarsh Island; see *Reminiscences of Arand VanderVeen, M.D.* (Grand Haven, MI.), Bentley Historical Library for "Some. . ."; *Camp Kettle*, USAMHI, 100th Pennsylvania Collection, Carlysle Barracks, No.'s 11 and 12, for the brigade's reaction to the return of the 8th Michigan from their Whitmarsh Island fight.

17. Beecher, *First Light Connecticut Battery*, pp. 132-33 for 1st Connecticut's Beaufort departure; Todd, *The 79th Highlanders*, pp. 132-33 for the Highlanders' departure, and p. 133 for "early. . ." Ella Lonn, *Foreigners in the Union Army and Navy* (Baton Rouge: LSU Press, 1951), p. 130, reveals that Irish recruits would eventually outnumber the Scotch in most of the companies, but the regiment would manage to retain its Scottish flavor. Johnston, Terry A. Jr., *"Him on the One Side, and Me on the Other": The Civil War Letters of Alexander Campbell, Seventy-Ninth New York Infantry Regiment and James Campbell, First South Carolina ("Charleston") Battalion*; Terry A. Johnston, Jr., May 1996, Author's Collection, p. 98 for "We think. . ." (Campbell to "Dear wife", 31 May 1862). In subsequent references to the Campbell letters, I have used Johnston's transcriptions.

18. Gavin, William, *The 100th Regiment Pennsylvania Volunteers* (Dayton, Ohio: Morningside, 1989), pp. 1-43 for Colonel Leasure and the early days of the Roundheads, p. 5 for origination of the name "Roundhead," and OR 6, pp. 59-61 for Leasure's report on the battle at Port Royal Ferry.

19. Stevens, *Life of*, p. 390 for the arrival of the Irish and the Germans. The 46th New York, some of them veterans of Germany's revolution in 1848, had developed an erratic reputation during their service in the theater. See OR 6, pp. 120-3 and Darling, *A Sad and Terrible Blunder*, p. 84 for two examples; Todd, *The 79th Highlanders*, p. 134 for "totally. . .," and p. 137 for "the war. . ."; ISP, Benham to Stevens, May 18, 1862, has Hamilton's Battery with Stevens as late as May 18, but with standing orders for transfer to Edisto.

20. Eldredge, Daniel, *The Third New Hampshire Volunteers and All About It* (Boston, MA.: E. B. Stillings and Company, 1893), p. 165 for the 3rd New Hampshire's crossing; "Report of Colonel Serrell, Vol. Engs. of Operations on James Island against Charleston So. Ca.," Record Group 77, Records of the Office of the Chief of Engineers, S.8820, National Archives hereafter Serrell, "Report," July 7, 1862, for "a floating pier. . ."

21. Denison, *Third Rhode Island Heavy Artillery*, pp. 1-87 for the 3rd Rhode Island Heavy Artillery's early history, and pp. 86-7 for the makeup of the 3rd's Edisto force; *Annual Report of the Adjutant General of Rhode Island* (Providence: Providence Press Co., 1865), p. 506 for the February 17, 1862, redesignation to heavy artillery; ibid., p. 507, describes one section of Company C as being mounted for the operation.

22. Eldredge, *The Third New Hampshire*, pp. 1-164 for 3rd New Hampshire's early history, and pp. 745-50 for a capsule history of Jackson. The officer had served in the 9th U.S. Infantry in Mexico and saw action at Churubusco, Molino del Rey, and Chapultepec.

23. Serrell, "Report," July 7, 1862, for "some Negro guides. . ."; Cadwell, *Old Sixth*, p. 39 for "several. . . ," "to. . ., " and "hotbed. . ."

24. Eldredge, *The Third New Hampshire*, p. 165 for "marched. . . ," and p. 166 for "gave. . . ," and also for the drunken appearances. Eldredge also provides temperature for the day; Cadwell, *Old Sixth*, p. 40, and Denison, *The Third Rhode Island Heavy Artillery*, p. 88 for lack of food; Price, Isiah, *History of the Ninety-Seventh Regiment Pennsylvania Volunteer Infantry* (Philadelphia, 1875), p. 112, for rumored death and equipment toss; Serrell, "Report," July 7, 1862 for the accident at the pier.

25. Eldredge, *The Third New Hampshire*, pp. 166-7 for the destruction of Sugar Mills plantation and the arrival of the storm, and ibid., p. 167 for "(I)t. . . ," and the continued hunger; Cadwell, *Old Sixth*, p. 40 for more storm description; Denison, *The Third Rhode Island Heavy Artillery*, p. 88 for "If you. . . ," and guards at the springs.

26. Eldredge, *The Third New Hampshire*, p. 167 for the review; Price, *Ninety Seventh Pennsylvania*, p. 112 for a view from the rear of the column.

27. Eldredge, *The Third New Hampshire*, p. 167 for the storm beginnings and the road conditions (in some cases, filled with 3 inches to a foot of water). Metcalf, Edwin, *Personal Incidents in the Early Campaigns of the Third Regiment Rhode Island Volunteers and the Tenth Army Corps* (Rhode Island Soldiers and Sailors Historical Society #9, Providence: Rider, 1879), p. 21 for, "My horse. . . ," and p. 22 for "Our little. . ."

28. Eldredge, *The Third New Hampshire*, p. 167 for "quite. . . ," and *Early Campaign*, p. 23 for "how. . . ," Cowley, Charles, *Leaves From A Lawyer's Life Afloat and Ashore* (Lowell, MA.: Penhollow Printing, 1879), p. 63 for "(We) arrived. . ." Cowley states the 6th suffered for want of cooking utensils for three weeks; Price, *Ninety Seventh Pennsylvania*, p. 112 for the arrival of the 97th Pennsylvania. The confusion of the operation has made the marching order of Horatio Wright's troops almost impossible to state categorically.

29. Todd, *The 79th Highlanders*, p. 137 for "(O)ld. . . ," and "the trip. . ."

30. Ibid., p. 137 for separation within the flotilla and discovery of the movement's intent.

31. Gavin, *100th Pennsylvania*, p. 80 for Roundhead detachment; Todd, *The 79th Highlanders*, p. 138 for "corral" and "fifty. . ."

32. Ibid., p. 138 for "'fiery'. . . ," and "strong picket"; pp. 138-9 for Elliot's advance.

33. Gavin, *100th Pennsylvania*, p. 80 for "It was. . . ," and "the countless. . ."

34. Todd, *The 79th Highlanders*, p. 139 for "a cap. . . ," and "claimed. . ."

35. Tracy, "Rebel Diary," p. 279 for the Federal appearance and resulting exchanges; *Charleston Courier*, May 6, 1862 describes the Seabrook house as "an elegant and commodious mansion, and is at present the headquarters of General Gist." See Pressley, "Wee Nee Volunteers," p. 136 for change in the Eutaw's camp.

36. Tracy, "Rebel Diary," p. 279 for Tracy's reconnaissance.

37. *OR* 14, pp. 534-5 for Pemberton's correspondence with his district commanders, p. 534 for Davis' requests, p. 535 for "dangerous," and p. 534 for Pemberton's orders to Evans.

39. *Charleston Mercury*, June 9, 1862, for details of Chichester's actions and "every appliance. . ." Abstracts of Troop Strengths notes the Gist Guards with 70 effectives on "62 April 2."

40. *Charleston Mercury*, June 9, 1862 for "were soon. . . ," "Your command. . . ," and continued details on the action.

41. Tracy, "Rebel Diary," p. 279 for the camp alert.

Chapter Four
First Blood

1. "Jordan," June 3, 1862, "Letter from Hilton Head," *Boston Herald*, June 17, 1862.

2. Daniel Leasure to "My dear wife," Daniel Leasure Papers, M. Gyla McDowell Collection, Pennsylvania State University, June 4, 1862, for Colonel Leasure's arrival.

3. Gavin, *100th Pennsylvania*, pp. 84-85, for details of the early morning advance.

4. The best map of 1862 Sol Legare Island accompanied Col. Edward Serrell's official report to the chief engineer of the army dated July 7, 1862. This map, which identifies the area north and east of the Legare buildings as a cotton field, can be found in file 1.107 Civil War Maps/National Archives. The location of the Legare house—which is not on the Serrell map—is best given in Ripley, Warren, ed., *Siege Train, The Journal of a Confederate Artilleryman in the Defence of Charleston* (Columbia, SC: University of South Carolina Press, 1986), pp. 143, 145, and 194. See Gavin, *100th Pennsylvania*, p. 86 for Cline's version of the same and "unmistakable. . ."

5. Ibid., p. 86 for "(T)hey broke. . . ," and "In a few. . ."

6. See ibid., pp. 85-7 for further details. Hazard Stevens describes this action, including the makeup of the Federal line, in *Papers of the Military Historical Society of Massachusetts*, vol. 9, pp. 135-6, hereafter referred to as Stevens, PMHSM. Roundhead Thomas Williams, Thomas Williams

Collection, USAMHI, p. 25, recalled that the 28th Massachusetts "fell back in confusion rallying behind us" before the Pennsylvanians fell back "behind a small rise." After engaging the Confederates for a time, Williams joined "A small party...ordered to advance to the houses."

7. Gavin, *100th Pennsylvania*, pp. 85-7 for continued details, p. 85 for "cut...," and "They kept..."; p. 87 for "to...," and "We were..." Stevens, *Life of*, p. 391 for the Confederate skirmishers on the marshline and the presence of a mounted officer leading the attack; Stevens, PMHSM, p. 135 for Stevens' view of the Roundhead movements. On p. 136, Stevens describes the Confederate attack ("they charged down the road..."), as taking a generally north to south direction. No map of the actual battle has surfaced.

8. *OR* 14, p. 29 for Capers' report of his advance, "until...," and "engaged..."; Capers, *The Soldier Bishop*, p. 53 for Lamar's warning.

9. *OR* 14, p. 29 for details on "poured...," "most...," "to cut...," and "I resolved..." In his report, Capers describes the isolated Federals as lining "the long hedge to the east" of the Legare buildings.

10. Ibid., p. 31 for "scene...," and pp. 30-1 for Gaillard's report. See Capers, *The Soldier Bishop*, pp. 53-4 for Caper's short exhortation and the beginning of the charge; Irish volunteers, p. 27 for "a strapping...," "like wire," and "an Irishman's..." Also see *Charleston Mercury*, June 4, 1862, for further details of the engagement.

11. *OR* 14, p. 30 for Capers' thinking, and p. 31 for Gaillard's report, including Walker's wounding; *Charleston Mercury*, June 4, 1862, for Bresnan's wounding; Capers, *The Soldier Bishop*, p. 54 and *Charleston Mercury*, June 4, 1862 for the Federal artillery fire.

12. Todd, *The 79th Highlanders*, p. 139 for "fall in..."; ibid., pp. 139-40 for further details of the Highlanders movements; *New York Herald*, June 24, 1862, for "scattered...," and the capturing of the wounded officer.

13. *OR* 14, pp. 27-8 for Howard's report.

14. Ibid., p. 30 for Capers' retreat.

15. Todd, *The 79th Highlanders*, p. 140 for "Clark...," and details of the afternoon advance. However, William Gage of Company A, *New York Herald*, June 24, 1862, claimed that "In this charge we lost one man named Clark...who fell wounded and was taken prisoner, but was rescued by his own company." Neither account dovetails completely with the known movements of the 79th New York on this day. It seems more likely that Clark had been shot the night before rather than having been wounded and captured in Legare's field on the 3rd.

16. Todd, *The 79th Highlanders*, pp. 140-2 for details of this confrontation, and p. 141 for "(A) few..."; *OR* 14, p. 28 for Keenan's spotting. Beecher, *Connecticut First Light Battery*, pp. 133-4 for the 1st Connecticut's arrival and advance to the front. Especially interesting is Porter's conversation with Hazard Stevens: "...if we meet the enemy we will action front and drive them before us."

17. Ibid., pp. 134-5 for this confrontation; ibid., p. 135 for "shower...," and "with considerable..."

18. Pressley, "Wee Nee Volunteers," p. 138 for "perfectly furious"; ibid., pp. 136-8 for Pressley's account of the Eutaw Battalion's confusing movements this day; Tracy, "Rebel Diary," p. 280 for Lamar's efforts and Gist's near-miss; Capers, *The Soldier Bishop*, p. 53 quotes Ellison Capers: ". . . why the regiments, which by that time came up and took position at River's, did not pull the guns out of the bog I cannot say."

19. Pressley, "Wee Nee Volunteers," p. 138 for the near-disaster with Hagood's men, "to hold. . . ," and "confidently. . ."

20. Ibid., pp. 138-9 for the weapons' discharge and Pressley's meeting with Mercer; ibid., p. 139 for "After. . . ," and "Well. . ." Mercer was evidently unaware that Hagood remained in Charleston.

21. Tracy, "Rebel Diary," p. 280 for "wet. . ."

22. Andrew Fitch to "Dear Father," Andrew Fitch Letters, Lewis Leigh Collection, USAMHI, June 10, 1862.

23. Todd, *The 79th Highlanders*, pp. 142-3 for Campbell's discovery and "Had. . ." Johnston, Campbell Thesis, pg. 2 gives an interesting account of the Campbell brothers' antebellum life in Charleston. Alexander was a stone cutter who moved from New York City to Charleston, where he worked on the Customs House. Both he and his brother enlisted in a local militia group. While he was stationed on Port Royal Island, Alexander went aboard the recently-seized *Planter* "and had a talk with the hands." One of the crew members recognized the Scotsman from his stay in Charleston, and they were soon engaged in a wide-ranging discussion. Ibid, p. 96 (Campbell to "Dear Brother," May 22, 1862).

24. Gavin, *100th Pennsylvania*, pp. 85-7 for details of Cline and his men's capture.

25. *OR* 14, pp. 535-6 for Pemberton's orders.

26. Ibid., pp. 536-8 for Pemberton's orders. *Charleston Mercury*, June 4, 1862, for the reluctant Federal prisoner (probably Captain Cline).

27. Pease, *Memoirs*, pp. 31-33 for details of Pease's adventures.

28. Ibid., p. 33.

Chapter Five
Sparring

1. *Charleston Mercury*, June 4, 1862, Grayson, *Diary of William Grayson*, p. 142 for "The talk. . ."

2. *OR* 14, p. 534 for Davis' requests; ibid., p. 539 for Davis' early troop requisitions; ibid., p. 540 for Davis' seeming retreat and the President's reply to Pickens. Within the reply lies the evidence of Pickens' June 3 dispatch. See ibid., pp. 540-1 for Pemberton's powder shortages; ibid., p. 540 for Pickens' solicitous offer of a liaison.

3. Pressley, "Wee Nee Volunteers," pp. 139-40 for "the men. . . ," and further details of the Eutaw Battalion's day.

4. Pease, *Memoirs*, pp. 33-4 for Pease's day and p. 34 for "Although. . ."

5. Todd, *The 79th Highlanders*, pp. 143-4 for the Highlanders' experiences and the cannon capture.

6. Gavin, *100th Pennsylvania*, p. 91 for "There is. . ."; George Leasure to Unknown, fragment found in Daniel Leasure Letters file (Box 2, file 15, McDowell Collection, PSU); Daniel Leasure to "My dear wife," June 4, 1862, for "They fought. . ."

7. *OR* 14, p. 539 for "to revive. . ."; Tracy, "Rebel War Diary," p. 280 for "Design. . ." Both Tracy and Pressley, the latter in "Wee Nee Volunteers," p. 140, describe the withdrawal ordered by Mercer.

8. *OR* 14, p. 539 for Pemberton's "gathering." See Unknown, "Diary of a Confederate soldier, May 25, 1861-October 18, 1863, Begins at Richmond, Madison Parish, Louisiana, concludes one mile from Chattanooga, TN., Confederate States of America Collection, Box 2C484, Folder 9, Eugene C. Barker Texas History Center, University of Texas in Austin, p. 40 for details on 4th Louisiana Battaalion. Although never officially designated, George P. Harrison's Brigade included his own 32nd Georgia, Gilbert William's 47th Georgia, and Lt. Col. John McEnery's 4th Louisiana Battalion. All had been serving near Savannah and arrived on James Island within days of Pemberton's request for troops. *Supplement to the Official Records* (Wilmington, N.C.: Broadfoot Publishing Company, 1994), pt. 2, vol. 23, p. 812 (hereafter cited as *SOR*), describes the battalion's trip from Savannah to Secessionville.

9. *Charleston Mercury*, June 5, 1862, for "criminal. . ." Woodward, C. Vann, *Mary Chesnut's Civil War* (New Haven and London: Yale University Press, 1981), p. 364 for "Landing. . ."

10. *OR* 14, p. 549 for exchanged between Davis and Pemberton. Lee to Davis, June 5, 1862, quoted from Dowdey, Clifford and Manarin, Louis H. eds., *The Wartime Papers of R. E. Lee* (NY: Bramhall House, 1961), p. 183-4 reads in part, "After much reflection I think if it was possible to reinforce Jackson strongly, it would change the character of the war. This can only be done by the troops in Georgia, South Carolina & North Carolina." Lee was considering the possibility of Jackson invading Maryland and Pennsylvania with his reinforced command. The forward elements of Alexander Lawton's Brigade reached Jackson on June 10. Tanner, Robert G., *Stonewall in the Valley* (Mechanicsburg, Pennsylvania.: Stackpole Books, 1996), p. 416.

11. Davis, ed., *Confederate General*, 6, pp. 174-5; Sifakis, *Who was Who*, p. 444; and Faust, ed., *Encyclopedia*, p. 487 for brief recountings of Hugh Mercer's life. Davis, *Confederate General*, 4, pp. 190-1 for William Duncan Smith.

12. *OR* 14, pp. 550-1 for Harrison's orders and the bounty offer.

13. Hagood, *Memoirs*, p. 90 for "half-drowned" and "I say. . ." Ibid., p. 90 for Hagood's memory of picket fire. Tracy, "Rebel Diary,", p. 280 for "Enemy. . ."

14. Davis, ed., *Atlas*, Plate XXIII, maps 6 and 7 for the James Island roadways; Pressley, "Wee Nee Volunteers," p. 140 for the Eutaw Battalion action and "No other casualties."

15. *OR* 14, p. 551 for Evans' report. Dunovant's unit is variously described as "the fine regiment of regulars," ibid., p. 515, "First Regiment Infantry," ibid., p. 551, and "1st Infantry," ibid., p. 591. He had commanded the 12th South Carolina, but remained in the theater when that regiment went north with Maxcy Gregg. See Chapter 1, note 15, supra.

16. Todd, *The 79th Highlanders*, p. 144 for details on "at intervals" and "would..."

17. *Wolverine Citizen*, June 21, 1862, for "...were ordered..."; Ely, *Diary of*, p. 36 for "The night..."

18. Another of the campaign's unknown quantities, the 28th Massachusetts left little of its record for posterity. Various sources provide some detail of the regiment's history, including Conyngham, *Irish Brigade*, p. 576; Fox, William F., *Regimental Losses in the Civil War* (Dayton, OH: Morningside, 1985), p. 118; Adjutant General's Report (MA.), pp. 296-300, Higginson, Thomas W., *Massachusetts in the Army and Navy During the War of 1862-1865*, 2 vols. (Boston, 1896), vol. 1, pp. 248-9; Bowen, James L., *Massachusetts in the War* (Springfield, 1889), pp. 419-421, and Tucker, ed., *The History of the Irish Brigade* (Fredricksburg,1995), p. 130-48.

Rumors of trouble in New York and Monteith's general incompetence—and an evident trouble with the bottle—come from the Adjutant General's Report (MA.), p. 300. and Tucker, ed., *Irish Brigade*, p. 130. Moore appears on the roster as the captain of Company A, 11th Massachusetts, from that regiment's inception, thus opening the possibility that Moore fought at First Bull Run. *Boston Herald*, "Letter from Port Royal," April 22, 1862 for "We have found...," and ibid., "Letter from Hilton Head," June 17, 1862, for "The 'Faugh-a-Ballahs...'". "Faugh A Ballagh" was an Irish battlecry which, loosely translated, meant "clear the way." See Gavin, *100th Pennsylvania*, p. 91, and Leasure to "My dear wife, June 4, 1862, for Leasure's pinning the blame on the 28th Massachusetts. Reverend Robert Browne referred disdainfully to the "28th Massachusetts, a foreign regiment for the "mistake" that resulted in Cline's capture. See Browne Letter to "My own dear wife," June 14, 1862. The Highlanders' opinion of the Irish regiment will become evident later in this book.

19. *OR* 14, pp. 550-1 for Pemberton's orders.

20. Stevens, *Life of*, pp. 392-3 for Isaac Stevens' view of Benham's urgings; ibid., p. 392 for "We shall..."

21. *OR* 14, p. 552 for S.O. #70 and related announcements. Grayson, *Diary of William Grayson*, pp. 142-3 for all quoted material.

22. Hagood, *Memoirs*, pp. 89-90 for the implementation of the "Advanced Forces" strategy. One artillery unit assigned to James Island was the six guns of the Macbeth Light Artillery, under the command of Capt. Robert Boyce. Johnson, Curt, *Artillery Hell* (College Station: Texas A&M University Press, 1995), p. 89, and Crute, *Confederate Units*, pp. 269-70.

23. Hagood., *Memoirs*, p. 90 for Hagood's concerns with the "haphazard" command arrangements on James; ibid., p. 89 for "best" regiments.

24. See Slemmons, J. H. Slemmons Diary, Michael Kraus collection, p.

57 for a humorous recounting of the Roundheads' day on Sol Legare: "Just as we were getting some coffee for supper & I had just diped a tin full bang goes a secesh cannon & a shell came whiaaing. Oh! you ought to hear em sing and see the boys scatter behind the trees and houses, and drop on the ground, Oh! I had to laugh a good deal." Serrell, "Report," June 6, 1862, for his report on the "small" reconnaissance; Cadwell, *Old Sixth*, pp. 40-1 for "cooking. . . ," Todd, The *79th Highlanders*, p. 144 for the weather. Metcalf, *Personal Incidents*. .*Third Rhode Island*, p. 23 for, "Battalion. . ."; Ely, *Diary of*, p. 36 for "Drying. . ."; Eldredge, *The Third New Hampshire*, p. 168 for "fine. . ."

25. Eldredge, *The Third New Hampshire*, p. 168 for the 3rd New Hampshire's crossing.

26. Todd, *The 79th Highlanders*, p. 145 for the Highlanders' actions. Slemmons, "Diary," p. 58 describes a lookout "on the top of the house in which the pickets headquarters are," which provided "a fine view of fort Sumpter" and the Charleston environs. He is probably referring to the Legare plantation house.

27. *OR* 14, pp. 552-3 for the talkative Northerner; ibid., p. 555 for "to move. . ."; ibid., pp. 553-4 for further Pemberton preparations.

28. Eldredge, *The Third New Hampshire*, p. 168 for "a real. . . ," and further details of the 3rd New Hampshire's first morning on Sol Legare Island.

29. Todd, *The 79th Highlanders*, pp. 145-6 for the Highlanders' advance.

30. Company A of the 7th Connecticut, and possibly Company's B and C, crossed to James Island on the 6th, and the rest of the regiment on the 7th. *SOR*, pt. 2, v. 3, p. 731. While these companies engaged in a reconnaissance northwest of Grimball's—still to be described—the remainder of the regiment made camp "within two and one-half miles of the enemy's lines." Walkley, *Seventh Connecticut*, p. 48, for "in a muddy. . . ," and "tender. . ."; Tourtellotte, *A History of Company K of the Seventh Connecticut volunteer Infantry in the Civil War*, p. 32, "in a floating. . ."

31. Todd, *The 79th Highlanders*, p. 145 for the appearance of the balloon. *New York Tribune*, June 17, 1862, for "discovered. . ." The *Tribune* reported that Starkweather made aerial reconnaissance's on the 7th, 8th, and 9th of June. Slemmons, "Diary," p. 59 for "It was. . ."

32. Serrell, "Report," June 7, 1862, for "that large bodies. . . ," and "a long line. . ." See ibid., for excellent detail of the reconnaissance. Price, *Ninety Seventh Pennsylvania*, p. 113, "difficult. . . ," and "promptness. . ."

33. Isaac Stevens mentions the Hawley/Lyons group in *OR* 14, p. 33. *SOR*, pt. 2, vol. 3, p. 731, places Company A in a "slight skirmish" on the 7th; p. 739 has Company B on a "reconnaissance as far as a church near Secessionville," and p. 746 puts Company C "in a reconnaissance on the enemy's right wing." See Brooks Map, NA Record Group 77b, HQ Map file, I-42, hereafter Brooks Map, for the location of the Grimball buildings. A second farm lane ran south from the buildings, crossed a small creek, and turned west towards the Stono. Here, one leg continued to the river while a second ran south to cross a tidal marsh on a causeway, then curved

east and north where it joined Hawley's route near its junction with the roadway to the Grimball's causeway.

34. Eldredge, *The Third New Hampshire*, p. 168 for "(B)linded...," "Language...," "sheds...," and "permanent." See Todd, *The 79th Highlanders*, p. 145 for the weather.

35. OR 14, pp. 553-5 for Pemberton's orders.

36. Ibid., p. 34 for Evans' report of this incident.

37. This reconnaissance germinated in the Benham-Stevens correspondence of June 6, 1862, Stevens, *Life of*, pp. 392-3. Although Isaac Stevens wanted to enlarge the operation to include a full-scale assault on the Confederate defenses, the operation eventually assumed less ambitious goals.

38. OR 14, pp. 33-4 for Stevens' report; *New York Tribune*, July 8, 1862 for this excellent description of the road running from Grimball's towards the Presbyterian Church and the Confederate lines. Ibid., for "girdled..."; *New York Herald*, June 17, 1862, for "second forest."

39. Ibid for "a galling fire," a "lively affair," and "unexplained..." See also, ibid., for Major Wright's wounding and the rattled state of the troops. OR 14, p. 33 for "a heavy..." *New York Tribune*, June 17, 1862 for Morrow's ankle sprain and horse wounding.

40. *New York Herald*, June 17, 1862, for naval fire; OR 14, p. 33 for "it prudent..."

41. *Charleston Mercury*, June 10, 1862, for "the sorry..."; ibid and Pressley, "Wee Nee Volunteers," p. 140 for the Confederate view of this skirmish.

42. Record Group 393, Expeditionary Corps, Letters sent and received, EC, General and Special Orders, EC, 2nd Brigade Correspondence, Department of the South, Letters sent and received, National Archives, Stevens to Fenton, et. al., June 7, 1862, gives Stevens' orders to his brigade and regimental commanders for "an armed reconnaissance" on the 8th. Slemmons, "Diary," for "in..."; OR 14, p. 33 for "two...," and details of the first reconnaissance on the Federal right. The remaining quotes come from the *New York Tribune*, 8 July, 1862 in a report dated June 24. The *Tribune* reporter did not accompany this reconnaissance but did observe the Tower Battery from a similar point two weeks later.

43. Eldredge, *The Third New Hampshire*, p. 169 for "(W)e saw...," and further details of the 3rd New Hampshire's movement; OR 14, p. 33 for "well directed..."

44. Stevens identifies the four prisoners as "a corporal and 3 privates of the Charleston Rifle volunteers." He is probably referring to the "Charleston Riflemen," a company in the Charleston Battalion. I assume Stevens erred slightly.

45. Walkley, *Seventh Connecticut*, Appendix, p. 11 for Woodford's adventure. Neither the 7th Connecticut nor the 28th Massachusetts was officially cited as part of this reconnaissance. The only evidence of their participation is in ibid., p. 48. One lingering question lies in Ely, *Diary of*, p. 36, which places the 7th Connecticut in a skirmish on Sol Legare Island on

June 7, where this incident could have occurred. Also recall that three companies of the 7th Connecticut, including Woodford's Company A, participated in the reconnaissance northwest of Grimball's on the 7th. For now, I accept, with reservation, Walkley's claim that Woodford's capture occurred on the 8th.

46. Eldredge, *The Third New Hampshire*, p. 169 for the 3rd New Hampshire's change of base; ibid., p. 169 for "did. . . ," and "the diaries. . ."

47. Tracy, "Rebel Diary," p. 280. Tracy mis-dated his entry for the 7th. The actions he describes more closely correlates with the actual events of the 8th.

48. OR 14, p. 556 for "a strong. . ."; ibid., p. 555 for "endeavor. . ."; Grayson, *Diary of William Grayson*, p. 143 for "So we. . ."

49. OR 14, p. 34 for Evans' description of "a sad catastrophe." Evans probably mistook the date of the accident, for Serrell's force witnessed it towards evening of the 7th. Serrell, "Report," June 7, 1862.

50. OR 14, p. 34 for Evans' report.

51. Price, *Ninety Seventh Pennsylvania*, p. 114 for the Legareville holding force and the 97th Pennsylvania's crossing to Grimball's. Cadwell, *Old Sixth*, p. 41 claims that the 6th Connecticut crossed on the 8th of June. All other evidence points to its movement being on the 9th, see Eldredge, *The Third New Hampshire*, p. 169 for the 6th Connecticut acting as a relief force for the 3rd New Hampshire and Price, *Ninety Seventh Pennsylvania*, p. 114 for the 6th Connecticut crossing with the 97th Pennsylvania. Eldredge, *The Third New Hampshire*, p. 169 for the bustle at Grimball's wharf. Price, *Ninety Seventh Pennsylvania*, p. 114 for the site of the 97th Pennsylvania's camp.

52. Denison, *The Third Rhode Island Heavy Artillery*, p. 89 for 3rd Rhode Island Heavy Artillery's crossing of the Stono and immediate picket duty. Metcalf, *Personal Incidents. . .Third Rhode Island*, pp. 24-27 for a fine description of the 3rd's first night on James Island.

53. Beecher, *Connecticut First Light Battery*, p. 140 for Chatfield's "in the face. . ." Chatfield claimed that the 1st Connecticut Light Battery covered his landing, but this seems unlikely. Metcalf, *Personal Incidents. . .Third Rhode Island*, p, 27-9 for the remaining quotes and Metcalf's full recounting of this incident.

54. Pressley, "Wee Nee Volunteers," p. 140 for the Eutaw Battalion's on picket. Pressley's date for this day is mistaken. The attack he places on the 9th actually occurred on the 10th. Working backwards, his account of June 8, with the Eutaw Battalion's 24-hour picket duty would have had to have occurred on the 9th. See Tracy, "Rebel Diary," p. 280 for "Enemy. . ." Again, Tracy had mis-dated this entry in his journal. See this chapter's footnote 44.

55. Ely, *Diary of*, p. 36 for "The enemy. . . ," and the movement of the 7th Connecticut.

56. *Charleston Mercury*, October 18, 1862 provides details of Thomas Lamar's civilian life and military service.

57. OR 14, p. 556 for "Don't allow. . ."
58. Ibid., p. 556 for Pemberton's warning to Gist.

Chapter Six
Prelude

1. OR 14, pp. 36-7 for Chatfield's report, and 37-8 for Hill's report; Price, *Ninety Seventh Pennsylvania*, p. 116 for the layout of the picket force and the noon skirmish.
2. Ibid., p. 116 for "the men. . . ," and "a terrific. . ."
3. OR 14, pp. 350-2 for Benham's orders. These evolutions display Benham's dangerous tendency to expect miraculous results from complicated maneuvers. The ability of three separate commands to coordinate their movements with each other while maneuvering in the darkness is hard to imagine. Add to this his hope that the navy would be able to support the inland thrusts with accurate shellfire, and you have the recipe for a disaster. The Confederates had enough close calls covering this land—recall the Eutaw Battalion/1st South Carolina face-off on June 3, and the Eutaw Battalion/24th South Carolina problem on the 5th—and they had held this area for over a year.
4. Hagood, *Memoirs*, p. 91 for Hagood's understanding of the attack's purpose and Smith's arrangements; Pressley, "Wee Nee Volunteers," pp. 140-1 for the Eutaw Battalion's involvement.
5. Hagood, *Memoirs*, p. 91 for the pre-battle jockeying; Pressley, "Wee Nee Volunteers," pp. 140-1 for the Eutaw Battalion's movements; *Charleston Mercury*, June 11, 1862, for the intensity of the shelling, which was clearly heard in the city. The length of the bombardment comes from Price, *Ninety Seventh Pennsylvania*, p. 116 (begins "about noon"), and *Charleston Mercury*, June 11, 1862 (the attack begins "At half past three).
6. Hagood, *Memoirs*, p. 91 for "almost. . . ," and the disordered nature of Williams' unit; Price, *Ninety Seventh Pennsylvania*, p. 116 for "confidently," the `within 10 yards' penetration, and the removal of the Confederate wounded; Denison, *The Third Rhode Island Heavy Artillery*, p. 90 for "Here. . ."; *Charleston Mercury*, June 24, 1862, for the first Confederate attack.
7. Price, *Ninety Seventh Pennsylvania*, pp. 116-17 for the Federal version of the attack, and ibid., p. 117 for "determined."
8. Ibid., p. 117 for "with. . . ," "rendered. . . ," and "the flashing. . ."; OR 14, p. 37 for "a deadly. . ." The Brooks Map identifies the area between the woods and the Union camps as a potato field and "Hard Ground-Grass."
9. Price, *Ninety Seventh Pennsylvania*, p. 119 for the gunboats' fire and Hamilton's Battery; *Charleston Mercury*, June 24, 1862, for more on Hamilton's guns; Denison, *The Third Rhode Island Heavy Artillery*, p. 90 for the arrival of the artillery, and ibid., p. 90 for "administered. . ."

10. Ibid., p. 90 for the drummer boys; *OR* 14, p. 35 for "a slight contusion"; Price, *Ninety Seventh Pennsylvania*, p. 118 for 97th Pennsylvania casualties.

11. *Charleston Mercury*, June 11, 1862, for "murderous" and "heavy"; ibid., for Col. Williams' actions; Hagood, *Memoirs*, p. 91 for artillery effectiveness; *Charleston Mercury*, June 12, 1862 for the Federal cover.

12. Hagood, *Memoirs*, p. 91 for the disengagement.

13. *Charleston Mercury*, June 12, 1862 for 47th Georgia's casualty list; Hagood, *Memoirs*, p. 90 for total losses; Davis, *Confederate General*, 5, p. 190 for "would. . ."; John Marszalek, ed., *The Diary of Miss Emma Holmes 1861-1866*, p. 177 has Miss Holmes writing, ". . .Gen. P. said angrily 'I believe I will arrest you, I will arrest you, you may consider yourself under arrest.' Nothing further was said, & he was released before the day was out."

14. Price, *Ninety Seventh Pennsylvania*, p. 118 for Confederate losses on the field and the talkative prisoner, and for "the men. . ."; *OR* 14, p. 37 for "too much. . ."; Ely, *Diary of*, p. 36 for "General Wright. . ."; Price, *Ninety Seventh Pennsylvania*, p. 119 for "tenacious. . . ," and p. 120 for the New York–Pennsylvania conversation.

15. Ibid., p. 120 for the 76th Pennsylvania's picket relief; Denison, *The Third Rhode Island Heavy Artillery*, p. 91 for "smarting. . ."

16. *ORN* 13, pp. 88-9 for Drayton's report containing all quoted material.

17. Alexander Campbell, letter dated June 10, 1862. Campbell Thesis.

18. *OR* 14, p. 46 for Hunter's orders to Benham, perhaps the most crucial document of the campaign. Hunter's decision to delay his Charleston assault until reinforcements arrived comes from *OR* 14, p. 42. Note, however, that Hunter wrote this well after the Secessionville battle, thus the possibility that Hunter was pinning a scapegoat for the repulse will always exist.

19. Ibid., p. 89 for Benham's reasons for deferring the attack and the time of the announcement; ibid., p. 352 for Wright's report; ISP, Stevens to "My dear wife," June 10, 1862 for "imbecile. . ." and "an ass. . ."; Stevens, *Life of*, p. 393 for the Mansfield remark, and p. 394 for the Benham–Wright feud; EC, Stevens to Sealy, June 10, 1862, for "The Surgeon. . . ," and Stevens to Benham, June 11, 1862, for "The men. . ."; ISP, Stevens to "My dear wife," June 11, 1862 for "Hunter has. . ." The freedmen regiment never saw service on James Island. See Richards, *Isaac Stevens*, pp. 364-379 for a full discussion of Stevens' negative views on arming former slaves.

20. Benham refers to his last meeting with Hunter in *OR* 14, p. 45; Stevens, *Life of*, p. 394 for "Those. . ."; Lusk, *War Letters*, p. 152 for "I believe. . ."

21. *Charleston Mercury*, June 12, 1862, for "heavy. . ."; "gallant. . ."; and "many. . ."

22. *OR* 14, p. 558 for Pemberton's orders to Evans, and ibid., p. 559 for the Pemberton–Randolph exchanges, including "if. . ." and "I not. . ."

23. Ibid., p. 559 for Pemberton's odd transmittal to Smith, which includes all quoted material. Pemberton also chose this moment to renew his complaints about Lamar's aggressiveness—"I shall get a little more powder tonight, but if it wasted by firing at gunboats from Secessionville it might as well not be here. I am informed Colonel Lamar has been returning their fire again. You must put a stop to this." Marszalek, *Diary of Emma Holmes*, p. 177 for Smith's request for written orders.

24. Grayson, *Diary of William Grayson*, p. 143 for "Doubts..." His diary inscription is actually dated the 10th of June. OR 14, p. 560 for the Miles letter, which includes all quoted material.

25. Ely, *Diary of*, p. 36 for the 8th Michigan's movements; Walkley, *Seventh Connecticut*, p. 49 for the 7th Connecticut's dash.

26. Price, *Ninety Seventh Pennsylvania*, p. 121 claims the gun calibers were two 32-pounders and one James gun. Serrell mapped the Grimball defenses for Horatio Wright to accompany a report filed July 7, 1862, and gave the calibers as quoted.

27. Tafft, Henry S., *Reminiscences of the Signal Service in the Civil War* (Providence, RI, 1899), p. 36 for "fully...," "once...," and the mistaken notion that the lookout was eighty feet high; Serrell, "Report," July 7, 1862, notes the correct height of the Grimball lookout and further describes the height of a later-built Sol Legare lookout as eighty feet. Tafft probably mistook the two, for the Sol Legare observatory was not built at the time of his ascension. In a related note, the engineers also built a signal station just south of the Grimball house. See Brooks Map.

28. Eldredge, *The Third New Hampshire*, p. 170 for the "spent ball". Metcalf, *Personal Incidents...Third Rhode Island*, p. 90 for the return of Williams' body.

29. OR 14, p. 559 for Pemberton's query.

30. Pressley, "Wee Nee Volunteers," p. 141 for the tree-felling duty. The location of the Hill's slave houses is given, among others, in Hagood, *Memoirs*, p. 99.

31. Ibid., p. 99 for the position of the Clark's Battery, named Battery Reed on this map. Willis "Skipper" Keith's on-site analysis of the area places the battery somewhat east of the Capers memorial marker. Pressley, "Wee Nee Volunteers," p. 141 for "The enemy..."

32. Ibid., p. 141 for the Eutaw Battalion's observations.

33. OR 14, p. 561 for Evans' transfer; Hagood, *Memoirs*, p. 93 mentions the transfer as occurring on June 14; Pressley, "Wee Nee Volunteers," p. 142 has Evans on James Island on the 12th; Tracy, "Rebel Diary," p. 280 also states that Evans took command on June 14.

34. Price, *Ninety Seventh Pennsylvania*, pp. 121-3 for a full recounting of this action.

35. Eldredge, *The Third New Hampshire*, p. 170 for the 3rd New Hampshire's cheering arrivals and quoted material "and our..."

36. Todd, *The 79th Highlanders*, p. 146 for "(T)here..."; Ely, *Diary of*, p. 36 for "up..." Slemmons, "Diary," p. 60 for "We have..."

37. Stevens, *Life of*, p. 399 for Stevens' and Wright's opinions of the

planned attack's direction. Stevens understood that Benham had given "preliminary orders" that the Confederate right would be the focus of the attack. However, an attack in that direction could have been construed as an assault on Fort Johnson, something expressly forbidden by Hunter's orders. No doubt, Benham chose the Secessionville area as the point of his attack for this very reason. See also, EC, Stevens to Benham, June 13, 1862, which provides Hazard Stevens' observations of the growing Confederate perimeter. In part, it reads, "A line of earthwork over half a mile long located in front of, or this side of the road from Grimball's to Fort Johnson and on the line between the extremity of the point on which we are planting a battery and Charleston was plainly visible. No guns to be seen however." Stevens is describing either the new line of abatis on the Hill peninsula or the main Confederate defenses further north and east.

38. Grayson, *Diary of William Grayson*, p. 143 for the removal of St. Michael's bells. Either the authorities were trying to save them, or the bells were to be used to manufacture cannon.

39. See Serrell, "Report," July 7, 1862 for the length of the infantry parapet. The Brooks Map identifies the units manning the parapet, from left to right, as the 3rd New Hampshire and 3rd Rhode Island, 47th New York, 6th Connecticut, and 45th and 76th Pennsylvania. Lying on the Stono just south of the Grimball building was the 97th Pennsylvania and the "vol. Eng. (Engineers) Camp." Eldredge, *The Third New Hampshire*, p. 170 for "an unusually...," and p. 171 for "I find..."; Price, *Ninety Seventh Pennsylvania*, p. 123 for "The Rebel..."

40. Todd, *The 79th Highlanders*, p. 146 for the Highlanders' detail and for "with...," "we...," and "the breath..."; Campbell letter, June 13, 1862, for "Just as..."

41. See footnotes 38 and 39 for evidence of Lamar's increased shelling.

42. Ely, *Diary of*, p. 36 for the 8th Michigan's day.

43. OR 14, pp. 39-40 for reports of the "Affair" and "a small..."

44. Todd, *The 79th Highlanders*, pp. 146-7 for the Highlanders' efforts, and p. 147 for quoted material; William Todd to "My Dear Parints," June 16 through July 6, 1862, New York Historical Society, June 16, for the presence of the James gun on Tybee Island; Ely, *Diary of*, p. 36 for the sleeping officer.

45. Eldredge, *The Third New Hampshire*, p. 171 for the 3rd New Hampshire's activity and quoted material. The Brooks Map provides a wealth of data on the Federal camp at Grimball's. The hospital mentioned in Eldredge was probably in one of three places, all of which Brooks marked well. Two sets of "Negro quarters" appear on the map, one lining the southern bank of the small creek that bisected the Grimball plain, and another hugging the Stono north of the plantation buildings. Another group of buildings marked "Hospital" stood about 1000 feet south of the creek on a small piece of high ground surrounded by a tidal marsh.

46. Pressley, "Wee Nee Volunteers," p. 142 for the Eutaw Battalion's movements and the quoted material.

47. Crute, *Confederate Units*, p. 257 for a short history of the unit. The

Pee Dee Battalion was formed in Georgetown and arrived in the Charleston area on April 25, 1862. See Compiled Service Records of South Carolina Soldiers, South Carolina State Archives, Combined Service Records of the 26th South Carolina, the unit that Smith's battalion eventually joined. *Charleston Mercury*, June 16, 1862, for "old...," and the identity of Andrews. Word of his death made the rounds, as both Tracy, "Rebel Diary," p. 280, and Pressley, "Wee Nee Volunteers," p. 142 mention the incident. Pressley notes the five tents.

48. Tracy, "Rebel Diary," p. 280 for "Vigorous" and "(F)iring..."; Pressley, "Wee Nee Volunteers," p. 142 for firing into the night.

49. Ibid., p. 142 for the Eutaw Battalion's movement and the burning of the Dill house; *Charleston Mercury*, June 16, 1862, for the time of the "bright glare" to the north. See SOR 23, p. 812 for the 4th Louisiana Battalion's losses.

50. Cadwell, *Old Sixth*, pp. 41-2 for quoted material.

51. See footnote 33 for Evans' arrival. Hagood, *Memoirs*, p. 93 for "considerable...," and p. 92 and Sorrel, Brig. Gen. G. Moxley, *Recollections of a Confederate Staff Officer*, Bell Wiley, ed. (Wilmington, NC: Broadfoot, 1987), pp. 93-4 for two of many accusations concerning Evans' drinking problem. Thomas Pelot letter to Lalla Pelot, Lalla Pelot Papers; Duke University Library, September 15, 1861 for "the best..."

52. Hagood, *Memoirs*, pp. 84-6 for Hagood's survey of the James Island defenses, upon which this description is based, and ibid., p. 85 for map location of Royall's; ibid., p. 84 for "slight,' and p. 86 for "the redans..."; *Charleston Courier*, May 6, 1862, hints that the owners of the plantations in the nearby parishes may have been reluctant to loan their slaves to the James Island work parties. After praising the efforts of some owners, the writer complains, "If other parts of the State had done as well, we would now have been impregnable."

53. Woodward, *Mary Chesnut's Diary*, p. 385 for "he ought..." Mary Chesnut wrote this in her diary on June 13, 1862.

54. Stevens, *Life of*, pp. 397-8 for Hazard Stevens' recounting of this story and quoted material.

Chapter Seven
Positions, Places

1. Tracy, "Rebel Diary," p. 280 for "similar..."; Jones, "Letters from Fort Sumter," *SHSP*, 12, p. 6 for a good description of the state of the Tower Battery and the garrison.

2. Jones, "Letters," pp. 5-7 for Jones' entire letter, and ibid., p. 7 for the tree-climbing and "(L)ed on..."

3. The location of the Pee Dee and Charleston Battalion's camps are reasoned guesses based upon a number of factors. The Pee Dee camp was probably closer to the fort, since they were the first to reinforce the garrison at the beginning of the battle. Also, Ripley's "Charleston in the Civil

War," *The News and Courier* and *Charleston Evening Post* (Charleston, S.C.), p. 31, hereafter Ripley, "Charleston," shows a detailed map of the battle area that includes the location of the Charleston Battalion's camp. Bonneau's gunboat had anchored near the southern flank of the fort coincident with the Federals' landing on the island, and had remained there until the night of June 15. OR 14, p. 96. Eldredge, in *The Third New Hampshire*, pp. 173-4 describes the buildings behind the right flank as "barracks"; Hawley, in OR 14, p. 1007, mentions "the window in the gable of the little house in the earthwork." The map in Ripley, "Charleston," p. 31 points out the houses lining this flank.

4. Two good diagrams of the Tower Battery exist. One is reproduced in Burton, *Siege of Charleston*, p. 109, which shows the fort close to its June 1862 state, although some later improvements—the new bombproof, among others—had been added. The second is in Gillmore, Quincy A., "Supplementary Report to Engineer and Artillery Operations against the Defences of Charleston Harbor in 1863," Professional Papers, Corps of Engineers USA, No. 16-Supplement (New York: D. Van Nostrand, 1868), Plate IV. This shows the fort with an extended right wing. The hand drawn map upon which the Gillmore map is based still exists, in NA Record group 77: Records of the Office of the Chief Engineer, Drawer 193-4, sheet K-17. It is one of the few official maps that locates the exact position of the tower and also reveals the location of two pivot positions along the battery's front. I've combined this information with the Burton Map, which shows a gun platform to the right center of the front, to estimate the position of the pivot-mounted columbiad on the morning of June 16. The roadway along the left wing is plainly visible on the Burton map. Stevens, *Life of*, p. 395 and Pressley, "Wee Nee Volunteers," p. 145 give excellent descriptions of the battery at the time of the battle. Ripley's "Charleston," p. 31 was the first to describe the shape of the fort as a letter "M"; Capers, *CMH*, 6, p. 86 for "thick. . ."; Stevens, *Life of*, p. 396 gives a fine description of the swamp lines, although he errs in his directions; Ripley's "Charleston," p. 37 for "pluff" mud, and the map on p. 31 for some idea of the foliage.

5. Lamar's official report, OR 14, pp. 93-6, mentions "the 8-in columbiad"; "the rifled 24-pounder"; "two rifled 24-pounders"; "the 18-pounders" and a mortar. The confusion arises as to whether the single 24-pounder is one of the "two rifled 24-pounders," or in a position by itself. I chose to separate them, but this is and only can be, an educated guess. Jones, "Letters," p. 7 for quoted material; *Charleston Courier*, June 18, 1862 for the footbridge as a Federal target; ibid also describes the intensity of the Federal artillery barrage and the presence of trenches.

6. Hagood, in OR 14, p. 98, states that Lamar's pickets "covered the space from the Secessionville road to the marsh on the left of our lines." The Rivers House anchored this section of the picket line. At the time of the battle, the Battery Island Road jogged to the northeast just north of the Rivers House in order to run along the eastern edge of a marshy finger of Simpson's Creek. It then crossed the marsh on a causeway near the road's

junction with the Grimball farm lane. Today, the road bypasses the jog by running directly north, although some locals recall vestiges of its former route. See Davis, ed., *Atlas*, plate XXIII, no. 6 and 7, and plate CXXXI, no.1, for the jog in the road; *OR* 14, p. 95 gives the armament in the Clark House Battery as "two smooth-bore 24-pounder guns."

7. *SOR* pt. 1, vol. 3, p. 101, places the 47th Georgia "as a support or guard to a body of axemen engaged in felling a piece of woods and forming an abatis between the battery (Lamar's) and a road running parallel with and near the skirt of woods, which we entered on Tuesday evening, June 10, and came upon the enemy and in such strong numbers." Since no line of abatis separated the Tower Battery from Battery Island Road, I assume Adjutant Williams simply misapprehended the lay of the land. It's quite possible that he couldn't see the swamp lying between the Hill's peninsula and the Secessionville peninsula. If that were the case, he could then assume that the abatis was the only barrier between the fort and the road. Pressley, "Wee Nee Volunteers," p. 142 for the Eutaw Battalion's' respite on June 15 and all quoted material. Pressley actually mentions two religious services, the second will be described later.

8. *OR* 14, p. 567 for "I fear...," "inadequate," and "To furnish..."
9. Ibid., p. 567 for "I am..."
10. Todd, *The 79th Highlanders*, p. 147 for "They..."
11. Ely, *Diary of*, p. 36 for "The same..."; Serrell, "Report," July 7, 1862 for "revetted...," and "two 42 lb..."; Denison, *The Third Rhode Island Heavy Artillery*, p. 91 for "Battery Lamar..."; Slemmons, "Diary," p. 60 for "I have..."
12. Todd, *The 79th Highlanders*, p. 147 for the Highlanders' concerns.
13. Eldredge, *The Third New Hampshire*, p. 171 for "dreadful hurry" and "It really..."
14. ISP, Stevens to "My dear wife," June 15, 1862, for "an evil hour," "they...," and "We..."
15. The details of this meeting will be discussed in Chapter 11. Stevens, *Military Operations in South Carolina*, p. 141 places the meeting aboard the Delaware.
16. Eldredge, *The Third New Hampshire*, p. 171 for "Two...," and the Hampshire pickets; Todd, *The 79th Highlanders*, p. 147 for "little General," and ibid., p. 148 for missing mess mates; Copp, Elbridge, *Reminiscences of the War of the Rebellion* (Nashua, New Hampshire: Telegraph Publishing Company, 1911), p. 132 for "Before..."
17. Porter, A. Toomer, *Led On! Step by Step* (NY: G. P. Putnam's Sons-The Knickerbocker Press, 1899), p. 138 for "We..."
18. Todd, *The 79th Highlanders*, p. 150-1 for the wake-up call. Todd, p. 150, gives 2:00 a.m. as wake-up hour, almost most others disagree. Fenton in *OR* 14, p. 64, gives 1:00 a.m. as wake up, and 2:00 a.m. as "in line." Hawley, ibid., p. 67, and Graves, ibid., p. 70, support Fenton's timeline. Leasure claims that his column started moving at 1:20 a.m., ibid., p. 72. Morrison, ibid., p. 75, basically agrees, while Rockwell, ibid., p. 82, states his men were moving by 2:30 a.m.

19. See ibid., p. 70 for the "Forlorn Hope's" orders; Stevens, *Life of*, p. 402, for the make-up of the advance; OR 14, p. 59, for Lusk's assignment. See note 20, below, for the possibility that Fenton didn't accompany the advance.

20. Beecher, *Connecticut First Light Battery*, p. 144 for Rockwell's disturbing meeting with Stevens, the "muffled wheels," and all quoted material.

21. OR 14, pp. 71-2 for Leasure's order of battle, and p. 73 for the scattered nature of the pickets. See also, ibid., p. 83 for the 3rd Rhode Island Heavy Artillery's relief of the Roundheads at the "battery in advance of the First Brigade."

22. Letter, *Flint Democrat*, July 3, 1862, claimed that Fenton was "sick and not able to sit upon his horse when we left the camp, but overtook us before we reached the field." The letter's probable author (signed "B") is Lt. Horatio Belcher. The account describes the actions of Company G—Belcher's company—and he was the last to leave the field. Fenton, although admitting that he was serving "in violation of the laws of health," Fenton letter to Stevens, Diary of Wm. M. Fenton, 1861-1863, and Material Relating to 8th Michigan Infantry, Flint, Michican Public Library, June 20, 1862, never mentions that he tardily joined the march. Most accounts of the march, including Hawley's in OR 14, p. 67, placed the 7th Connecticut second in line. In late August, Hawley described the exchange between the 7th Connecticut and the 28th Massachusetts, as well as his conversation with Belcher. Ibid., p. 1006.

23. Eldredge, *The Third New Hampshire*, p. 172 for 2:00 a.m. wakeup and the scattered Hampshire pickets; Denison, *The Third Rhode Island Heavy Artillery*, p. 92, for 3rd Rhode Island Heavy Artillery's lack of breakfast. Both Metcalf, OR 14, p. 83, and Jackson, ibid., p. 78, noted 3:00 a.m. as the start of the march. Horatio Wright, ibid., p. 54, gives the order of battle. He had taken the 97th Pennsylvania from Chatfield's Brigade, and probably Hamilton's section from Welsh's Brigade, and reassigned both to William's attack force. I say "probably" because there is no documentation concerning Wright's brigades for the days immediately prior to the battle, but Hamilton's Battery is listed as part of Welsh's Brigade on June 30, 1862. Ibid., p. 362.

24. Ibid., p. 54 for Wright's thinking; Eldredge, *The Third New Hampshire*, p. 172 for picket relief, and p. 173 for "quite. . ."; Copp, *Reminiscences*, p. 134 for "stack arms," and pp. 134-5 for biscuit incident; OR 14, p. 54 for Wright's recollection of the first shots.

25. Ibid., p. 96 for "although. . . ," and Lamar's admission that his men didn't sleep on their arms; *Charleston Courier*, June 18, 1862 for the Battalions' reinforcement of the work parties.

26. Evans claimed, OR 14, p. 91, that Lamar informed him on June 15 that an attack was expected either that night or the next morning. That Evans only sent 100 men to reinforce the fort belies this claim. If he believed such an attack was imminent, he would have sent more men. More likely, Evans was surprised by the attack. Another point of contention af-

ter the battle was the nature of the Confederate picket force in front of Secessionville, and its response to the Federal attack. In a note to the *Charleston Mercury* dated June 24, Lt. Col. Smith of the Pee Dee Battalion stated that "The pickets from Secessionville were commanded by Capt. Smart, of my Battalion. Capt. Simons, of the Charleston Battalion, was also on duty with his company." No one from Simons' unit left an account of the morning's action, so their whereabouts are apparently lost to history. To further confuse the issue, Adjutant Benjamin Williams of the 47th Georgia claimed that one company and part of another were "stationed as pickets near the Rivers House..." *SOR* pt. 1, vol. 3, p. 101. Most likely, the Georgians spent the night somewhere north of the Rivers House. Although Lamar doesn't mention it in his official report, he admitted to Johnson Hagood (Hagood, *Memoirs*, p. 94), that he fell asleep on his post.

27. Ibid., p. 93 gives the picket alignment and Hagood's own position that night. See *OR* 14, p. 102 for Stevens' recollection.

28. B. F. Miller, Lt. Col. Smith's adjutant, reported that "Brevet Second Lieutenant Sarvis and Privates Wm. Russ and S. M. Morgan" as "Captured on Picket," *Charleston Mercury*, June 17, 1862. Smith, in Report of Lieutenant Colonel A. D. Smith, June 19, 1862, reported Sarvis "and Wm. Buss and F. M. Jordan...captured on picket." All Union accounts claim four captures in this first rush, the details of which are still forthcoming.

29. James C. Wilson joined the 8th Michigan as its surgeon in March. His letter to the *Flint Wolverine Citizen*, July 26, 1862, describes both the halt "to await more clear daylight" and Graves subsequent action. One of the wounded Unionists had a severed femoral artery that nearly hemorrhaged. See Pease, *Memoirs*, p. 35 for the short rest and the picket fire; Pease thought two Michiganders were killed by this fire. Graves, *OR* 14, p. 70, reported five wounded by two Confederate shots. See ibid., for Graves' description of the capture of the enemy pickets. Todd, *The 79th Highlanders*, p. 153 for the feared lack of surprise.

30. Pease, *Memoirs*, p. 35 for the 8th Michigan's formation; *OR* 14, p. 65 for Fenton's arrival and observation, and ibid., p. 70, for Graves' observations and "ready..."; Orrin Bump, *Personal Account of Private Orrin Bump, 8th Michigan Infantry*, Bentley Historical Library, for "heard...," and "Every discharge..." Lieutenant George Turner letter, Company A, *Flint Wolverine Citizen*, July 5, 1862 for "We passed over the rifle pits..."; Isaac Stevens, in *OR* 14, p. 59, reported that the Michigan "forlorn hope" was 40 feet in front of the regiment, and that the entire force was 100 yards from the front of the battery when the Confederate artillery opened.

31. Ibid., p. 98 for Jamison's arrival at the battery, and ibid., pp. 94-5 for Lamar's recollections of the first moments of the battery's defense. Hagood, *Memoirs*, p. 94 claims that Lamar was "Aroused by the sentinal over the guns." The pickets that just beat the Michiganders to the fort were probably Simons' group from the Charleston Battalion (see note 24). Ibid., p. 94 claims that the pickets "fled without firing a shot." Smith, however, states "Both officers (Smart and Simons)...gave notice of the approach of the enemy to the batteries." Smith to *Charleston Mercury*, June

24, 1862. While various sources support both positions, most sources do place Simons in the fort during the earliest stages of the battle. See *OR* 14, p. 99 for "a murderous. . ."

There was also some question concerning the activity of the Charleston and Pee Dee Battalions at this time. Early accounts (e.g., *Charleston Courier*, June 18, 1862; *Charleston Mercury*, June 18, 1862), stated that both units had labored through the night and were still working when they were ordered to "return to their quarters, arm themselves and return to their battery, (Lamar's)." Later, more accurate accounts place them in their camps. "The captain came to our tents about four o'clock this morning and hastily awoke us." *Charleston Mercury*, June 20, 1862.

32. *OR* 14, p. 94 for quoted material. Although the majority of Confederate accounts (e.g., Capers, *CMH*, p. 87; Hagood, *Memoirs*, p. 94, et. al.), have Lamar sighting and firing the Columbiad, Humbert disputed the claim. *Charleston Mercury*, June 20, 1862. In his response, the lieutenant asserts, "I fired the first gun myself. . ." It is impossible to reconcile the accounts.

33. Coleman, Philip, "Philip Coleman Speech to the 1st Congregational Church of Washington D.C., October 21, 1898." Transcript in the possession of Catherine Fishback, Fredricksburg, Virginia, p. 3 for quoted material; George Newell letter, *Flint Wolverine Citizen*, 5 July 1862, for the destruction of the horseflesh. Newell was a 1st lieutenant in Company A.

34. *OR* 14, p. 71 for "Come on, boys." Stevens, *Life of*, p. 404 for same and Lyons' wounding; *OR* 14, p. 60 for the location of Lyons' wounding.

35. Newell letter, *Flint Wolverine Citizen*, July 5, 1862 for Donohue's wounding and "You cannot. . ."; ibid., July 12, 1862 for "pierced. . ."

36. G. B. Fuller letter, *Jackson Weekly Citizen*, July 9, 1862, for "a shower. . . ," "to the right. . . ," and "or any others." W. E. C. letter, *Flint Wolverine Citizen*, July 5, 1862, for "perfectly horrible. . ."; Bump, *Personal Account*, for ". . . by the assistance. . ."

37. *Detroit Free Press*, June 30, 1862, for Demond's exploits; Belcher letter, July 3, 1862 for Curtis "then fight. . . ," and Tracy "fought like. . ."; Wilson letter, July 26, 1862, for suppressed Confederate artillery fire; *Charleston Mercury*, June 24, 1862, for "demanding. . ."

38. Lamar, in *OR* 14, p. 94, recalled the heavy fire from his left flank; George Newell letter, July 5, 1862, for "to put. . ."; Wilson letter, July 26, 1862 for "while. . ."; Bump, *Personal Account*, for "(I)n hand. . ."

39. Pease, *Memoirs*, p. 35-6 for all quoted material.

40 Ibid., p. 36 for all quoted material.

41. *OR* 14, p. 94 for the Pee Dee's arrival. They were also called "Smith's Battalion.".

42. Ibid., pp. 94-5 for the Pee Dee's response. The *Charleston Mercury*, June 24, 1862, describes the rush as having no time for "accurate formation of companies, but every man flew to his post. . ."

43. Ibid., p. 95 for "refused. . ." and the weapon problem.

44. *Charleston Courier*, June 17, 1862, provides the details of the deaths of Baggott and Reed. *Charleston Mercury*, June 20, 1862, has W. C. Barber,

the Acting Adjutant, First Regiment Artillery, South Carolina volunteers, identifying Company B as coming from the Barnwell District and Company J as coming from Orangeburg. *Charleston Mercury*, June 28, 1862, for "like beeves."

45. Bellinger's account of this action and all quoted material comes from the *Charleston Mercury*, June 28, 1862, which in fact paraphrases a letter the lieutenant wrote "to his relatives" after the battle.

46. *OR* 14, p. 94 for Lamar's version of Gaillard's arrival. *Charleston Mercury*, June 19, 1862, provides the details of King's and Henry Valentine's wounding. This account also claims that Isaac Valentine was "instantly killed by the fire of the enemy." However, the *Charleston Courier*, June 18, 1862 differs concerning Valentine: ". . .after receiving his death wound, (he) stated that he felt no apprehension of death (but) had one wish that he might see his family before he died for his country." *Charleston Mercury*, June 28, 1862, for "poured. . ."

47. *Charleston Courier*, June 18, 1862, for the Campbell/Tennant action. *Charleston Mercury*, June 28, 1862, for Bellinger et. al. *Charleston Mercury*, June 19, 1862, for Parker's death and Edgerton's wounding. Edgerton would die early Tuesday morning. Ibid., for Poznanski's presentiment and death. Poznanski' father—the controversial leader of Charleston's Beth Elohim Congregation from 1837 to 1850—has been called "the first Jewish Reform religious leader in America." Breibart, Solomon, *The Rev. Mr. Gustavus Poznanski—First American Jewish Reform Minister* (Charleston, South Carolina: Kahal Kadosh Beth Elohim, 1979), p. 1.

48. *Irish Volunteers*, p. 27 for this unit's actions.

49. *Charleston Mercury*, June 24, 1862, for the Oliver/Moseley action, Keitt's encouragement, and all quoted material. See *OR* p. 95 for Lamar's acknowledgement of Bonneau's service at the columbiad.

50. *OR* 14, p. 1009 for Hawley's map of the 7th Connecticut's movements. Ibid., p. 67 for "excellant" and p. 1007 for "clambering. . ." Tourtellotte, *Company K. . .Seventh Connecticut*, p. 33 for "had. . ."

51. *OR* 14, p. 1007 for Hawley's view of the "little house," and the 7th Connecticut's collision with the marsh; Rowley letter to his "Parints," John Rowley Letter, Author's Collection, June 17, 1862, for "Their rifle pits. . . ," and "doing. . ." Tourtellotte, *Company K. . .Seventh Connecticut*, p. 34 for "(I)t was. . ."

52. *OR* 14, pp. 67-8 for Hitchcock and Atwell's attack. McCaslin, Richard B., *Portraits of Conflict, A Photographic History of South Carolina in the Civil War* (Fayetteville, Arkansas: University of Arkansas Press, 1994), p. 134 for "evidently. . ."; Rowley for "It was. . ."

53. *OR* 14, p. 68 and p. 1007 for the arrival of the 28th Massachusetts.

54. Rowley for "the shells. . .," "but the. . .," and Gilbert's wounding. *OR* 14, p. 68 for Hooten and Upson; *Edgefield South Carolina Advertiser*, July 23, 1862, for "junk bottle." Tourtellotte, *Company K. . .Seventh Connecticut*, p. 34 for Corbin, Hibbard, and St. Lyon.

55. *OR* 14, p. 1007 for Hawley's efforts to maneuver his regiment and p.

68 for "the heaviest. . ."; Tourtellotte, *Company K. . .Seventh Connecticut*, p. 33 for "by fits. . ."

56. *OR* 14, p. 69 for "in column. . ."; Michael McGuinnis File (McGuinnis Pension File, NARA Pension Request, September 17, 1887, for "deep furrows. . ."; Hiram Nason letter to Mr. Moses Nason (Nason Pension File, NARA, June 22, 1862, for "shot and shell. . ."; Charles McVey Pension Record, McVey Pension File, NARA, February 17, 1863 for "filled. . .". See the *Boston Herald*, June 30, 1862, for the surprising discovery of the Confederate fort. Stroud, David V, *Civil War Sword and Revolver Presentations* (Pinecrest Publishing Company, n.d.), p. 42, for Barrett's wounding and "smashed. . ."; Michael Campbell Pension File, NARA, request, January 27, 1888, for Campbell's actions.

57. Nason letter to Mr. Moses Nason, June 22, 1862, for "arms legs. . .," and further descriptions; *National Tribune*, January 18, 1917, relates the later discovery of the 28th Massachusetts' eagle by a Roundhead officer; Welsh, Peter, *Irish Green & Union Blue* (NY: Fordham Univ. Press, 1986), p. 83, and letter from "C," *Boston Herald*, June 30, 1862, for Sgt. McDonald's death. The 28th's disintegration is described by a number of eyewitnesses, perhaps the most damning of which is Denison, *Third New Hampshire*, p. 103: "the Twenty-Eighth Massachusetts came back past us in a broken condition." At this point, the 3rd New Hampshire was near the Battery Island Road. See the George Cartwright letter to Massachusetts Governor John Andrew, *Correspondence of the 28th Regt.* (Massachusetts), State Library of Massachusetts, August 3, 1862, hints at Moore's dereliction of duty. We will return to this subject later.

58. John MacDonald Pension File (NARA), for MacDonald's actions. William Kerrigan deposition, July 24, 1865, (Hugh Gallagher Pension File, NARA) for Kerrigan and Gallagher experiences. G. B. Fuller letter, June 19, 1862, for hat-waving, Cartwright's presence at the front, and "as soon. . ."

59. Ibid for all quoted material.

60. Guild's wounding is described in both the Newall letter and Turner letter published in the *Flint Wolverine Citizen*, July 5, 1862. In contrast, Robertson, *Michigan In The War* (Lansing Mi: W.S. George, 1880), p. 123 claims that Guild "was struck by a shot and fell over the wall into the rebel hands. . ." Doyle's actions are taken from the *Detroit Free Press*, June 30, 1862. Aitkin letter, *Flint Wolverine Citizen*, July 12, 1862, for Pratt's wounding. Although Pratt had written a family friend "that a shadow was creeping over him" (ISP, R.A. Wright to Stevens, June 30, 1862), he survived both his wounding and captivity only to die in Kentucky when his horse accidentally threw him. Robertson, *Michigan in the War*, pp. 111-112.

Chapter Eight
Fields of Fire

1. *OR* 14, p. 102 for Stevens' movements and "On reaching. . ."
2. Ibid., p. 99 for Hagood's report and "to the. . ." *SOR* pt. 1, vol. 3, p. 101, for the presence of the 47th Georgia's Company B at Artillery Crossroads "on the morning of June 16. . ." The Macbeth Artillery was also called Boyce's Battery. Johnson, *Artillery Hell*, p. 89.
3. *OR* 14, p. 103 for Simonton's report. He and the Eutaw Battalion probably advanced on the Dill's Bluff Road to the King's Highway on their way to Artillery Crossroads. See Pressley, "Wee Nee Volunteers," p. 143 for march route and "under arms. . ."; Augustine Smyth letter, June 17, 1862, for "at 'quick'," "a shout. . .," and the presence of the creek.
4. *OR* 14, p. 100 for McEnery's report and "(A)fter. . ."
5. Ibid., p. 95 for Lamar's account of Smith's actions. Lamar placed Smith's heroic efforts after the first Federal charge and "while they were on their second charge."
6. *New York Times*, June 28, 1862 for "just as. . . ," and length of intervening distance; Todd, *The 79th Highlanders*, p. 153 for the 8th Michigan's cheer, the opening of the artillery ("in or near. . .), and "after only. . ." The unevenness of the terrain is universally acknowledged—*New York Times*, June 28, 1862; *OR* 14, p. 75. See the *New York Times* for Isaac Stevens' presence in the first field. See *OR* 14, p. 72 for the two-company advance.
7. Todd to "My Dear Parints," June 16, 1862, for "a complete. . ." In *OR* 14, p. 72, Leasure recalls the difficulty that the succeeding Highlander companies had in catching up to Morrison's people. The account of the collision between the Highlanders and the Irish is colorfully if not prejudicially given in Todd, *The 79th Highlanders*, pp. 154-5. Quoted material is also from ibid. There is no doubt that sections of the 28th performed poorly at Secessionville. Still, Todd's description of their total breakdown must be taken with a grain of salt, if not a shot of Irish whiskey.
8. Ibid., p. 154 for quoted material. See *OR* 14, p. 72 for Leasure's difficulty with the horses. Not all Highlander accounts recall this halt. It is probable that Morrison paused at this hedge to allow the trailing companies to catch up to the advance. Thus, the trailers remembered the attack as a single rush from the first hedge, while the advance recalled a pause before the attack was delivered.
9. Todd to "My Dear Parints," credits the Connecticut guns for diverting enemy attention enough to allow the Highlanders a relatively easy crossing of the first field. See ibid., for "The inside. . ." Todd, *The 79th Highlanders*, p. 155, for "encountered" and "we hurried. . ." *New York Times*, June 28, 1862, for "The grape. . ." See *OR* 14, p. 1007 for Hawley's version of the encounter. See Coleman Speech, p. 5, for "A second. . ."; Gavin, *100th Pennsylvania*, p. 100 for "bellowed. . ."
10. *OR* 14, p. 72 and Gavin, *100th Pennsylvania*, p. 100 for Leasure's reports.
11. Todd to "My Dear Parints," for "cheering. . ." and the location of the

color guard. Todd was a member of this unit. Todd, *The 79th Highlanders*, p. 155, for "lustily" and the route of the attack. *New York Times*, June 28, 1862, for "without..."

12. Unknown, 4th Louisiana Battalion Diary, p. 45 for quoted material.

13. Todd, *The 79th Highlanders*, p. 157, for Morrison's conference with his officers.

14. Ibid., pp. 157-158, for the Highlanders' anger with the lack of support. Todd to "My Dear Parints," June 16, 1862, for "the blood...," and "I never..." *New York Times*, June 28, 1862, for "by one...," "unseen," and more reaction to the regiment's isolation. *OR* 14, p. 76 for "fierce..."

15. Ibid., pp. 76-7 for Leckey's report.

16. Ibid., p. 77 for Leckey's version of his orders and "forward..."; Slemmons, "James Island Campaign," as quoted in Stevenson, J. C., *History of the Roundheads*, M. Gyla McDowell Collection, Penn State University, for "rebel..."

17. Ibid., for "running..."; Slemmons, "Diary," p. 61, for "(the) cotton field..." From his position in the charge, Slemmons could see "whole lines in front of us go down," victims of Confederate artillery.

18. Gavin, *100th Pennsylvania*, pp. 98-105 reprints Daniel Leasure's personal account of the battle. All quoted material comes from this letter to his daughter. The "Camp Kettle" was a regimental newspaper published for the Roundheads. In Issue No. 4, the soldier is advised, "Learn to drop on the instant, to avoid the discharge from a battery." Camp Kettle, US-AMHI, 100th Pennsylvania Collection, Carlysle Barracks.

19. Lt. Philo Morton letter to Mr. Jn. McCaskey, Shriber Collection, Memphis Tennessee, June 18, 1862, for "under...," and "tore..."; Sgt. John P. Wilson letter to his sister Eleanor, Carolyn Shriber Collection, Memphis Tennessee, June 22, 1862, for "fell..."

20. *OR* 14, p. 77 for "within..."; Wilson letter for "the rebels...," "to avoid...," "Several...," "to see...," "balls...," and "We could..."; Morton letter for "We fought..."

21. *OR* 14, pp. 74-75 for Rosa's official report, and ibid., p. 73 for Leasure's report on the action. One of the difficulties in telling the full story of the battle of Secessionville is the lack of primary material on the 46th New York. This German regiment left few, if any, reminiscences of the campaign. The language barrier might have had something to do with this. Stevens, *Life of*, p. 406 adds some detail.

22. *Charleston Mercury*, June 20, 1862, for Hudson's and Miller's actions.

23. *Irish volunteers*, p. 27 for Allemong's actions. The *Charleston Mercury*, June 17, 1862, listed Humbert as "slightly wounded."Ibid., June 24, 1862, claims "Humbert received quite an injury by the concussion produced by his gun...The blow rendered him unfit for work." Command of the Columbiad supposedly devolved upon Lt. T. P. Oliver. Humbert, however, states that he wasn't wounded and remained at his post for the entire battle. *Charleston Mercury*, June 20, 1862. Ibid., June 19, 1862, reports Howard's death.

24. *Irish Volunteers*, p. 27 for Henery's death ("a Minie ball. . .entered under the left ear"). *Charleston Mercury*, June 19, 1862, for "desperate. . ."; *Charleston Courier*, June 18, 1862, for Miles' death.

25. Both Gaillard's and Lamar's woundings were first described in the *Charleston Mercury*, June 17, 1862. Ibid., June 18, 1862, adds further details to Lamar's wound and the reaction of his men. *Charleston Courier*, June 17, 1862, states that Gaillard "was wounded in the knee. . ." *OR* 14, p. 94 for "A third. . ."

26. Beecher, *Connecticut First Light Battery*, p. 148 for quoted material.

27. Ibid., p. 148 for all quoted material.

28. Ibid., pp. 148-9 for quoted material an the battery's view of the beginnings of the withdrawal.

29. Stevens, *Life of*, p. 406 for quoted material, and ibid., p. 409 for Stevens' request for support. *OR* 14, p. 60 for Isaac Stevens' report on the action. Pease, *Memoirs*, p. 181 reproduces two notes from Isaac Stevens to Henry Benham made on the battlefield. The first, which was probably written around this time, states, "Gen. Benham: My troops are withdrawn under cover of the hedge, and are in tolerable order. Hedge about 500 yards from the fort. The advance companies mounted the parapet, but support did not follow closely enough." Later, Benham would use this note to fault Stevens' dispositions. The second note was probably sent soon after the first, but before Williams and Wright advanced to the north. It read, "Gen. Benham: Unless supported on the left, I cannot charge the enemy. My command is perfectly quiet and in hand, but they must pass over a perfectly exposed place of 800 yards with a well-built parapet before them. I do not think it possible to charge the work."

30. Stevens, *Life of*, p. 407 for "Not. . ."; "heavy. . ."; and the description of the 7th Connecticut; *OR* 14, p. 1007, for "The General. . ."

31. Tourtellotte, *Company K. . .Seventh Connecticut*, p. 34, for Elliot's action.

32. Todd, *The 79th Highlanders*, p. 157, for "not. . . ," and Van Horsen's exploits. The private's unlikely capture is inaccurately recounted a number of ways. Alexander Campbell's letter to his wife, June 16, 1862, is an example: "Some of the 79th pulled two or three of the rebels out of the fort by the hair of the head." Campbell's letter also relates Daniel Lawrence's wounding, although he spells the last name Lorrance. Todd to "My Dear Parints," June 16, 1862, for "The prisoner. . ." *New York Times*, June 28, 1862 for "made. . . ," and "succeeded. . ."

33. Gavin, *100th Pennsylvania*, pp. 101-2 for quoted material.

34. See ibid., p. 102 for Leasure's version of this retreat. Stevens, *Life of*, p. 407 for "But. . . ," and his view of the withdrawal. Michigan private Orrin Bump remembered the retreat somewhat differently: ". . .fortunately our artillery gained a position from which they could shell the enemy over us, and at every discharge of our cannon, the rebs would dodge down behind their fort and we would pop up from behind cotton rows and make our best time to the rear, by successive movements, a portion of us got off the field." Bump may be one of the Michiganders that remained near the

fort for the duration of the battle and is thus relating the final Federal retreat from the field. However, his description—especially the use of artillery—more closely describes the first retreat. See note 37 for the Confederate view of the Union retreat.

35. Todd, *The 79th Highlanders*, p. 159 for "A close. . ." *OR* 14, p. 71 for "a portion." Ralph Ely was the only Michigan captain not felled by Confederate fire.

36. Todd, *The 79th Highlanders*, p. 159 for Williams' advance from the Highlanders' perspective.

37. *Charleston Courier*, June 18, 1862, for "Under. . ."

38. *OR* 14, p. 52 for Benham's conception of Williams' and Wright's function. Also see ibid., pp. 54-55, p. 60, and Stevens, *Life of*, p. 408, for the transfer of Williams to Stevens, and Isaac Stevens' understanding of the left column's tactical purpose.

39. Denison, *The Third Rhode Island Heavy Artillery*, p. 103 for "full blast," and "in a . . ."; ibid., p. 93, for "no better. . ." The Rhode Islanders probably entered the Battery Island Road just south of its junction with the Grimball farm lane.

40. Ibid., p. 103 for all quoted material. Stevens noted that Williams' ADC reported for orders soon after "the line at the advanced hedge had been formed and the regiments at the second hedge were forming, (and) that Colonel Williams' advance was to be seen to our left. . ." The general's response was for Williams "to maintain the position he had taken on that flank, and to do the best, in concert with our attack, the circumstances of the ground permitted." *OR* p. 60. For his part, Williams desired to suppress the fire of the Tower Battery "while General Stevens made his second advance." Ibid., p. 78.

41. Eldredge, *The Third New Hampshire*, p. 173 for "Well. . ." Copp, *Reminiscences of the War of the Rebellion*, pp. 134-135, for the prelude to battle, and ibid., p. 135 for "Take arms."

42. Ibid., p. 136 for the "guying," and p. 139, for "a wall. . ."

43. Eldredge, *The Third New Hampshire*, p. 173, for "rapidly," Cassidy's wounding, "forward. . . ," and "we. . ." See *OR* pp. 78-79, for Jackson's confusion and the two-company detachment.

44. In his report, *OR* 14, p. 79, Jackson implies that the two New Hampshire companies that arrived at the slave shanties opened immediately upon the Tower Battery. Given the distance the main body of the regiment had to cover, some time had to elapse before it joined in the detachment's firing. Eldredge, *The Third New Hampshire*, p. 174, for all quoted material.

45. Copp, *Reminiscences*, p. 139, for "deadly. . . ," and ibid., p. 140, for "sometimes. . .," and the irregularities of the ground. Eldredge, *The Third New Hampshire*, pp. 174-175, for various reactions to the intervening swamp. *OR* 14, p. 79, quotes Jackson: ". . .one shot from which (battery) killed a captain and non-commissioned officer." Carleton was the only New Hampshire captain to die. He survived the retreat only to succumb in a field hospital.

46. *OR* 14, p. 94 for "They made..." *Charleston Mercury*, June 18, 1862, for "a small...," "the contest...," and the three regiment estimate.

47. *OR* 14, p. 94, quotes Lamar: "...I never ceased to give orders to my batteries." However, the *Charleston Mercury*, June 18, 1862, states, "(Lamar) was carried off as soon as practicable."

48. *OR* 14, p. 94, gives the transfer of command.

49. *Charleston Mercury*, June 24, 1862, gives a harrowing description of the near-collapse of the Confederate defense.

50. *OR* 14, p. 100, for "on...," and ibid., p. 101, for "outer..." H. J. Lea, "The Fourth Louisiana Battalion at the Battle of Secessionville, S.C.," *Confederate Veteran*, 40 vols. (Harrisburg, Pennsylvania), 31, p. 14, for "about one hundred..." *Charleston Mercury*, June 18, 1862, for Hudson's guidance of the Louisianans. Ibid., June 19, 1862, for the final rush to the fort, and "Remember Butler." Union Maj. Gen. Benjamin Butler had angered the South in general and the Louisianans in particular with his blunt governing of occupied New Orleans.

51. (Unknown) 4th Louisiana Battalion Diary, p. 46, for "Out batt..." and "after..." *OR* 14, p. 101, for "At this point...," and "finally..." See also Lea, "The Fourth Louisiana Battalion," p. 15, for "was shot...," "It seemed...," and the falling of Reagan. *Charleston Mercury*, June 19, 1862, for "(We) poured..." I note here that Lea pointedly asserted that Lt. Ike Doyle of the Franklin Life Guard died in the battle, a contradiction of all published reports of the 4th Louisiana Battalion's casualties. In fact, Doyle became the brunt of a humorous poem that circulated through the 4th's camp later that summer. In part, the verse read: "He (Doyle) turned on his pivot swung around like a gate and made strides from the field from six feet to eight." The poem in its entirety, including the opening line, "We went to Secessionville a disturbance to quell," appears in an Unknown, 4th Louisiana Battalion Diary, August 5, 1862.

52. *OR* 14, p. 101 for "an incessant"; *Charleston Mercury*, June 19, 1862, quotes the 4th's Adjutant: "Three of our boys, viz: Mike Green, Chas. Setzer and Thos. Dunham, took charge of, and worked effectively, one of the guns."

53. *OR* 14, p. 79, for "good effect," "opened...," and "Their being..." Eldredge, *The Third New Hampshire*, p. 174, for "firing."

54. *OR* 14, p. 79, for "(W)e could..." Eldredge, *The Third New Hampshire*, p. 174, for "so hot...," and "The shrieks..." Copp, *Reminiscences*, pp. 141-142, for "striking...," and ibid., p. 142, for the ramrod launchings.

55. Ibid., p. 143, for Moore's wounding, Wadworth's assistance, and (among other details) Carleton's transportation. *OR* 14, p. 80, for Jackson's view of Dow.

56. Copp, *Reminiscences*, p. 143 for the arrival of the retreat orders ("to retire..."), and ibid., pp. 143-144, for the 3rd New Hampshire's retreat and the arrival of Hamilton's Battery.

57. Todd to "My Dear Parints," June 16, 1862, for "the roar..."; Pease, *Memoirs*, p. 37, for quoted material.

58. *OR* 14, pp. 1013-1014 for all quoted material.

59. Capers, *Soldier-Bishop*, pp. 54-55, for Ellison Capers traveling "via the crossroads...," "off the...," "double shelled," and "let the..." *OR* 14, p. 1014, for the remaining quoted material.

60. Capers, *Soldier Bishop*, p. 55, for Evans' location. From the tone and substance of Capers' letter to his wife describing the battle, see Cisco, Walter Brian, *States Rights Gist* (Shippensburg, PA., White Mane Publishing Co., 1991), pp. 79-80. Capers regarded Evans as a coward for holding back near Clark's House and avoiding the main action. Capers also states that Evans "drinks to excess," possibly referring to the general's state the morning of the battle. *OR* 14, p. 1014, for "We fired...," and ibid., p. 91, for "piercing."

61. Ibid., p. 102, for Stevens' report, and "(T)his position..." Evidently, the tree-felling operation east of the Battery Island Road had not been completed. Stevens makes an obvious distinction between the abatis and the "heavy thicket." The differing nature of the obstructions here helps explain the resulting confusion.

62. Pressley, "Wee Nee Volunteers," p. 143, for "immediately..." The Eutaw Battalion's position has been variously described as "on the outer edge of a low wood the large trees having been felled." See John Sheppard to his mother, Sheppard Family Papers, edited by Susan Smyth Bennett; South Caroliniana Library, June 17, 1862, "behind a hedge"; S. Van Vector Breese to Pinckney Bull, S. Van Vector Breese Letters, Tim Bradshaw Collection, Columbia, S.C., June 17, 1862, and "behind the felled thicket," *OR* 14, p. 99. See also ibid., p. 99, for Jeter's position and Hagood's observations. Hagood, *Memoirs*, p. 95, for more on Hagood's tactical considerations and his planned attack on the Federal artillery piece.

63. *OR* 14, p. 99 for "a heavy..." *SOR* pt. vol 3, p. 102 for "terribly crushing..." Pressley, "Wee Nee Volunteers," p. 143, for Stevens' admonitions. Hagood, *Memoirs*, p. 96, describes the Federal attack as "handsomely repulsed...except one portion."

64. Pressley, "Wee Nee Volunteers," p. 143 for "The Eutaws..."; Sheppard, June 17, 1862, for "Scarcely had...," and "(T)hey told..."; and see Augustine Smyth to 'Aunt Janey," June 17, 1862, for "volley after volley...," and "just as..."

65. *Charleston Mercury*, June 19, 1862, for "was instantly...," and "cut down..." Smyth, June 17, 1862, for "Don't fire..." A number of Confederates recalled similar shouts. See ibid., for the arrival of the Rhode Islanders, an incident repeated in Sheppard, June 17, 1862, Sheppard to his mother, June 22, 1862, and Breese, June 17, 1862. Ibid for Jervey's kill and "an Irishman." Jervey's action is recounted in Pressley, "Wee Nee Volunteers," p. 143.

66. Sheppard, June 17, 1862, for the breast plate incident, and for "who had..." Smyth, June 17, 1862, for "Soon...," and "sad..."

67. Porter, *Led On*, pp. 140-141, for "(Y)oung Christopher Trumbo..." and the list of the Eutaw Battalion dead. Reverend Porter and Dr. Ravenel, the Eutaw Battalion surgeon, had both ridden to the battlefront in the wake of the Eutaw Battalion's advance. Ravenel soon withdrew to estab-

lish a field hospital, while Porter helped evacuate the wounded. The chaplain enjoyed one light moment when Johnson Hagood tried to order him away from the front: "'Well,' I replied, 'you are not my Colonel and I will not obey you.' We both laughed, though the situation was pretty serious." Ibid., p. 140.

68. Pressley, "Wee Nee Volunteers," p. 144, for Pressley's movements and quoted material.

69. Denison, *The Third Rhode Island Heavy Artillery*, p. 103, for quotes on "Boys. . . ," Bartholomew's wounding ("shot through the loin"), and "laying. . ."; and see ibid., p. 94, for "double-quick," "cheering. . . ," and "Let. . ." See OR 14, p. 83, for "to capture. . ."

70. Ibid., p. 103, for Metcalf's orders and all quoted material. See Serrell, "Report," July 7, 1862, for the advance of the engineers. Five companies of Serrell's engineers were supporting Welsh's Brigade when Serrell called for volunteers to assist the Rhode Island assault. The engineers remained at the front until the 3rd Rhode Island Heavy Artillery was withdrawn.

71. Denison, *The Third Rhode Island Heavy Artillery*, p. 102, for Mulligan's exploits and all quoted material.

72. OR 14, p. 84, for "I deemed. . . ," and "slowly. . ."

73. Pressley, "Wee Nee Volunteers," p. 143, for "Our fire. . ." Ibid., pp. 143-144, for Sellars probe, and p. 144 for the Federal artillery fire. For more on the latter, see Smyth, June 17, 1862, and Sheppard, June 22, 1862. See Capers, *CMH*, p. 837, for Simons' wounding.

74. OR 14, p. 55, for "hotly. . . ," and Wright's report; Price, *Ninety Seventh Pennsylvania*, p. 124, for the 97th Pennsylvania's initial movement, and ibid., p. 124, for "inequality. . . ," and "to avoid. . ."

75. Cartwright to Andrew, *Correspondence of the 28th Regt. (MA)*; State Library of Massachusetts, August 3, 1862. Cartwright goes on to describe two more times that he commanded the regiment before Moore finally resigned in July. The only other reference to this incident, oblique as it is, is in Conyngham, *Irish Brigade*, p. 587: Cartwright "commanded the regiment during the latter part of the battle of James Island. . ." Moore would eventually resign on July 25, 1862. Wright never commented officially on his highly unusual action.

Chapter Nine
". . .A Disturbance to Quell. . ."

1. According to Horatio Wright, OR 14, p. 54, Benham had joined his column "just after or about the time I gave the order for the advance from camp. . ." Benham then "assumed command of the column. . . ."; ibid., p. 55, places their arrival at the front at the time "the command of General Stevens was falling back."

2. Ibid., p. 82, for "in good order" and "constantly. . ." Also see Beecher, *Connecticut First Light Battery*, p. 150, for the 1st Connecticut Light

Battery on the Battery Island Road. See *OR* 14, p. 71, for Fenton's description of the 8th Michigan after its withdrawal.

3. Gavin, *100th Pennsylvania*, pp. 102-103, for Leasure's reformation efforts. Sergeant John P. Wilson to his sister Eleanor, June 22, 1862, for "I did..." *National Tribune*, January 18, 1917, for Collins' discovery of the eagle; *OR* 14, pp. 74-75, for Rosa's movements. The 46th New York may have taken the retreating 7th Connecticut's place in line, as Rosa recalls forming up to the right of the 79th New York. It is possible that the Highlanders withdrew only after the the 46th New York arrived.

4. See Todd to "My Dear Parints," June 16, 1862, for "Only 3..." and "was..." Todd, *The 79th Highlanders*, p. 160, for "prepared..." and "heroism..." Ibid., for Stevens' reference to Wright's delays and the time. It was probably sometime between 6:30 and 7:30 a.m.

5. Corporal John Burwell was initially reported as "wounded & missing," *Flint Wolverine Citizen*, July 5, 1862. His body, like many others, was neither recovered nor identified. See Coleman Speech, pp. 5-6, for quoted material. Coleman identified the officer who helped him as "The Captain of Company A of the 8th Maine." Two problems exist with his identification. First, the 8th Maine was not on James Island during this campaign, and second, if he made the most likely mistake and was in fact referring to the 8th Michigan, the "Captain of Company A" would have been Simon Guild, who by this time was lying up by the fort either badly wounded or dead. The officer will probably remain unidentified.

6. Ibid., p. 6 for quoted material.

7. Robert Audley Browne, Robert Browne Papers, M. Gyla McDowell Collection, PSU Letter to "My own dear wife" June 17, 1862, for "Many..." and "direct(ing)..."

8. Gavin, *100th Pennsylvania*, pp. 102-103, for Leasure's efforts; ibid., p. 103, for "hold..."; ibid., p. 102, for "insisting..."

9. Beecher, *Connecticut First Light Battery*, p. 151, for the state of mind of the Connecticut gunners; *OR* 14, p. 68, for "a few..."; Todd, *The 79th Highlanders*, p. 160, for "Orders..." See note 10, below, for Stevens' presence.

10. Todd, *The 79th Highlanders*, p. 160, for "pale..," "even...," and "Follow..." Morrison described the 7th Connecticut "on the right," *OR* 14, p. 76, during this attack; Hawley's map of the action, ibid., p. 1009, shows the 7th's eventual position on the right of the line; Beecher, *Connecticut First Light Battery*, p. 151, for "Connecticut boys..." and "a wild..." The broken elements of the 28th Massachusetts were milling about the Battery Island Road north of Stevens' vantage point. *OR* 14, p. 61.

11. Beecher, *Connecticut First Light Battery*, p. 151, for quoted material.

12. Major Leckey claimed in *OR* 14, p. 77, that Capt. Hazard Stevens issued the order moving the Roundhead right. Beecher, *Connecticut First Light Battery*, p. 151, for "breathlessly"; Ibid., pp. 151-152, for Hawley's work with the gun crews; *OR* 14, p. 68 for the 7th Connecticut's assistance with the guns.

13. Beecher, *Connecticut First Light Battery*, pp. 152-157, for all quoted

materia;. Todd, *The 79th Highlanders*, p. 161, for the pistol shots ending the horses' misery.

14. Ibid., pp. 160-161, for all quoted material except Beecher, *Connecticut First Light Battery*, p. 158, for "plowed. . ."

15. Gavin, *100th Pennsylvania*, pp. 103-104, for Leasure's observations and quotation. Leasure was mistaken as to a Confederate withdrawal.

16. The felling of a Confederate posted in the observation tower is best told in Beecher, *Connecticut First Light Battery*, p. 154. Interestingly, Beecher portrays this incident along with the destruction of the battery mounts in a colorful but somewhat inaccurate illustration of the battle. Ibid., p. 156. See also ibid., p. 158, for the fleshy officer, and p. 159, for "Fowler. . ."; Lusk, *War Letters*, p. 157, for "I looked. . ."

17. Tafft, *Signal Service*, pp. 39-40, for all quoted material.

18. Ibid., p. 40, for quoted material.

19. *ORN* Series I, 13, pp. 104-105, for Drayton's report and all quoted material.

20. Ibid., pp. 107-108, for Lieutenant Gillis' report.

21. Stevens, *Life of*, p. 410, for "reformed. . ."; *OR* 14, p. 52, for "a useless. . ." and "reconnaissance. . ."; Tafft, *Signal Service*, p. 40, for "declined. . ."

22. Ibid., p. 40, for the "coward" reference.

23. Price, *Ninety Seventh Pennsylvania*, p. 125, for "in perfect order. . ."; Eldredge, *The Third New Hampshire*, p. 174, mentions "a sharp artillery fire, participated in by our gunboats on the Stono."

24. *OR* 14, p. 61, for the staff report of Benham's withdrawal orders. Stevens, *Life of*, p. 410, for the "rebel cheers" and the "redoubled" rebel artillery fire.

25. Tafft, *Signal Service*, p. 40, for Tafft's return.

26. Gavin, *100th Pennsylvania*, pp. 103-104, for all quoted material.

27. Beecher, *Connecticut First Light Battery*, pp. 158-160, for the 1st Connecticut Light Battery's retreat. See *OR* 14, p. 83, for Rockwell's computation of 500 rounds fired during the battle.

28. Todd, *The 79th Highlanders*, p. 161, for the Highlander concerns. OR 77, for "slowly. . ."; ibid., p. 68, for "moved. . ."; Sgt. John P. Watson to his sister Eleanor McDowell, M. Gyla, Manuscript History of the Roundheads, M. Gyla McDowell Collection, PSU, June 22, 1862, for "(Y)ou never. . ."; *National Tribune*, January 18, 1917, for Collins' burial of the eagle and "(P)robably some Confederate. . ."

29. Gavin, *100th Pennsylvania*, p. 106, for quoted material.

30. Stevens, *Life of*, p. 411, for Belcher's actions. Belcher stated, "I was ordered. . .to bring them (the remnants of the 8th Michigan) off as a rear guard." Pease, *Memoirs*, pp. 37-38, for Pease's experiences and all quoted material.

31. Ibid., p. 39 for Pease's capture.

32. Beecher, *Connecticut First Light Battery*, p. 160, for Griswold's experience with Fenton.

33. Coleman Speech, pp. 6-8, for quoted material.

34. Belcher letter, *Flint Democrat*, July 3, 1862, for Belcher's description of the firing of the buildings. *OR* 14, p. 62, has Isaac Stevens stating that Belcher "was the last man to leave the field."
35. *Charleston Mercury*, June 19, 1862, for the details of Edwards' death. *Charleston Courier*, June 18, 1862, describes Edwards as "Among the last to fall. . ."
36. Ibid for "gave. . ." and the lowering of the Federal battle flag.
37. *Charleston Mercury*, June 20, 1862, for Bonneau's remarks; ibid., June 19, 1862, for the 4th Louisiana Battalion's actions after the Federal withdrawal.
38. *OR* 14, p. 90, for the Confederate casualty reports.
39. Ibid., 101, for McEnery's totals; ibid., p. 96, for Lamar's estimates.
40. Sheppard letter, June 22, 1862, for "The scene. . ." Smyth letter, June 17, 1862, for "such a scene. . ."
41. Pressley, "Wee Nee Volunteers," p. 146, for "showing. . ."
42. *OR* 14, pp. 98-100, for Hagood's report; ibid., p. 90, for the casualty report. Stevens, *Life of*, map facing p. 402, shows the two Georgia regiments massed on the Battery Island Road north of the Confederate defensive perimeter. The recent discovery of the 47th Georgia's report on the engagement, printed in *SOR*, pt. 1, vol. 3, pp. 101-102, states, "We were not permitted to engage in the fight, though the Forty-seventh was anxious and eager for the fray, and longed only for an opportunity to avenge the death of their comrades, who so gallantly fell in the attempt to charge the entrenchments of the enemy on the evening of June 10. . .(O)ur brave men nobly stood their ground and maintained their position, while shot and shell flew thick around them."
43. *OR* 14, p. 98, for Goodlette's report; ibid., p. 101, for McEnery's surrender of command, which he put "about 12 m(idday)." Unknown, 4th Louisiana Battalion Diary, p. 46, for "(O)ur boys. . ."; Pease, *Memoirs*, p. 39, for "50 or 60. . . ," "You. . ," "as. . . ," "(Q)uite. . . ," and "plenty. . ." ; Capers, *CMH*, p. 599, for "offering. . ."
44. *Charleston Mercury*, June 17, 1862, places Simons in charge of the prisoners.
45. Denison, *The Third Rhode Island Heavy Artillery*, p. 103, for Batchellor's post-battle experiences and all quoted material.
46. *OR* 14, pp. 91-92, for the Evans–Pemberton inspection of the Tower Battery and subsequent actions.
47. Hayes, James, *James and Related Sea Islands* (Charleston, 1978), p. 123, and "Biographical Sketch of Dr. Robert Lebby," Irving A. Watson, Physicians and Surgeons of America (Concord, 1896), places Lebby and his wife at Secessionville after the battle. Stoney, Recollections of John Safford Stoney, Confederate Surgeon, *SCHM*, October 1959, p. 216, also places Stoney, along with "Bellinger, (and) Mr. Simpson," in the village after the fight.
48. Denison, *Third Rhode Island Heavy Artillery*, p. 99, for "in a . . ."; Slemmons, "Diary," p. 61, for "(T)hey had. . ."; Beecher, *Connecticut First Light Battery*, p. 167, for "Old. . ." and "our troops. . ."

49. Todd, *The 79th Highlanders*, p. 161, for "a strong..." Wm. Magill to "Dear Mother," Michael Kraus collection, June 18, 1862, descibes Magill's week-long bout with fever, chills, and dysentery. He wrote, "On Monday the 16th I resigned my couch to a wounded man who had his leg amputated and I was able during the afternoon to nerse the wound as the Hospital was soon filled up."

50. *OR* 14, p. 51, for Union casualty reports, ibid., p. 63, for the "Special arms" casualties and ibid., p. 83, for "detailed..." The Rhode Islander was probably serving the battery at the eastern tip of Sol Legare Island.

51. Ibid., p. 51.

52. Denison, *The Third Rhode Island Heavy Artillery*, p. 103, for a description of the gathered crowd, the route to the prison, and "shouts..."; *Charleston Mercury*, June 17, 1862, for the time of the prisoners' arrival, "Nearly...," and "Matt Peel's..."

53. Pease, *Memoirs*, p. 39, for "(Q)uite...," and p. 40, for "almost..."

54. Todd to "My Dear Parints," June 16, 1862, for "there was..." Campbell to his wife, June 16, 1862, for all quoted material.

55. *OR* 14, pp. 51-53, for Benham's report, which contains all quoted material. Other reports included in ibid., include Chatfield's (p. 56), Welsh's (pp. 57-58), Hawley's (p. 67), and Graves'(pp. 70-71).

56. Campbell to his wife, Campbell Family Papers, South Carolina Department of Archives and History, June 25, 1862.

Chapter Ten
After Action

1. W. E. C. letter, *Flint Wolverine Citizen*, July 5, 1862, for "We are..."; Turner letter, ibid., for "The Michigan..."; Rowley letter, June 17, 1862, for "just what..."; Elmer Packard to Hiram Burgess, Ralph Ely Pension File, NARA, June 17, 1862, for "Dear sir..."

2. Slemmons, "Diary," p. 62, for "It has..."; Todd, *The 79th Highlanders*, p. 164, for "horrible conditions"; Lusk, p. 156-157, for Lusk's letter to his mother. Some of Lusk's words were so strong (such as "as a coward...liar," and "blasted reputation...knave,") that his family blotted them out from the letter's transcript. Lusk's originals, which include the edited phrases, are located at Yale University Library, Manuscripts and Archives in the Civil War MCC Collection, Mss No. 615.

3. Eldredge, *The Third New Hampshire*, p. 180, for Holbrook and the lively corpse.

4. *Charleston Mercury*, June 17, 1862, for "(T)he ancient fame..."

5. Ibid., for "The foe..."; Woodward, *Mary Chesnut's Civil War*, p. 390, for "Scotchmen..."; *Charleston Courier*, June 17, 1862, for the names of the steamers.

6. Ibid., June 18, 1862, for a copy of Pemberton's "Congratulatory Order.

7. Edward Smith Tennant to his wife, Edward Smith Tennent Papers, South Caroliniana Library, June 17, 1862, for "On Monday..." Mary

Chesnut heard that "Dr. Tennent proved himself a crack shot at Secessionville. They handed him rifles loaded, in rapid succession. And at the point he aimed were found thirty dead men." Woodward, ed., *Mary Chesnut's Civil War*, p. 390.

8. Capers to his wife, June 17, 1862, as quoted in Cisco, *Gist*, pp. 79-80, for Capers' ferocious attitude towards Nathan Evans.

9. Pressley, "Wee Nee Volunteers," p. 146, for quoted material.

10. Pease, *Memoirs*, pp. 39-41, for all quoted material. Dart survived his operation and was eventually exchanged.

11. Benjamin Pease rejoined the 8th Michigan and served for the duration of the war. He mustered out of the regiment on May 1, 1865, as a 1st lieutenant.

12. Fenton "respectfully," *OR* 14, p. 66, deferred to Moore's report of the battle; ibid., pp. 69-70, for Fenton's report; ibid., pp. 71-74, for Leasure's report; Cartwright to Andrew, August 3, 1862, for Cartwright's obvious displeasure with Moore's actions—the major underlines "when Col Moore again assumed the Comd."

13. Tourtellotte, *Company K. . .Seventh Connecticut*, p. 34, for Hibbard's death.

14. *Charleston Mercury*, June 18, 1862, for Henry King's death.

15. *OR* 14, p. 568, for Pemberton's two messages.

16. The location of the burial trench has long been a source of controversy. The Nomination Form for the Secessionville Historic District's inclusion in the National Register of Historic Places, Author's Collection, identifies the "Union Grave Site" at the very western edge of the district's boundary somewhat south of the post-war Fort Lamar Road. See Pressley, "Wee Nee Volunteers," pp. 146-147, for the details of Goodlette's confrontation with the Federals.

17. James Campbell to Alexander Campbell, Campbell Thesis, June 18, 1862, for all quoted material.

18. Eldredge, *The Third New Hampshire*, p. 180, for Benham's congratulatory note; Serrell, "Report," July 7, 1862, for Serrell's rise to chief engineer.

19. Ibid., for the Ben Deford reference; *OR* 14, p. 51, for Wright's casualties.

20. Du Pont, *Letters*, p. 118, for details of the dinner and all quoted material.

21. *OR* 14, pp. 353-354, for both of Hunter's reports to Stanton.

22. Du Pont, *Letters*, p. 123: "news came last night by a transport steamer."

23. Ibid., p. 123-124, for Du Pont's version of the reports including all quoted material.

24. Pressley, "Wee Nee Volunteers," p. 147, for "The enemy. . ." and "terrific."

25. Ely, *Diary of*, p. 37, for quoted material; Moore to "General," Correspondence of the 28th Regt. (MA); State Library of Massachusetts, June 19, 1862, for "Please. . ." *Boston Herald*, June 30, 1862, for "Letter

from the 28th Massachusetts Regiment." *Edgefield Advertiser*, July 23, 1862, for "Sav. Rep.," the 7th Connecticut letter writer. This letter was found in the abandoned Federal camps by Confederate pickets.

26. Eldredge, *The Third New Hampshire*, p. 181, for the departure of the *Ben Deford*; Coleman Speech, p. 9, for Private Coleman's post-operative hospital experience; Browne to "My own dear Davie," Robert Browne Papers, M. Gyla McDowell Collection, PSU, June 21, 1862, for "was crowded..." and reference to the afternoon storm.

27. Eldredge, *The Third New Hampshire*, p. 181, for some detail of Benham's orders. OR 14, p. 356, for Wright's response to Benham.

28. Eldredge, *The Third New Hampshire*, p. 181, for camp rumors; Wm. Magill to "Dear Mother," June 18, 1862, for "There will..."

29. OR 14, p. 355, for Hunter's orders to Horatio Wright.

30. Du Pont, p. 128, for Benham's version of the meeting, as related to Du Pont through John Rodgers.

31. OR 14, p. 63, for "I desire..."; Todd to "My Dear Parints," June 16, 1862, reiterates Stevens' stand nearly verbatim and adds the intriguing detail that Stevens was overheard arguing his case to Benham soon after the battle.

32. Ibid., pp. 125-127, for Ely's take on the battle including all quoted material.

33. Ibid., pp. 126-127, for Du Pont's reactions to the reports.

34. OR 14, pp. 44-46, for Benham's addendum. The general claimed in his official report, ibid., p. 51, that Hunter's approval for a reconnaissance in force was given "upon the 11th instant." However, in his addendum, Benham states that Hunter's assent was given "upon the evening prior to his leaving," which would have been June 10.

35. Du Pont, *Letters*, p. 128, for "crushed but calm."

36. Fenton to Stevens, William Fenton Pension File, NARA, June 20, 1862, for all quoted material.

37. Serrell, "Report," July 7, 1862, for the height of the observatory. Another platform 80 feet high had been built near the eastern point of Sol Legare Island. Todd, *The 79th Highlanders*, pp. 164-165, for "so near..." and Kinnear's death.

38. OR 14, pp. 357-358, for Wright's two communications. Ibid., p. 64, has Stevens referring to Wright as "Commanding U. S. Forces, James Island, S.C.," in a report date June 19. Evidently Stevens heard of Benham's removal and Wright's ascension before he received offical notification. Serrell, "Report," June 18, 1862, for Serrell's analysis of the James Island defenses.

39. ISP, Stevens to "My dear wife," June 20, 1862, for "This is..."

40. *New York Times*, June 29, 1862, for a reprint of "Palmetto's" dispatch, which includes all quoted material.

41. *Charleston Mercury*, June 21, 1862, for "A Son of the Soil's" letter. Hatch commanded "A Corps of Signal men...distributed at Morris Island, Fort Sumter, Fort Moultrie..." Order Book, Headquarters 2nd Military District, May 17, 1862. Krick, *Lee's Colonels*, p. 187, states that Hatch "re-

mained in South Carolina service" and survived the war. Porter, *Led on*, p. 139, states that Hatch died on January 12, 1897.

Chapter Eleven
Exit

1. Serrell, "Report," July 7, 1862, for an interesting discussion of the Confederate artillery projectiles, including the possibility that Lamar's 8-inch columbiad burst on the morning of June 18. Todd, *The 79th Highlanders*, p. 165, for the sword presentation ceremony. Around this time, Stevens described Benham as "Poor, blustering, blundering, unscrupulous, foolish" and claimed that "Six hundred to seven hundred killed & wounded cry out against him!" ISP, Stevens to "My Dear Wife," June 30, 1862. The vehemence of much of Isaac Stevens' commentary concerning Benham is startling. Ely, *Diary of*, p. 37, for "the men. . .";. ibid., p. 38, for "The Regiment. . ." *Flint Wolverine Citizen*, July 5, 1862, for the number of Michigan effectives.

2. Du Pont, *Letters*, pp. 150-151, note 2, for Drayton's observations, which includes his belief that Wright could have taken Charleston by regular approaches. Drayton was highly impressed with the works Wright had completed and mounted in just five days. Serrell, "Report," July 7, 1862, and accompanying map details the entire Federal perimeter just prior to the evacuation. Pressley, "Wee Nee Volunteers," pp. 147-148, for details of the renewed artillery fire. The entry in the Unknown, 4th Louisiana Battalion Diary for "July 2, 1862," notes that the Tower Battery now had "eight or ten more guns." Todd, *The 79th Highlanders*, p. 166, for the Federal view of the renewal. Todd to "My Dear Parints," June 30, 1862, states that "about 5.p.m. . .the first shell struck inside the fort instantly killing one of the 6th co and slightly wounding one of our co. . ."

3. OR 14, pp. 42-43, for Hunter's report; ibid., p. 361, for Wright's reply to Hunter's abandonment order.

4. Du Pont, *Letters*, pp. 149-151, for Drayton's ire; ibid., p. 151, for Du Pont's "the finest. . ." Drayton was upset with Benham well before the abandonment of James Island was announced. Du Pont wrote on June 22, that Drayton felt "if putting coals of fire on a man's head punished him, this one (Benham) had a full dose." Ibid., p. 132.

5. Serrell, "Report," July 1862, for "It is. . ."; Du Pont, *Letters*, pp. 150-151, for Stevens' dissatisfaction; Russell Duncan, ed., *Robert G. Shaw: Blue-Eyed Child of Fortune* (Athens, 1992), p. 222, for quoted material. Shaw would be killed leading the assault on Battery Wagner in July of 1863 as the colonel of the 54th Massachusetts.

6. Pressley, "Wee Nee Volunteers," pp. 148-149, for the Confederate view of the arriving Federal vessels. Crawford quoted in *Recollections and Reminiscenes, 1861-1865*, 2 vols. (Columbia, 1991), 2, p. 143. See Unknown, 4th Louisiana Battalion Diary, "July 2nd 1862," entry for "Houses. . ."; Augustine Smythe to Unknown, Augustine Smyth Papers;

Charleston Historical Society, June 26, 1862 for "One poor..."

7. *OR* p. 108, for "very..." Eldredge, *The Third New Hampshire*, p. 183, for the cavalry departure. Ibid., p. 187, for the 3rd New Hampshire's departure; Todd, *The 79th Highlanders*, pp. 166-168, for the use of "quaker" guns and details of the 79th New York's departure; ibid., p. 168, for "the popular..."; Todd to "My Dear Parints," July 6, 1862, for "(E)verything..." and the departure of the 1st Connecticut Light Artillery; Alexander Campbell to his Wife, Campbell Family Papers, South Carolina Department of Archives and History, July 15, 1862, for James' last attempt to contact his brother. Alexander Campbell resigned his commission less than a year later and left the army "thoroughly disillusioned," Power, *SCHM*, 95, April 2, 1994, p. 137, but he would keep in touch with his brother James throughout and after the war. See Johnston, Campbell Thesis, pp. 161-86, for their correspondence.

8. Ely, *Diary of*, p. 38, for all quoted material. Fenton Diary, July 5 entry for details of the 8th Michigan's departure and the 28th Massachusetts' arrival on July 6; Slemmons, "Diary," p. 65, places the private's Roundhead company on Battery Island on July 7. See *OR* 14, pp. 107-110, for Wright's various reports on the evacuation. The last of his troops reached Edisto "about 8 p.m. on the evening of the 7th instant..."

9. Pressley, "Wee Nee Volunteers," pp. 149-151, for the Confederate view of the last few days of the Federal occupation of James Island; see Tracy, "Rebel Diary," p. 281, for another view of the Federal retrograde; Unknown, 4th Louisiana Battalion Diary, "July 4th 1862," entry for "the glorous fourth..." and the Confederate artillery salute ("The Confederates fired a salute this noon from all the Batters and finishing with the big guns of Fort Sumter...").

10. Ibid., places Confederate troops near Grimball's on July 5; Tracy, "Rebel Diary," p. 281; mentions Duncan's near-capture by a "party probably from the gunboats." The incident occurred near the former Battery Wright; *New York Tribune*, July 8, 1862, for the signposts and Williams' grave; *Charleston Mercury*, July 4, 1862, for "affecting sentence..."

11. Tracy, "Rebel Diary," p. 281, for "Enemy known..."; Pressley, "Wee Nee Volunteers," p. 150, for the re-occupation of Battery Island.

12. *OR* 14, p. 44, for Stevens' and Wright's responses to Benham's addendum.

13. Ibid., p. 43, for "this department..."; pp. 48-50, for Stevens' version of the June 15 meeting, including all quoted material.

14. Ibid.

15. *New York Times*, July 16, 1862.

16. *OR* 14, pp. 988-990, for Benham's response to Stevens.

17. Ibid.

18. Ibid., pp. 987-988, for Stevens' reply. It is instructive to compare the two maps that accompany the reports in the *Official Records* (Plate XXIII, nos. 6 and 7). Map 6 refers to the main body of reports while Map 7 accompanies the documents dealing with the Benham-Stevens controversy. The only real difference between the two documents is the placement of the

two generals' respective field headquarters on Map 7. Benham probably added these to make it seem as though he was closer to the front than Stevens. Bache wrote Stevens at least four times between July 3 and July 24, to update him on Washington's position in the controversy and urge him to ignore Benham's "slanders." Stevens also wrote to Lincoln on July 8 to urge his troops' transfer to Virginia, almost at the exact same time Lincoln independently decided to do the same. ISP, Stevens to Abraham Lincoln, July 8, 1862. ISP, Wright to Stevens, August 9, 1862, for "shall be ready..."

19. *OR* 14, pp. 979-1013, for the correspondence relating to Benham's revocation of command and eventual reinstatement. Michael Burlingame, *The Inner World of Abraham Lincoln* (Urbana and Chicago, 1994), p. 197, for Lincoln's anger with Benham's equivocations.

20. Henry W. Benham, "Brief Report of Services in Action of Genl. H. W. Benham," Benham file, National Archives, pp. 3-4, for all quoted material.

21. Stephen Minot Weld, *War Diary and Letters of Stephen Minot Weld, 1861-1865* (Boston, 1979), pp. 188-189, and 199-200, for Weld's observations. Weld originally liked and respected Benham, but quickly grew to find the general "a man of a great deal of brain, but with an inordinate amount of vanity, and exceedingly nervous and irritable." Ibid., p. 199.

22. William Marvel, *Burnside* (Chapel Hill, 1991), p. 98, for "the force...."; Todd, *The 79th Highlanders*, p. 220, for the death of Isaac Stevens; ibid., p. 221, for "By—!..."; Daniel Leasure, "Address," pp. 141-142, for Leasure's view of Isaac Stevens.

23. Stevens, *Life of*, p. 500.

24. *SOR*, pt. II, vol. 28, p. 687, for "(We) behaved..."; Todd, *The 79th Highlanders*, p. 155, and p. 220, for the bravery of the 28th Massachusetts at Chantilly. Conyngham, *Irish Brigade*, , p. 587, for Cartwright's subsequent service; ibid., pp. 576-589, for a history of the 28th Massachusetts. A recently published compilation of essays, see Tucker, *The History of the Irish Brigade*, for a short history of the 28th's service with that esteemed brigade.

25. Eldredge remains the finest source on the 3rd New Hampshire and one of the war's best regimentals. Eldredge, *The Third New Hampshire*, pp. 312-335, for the 3rd's participation in the attack on Battery Wagner. See ibid., pp. 459-573, for the 3rd's service in Virginia including the Bermuda Hundred campaign.

26. Both Gavin and Todd provide excellent service accounts of the Roundheads and the Highlanders, respectively. See *Record of Service of Michigan volunteers in the Civil War*, 8, for the rolls and a brief history of the 8th Michigan. The 8th is one of the many fighting regiments, both Southern and Northern, whose service to its country has gone largely, and unfortunately, undocumented. David Morrison became the 79th New York's colonel after Second Manassas, and led the regiment for the remainder of the war. Todd, *The 79th Highlanders*, p. 389, for "Remember James Island"; VanderVeen for "The 79th..." On a related subject, both the 79th New York and the 100th Pennsylvania made curious choices in locating

their battlefield memorials. The Roundheads constructed an impressive monument near the Otto farm at Antietam, even though they suffered but four casualties on the war's bloodiest day. Even more unusual is the placement of the 79th's memorial near the site of Fort Sanders in Knoxville, Tennessee. Fighting behind well-placed and strongly-constructed walls, the Highlanders only took nine casualties during James Longstreet's attack. Today, the monument stands rather awkwardly on a Knoxville street corner. The 8th Michigan never constructed a battlefield memorial.

27. Faust, ed., *Encyclopedia*, p. 376, and Sifakis, *Who Was Who*, pp. 327-328, for Hunter's career; Faust, ed., *Encyclopedia*, p. 844, and Sifakis, *Who Was Who*, pp. 732-733, for more on Horatio Wright; *Record of Service of Michigan volunteers in the Civil War*, p. 52, for Fenton's service record; Gavin, *100th Pennsylvania*, p. 418, for Leasure's wounding at Spotsylvania and pp. 557-560, for Leasure's departure from the Roundheads.

28. Faust, ed., *Encyclopedia*, p. 230, and Sikfakis, *Who Was Who*, pp. 195-196, for Du Pont's life. Du Pont left an incredible array of letters, quoted at length in this work, that will forever serve to illuminate the machinations of the Southern Expedition.

29. *Charleston Mercury*, June 23, 1862, for Evans' note. Ibid., June 24, 1862, for Eyewitness' rejoinder; Hagood, *Memoirs*, p. 97, for Hagood's reflections on Nathan "Shanks" Evans and nod to William Duncan Smith; Crute, *Confederate Units*, p. 264, for a brief history of the 22nd South Carolina; Faust, ed., *Encyclopedia*, p. 248, and Sifakis, *Who Was Who*, p. 208, for Nathan Evans' career; Krick, *Lee's Colonels*, pp. 162-163, for Goodlett's "cashiering."

30. *OR* 14, pp. 86-90, for Pemberton's full report on the James Island campaign; *Charleston Courier*, June 26, 1862, as quoted in Ballard, *Pemberton*, p. 106, for "Be assured. . ." See ibid., pp. 106-114, for an excellent analysis of Pemberton's last days in South Carolina.

31. Davis, ed., *Confederate General*, 5, pp. 190-191, for Smith's subsequent record. Cisco, *Gist*, provides the only full-length study of State Rights Gist's life. Ellison Capers' son, Walter, wrote *The Soldier-Bishop*, the only book-length examination of this remarkable man. Walkley, *Seventh Connecticut*, Appendix pp. 11-12, for Capers' letter to Woodford's widow.

32. Arthur W. Bergeron Jr., *Guide to Louisiana Confederate Military Units, 1862-1865*, pp. 157-158, for a brief overview of the 4th Louisiana Battalion's service record; *SOR*, pt. 2, vol. 23, p. 812, for the 4th's service record.

33. Crute, *Confederate Units*, pp. 265-266, for a short history of the Eutaw Battalion; ibid., p. 257 and p. 266, for the Pee Dee Battalion's service record.

34. Ibid., pp. 246-247 and p. 266, for the Charleston Battalion's record. One of the five Confederates captured at Battery Wagner was James Campbell, who then spent the next two years imprisoned in various Northern prisoner of war camps. He returned to Charleston after the war and lived another fifty years. Power, *SCHM*, 95, No. 2 (April, 1994), p. 138,

27n. See Johnston, Campbell Thesis, pp. 177-86, for the brothers' post-war experiences.

35. Hagood, *Memoirs*, p. 11, for "Out of. . ." Johnson Hagood's *Memoirs of the War of Secession* has often been dismissed as a wordy reminiscence by a minor player (see Faust, ed., *Encyclopedia*, pp. 331-332). Those studying Confederate efforts in South Carolina obviously feel otherwise.

36. Crute, *Confederate Units*, p. 249, for the unit's service record. *Edgefield Advertiser*, Oct 22, 1862, for Lamar's October 4, 1862, declining of the proffered candidacy and reactions of the Edgefield district to his death. Included in this account is a listing of Lamar's final escort, which included Maj. David Ramsey and Surgeon Robert Lebby. *Charleston Mercury* and *Charleston Courier*, October 18, 1862, for Lamar's death. Most of the details come from the *Mercury's* coverage. My thanks to Judge John B. Lewis of Raleigh, NC, a descendent of Colonel Lamar, for filling in important gaps in Lamar's personal history.

Bibliography

MANUSCRIPTS

Patrick Brennan Collection, Chicago
   Kearny, Philip. Letter to Marsena Patrick, 29 May 1861.
   John Rowley Letter
   Confederate Order Book
   Henry Benham to John L. Goldsborough, 23 May 1862
   John L. Goldsborough to "My Dear Wife, 24 May 1862
Tim Bradshaw Collection (Columbia, S.C.)
   S. Van Vector Breese Letters
Charleston Historical Society, Charleston
   Augustine Smyth Papers
Bill Compton Collection, Oakland, California
   Civil War Memoirs of Benjamin F. Pease.
Duke University Library
   Lalla Pelot Papers
Roger Durham Collection (Hinesville, Ga.)
   William Daniel Dixon Journal
Catherine Fishback Collection. Fredericksburg, VA.
   Philip Coleman Speech, transcript, to the 1st Congregational Church of Washington D.C., Oct ober 21, 1898.
Michael Kraus Collection
   J.H. Slemmons Diary
   Wm. Magill Letters, June 18, 1862
Louisiana State Library
   4th Louisiana Battalion Unit Papers
State Library of Massachusetts
   Correspondence of the 28th Regt. (Mass).
Civil War Flags—Michigan. Report submitted by Mary Jo Verran to the Michigan State Capitol Committee (1991). Mary Jo Verran Collection
Flint (Michigan) Public Library
   Diary of Wm. M. Fenton 1861-1863 and Material Relating to 8th Michigan Infantry
State Archives of Michigan
   Daniel Dillabough Letters
   Service Records of the 8th Michigan
University of Michigan
   Bentley Historical Library
      Solomon Kroll Letters
      Personal Account of Private Orrin Bump, 8th Michigan Infantry
      Reminiscence of Arand VanderVeen, M.D. (Grand Haven, Mich.)
National Archives, Washington, DC.
   Benham, Henry W. "Brief Report of Services in Action of Genl. H.W. Benham," Benham file,
William Fenton File
Ralph Ely File
Michael McGuinnis File
Hiram Nason File

Charles McVey File
Michael Campbell File
John MacDonald File
Hugh Gallagher File
Report of Col Serrell Vol. Engs. of Operations on James Island against Charleston So. Ca.; Record Group 77, Records of the Office of the Chief of Engineers; S.8820, National Archives
Record Group 393; Expeditionary Corps, Letters sent and received; EC, General and Special Orders; EC, 2nd Brigade Correspondence; Department of the South, Letters sent and received.
New York Historical Society
   William Todd Letters
Penn State University
   M. Gyla McDowell Collection
   Stevenson, J. C. "History of the Roundheads,"
   Daniel Leasure Papers
   George Leasure Papers
   Robert Browne Papers
   Thomas Hamilton Papers
   McDowell, M. Gyla. Manuscript, "History of the Roundheads"
Carolyn Shriber Collection, Memphis
   Philo Morton Letters
   John Wilson Letters
Floye Smith Collection, Oak Ridge, Louisiana
   McEnery Family Tree
South Carolina Department of Archives and History
   Campbell Family Papers.
South Carolina State Archives
   Abstracts of Troop Strengths
   Compiled Service Records of South Carolina Soldiers
   1st (Hagood's) South Carolina
   Charleston Battalion (later 27th South Carolina)
   Pee Dee Battalion (later 26th South Carolina)
   21st South Carolina
   22nd South Carolina
   24th South Carolina
   Eutaw Battalion (later 25th South Carolina)
   1st (later 2nd) South Carolina Artillery (Lamar's)
South Caroliniana Library
   Ellison Capers Papers
   Sheppard Family Papers (edited by Susan Smyth Bennett)
   Edward Smith Tennent Papers
University of Texas in Austin
   Eugene C. Barker Texas History Center
     "Diary of a Confederate soldier, May 25, 1861-October 18, 1863. Begins at Richmond, Madison Parish, Louisiana. concludes one mile from Chattanooga, Tenn." Confederate States of America Collection, Box 2C484, Folder 9
United States Military History Institute, Carlisle Barracks, Pennsylvania
   Camp Kettle
   Thomas Williams Collection
   Smith Family (1st Mass. Cav.)
   Andrew Fitch Letters. Lewis Leigh Collection
   Frederick Petit Correspondence, CWTI Collection

Henry Applegate Letter. CWTI Collection
Charles Legg Letters (1st Mass. Cav.). Lewis Leigh Collection
Robert Browne Letters
Mary Jo Verran Collection
John Rice Burwell Letters
University of Washington in Seattle
  Allen Library
    Isaac I. Stevens Papers
Yale University Library
  Civil War MSS Collection
  William Thompson Lusk Papers (Mss No. 615)

NEWSPAPERS

Newport (RI) Mercury
Newport (RI) Daily News
Wolverine Citizen (Flint, MI)
Jackson (MI) Weekly Citizen
Detroit Free Press
Detroit Daily Advertiser
New York Commercial Advertiser
The Democrat (Flint, MI)
Charleston (SC) Mercury
Charleston (SC) Courier
Augusta (GA) Constitution
The Island Gazette (Savannah, GA)
The Savannah (GA) Republican
New York Tribune
New York Times
New York Herald
Horry (SC) Dispatch
Edgefield (SC) Advertiser
Marion (SC) Star
Georgetown (SC) Times
Boston Herald
Boston Pilot

OFFICIAL PUBLICATIONS

Adjutant General's Office-Connecticutt; Catalogue of Connecticutt Volunteer Organizations in the Service of the United States, 1861-1865. Hartford (Conn): Brown & Gross, 1869.
Adjutant-General's Office-Massachusetts. *Massachusetts Soldiers, Sailors, and Marines in the Great Civil War.* Norwood (Mass): Norwood Press, 1931.
Adjutant General's Office-New Hampshire. *Revised Register of Soldiers and Sailors of the Rebellion, 1861-1866.* Concord (NH): Ira C. Evans, 1895.
Annual Report of the Adjutant General of Rhode Island. Providence: Providence Press Co., 1865.
Adjutant General's Office-Rhode Island. *Names of Officers, Soldiers and Seamen in Rhode Island Regiments Who Lost Their Lives in the Defense of their Country in the Suppression of the Late Rebellion.* Providence: Providence Press, 1869.

Official Register of Rhode Island Officers and Soldiers Who Served in the United States Army and Navy from 1861 to 1866. Providence: General Assembly, 1866.
Report of The Joint Committee on the Conduct of the War, Part III; Government Printing Office, Washington, D.C.: 1863.
Rhode Island Adjutant General Report. Providence (RI): Providence Press Company, 1866.
Supplement to the Official Records. Wilmington, N.C.: Broadfoot Publishing Co., 1994.
United States Department of Agriculture Aerial Photographs- No.'s 45019-178-82 and 45019-178-83. Aeriel Photography Field Office, Salt Lake City, Utah.
United States Department of the Interior Geological Survey-James Island Quadrangle, 1959.
US War Department. *The War of the Rebellion: A Compilation of the Official Records of the Union and Confederate Navies.* Washington, D.C.: US Government Printing Office, 1896.
US War Department. *The War of the Rebellion. A Compilation of the Official Records of the Union and Confederate Armies.* 128 vols. Washington, D.C.: US Government Printing Office, 1880-1901.

PRIMARY ACCOUNTS

Ammen, Rear Admiral Daniel: *The Navy in the Civil War-The Atlantic Coast.* New York: Chas. Scribners Sons, 1898
———; *The Old Navy and the New.* Philadelphia: J.B. Lippincott Co., 1891
Anderson, Maj. Edward C.; *Confederate Foreign Agent.* University (Alabama): Confederate Publishing Company 1976
Andrews, W. H. *Footprints of a Regiment: A Recollection of the First Georgia Regulars 1861-1865.* Edited by Richard McMurry. Atlanta: Longstreet Press, 1992
Bates, Samuel. *History of Pennsylvania Volunteers, Vol. III.* Harrisburg: B. Singerly State Printer, 1870
Bedel, John. *Historical Sketch of the Third Regiment, New Hampshire Volunteers.* The Granite Monthly, 3 (Sept 1880): pp. 516-34
Beecher, Herbert W. *History of the First Light Battery Connecticutt Volunteers, 1861-1865.* New York: A.T. De La Mare Ptg. and Pub.
Booth, Andrew B. *Records of Louisiana Confederate Soldiers and Louisiana Confederate Commands.* Spartanburg (South Carolina): Reprint Co. 1984
Bowen, James L. *Massachusetts in the War, 1861-1865.* Springfield (Mass): Clark W. Bryan 1889.
Buel, Clarence and Johnson, Robert (eds.) *Battles and Leaders of the Civil War.* NY: Century Company, 1884-9.
Cadwell, Charles K. *The Old Sixth Regiment.* New Haven: Tuttle, Morehouse & Taylor 1875.
Capers, Ellison. *Confederate Military History Extended Edition-South Carolina.* (Reprint) Wilmington, N.C.: Broadfoot, 1987.
Carlton, William J. *Company D of the Forty-Eighty Regiment New York State Volunteers 1861-5.* Privately Printed, 1892.
Confederate Military History, Extended Edition—Louisiana, vol. 13. Wilmington (NC): Broadfoot Publishing 1987.
Confederate Veteran (Reprint). Harrisburg (Pa): NHS
Conyngham, D. P. *The Irish Brigade and Its Campaigns.* NY: William McSorely, 1867.

Copp, Elbridge. *Reminiscences of the War of the Rebellion.* Nashua, NH: Telegraph Publishing Co. 1911.
Cowley, Charles. *Leaves From A Lawyer's Life Afloat and Ashore.* Lowell (Mass.): Penhollow Printing, 1879.
———. *The Career of Gen. Robert Smalls: Individual Biography* (Newberry Library) Originally published Lowell, Mass., 1882.
Crater, Lewis. *History of the Fiftieth Regiment Pennsylvania Veteran Volunteers 1861-65.* Reading, Pa.: Coleman Printing House 1884.
Crowinshield, Benjamin W. *A History of the First Regiment of Massachusetts Cavalry Volunteers.* Boston and New York: Houghton, Mifflin and Company 1891.
Denison, Frederick. *Shot and Shell: The Third Rhode Island Heavy Artillery In The War of The Rebellion.* Providence: JA and RA Reid 1879.
Dowdey, Clifford and Manarin, Louis H. eds. Robert E. Lee. NY, 1965.
———. *The Wartime Papers of R.E. Lee.* NY: Bramhall House 1961.
Du Pont, Samuel Francis (Hayes, John D. ed.). *A Selection From His Civil War Letters.* Ithaca, NY: Cornell 1969.
Dyer, Frederick H. *A Compendium of the War of the Rebellion.* Dayton, Ohio: Morningside, 1979.
Eldredge, Daniel. *The Third New Hampshire Volunteers and All About It.* Boston (Mass.): E. B. Stillings and Company, 1893.
Ely, Ralph. *The Diary of Captain Ralph Ely of the Eighth Michigan Infantry.* Mount Pleasant (Michigan): Central Michigan University Press, 1965.
Gavin, William. *The 100th Regiment Pennsylvania Volunteers.* Dayton, Ohio: Morningside 1989.
Gillmore, Q.A. *Supplementary Report to Engineer and Artillery Operations against the Defences of Charleston Harbor in 1863* (Professional Papers, Corps of Engineers USA, No. 16-Supplement). New York: D. Van Nostrand, 1868.
Hagood, Johnson. *Memoirs of the War of Secession.* Columbia (S.C.): The State Company, 1910.
Higginson, Thomas W. *Massachusetts in the Army and Navy During the War of 1861-65.* Boston: Wright & Potter, 1896.
Inglesby, Charles. *Historical Sketch of the First Regiment of South Carolina Artillery (Regulars).* Columbia: Walker, Evans & Cogswell 1893.
Izlar, William Valmore. *A Sketch of the War Record of the Edisto Rifles, 1861-1865.* Columbia S.C.: The State Company 1914.
Johnson, John. *The Defense of Charleston Harbor;* Charleston, South Carolina. Walker Evans & Cogswell, 1890.
Johnston, Terry A., Jr. *"Him on One Side, Me on the Other": The Civil War Letters of Alexander Campbell, Seventy-Ninth New York Infantry Regiment and James Campbell, First South Carolina ("Charleston Battalion").* Master's Thesis, Clemson University.
Leasure, Daniel. "Address By Col. Daniel Leasure." MOLLUS, Minnesota Commandery ("Glimpses of a Nation's Struggle") St. Paul (Minn.) 1887.
Lusk, William Thompson. *War Letters of William Thompson Lusk.* New York: Privately Published 1911.
Marszalek, John F. (ed.) *The Diary of Miss Emma Holmes 1861-1866.* Baton Rouge and London: LSU Press, 1979.
Metcalf, Edwin. *Personal Incidents in the Early Campaigns of the Third Regiment Rhode Island Volunteers and the Tenth Army Corps.* Rhode Island Soldiers and Sailors Historical Society #9; Providence: Rider 1879.
Mixson, Frank M. *Reminiscences of a Private.* Columbia (SC): The State Co., 1910.
Moore, Frank. *Rebellion Record,* Twelve Volumes. New York: G.P. Putnam, 1863.

Nichols, James. *Perry's Saints*. Boston: D. Lathrop 1886.
Nichols, G.W. *A Soldier's Story of His Regiment*. Privately Published.
Palmer, Abraham J. *The History of the Forty-Eighth Regiment New York State Volunteers*. Brooklyn and New York: Dillingham, 1885.
Petit, Frederick. *Infantryman Petit*. Shippensburg (Pa.): White Mane, 1990.
Porter, A. Toomer. *Led On! Step by Step*. NY: G. P. Putnam's Sons-The Knickerbocker Press, 1899.
Price, Isiah. *History of the Ninety-Seventh Regiment Pennsylvania Volunteer Infantry*. Philadelphia (Subscription) 1875.
Ripley, Warren (ed.). *Siege Train, The Journal of a Confederate Artilleryman in the Defence of Charleston*. Columbia (S.C.): University of South Carolina Press, 1986.
Shaw, Robert G., (Duncan, Russell (ed.). *Blue-Eyed Child of Fortune*. Athens, (Ga.): University of Georgia Press, 1992.
Sherwood, W. Cullen. *The Nelson Artillery Lamkin and Rives Batteries*. Lynchburg, Va.: H.E. Howard 1991.
Sorrel, Brig. Gen. G. Moxley. *Recollections of a Confederate Staff Officer*, Bell Wiley (ed.). Wilmington, NC: Broadfoot (Reprint) 1987.
Southern Historical Society Papers. 52 Volumes. Richmond, Virginia: Southern Historical Society, 1876-1959.
State Division of Confederate Pensions and Records (Georgia). *Roster of the Confederate Soldiers of Georgia, 1861-1865*. Vol. 5 Hapeville (Ga.): Longino & Porter, 1959.
Stevens, Hazard. *Papers of the Military Historical Society of Massachusetts*. (Reprint) Wilmington N.C.: Broadfoot 1989.
Stevens, Hazard. *The Life of Isaac Ingalls Stevens*. Boston: Houghton Mifflin, 1900.
Tafft, Henry S. *Reminiscences of the Signal Service in the Civil War*. RISSHA Fifth Series #9 Providence: Published by the Society 1899.
Thompson & Means (eds.). *Confidential Correspondence of Gustavus V. Fox*. New York: Naval Institute Society-De Vinne Press, 1918.
Todd, William. *The Seventy-Ninth Highlanders New York Volunteers*. Albany (NY): Brandow, Barton & Company, 1886.
Tourtellotte, Jerome. *A History of Company K of the Seventh Connecticutt Volunteer Infantry in the Civil War*. (SL) 1910.
(various). *The Irish Volunteers*. Charleston (S.C.): The News and Courier Book and Job Presses, 1878.
(various). *An Historical Sketch of the Washington Light Infantry of Charleston S.C.* New York: D. Appleton 1875.
(various). *Recollections and Reminiscenes, 1861-1865*, vol. 2. South Carolina Division UDC: Columbia, South Carolina 1991.
Walkley, Stephen, Jr. *History of the Seventh Connecticut Volunteer Infantry, Hawley's Brigade, Terry's Division, Tenth Army Corps, 1861-1865*. Hartford (CT): 1905.
Weld, Stephen Minot. *War Diary and Letters of Stephen Minot Weld, 1861-1865*. 2nd Ed.. Massachusetts Historical Society, Boston 1979.
Welsh, Peter. *Irish Green & Union Blue*. NY: Fordham Univ. Press, 1986.
Woodward, C. Vann. *Mary Chesnut's Civil War*. New Haven: Yale Univ. Press, 1981.

SECONDARY SOURCES

Ballard, Michael B. *Pemberton, A Biography*. Jackson (Mississippi): University Press of Mississippi, 1991.

Burton Burton, William L. "Irish Regiments in the Union Army: The Massachusetts Experience." *Historical Journal of Massachusetts*, vol. 11, June 1983. The Neale Publishing Company, 1912.

Carse, Robert. *Department of the South: Hilton Head in the Civil War.* Columbia: The State Printing Company, 1961.

Cauthen, Charles Edward. *South Carolina Goes To War 1860-65.* Chapel Hill: UNC Press, 1950 (James Sprunt Studies in History and Political Science).Cisco, Walter Brian. *States Rights Gist.* Shippensburg (Pa.): White Mane Publishing Co., 1991.

Conrad, James L. "The Sad History of 'Shanks' Evans." *CWTI*, vol. XXII, No. 5 (Sept. 1983)

———.*Ruin: The William Bull Pringles and the Death of the South Carolina Rice Culture, 1800-1884.* Privately Published, Revised 1994.

———. *Jewel of the Cotton Fields.* Mt. Pleasant, South Carolina. Richard Cote & Associates, 1995.

Crute, Jr., Joseph H. *Units of the Confederate States Army.* Midlothian (Va.): Derwent Books, 1987.

Darling, Roger. *A Sad and Terrible Blunder.* Vienna (Va.): Potomac Western, 1990.

Davis, C. H. *Life of Charles Henry Davis, Rear Admiral, 1807-1877.* Boston, 1899.

Davis, William C. (ed.). *The Confederate General.* Harrisburg, Pa.: NHS, 1991.

Du Pont, H. A. *Samuel Francis Du Pont-A Biography.* NY: National Americana Society, 1926.

Ellis, E. Detreville. *Nathaniel Lebby—Patriot and Some of his Descendants.* (N.P.) Chevy Chase, MD.: 1967.

Faust, Patricia (ed.). *Historical Times Illustrated Encyclopedia of the Civil War.* NY: Harper & Row, 1986.

Fox, William F. *Regimental Losses in the American Civil War, 1861-1865.* Albany: Albany Publishing Co., 1889.

Freeman, Douglas Southall. *R.E. Lee.* NY: Scribners, 1934.

Glatthaar, Joseph T. *Partners in Command.* NY: Free Press, 1994.

Gragg, Rod. "A Bloody Half-Hour." *CWTI*, vol. XXXII, No. 6 (January/February 1994).

Hawes, Lilla Mills (ed.). *Collections of the Georgia Historical Society.* Savannah, (Ga.): Georgian Historical Society, 1964.

Hayes, James P. *James and Related Sea Islands.* Charleston: W. Evans & Cogswell, 1978.

Hennessy, John. *The First Battle of Manassas.* Lynchburg (Va.): H.E. Howard, 1989.

———. *Return To Bull Run. The Battle of Second Manassas.* NY: Simon & Schuster, 1993.

Johnson, Curt, and Anderson. *Artillery Hell.* College Station: Texas A&M University Press, 1995.

Jones, Charles E. *Georgia In The War, 1861-1865.* Atlanta: Foot & Davies, 1909.

Krick, Robert. *Lee's Colonels.* Dayton, Ohio: Morningside 1992.

Lattimore, Ralston B. *Fort Pulaski National Monument.* Washington, D.C.: National Park Service Historical Handbook Series, 1954.

Lawrence, Alexander A. *A Present For Mr. Lincoln.* Macon: The Ardivan Press 1961.

Marvel, William. *Burnside.* Chapel Hill: University of North Carolina Press, 1991.

McCaslin, Richard B. *Portraits of Conflict, A Photographic History of South Carolina in the Civil War.*

———. *Arkansas:* University of Arkansas Press, 1994.

Middlekauff, Robert. *The Glorious Cause.* Oxford and NY: Oxford, 1982.

Miller, William J. (ed.). *The Peninsula Campaign of 1862: Yorktown to the Seven Days*, Vol. 1. Campbell (CA.): Savas Publishing Co. 1993.

Nash, Howard P., Jr. "The Ignominious Stone Fleet." *CWTI*, vol. III, No. 3 (June 1964)
North South Trader's Civil War. vol. XIX, No. 3. (May-June 1992. Issue 117).
Patterson, Gerald A. and Nye, Wilbur S. "The Battle of Secessionville." *CWTI* Vol. VII, No. 6 (October 1968).
Phisterer, Frederick. *New York in the War of the Rebellion, 1861-1865*. Albany (NY): Weed and Parsons 1891.
Power, J. Tracy. "'I Hope To God That He And I Will Get Safe Through It Al': Alexander and James Campbell's Civil War." Speech to Charleston Civil War Round Table, March 10, 1992.
———. "An Affair of Outposts, in which the Subordinate Officers and the Troops on the Spot Did the Best They Could": The Battle of Secessionville, 16 June 1862. *Civil War History*, XXXVIII: 2 (June 1992).
———. "Brother Against Brother: Alexander and James Campbell's Civil War." *South Carolina Historical Magazine*, 95 No. 2 (April 1994).
Preservation Consultants, Inc. *James Island and Johns Island Historical and Architectural Inventory*. Charleston: South Carolina Department of Archives and History, 1989
Reed, Rowena. *Combined Operations in the Civil War*. Annapolis, Md.: Naval Institute Press, 1978.
Richards, Kent. *Isaac I. Stevens: Young Man In A Hurry*. Provo, Utah: Brigham Young University Press, 1978.
Robertson, John. *Michigan in the War*. Lansing (Mi): W.S. George 1880.
Salley Jr., A.S. (compiler). *South Carolina Troops in Confederate Service*. Columbia South Carolina: R.L. Bryan Co., 1913.
Sears, Stephen W. *George B. McClellan, The Young Napoleon*. Ticknor & Fields, 1988.
Sifakis, Stewart. *Who Was Who in the Civil War*. NY: Facts On File, 1988.
Stroud, David V. *Civil War Sword and Revolver Presentations*. Pinecrest Publishing Company (N.D.).
Tanner, Robert G. *Stonewall in the Valley*. Mechanicsburg, Pa.: Stackpole Books, 1996.
Tucker, Philip T., ed., *The History of the Irish Brigade*. Fredricksburg, Va., Sgt. Kirkland's Museum and Historical Society, Inc., 1995.
Uya, Okon Edet. *From Slavery To Public Service-Robert Smalls 1839-1915*. New York: Oxford University Press, 1971.
(various), *Charleston in the Civil War. The News and Courier and Charleston Evening Post.*Charleston, S.C.
(various), *Biographical Register of the Officers and Graduates of the U.S. Military Academy 1802-1867*. Boston & New York: Houghton Mifflin & Co., (The Riverside Press, Cambridge) 1891.
(various). *The South Carolina Historical Magazine*. South Carolina Historical Society. Charleston, South Carolina.
Waite, Otis. *New Hampshire in the Great Rebellion*. Claremont (NH): Tracy, Chase, 1870.
Watson, Irving A. *Physicians and Surgeons of America*. Concord, NH: Republican Press Association, 1896.
Wegner, Dana: "The Port Royal Working Parties." *CWTI*, vol. XV, No. 8 (December 1976).
Woodman, John E. "The Stone Fleet," *American Neptune*. XXI, October 1961.
Woodward, C. Vann. *Mary Chesnut's Civil War*. New Haven and London: Yale University Press, 1981.
Young, Mel. *Where They Lie*. Lanham, New York, London: University Press of America.

INDEX

Aberpoolie Creek, 105, 118
Adams Run, 11, 71, 89, 101, 145-146, 321n
Aitken, Pvt. W. H., 193
Alabama Troops, *4th Infantry*, 35
Alabama, 91
Allemong, Lt. —, 211
Alston, Abraham, 324n
Andrew, Governor John, 351n
Andrew, Pvt. John, 152
Andrews, Sgt. William H., 325n, 344n
Antietam, Maryland, Battle of, 299-300, 367n
Applegate, Henry, 1, 3
Appomattox Court House, Virginia, 301, 303
Army of Northern Virginia, 304
Army of Tennessee, 303-305
Army of the Potomac, 8, 93, 297-298
Artillery Crossroads, 100, 105, 114, 144, 196, 230, 307, 352n
Ashepoo River, 3, 11, 14
Ashley River, 3
Atwell, Lt. —, 187
Augusta, Georgia, 14, 22

Bache, Alexander, 5, 296
Baggott, Sgt. —, 183, 212, 349n
Ball's Bluff, Virginia, Battle of, 97, 123
Balloons, 109, 327n, 337n
Bamberg, South Carolina, 19
Bannon, Lt. Nichols, 191
Barber, Adjutant W. C., 349n
Bartholomew, Lt. E. S., 237, 358n
Batchellor, Sgt. James, 238
Batchellor, John, 262
Battery Island, 10, 19, 23-24, 29, 31, 34-35, 38-40, 54-56, 68-69, 71, 85, 91, 100, 106, 109, 112, 143, 291-292, 321n, 326n, 329n, 366n
Battery Island Causeway, 39
Battery Island Road, 34, 76, 79, 86, 100, 105, 115, 125, 127, 144, 159-160, 167, 169, 196, 208, 212, 219, 222, 229, 232-233, 239-242, 252-253, 256-257, 273, 345n-346n, 351n, 355n, 357n-359n, 361n
Battery Lamar (Tower Battery), 161
Battery Reed, 306, 342n
Battery Stevens, 288
Battery Wagner, 300, 305, 365n, 367n-368n
Battery Williams, 288
Battery Wright, 287-288
Bay Point, 62, 323n
Beaufort Artillery, 49, 51
Beaufort River, 27, 59
Beaufort, South Carolina, xiii, 3, 5, 23, 27, 59-60, 91, 293
Beauregard, Gen. Pierre G. T., 160, 303
Bee, Gen. Bernard, 17, 35
Belcher, Lt. Horatio, 165, 255-257, 347n, 360n, 255
Bell, Lt. Col. Louis, 21
Bellinger, Lt. John A., 173, 183-184, 350n
Bellinger, Pvt. Vincent, 185
Ben Deford, 276, 279-280, 291
Benham, Gen. Henry, xiv, 5-6, 8-9, 22, 33, 41-45, 47-48, 51, 59, 65-67, 103-104, 111-112, 117, 125, 127, 137-141, 143, 147, 155, 161-162, 165, 213, 218, 241, 246, 251-254, 259, 263-264, 266-267, 269-270, 274, 276-283, 288, 292-298, 319n-320n, 326n-327n, 336n, 338n,

340n-343n, 354n-355n, 358n, 360n, 362n, 364n-367n, *photo*, 2
Bermuda Hundred, 300
USS Bibb, 40-41
Big Folly Creek, 29, 31, 158, 251
Blake, Capt. Julius, 258
Blum, Lt. R. A., 233-234
Boggott, Sgt. James, 172
Bonneau, Capt. F. N., 55-57, 158, 167, 185, 258, 345n, 350n, 361n
Boston Herald, 279
Bounty and Furlough Act, 19
Boutelle, Charles, 38, 40
Boyce, Capt. Robert, 196, 336n
Bradford, John, 40-41
Brayton, Lt. —, 237
Breckinridge, Gen. John C., 8
Breese, Pvt. S. Van Vector, 234
Brenholts, Lt. Col. —, 47
Brickyard Creek, 23, 27
Broad River, 3, 59
Brown, Maj. J. W., 58
Browne, Chaplain Robert, 245, 336n
Bull Bay, South Carolina, 3
Bump, Pvt. Orrin, 193, 354n
Burgess, Pvt. Clarkson, 270
Burnside, Gen. Ambrose E., 71, 93, 97
Burnside's Expedition, 296
Burwell, Cpl. John R., 1, 244, 359n
Butler, Gen. Benjamin F., 97, 356n

Calhoun Guards, 85, 211
Cameron, Simon, 8
Camp Mercer, 97
Camp Road, 34
Campbell, Pvt. Alexander, 8, 138, 215, 266, 275-276, 290-291, 334n, 341n, 354n, 366n
Campbell, Lt. James, 88, 138, 184, 215, 275-276, 290, 366n, 368n

Campbell, Michael, 191
Campbell, Pvt. Alexander, 60
Cannon, Lt. —, 4
Capers, Lt. Col. Ellison, 17-18, 35-36, 39, 73, 79-80, 82-84, 86, 230-232, 272, 303-304, 308, 322n, 333n-334n, 342n, 345n, 356n-357n, 362n, 368n, *photo*, 18
Carlton, Capt. Ralph, 223, 229, 355n-356n
Carnifex Ferry, West Virginia, Battle of, 8
Cartwright, Maj. George, 102, 193, 240, 255, 273, 299, 351n, 363n, 367n
Cassidy, James, 222
Chancellorsville Campaign, 298
Chantilly, Virginia, Battle of, 297-299
Chapman's Fort, 11
Chapman, Pvt. Thomas N., 236
Charleston Arsenal, 112
Charleston Battalion, 20, 57, 79-80, 82-83, 88, 116, 138, 152-154, 158, 184-185, 211, 215, 218, 224, 259, 262, 266, 272, 274, 304-306, 308, 338n, 344n, 348n, 368n
Charleston Courier, 270, 303, 344n
Charleston Harbor, 24-26, 29, 34, 98, 143, 262
Charleston Light Dragoons, 50
Charleston Mercury, 93, 97, 114, 141, 186, 270, 285, 302, 328n, 344n
Charleston Riflemen, 20, 116, 258, 338n
Charleston, South Carolina, xii-xiv, 3, 6, 9-11, 14, 16-20, 22-27, 31, 34-35, 38, 41-42, 44-45, 48, 53-55, 57-59, 62-65, 69-71, 75, 89-90, 93-94, 96-98, 104, 106, 108, 111-112, 116, 118, 120-121, 125, 138-142, 145-147, 155-156, 160-161, 167-168, 174, 186, 241, 250, 259, 262-263, 265, 272-274, 277-279, 281, 284-

285, 288, 292, 296, 300, 302-306, 326n-327n, 334n, 337n, 343n-345n, 349n, 365n
Charleston-Savannah Railroad, xiii, 3, 14, 48
Chatfield, Col. John, 63, 65, 120, 125, 136, 219, 241, 266, 339n-340n, 362n
Chatfield's Brigade, 166, 239, 347n
Chesnut, James, 53-54, 329n
Chesnut, Mary, 93, 344n
Chesterfield, 55-57, 329n
Chichester, Capt. C. E., 71-73, 79-80, 84, 87, 90, 332n
Chisholm, Samuel, 324n
Christ, Col. Benjamin, 46-47, 50-51, 61, 328n
Church Flats, South Carolina, 3, 11, 16, 101
Church, Capt. Benjamin, 176, 265
Circular Church, Charleston, 104
Citadel, 16-18, 20, 90
Citadel Cadets, 90
Clark Family House, 32-33, 145, 159, 231, 304, 306, 333n, 346n, 357n
Clark's Battery, 232, 308, 342n
Cline, Capt. James, 76, 78-79, 83, 89, 103, 336n
Coleman, Pvt. Philip, 174, 201, 244-245, 257, 280, 359n, 363n
Coles Island, xiii, 9-10, 16-19, 23-25, 27, 31, 34-36, 38-39, 41, 53-54, 69, 99, 155, 321n-324n, 326n
Collins, Lt. —, 5
Collins, Sgt. Walter, 242, 255
Colquitt, Col. Peyton H., 14, 263, 306
Columbia, South Carolina, 16, 147
Combahee River, 3, 52
Cook, Pvt. Foster, 238

Connecticut Troops, *1st Light Artillery*, 45-47, 60-61, 85, 164, 212-213, 242, 246, 254, 264, 333n, 339n, 358n, 366n, *6th Infantry*, 21, 44, 63, 65, 105, 119-120, 153, 166, 291, 300, 327n, 339n, 343n, *7th Infantry*, 21, 44-45, 62, 109-110, 116, 121, 140, 143, 151, 164-165, 186-187, 189-191, 193, 199, 209, 213-214, 216, 242, 246, 255, 264, 266, 269, 274, 279, 291, 300, 304, 308, 337n-339n, 342n, 347n, 350n, 354n, 359n, 363n
Coosaw Ferry, 3
Coosaw River, xiii, 23, 27, 46-47, 50-51, 251
Coosawhatchie River, 3
Copp, Sgt. Elbridge J., 116, 220, 223
Corbin, Pvt. George, 189
Corcoran, Cpl. Edward, 134
Corinth, Mississippi, 11, 97
Corrick's Ford, West Virginia, Battle of, 6
Cosmopolitan, 66, 91, 290-291
Crater, Battle of the, 301, 305
Crawford, Sgt. S. M., 288
Cumming's Point, 1
Curtis, Pvt. Emory, 177

Dart, Pvt. Edward, 273, 363n
Daufuskie Island, 21, 44
Davis, Jefferson, 10, 14, 20, 71, 93-94, 97, 108, 160, 321n, 332n, 335n
Davis, Quartermaster Thomas, 40
Delaware, 44, 125, 139, 162, 291
Demond, Pvt. William, 177
Department of Georgia, 103
Department of Georgia and South Carolina, 9
Department of Kansas, 22
Department of Mississippi, 2

Department of the Ohio, 6
Department of the South, 9, 11, 22, 300-301, 320n
Dill's Bluff, 34
Dill's Bluff Road, 154, 352n
Dill's Branch Road, 70, 196
Dill's House, 153, 344n
District of Georgia, 14
District, 1st Military, 9, 57, 303
District, 2nd Military, 9, 57
District, 3rd Military, 14, 55, 57
District, 4th Military, 11, 57
District, 5th Military, 14
Dixon Island, 23, 39, 55-56
Dixon Island Footbridge, 39
Donelson, Gen. Daniel, 11, 321n
Donohue, Lt. James, 115-116, 176
Donovant's Regiment, 101
Dow, Capt. Robert C., 229
Doyle, Lt. Ike, 356n
Doyle, Capt. Richard, 169, 193, 296
Drayton, Capt. Percival, 137-138, 162, 251, 288, 295, 341, 360n, 365n
Drayton, Col. Thomas, 57-58, 71, 89
Du Pont, Capt. Samuel F., xii-xiii, 3, 8, 26-27, 29, 38, 41-43, 137-138, 277-278, 283, 288, 301-302, 319n, 323n-324n, 326n-327n, 364n-365n, 368n
Duncan, Maj. W. H., 87, 94, 292
Dunn, Pvt. Henry, 134

Early, Gen. Jubal A., 99
Early's Brigade, 99
Edgerton, Pvt. Samuel, 185, 350n
Edisto, South Carolina, 44, 366n
Edisto Island, 20-21, 42-44, 62-63, 65-66, 68, 140, 288, 327n, 330n
Edisto River, 11, 327n
Edisto Rifles, 19

Edward, Lt. J. J., 258-259, 360n
Eldridge, Pvt. Daniel, 227, 367n
Ellen, 138, 251-252
Elliot, Capt. Stephen, 49, 69-70, 76, 78-79, 354n
Elliot, Pvt. Thomas, 214, 274
Elliot's Cut, 10, 24, 29, 54-55
Ely, Capt. Ralph, 96, 102, 151, 169, 279-280, 282, 287, 291, 355n, 364n
Engineering Brigade, 298
Ericsson, 292
Etiwan, 25, 272
Eutaw Battalion, 19, 36, 57, 70, 86-87, 90, 100, 105, 114, 120, 127, 130, 142, 144-145, 152-154, 160, 163, 168, 196, 230, 232-234, 236, 239, 260-262, 273, 278, 289, 292, 304, 308, 322n, 326n, 334n-335n, 339n-340n, 342n-344n, 346n, 352n, 357n, 368n
Evans, Gen. Nathan, 11-12, 14, 16, 54, 57, 71, 89-90, 101, 118-119, 123, 141, 144-146, 154-155, 160, 167-168, 172, 195, 231, 262-263, 272, 300, 302, 304, 321n, 332n, 336n, 338n-339n, 341n-342n, 344n, 347n, 356n-357n, 361n-362n, photo, 13
Fenton, Col. William M., 59-60, 62, 91, 163, 165, 171, 174, 190, 198, 212, 242, 244, 253, 256, 273, 283, 301, 330n, 346n-347n 364n, 368n, photo, 164
Fenton's Brigade, 165, 212
Fenwick Island, 323n
Fernandina, Florida, 20-21, 288
First Division Headquarters Brigade, 44
First Military District of South Carolina, 103, 154
Fitch, Pvt. Andrew, 88
Floyd, John, Gen., 8

Folly Island, 16, 31
Folly River, 29, 39, 70-72
Fort Clinch, 27
Fort Donelson, 321n
Fort Fisher, 304
Fort Jackson, 97
Fort Johnson, 19, 25, 31-32, 34-35, 38, 89, 100, 121, 125, 139, 143, 168, 262, 265, 281, 326n, 343n
Fort Lamar, 305, 308, *photo*, 307
Fort Monroe, 13
Fort Moultrie, xii, 54, 58, 326n, 364n
Fort Pemberton, 33-34, 55, 58, 100, 103, 155, 307
Fort Pulaski, xiii-xiv, 1, 4-5, 10-11, 14, 21, 44-45, 60, 62, 143, 148, 288, 297, 320n, 327n
Fort Ripley, 24-25
Fort Sanders, Knoxville, Tennessee, 367n
Fort Sumter, xi, xiv, 16-18, 26, 32, 53-54, 58, 89, 115-116, 121, 139, 157-158, 301, 303, 324n, 326n, 344n, 364n
Franklin Life Guard, 22, 356n
Franklin, Tennessee, Battle of, 303
Fredericksburg, Virginia, Battle of, 299
Freer's Store, 105
Freer, Edward H., 325n
Fuller, Lt. G. B., 176, 193

Gadsen, Jr., Pvt. Thomas, 234
Gage, Pvt. William, 333
Gaillard, Col. Peter, 20, 57, 80, 82, 172, 184, 211, 224, 305-306, 322n, 333n, 350n, 353n, 354n
Gaillard's Battalion, 172
Gallagher, Pvt. Hugh, 193
Gardens Corner, South Carolina, 3, 46-51, 328n
Garnett, Gen. Robert, 6

General Burnside, 91
Georgetown, South Carolina, 9-11
Georgia Legion, 50
Georgia Troops, *13th Infantry*, 60, *32nd Infantry*, 97, 99, 335n, *46th Infantry*, 263, 306, *47th Infantry*, 97, 127, 130, 135, 141, 144, 154, 160, 167, 196, 232-233, 261, 292, 335n, 341n, 346n, 348n, 352n, 361n, *51st Infantry*, 51, 261
Gettysburg, Pennsylvania, Battle of, 299
Gilbert, Pvt. Charles, 189
Gilliland, Lt. Joseph, 246
Gillis, Lt., 252, 360n
Gillmore, Capt. Quincy A., xiv, 10, 21, 62, 297, 345n
Girardeau, Reverend John, 261
Gist, Gen. States Rights, 10, 35-36, 39, 55, 70-73, 79, 86, 90, 96, 99-100, 117, 121, 123, 142, 153-154, 263, 272, 274, 303, 326n, 326n, 329n, 340n, 368n, *photo*, 35
Gist Guards, 71, 332n
Goddard, Doctor P. C., 50
Goldsborough, Capt. John R., 43, 327n
Goodlette, Maj. Spartan, 259, 275, 302, 261, 263
Gradine, Alfred, 324n
Graham, Lt. Benjamin, 11, 233, 261
Grant, Gen. Ulysses S., 300, 303
Graves, Lt. Col. Frank, 164, 169, 171, 174, 216, 265-266, 346n
Grayson, William J., 24, 58, 142
Greer, Lt. Richard, 234, 236
Gregg, Gen. Maxcy, 11, 14, 20, 336n
Gregorie, Capt. J. W., 33
Grimball Family, 32, 34
Grimball Causeway, 34, 110, 113, 117, 119, 338n

Grimball Plantation, 55-56, 70, 86-87, 100, 110-114, 117-120, 125, 127, 130, 142-148, 150, 152-153, 157, 161,162, 166, 253, 266, 280, 284, 288, 290-292, 337n, 338n-339n, 342n-343n, 345n
Grimball, Thomas H., 325n
Griswold, Pvt. ?, 247, 256-257
Guild, Capt. Simon, 176, 193, 265, 351n, 359n
Guss, Col. H. R., 125, 132, 137, 253

Hagood, Col. Johnson, 16-20, 36, 87, 100, 104-105, 127, 130, 135, 142, 154-155, 160, 167-168, 195-196, 230, 232, 234, 236, 260-261, 263, 274, 302, 305, 321n, 322n, 326n, 329n, 334n-336n, 342n, 345n, 348n, 357n, 368n, photo, 15
Hagood's Brigade, 300, 304-305, 322n
Hale, 138, 251-252
Halleck, Gen. Henry W., 22, 297
Hamilton, Capt. John, 62-63, 134, 229, 241, 250, 290
Hamilton's Battery, 119-120, 166, 240, 291, 330n, 340n, 347n, 356n
Hampton, Gen. Wade, 305
Hardee, Gen. William J., 160
Hardeeville, South Carolina, 48, 71, 89, 319n
Harrison, George P., 99, 335n
Harrison's Brigade, 97, 335n
Hatch, Col. Lewis, 33, 272, 285, 325n-326n, 364n
Hawley, Lt. Col. Joseph, 45, 110-111, 113, 164, 186-187, 189-190, 199, 214, 216, 246, 255, 266, 300-301, 337n-338n, 345n-347n, 350n, 359n
Hayes, Pvt. Patrick, 112
Haynes, Sgt. ?, 189

Henery, Sgt. Robert, 211
Heyward, Capt. Blake, 48
Hibbard, Pvt. Andrews, 189, 214, 274
Higgenson, Maj. ?, 46
Hill Family, 32
Hill Plantation, 145, 230-232, 240, 253
Hill, Washington, 325n
Hills, Capt. Francis, 125
Hilton Head, South Carolina, xiii, 1, 5, 17, 20-21, 43-44, 56, 61-62, 65, 102-103, 139-141, 146-147, 151, 276-277, 279-280, 283, 288, 290-291, 293, 295, 323n
Hitchcock, Capt. Edwin, 187
Holly, Pvt. —, 248
Holmes, James W., 325n
Holt, Joseph, 297
Honduras, 60
Hooten, Lt. —, 189
Howard, Lt. O. H., 83
Howard, Pvt. D., 211
Hudson, Maj. J. H., 209, 225
Huger, Gen. Benjamin, 160
Humbert, Lt. J. B., 173, 185, 211, 258, 349n
Humbert, Lt. T. P. Oliver, 353n
Hunter, Gen. David, xi, 5, 8, 20-22, 27, 32-33, 41-44, 59, 75, 97, 102, 104, 111, 113, 117, 125, 139-141, 147, 151, 161, 266-267, 277-278, 280-284, 288, 292-297, 301, 320n, 322n-323n, 341n, 343n, photo, 21

Irish Brigade, 102, 299
Irish Volunteers, 20, 82, 185, 211
Jackson, Abraham, 324n
Jackson, Lt. Col. John H., 65, 220, 222-223 227, 229, 300, 355n, photo, 64
Jackson, Gen. Thomas J., 98, 298, 302
Jackson, Mississippi, Battle of, 300

James Island, South Carolina, xiii, 3, 10, 14, 18-19, 23-24, 29, 31-36, 38-39, 42, 45, 55-56, 58, 69, 72-73, 84, 90, 93-94, 97-101, 104-105, 112, 116-121, 139-148, 151, 154-155, 157, 167, 172, 195, 263, 265, 274, 276-278, 280-281, 284, 287-288, 291-293, 298, 300-307, 325n, 326n, 335n-337n, 342n, 344n, 358n-359n, 364n-366n, 368n

James Island Campaign, 303, 353n

James Island Creek, 29, 31, 34, 274

James Island Presbyterian Church, 100

Jamison, Capt. Joshua, 172-173, 183, 209, 348n

Jervey, Pvt. Bill, 234

Jeter, Lt. —, 196, 232-233

Johns Island, 38, 54, 65-66, 68-69, 93, 97, 105, 110-112, 118-119, 123, 141, 284, 325n

Johnson, Lt. William, 173

Johnston, Gen. Joseph E., 305

Jones, Capt. —, 39-40

Jones, David, 324n

Jones, Lt. Iredell, 157, 159

Kearny, Gen. Philip, 299

Keenan, Lt. —, 83

Keitt, Capt. G. D., 157, 186

Kemble, Maj. George, *photo,* 107

Kerrigan, Sgt. William, 193

Kiawah Island, 16, 31, 69

Kiawah River, 38, 56

King's Highway, 34, 70, 100, 105, 154, 196-197, 225, 352n

King, Capt. Henry, 184, 259, 274, 350n, 363n

Kinnear, Lt. James, 205, 284

Kitching, Lt. J. B., 230-232

Knoxville, Tennessee, Battle of, 300, 367n

Lamar, Col. Thomas G., 19, 35, 57, 79, 86, 121, 123, 150, 152-153, 157-158, 161, 167-168, 172-173, 181, 183-184, 195, 197, 201, 211-212, 218, 223-224, 227, 230, 259, 261-262, 272, 305-306, 308, 339n, 341n-343n, 345n-350n, 352n-355n, 361n, 365n, 369n, *photo,* 122

Lamar's Artillery, 19, 35, 305

Lanahan, Jerry, 237

Lancaster, Lt. J. W., 173

Lanneau, Sgt. FLeetwood, 234, 236

Laurel Hill, WV., Battle of, 6

Lawrence, Pvt. Daniel, 215, 354n

Lawton, Gen. Alexander, 14, 57, 71, 89-90, 98-99, 103, 335n

Lawton's Brigade, 90, 335n

Lawton, Pvt. C. J., 50

Lawton House, 168, 195, 231

Leary, Pvt. Jacob, 208

Leasure, Col. Daniel, 61-62, 75, 96, 165, 198-199, 201, 205-206, 208-209, 215-216, 218, 241-242, 245-246, 248, 250, 253-255, 274, 299, 301, 330n, 332n, 335n-336n, 347n, 352n-353n, 359n, 367n-368n, *photo,* 61

Lebby, Doctor Robert, 263, 361n, 369n

Leckey, Maj. David, 205, 208, 254, 308, 353n

Lee, Gen. Robert E., xiii, 9-11, 14, 33, 35, 53-55, 58-59, 90, 93-94, 142, 301-302, 304-305, 320n-321n, 329n, 335n

Legare Plantation, 76, 78-80, 82-84, 89-90, 95, 108-109, 112, 143, 153, 155, 332n-333n, 337n

Legareville, South Carolina, 38, 65, 67-69, 90, 101, 103, 105-106, 109-110, 118-119, 123, 339n
Lesesne, Lt. F. J., 100
Lexington, Virginia, 301
Lighthouse Creek, 29, 31, 138
Lighthouse Inlet, 33
Lilley, William, 5
Lincoln, Abraham, xii, 6, 20-21, 43, 296-298, 301, 367n
Little Edisto Island, 21
Little Folly Creek, 31
Long Island, 31
Longstreet, Gen. James, 160, 368n
Lord, Pvt. —, 246
Louisiana Troops, *4th Infantry Battalion*, 97, 105, 127, 130, 135, 153-154, 196-197, 225-226, 259, 263, 304, 306, 335n, 344n, 352n, 356n, 361n, 365n, 368n
Lucas, Maj. J. J., 16, 24, 34
Lucas' Battery, 18, 321n
Lusk, Lt. William T., 141, 164, 250, 270, 346n, 362n, *photo*, 107
Lynchburg, Virginia, Battle of, 301
Lyons, Lt. Benjamin, 110, 164, 174, 213, *photo*, 107
Lyon, Capt. Ephraim, 181
Macbeth Light Artillery, 58, 196, 336n, 352n
MacDonald, Capt., 125
Magruder, Gen. John, 160
Maine Troops, *9th Infantry*, 21
Manassas, First Battle of, 17, 22, 35, 60, 101, 303, 336n
Manassas, Second Battle of, 297, 299, 300, 367n
Manigault, Col. Arthur M., 9, 321n
Mansfield, Gen. Joseph, 140

Marchand, Commander J. B., 38, 42, 326n
Marion Men of Combahee, 48
Marion Rifles, 80
Massachusetts Troops, *1st Infantry*, 21-22, 44, 46, 60, 62-63, 66, 110, 112-113, 119, 165-166, 277, 327n, *2nd Infantry*, 288, *3rd Cavalry*, 264, *11th Infantry*, 103, 336n, *28th Infantry*, 21-22, 44, 62, 69, 76, 78, 88, 102-103, 116, 164-165, 189-191, 193, 199, 206, 209, 213, 219, 240, 242, 255-256, 264, 273, 279, 287, 291, 299, 308, 323n, 327n, 333n, 336n, 338n, 347n, 350n-351n, 352n, 359n, 366n-367n
Mattano, 106
Mayflower, 119
Mayo, Pvt. Napoleon, 265
McCasky, Sgt. James, 208
McClellan, Gen. George B., 6, 8, 90, 93, 98, 140, 288, 302, 323n
McDonald, Cpl. John, 193
McDonald, Sgt. John J., 191, 351n
McEnery, Lt. Col. John, 105, 127, 135, 154, 168, 196, 197, 225-227, 258-259, 261, 304, 335n, 361n
McVey, Pvt. Charles, 191
Meagher, Gen. Thomas F., 102
Means, Col. John Hugh, 49-50
Meeting Street, Charleston, 118
Mellinchamp, Reverend, 87
Mercer, Gen. Hugh, 14, 55, 57, 87, 90, 95-96, 98-99, 103-104, 112, 117, 329n, 334n, 335n
Metcalf, Lt. Col. Edwin, 65, 67, 105, 119-120, 219, 237-238, 358n
Michigan Troops, *8th Infantry*, 1, 21-23, 27, 45, 59-60, 62, 90-91, 95-96, 102, 111, 117, 121, 143, 150-151,

163, 165, 169, 171, 174, 176-177, 180, 186-187, 190, 193, 197-199, 201, 206, 208, 213, 216, 242, 244, 255-257, 265-266, 270, 273, 278-280, 283, 287, 291, 296, 300-301, 305, 308, 330n, 342n-343n, 347n-348n, 352n, 358n, 360n, 363n, 366n-368n

Middle Ground Battery, 24
Miles, Capt. F. T., 211
Miles, William P., 142
Military District of Georgia, 57
Miller, Adjutant B. F., 209, 211, 348n
Moffatt, Sgt. Robert, 79, 89
Monteith, Col. William, 102, 336n
Moore, Lt. Col. McClelland, 62, 103, 164, 190, 240, 255, 273, 279, 336n, 356n, 358n, 363n
Moore, Sgt, 229
Morgan, Maj. Joseph, 48
Morgan, Pvt. S. M., 348n
Morris, Gen. T. A., 6, 16-17, 26, 31, 55, 57, 121, 304-305, 326n, 364n
Morrison, Lt. Col. David, 69, 165, 195, 198, 201, 203, 246, 248, 296, 299, 352n, 367n
Morrow, Col. J. H., 113-114
Morton, Lt. Philo, 208
Moseley, Lt. J. W., 172, 185
Mt. Pleasant, South Carolina, 10
Mulligan, Pvt. John, 238

Nason, Sgt. Hiram, 191, 193, 351n
Nesmith, James, Oregon Senator, 9
New Hampshire Troops, *3rd Infantry,* 21, 44, 62-63, 65, 67, 106, 108-109, 111, 115-117, 119, 144, 146, 148, 152, 161-162, 166, 219-220, 222, 224-225, 227, 237-238, 240, 253, 262, 269, 290, 300, 304, 330n,

338n-339n, 342n-343n, 351n, 356n, 365n, 367n
New Orleans, Louisiana, 97
New York Times, 294-295
New York Tribune, 53
New York Troops, *3rd Infantry,* 223, 227, 229, 276, 308, 337n, *12th State Militia,* 102, *46th Infantry,* 21, 62, 102, 112-113, 165, 208-209, 213, 242, 245-246, 254, 264, 291, 305, 330n, 353n, 358n, 359n, *47th Infantry,* 21, 63, 125, 132, 134, 137, 166, 239, 343n, *48th Infantry,* 21, 45, *79th Infantry,* 8, 21, 45, 60, 69, 76, 78-79, 83-85, 88, 95-96, 101-103, 106, 108-109, 111, 117, 121, 138, 151, 161, 163, 165, 195, 197-199, 201, 203, 205-206, 208, 213-216, 218, 242, 244, 246, 248, 254, 264, 270, 275, 278, 284, 287-288, 290-291, 294, 296, 298-300, 308, 323n, 328n, 333n, 353n, 359n, 366n-367n
Newall, Lt. George, 177, 193, 351n
Newport News, Virginia, 298
Newtown Cut, 29, 33-35, 90, 104-105, 121, 154, 195
Nickels, Lt. J. F., 26
North Edisto River, 3

O'Rorke, Lt. P. H., 115
Oketie River, 14
Oliver, Lt. T. P., 185
Olustee, Battle of, 301
USS Onward, 26
USS Ottawa, 38, 40-41, 56
Otter Island, 21, 44
Ouchita Rebels, 226
Overland Campaign, 299-300
Overton, Pvt. Adelbert, 256

Packard, Pvt. Elmer, 270
Palmetto Battalion, 57
Parker, Pvt. Thomas, 185, 350n
Parrott, Commander E. G., 26
USS *Pawnee*, 251
Pease, Pvt. Benjamin, 22, 23, 91, 95, 180-181, 230, 256, 261-262, 266, 273, 323n, 348n, 360n, 363n
Pee Dee Battalion, 152, 154, 167-168, 181, 183-185, 197, 209, 211, 225, 259, 300, 302, 304-305, 308, 343n-344n, 348n-349n, 368n
Pelican Regiment, 304
Pemberton, Gen. John C., 9-14, 16, 20, 23-24, 33, 36, 48, 53-55, 57-59, 71, 89-90, 93-94, 96-99, 103-104, 106, 108, 111-112, 117-118, 121, 123, 127, 136, 141-142, 144-146, 153-154, 160, 263, 272, 274, 284, 300, 303, 320n-321n, 328n-329n, 332n, 334n-335n, 337n-338n, 340n-341n, 361n-363n, 368n, *photo*, 12
USS *Pembina*, 38, 55-56
Peninsula Campaign, 93, 98
Pennsylvania Troops, *45th Infantry*, 21, 63, 125, 132, 151, 166, 276, 323n, 343n, *50th Infantry*, 21, 45-46, 61, *55th Infantry*, 21, 62, *76th Infantry*, 21, 63, 65, 137, 300, 304, 341, 343n, *79th Infantry*, 110, 252, *97th Infantry*, 21, 63, 68, 119, 125, 132, 134, 136-137, 146, 166, 239-240, 253, 276, 291, 304, 331n, 339n, 343n, 347n, *100th Infantry*, 21, 47, 60-62, 69-70, 75-76, 78-79, 82-85, 89, 102-103, 106, 109, 147, 165, 205-206, 208-209, 213, 241-242, 245, 254, 264, 270, 280, 290-291, 299-301, 305, 353n, 367n
Perry, Col. James, 45, 327n

Petersburg, Virginia, 301
Pettigrew, Gen. Johnston, 18
Phillip's Georgia Legion, 51
Phillips, Lt. Col. William, 50
Pickens, Governor Francis, 10-11, 14, 16, 20, 53-55, 58, 94, 121, 160, 321n, 329n, 334n
Pinckney Island, 151
Planter, 24-27, 35, 38, 63, 324n, 334n
Pocotaligo, South Carolina, 3, 5, 9, 45-52, 58, 328n
Port Royal, xi, xiii, 1, 5, 8, 26, 32-33 38, 42, 62, 288, 291, 319n
Port Royal Ferry, xiii, 1, 8, 23, 46-48, 50-51, 61, 83, 102, 330n
Port Royal Island, 1, 3, 21, 23, 45, 48, 51-52, 59, 334n
Port Royal Sound, 27, 59, 68
Porter, Rev. A. Toomer, 160, 163, 236, 288, 357n
Porter, Capt. B. F., *photo*, 107
Porter, Lt. S. E., 85-86, 212-213, 333n
Potter, Lt. Isaac, 237
Poznanski, Jr., Pvt. Gustavus, 185, 350n
Pratt, Capt. Gilbert, 176, 193, 265
Presbyterian Episcopal Church, 105, 114, 120, 127, 146, 152, 168, 196, 307, 338n
Pressley, Maj. John, 86-88, 101, 152, 236, 260-261, 278, 321n, 325n, 334n-335n, 340n, 342n, 345n, 352n, 365n
Preston Light Artillery, 86, 114, 120, 127

Raccoon Island, 323n
Ramsey, Maj. David, 305, 369n
Rantowles Bridge, 11
Reagan, Pvt. John, 226
Reed, Capt. Samuel, 157, 183, 306, 349n

Reynolds, Gen. John F., 298
Rhode Island Troops, *3rd Heavy Artillery*, 21, 43-44, 62-63, 65, 67-68, 105, 119-120, 134, 151, 165-166, 219-220, 227, 229, 237-240, 253, 264, 276, 308, 331n, 339n, 343n, 347n, 358n
Rich, Col. Richforth, 21
Richmond Dispatch, 284
Ripley, Gen. Roswell, 9-12, 14, 16, 18, 24, 33-35, 39, 53-55, 57-58, 303, 321n, 325n-326n, 329n, 344n-345n
Rivers Causeway, 39, 72, 79, 84, 86, 89-90, 115-116, 121, 125, 150, 155, 159, 163, 168, 197, 254, 269, 288, 292
Rivers House, 79, 100, 105, 116, 144, 159, 167-168, 172, 205, 244-245, 254-255, 257-258, 273, 345n, 348n
Rivers, Horace, 325n
Robertson, Lt. Thomas, 205
Rockwell, Capt. Alfred P., 160, 164-165, 212, 242, 246, 250, 254, 347n
Rockwell's Battery, 168, 246, 256
Rogers, Capt. —, 237-238
Rodgers, Capt. C. R. P., 42-43
Rodgers, Capt. John 282-283, 288
Rosa, Col. Rudolph, 62, 165, 208-209, 242, 264, 359n
Rosecrans, Gen. William S., 6, 8, 141, 282
Royall House 154, 168
Russ, Pvt. William, 348n
Rutledge Mounted Riflemen, 48, 50
Ryan, Capt. W. H., 82, 185

Sargent, Capt. Lucius, 165
Sarvis, Lt. —, 168, 348n
Savage, Pvt. Walter, 256

Savannah, Georgia, xii-xiv, 3, 9, 11, 27, 48, 58-59, 71, 89, 96-99, 103, 112, 117, 142, 319n, 327n, 335n
Savannah Creek, 158
Savannah River, xiii, 1-3, 97
Savannah Road, 159
Scranton, Capt. —, 246
Screven's Canal, 48-49
Sea Island, 31
Seabrook House, 70, 101
Seabrook Island, 31, 63, 65, 90
Seabrook William B., 325n
Secessionville, South Carolina, 32-36, 39, 57, 70, 72, 79-80, 84, 86, 89-90, 96-97, 99-100, 103-104, 108, 112, 115-116, 121, 130, 138, 143-145, 147-148, 150, 152, 154, 157-158, 160-162, 172, 181, 186, 195-196, 219, 225, 227, 230, 232, 251, 260-263, 265-267, 273, 277-278, 283, 288, 293, 295, 305, 308, 325n, 335n, 337n, 341n-343n, 345n, 347n-348n, 356n, 361n, 363n
Secessionville, South Carolina, Battle of, 267, 270, 274, 278-279 281, 285, 288, 294, 296-297 299-305, 307, 352n-353n, 356n
Secessionville Causeway, 87, 225
Secessionville Peninsula, 306, 346n
Sedgwick, Gen. John, 298, 301
Sellars, Capt. —, 239
Serrell, Capt. Edward, 44, 63, 66, 110, 143, 148, 161, 164, 166, 212, 220, 237, 276, 280, 288, 330n-332n, 337n, 339n, 342n-343n, 358n, 364n-365n
Seven Days Battles, 302
Seward, Lt. —, 168, 212-213
Shaw, Col. Robert Gould, 288, 365n
Shelton, Pvt. William, 185

Shenandoah Valley Campaign, 301
Sheppard, Benjamin, 260
Sheppard, Pvt. John, 233-234
Sheridan, Gen. Philip H., 301
Sherman, Gen. Thomas W. xiii-xiv, 3-6, 32-33, 62, 319n, 323n
Sherman, Gen. William T., 303, 305-306
Shiloh, Tennessee, Battle of, 1, 11
Sigwald, Capt. ?, 80
Simons, Capt. T. Y., 173 262, 239, 348n
Simonton, Lt. Col. Charles H., 36, 57, 86, 94, 105, 120, 152, 168, 196-197, 230, 232-233, 288, 352n, photo, 37
Simpson Creek, 158, 345n
Sisson, Maj. H. T., 219
Slaughter, Col. William, 51
Slemmons, Pvt. J. H. 205, 206, 208, 264, 366n
Smalls, John, 324n
Smalls, Robert, 25-27, 32, 42, 324n
Smart, Capt. —, 348n
Smith, Lt. Col. Alexander D., 152, 158, 167, 172, 181, 183, 197, 303-304, 308, 344n, 348n, 352n
Smith, Gen. William Duncan, 14, 89, 99, 103-105, 108, 112, 118, 127, 130, 136, 142, 144, 146, 154, 231, 272, 274, 302-303, 306, 341n-342n, photo, 98
Smyth, Pvt. Augustine, 233, 236, 260, 329n
Sol Legare Island, 23, 31, 34, 39-40, 68-72, 75-76, 79, 86, 88, 93-94, 96, 99, 103-104, 106, 108-109, 111-112, 116-118, 121, 136, 143, 147-148, 150, 159, 162, 165, 191, 198, 205, 254-255, 257, 280, 283, 288, 291-292, 307, 332n, 337n-338n, 342n, 362n

South Atlantic Blockading Squadron, 324n
South Carolina Department of the Military, 53
South Carolina Military Academy, 16-18, 20, 90
South Carolina Troops, *1st Artillery Battalion*, 57, 121, 263, 349n, *1st Cavalry*, 48, *1st Infantry*, 15-20, 87, 105, 127, 154, 167, 195-196, 230, 232, 261, 292, 321n-322n, 340n, *2nd Artillery Battalion*, 59, 305, *3rd Cavalry*, 58, *9th Battalion*, 152, 158, 181, *10th Infantry*, 10, *11th Battalion*, 49, 322n, *12th Infantry*, 14, 336n, *13th Infantry*, 14, *14th Infantry*, 14, *17th Infantry*, 49, 118, *17th Militia*, 20, *21st Infantry*, 300, *22nd Infantry*, 144-145, 167, 172, 259, 261, 263, 288, 300, 302-303, 305, *23rd Infantry*, 261, *24th Infantry*, 17-18 23-24, 27, 35, 39, 41, 57, 79, 82-83, 100, 105, 154, 167, 195, 230, 232-233, 260, 303, 308, 322n, 340n, *25th Infantry*, 300, 304, *26th Infantry*, 304, 344n, *27th Infantry*, 305
South Edisto River, 11
South Mountain, Maryland, Battle of, 300
Southeast Atlantic Blockading Squadron, 301
Southern Expedition 323n, 368n
Spotsylvania Court House, Virginia, Battle of, 300-301, 368n
St. Lyon, Pvt. Edward, 189
St. Michael's Church, 147, 343n
Stanton, Edwin M., 22, 277, 297
Starkweather, Capt. ?, 109, 337n
Stevens' Brigade, 61-62, 114

Stevens' Division, 42, 75, 101, 106, 112, 161, 165, 223, 230, 252, 257, 300
Stevens, Col. Clement H., 17-18, 23-24, 35, 39-40, 57, 105, 154, 167-168, 195, 230, 232-233, 236, 239, 260, 322n, 338n, *photo*, 17
Stevens, Capt. Hazard, 5, 8, 78, 112, 115, 155, 162, 213-214, 216, 332n-333n, 343n-344n, 359n, *photo*, 107
Stevens, Gen. Isaac, 3-6, 8-9, 21, 42, 45, 47-48, 51, 59-62, 69, 75, 93, 101-102, 104-106, 108, 115, 125, 127, 138, 140-141, 143, 147-148, 155, 157, 161-163, 165-166, 168-169, 198, 208-209, 212-213, 215, 218-220, 222, 230, 239, 241-242, 244-246, 250-253, 255, 257, 264, 267, 270, 273-274, 276, 281, 283-284, 287-288, 290, 292-299, 319n-320n, 322n-323n, 326n, 328n, 330n, 333n, 336n, 338n, 342n, 347n, 354n-355n, 357n-360n, 364n-367n, *photo*, 7, 107
Stockton, Samuel, 278, 280
Stokes, Maj. WIlliam, 50
Stoney, John S., 263
Stono Inlet, 16, 18, 24, 27, 38, 71, 91
Stono Naval Squadron, 137
Stono River, 3, 9-10, 23-24, 29, 31, 33-3, 36, 38-40, 42, 45, 53-57, 62, 65, 67-71, 80, 86, 91, 96, 100, 103, 106, 109-110, 117, 119, 123, 125, 127, 138, 144, 148, 150, 152-153, 232, 257, 263-264, 269-270, 276, 278, 280, 283, 288, 291-292, 307, 326n, 329n, 337n, 343n
Sumter Guards, 20, 184-185, 274
Swash Channel, 26

Tafft, Lt. Henry, 143, 250-253, 342n

Tavener, Lt. ?, 236
Tennent, Pvt. Edward S., 272, 362n
Tennant, Pvt. Josiah, 184
Terry, Gen. Alfred, 44, 327n
Todd, Sgt. William, 266, 352n
Tower Battery (Fort Lamar), 33-35, 58, 121, 145, 148, 150-153, 155, 157-159, 161, 167, 171-172, 183, 185, 187, 193, 197, 199, 201, 212, 214, 216, 218-220, 222-227, 230-232, 237, 239-240, 244, 246, 251, 257, 259, 263, 272, 274, 283, 288, 293, 297, 300, 302, 305, 308, 326n, 344n-346n, 355n, 361n, *photo*, 307
Tracy, Capt. Carlos, 71, 73, 96, 100, 117, 120, 153, 326n, 332n, 334n-335n, 339n, 344n
Tracy, Pvt. William, 177
Trenholm, Capt. —, 48
Trumbo, Pvt. Christopher, 236, 357n
Turner, Lt. George, 270, 348n, 351n
Turno, Gabriel, 324n
Tybee Island, xiii, 297, 343n

Unadilla, USS., 38, 40-41, 55-57, 83
Union Light Infantry, 20, 184, 211, 266
United States Troops, 3rd Artillery, Battery E, 62
Upson, Sgt. —, 189

Valentine, Henry, 184, 350n
Valentine, Cpl. Isaac, 184, 350n
Van dorn, Gen. Earl, 160
Van Horsen, Pvt. —, 215
Vanderbilt, 59, 290
Veile, Gen. Egbert, 21, 44, 327n
Vicksburg, Mississippi, 300, 303

Wabash, USS., 27, 277, 282
Wadmalaw Island, 54

Wadmalaw River, 3
Wadsorth, Sgt. David, 229, 356n
Wagner, Lt. Col. Thomas, 185, 224, 226, 305
Walker, Capt. J. H., 22, 259
Walker, Col. William S., 48, 49-51, 55, 57-58, 328n, 333n
Wappoo Cut, 3, 29, 31, 33, 109
Washington Light Infantry, 19, 232-234, 236, 260-261, photo, 37
Wassaw Sound, 43
Watson, Acting Master —, 26
Watson, Maj. Amasa, 174
Watson, Sgt. John P., 360n
Weld, Stephen Minot, 298
Welles, Gideon, 302
Welsh, Col. Thomas, 3, 166, 219, 241, 266
Welsh's Brigade, 166, 347n 358n
Whelan, Pvt. Rody, 82
White's South Carolina Battalion of Artillery, 34
White, Maj. E. B., 24, 34, 58, 90
Whitmarsh Island, 60, 102, 330n
Williams' Brigade, 125, 162, 218-219, 230, 239, 252-253
Williams, Adjutant Benjamin, 346n, 348n
Williams, Col. Gilbert W. M., 127, 130, 167, 335n, 341n
Williams, Col. Robert, 21, 44, 63, 134-135, 162, 166, 209, 218-219, 227, 240-241, 282, 293-294, 296-297, 347n, 354n-355n
Williams, Thomas, 332n-333n
Williams, Capt. William, 144, 130, 136, 292
Willstown, South Carolina, 11
Wilmington River, 327n
Wilson, Pvt. Hugh, 208

Windmill Point, 31
Winnsboro, Lea, 226
Wise, John, Gen., 8
Woodford, Pvt. Milton, 116-117, 303-304, 339n
Woolsey, Capt., 252
Wright, Maj. —, 113, 338n
Wright, Pvt. George, 134
Wright, Gen. Horatio, 21, 42, 62-63, 65-68, 93, 101, 109, 113, 119-120, 125, 127, 134, 136, 139-141, 143, 147-148, 162, 166, 214, 216, 218, 239-241, 244, 252, 267, 273, 276, 280-284, 287-288, 290-293, 295-296, 301, 342n, 347n, 354n-355n, 358n-359n, 364n, photo, 63
Wright's Division, 66-68, 93, 96, 101, 103-105, 119-120, 125, 136, 166, 253, 290

Yorktown, Virginia, Battle of, 14, 97

An Interview With Patrick Brennan

SPC: Why does the Battle of Secessionville deserve a full-length book?

PB: There is a surprisingly easy answer to that question. The battle didn't involve large numbers of troops—probably 6,600 Unionists and 1,000 Confederates. Based strictly on that fact, one might argue its relative importance. But, Secessionville represented the flash point that turned a successful Federal operation into a rather stunning Confederate victory and, in the process, redirected further Federal efforts against Charleston elsewhere. In addition, it broke at least one officer's career, and molded and shaped others that went on to serve in other theaters in larger actions. It was an important early war engagement. It was also, and few people realize this fact, the largest land battle ever fought in South Carolina.

SPC: Describe the events leading up to the battle.

PB: When Federal Maj. Gen. David Hunter assumed command of the Department of the South in April 1862, he promised his superiors that the Stars and Stripes would soon fly over Fort Sumter's ramparts. Of course, at that time Federal efforts were directed against Fort Pulaski near Savannah, Georgia. Hunter and his new second-in-command, Brig. Gen. Henry Benham, had no idea that Pulaski would fall so quickly after their arrival. Well, it did and suddenly these two newcomers were confronted with the difficult task of assaulting Charleston. Benham insisted on testing Charleston's southern flank, the defenses on James Island, and Hunter acquiesced. After a month of tortured preparations, the Federals landed on June 2 and established a bridgehead on Sol Legare Island.

SPC: Secessionville didn't take place until June 16. What transpired in the interim?

PB: Initially, the Federals simply consolidated their foothold. Later, they constructed a number of forward artillery positions that opposed a Confederate earthwork, the Tower Battery, near a clustering of planter summer homes called Secessionville. Another Union division landed on James Island proper and established a large fortified camp. Both sides maneuvered and clashed here and there, essentially preparing for what many knew was coming. After a week or so, Hunter decided his presence was demanded at Hilton Head, South Carolina, so he left Benham in command with strict orders not to force a battle until he returned. Benham defied these orders and launched his troops at the Tower Battery in the pre-dawn of June 16.

SPC: What were the Confederates doing during this period?

PB: To defend Charleston's southern flank, the Confederates had constructed an entrenched line that ran from Fort Pemberton on the Stono River to the Tower Battery in front of Secessionville. The authorities in Richmond, however, had been stripping the Charleston defenses of troops—remember, you have Shiloh/Corinth and the Peninsula Campaign occurring around the same time—and the defensive line itself was incomplete. Luckily, Col. Thomas Lamar was in command at the Tower Battery, and he had turned his earthwork into the strongest Confederate position on James Island. It was the linchpin of the city's southern defenses.

SPC: Describe the battle.

PB: Half the Federals—Gen. Isaac Stevens' six regiments—attacked the Tower Battery head on. The other half advanced against the battery's northern flank. Benham's reconnaissance was so poor, however, that he threw Stevens' force down a marsh-bound peninsula that telescoped directly into Lamar's guns. The peninsula was so narrow in front of the battery that the Federals could barely form a regimental front. Needless to say, the fighting became very confused, and in three hours of combat Lamar was able to beat back over 3,000 Federals with about 500 men.

SPC: What happened to the flanking force?

PB: Those troops advanced down the next peninsula to the north. When they turned to take the battery in flank, they found 125 yards of impassable swamp blocking their way. Although the Federals had some initial success sweeping the battery's right flank, they were eventually surrounded by Confederate troops reacting quickly to the attack.

SPC: So this was really Lamar's victory?

PB: Lamar deserves the lion's share of credit, but Col. Johnson Hagood deserves praise for his response to the attack. Upon hearing the opening guns, Hagood sent troops to reinforce the battery, then personally led the Confederate effort against the Federal flanking force. The Confederate theater commanders—Generals John C. Pemberton and Nathan "Shanks" Evans—had little to do with the battle, although Evans watched it from a second floor window of a nearby house!

SPC: Given the preponderance of numbers, isn't it surprising that Benham's men did not simply overwhelm the defenders?

PB: How many times do we talk about the importance of holding good ground? This was another example of it. Of course, the Confederate defenders joked afterwards that they could not afford to lose that morning because the women of Charleston wouldn't have let them back home!

SPC: So if the Federals had cracked the Tower Battery that morning, the Battle of Secessionville would be widely recognized within the Civil War community?

PB: Had the Federals succeeded that morning, two things would have happened. First, the Confederate defenses on James Island would have been seriously compromised, and second, the Federals would have gained a water route into Charleston Harbor that could have turned Morris Island and Fort Sumter. So yes, had Secessionville been a Federal victory, the battle would be better known. The stakes were enormous.

SPC: Who in the officer corps stands out as particularly interesting or worthy of further study?

PB: I found two officers intriguing. Isaac Stevens led a very interesting life, and Secessionville was just one of many intense moments for what seemed to be a very intense person. Luckily, his career is well documented. On the other hand, I wish I could have dug up more material on Thomas Lamar. His world appeared to be the exact opposite of Stevens'. While Lamar stayed primarily in South Carolina and Georgia, Stevens roamed all over the country. Lamar was basically a planter for most of his life, but Stevens engaged in all sorts of activities. Yet, they meet at Secessionville, this Rebel planter and Yankee explorer. There seems to be some undefinable linkage between the two men. Their respective behavior is remarkable.

SPC: What about Henry Benham?

PB: I really looked for someone somewhere to say something nice about the man. Nothing turned up.

SPC: Any thoughts on David Hunter?

PB: Someone will probably tackle Hunter eventually, but he would likely end up like Braxton Bragg's biographer, who found his subject so distasteful that he could not finish the project!

SPC: You mentioned that you wish you had more information on Lamar. Who else did you find fascinating yet enigmatic because of a dearth of material?

PB: Although there isn't a lot to go on, I think Lt. Col. Peter Gaillard of the Charleston Battalion fits that description. He is something of a mystery, no photo of him exists, and few if any papers have survived. A couple units also come to mind. First, the Pee Dee Battalion—actually the 9th South Carolina Battalion. Now they were a tough group. Another unit that deserves further study is the 46th New York. Unfortunately, the Germans didn't leave much in the way of first person accounts, either.

SPC: *Unlike many writers, you have walked every inch of the ground you write about. Why is that so important to you?*

PB: Terrain influences battle probably as much as any variable. Secessionville was no different. The terrain of James Island—the peninsulas, the marches, the forests and inlets—defined and shaped the campaign and battle. Walking that ground, even with the extensive modern intrusions, made it that much easier to write about Secessionville. Plus, who wouldn't want to spend a week in Charleston? (laughter)

SPC: *This is your first book. How did you go about researching a relatively obscure subject like the Battle of Secessionville?*

MB: Published accounts of the battle are rather scarce. I started with the *Official Records*, which is usually a good place to begin a project like this. After determining what was readily available, I began digging in the National Archives and then various state and local libraries, historical societies—even reenactment units. I found incredible amounts of information in contemporary newspapers, and also plugged into a network of regimental historians. I was also lucky enough to spend a lot of time in Charleston, where many South Carolinians graciously assisted me. Their help was invaluable.

SPC: *What are some of the really interesting or surprising manuscript sources you found during the course of your research.*

PB: That's hard to pin down. I have a natural tendency to empathize with the soldiers, and some of their stories were amazing. Michigander Benjamin Pease wrote a beautiful reminiscence of his service in South Carolina, including his wounding at Secessionville. I think it rivals anything I have seen from the perspective of the foot soldier. Likewise, fellow 8th Michigander Philip Coleman's account of the battle and his subsequent wounding is absolutely harrowing. There is another account that really captures the spirit of the fighting from within the battery that was published in one of the Charleston newspapers. It's one of those up-close and personal descriptions of the action. Unfortunately, it is signed by "Eyewitness." I'd love to know who "Eyewitness" was, but despite all of my research, I have no idea who penned it.

SPC: *Many people, myself included, find it interesting to learn how individual authors actually write their books. Douglas Southall Freeman, for example, would secure a single sheet of paper to a board and write epics! How did you write* Secessionville?

PB: I actually hand-wrote the entire first draft of this book on blank typing paper with a pencil. It took several months and I think it was about 500 pages when I finished. I am, by the way, computer literate!

SPC: *Then why a pencil and typing paper?*

PB: This may sound crazy, but I enjoyed the actual physical process of writing. Putting pencil to paper—the feel of the whole thing. It was highly enjoyable.

SPC: *Would you do it again on a second book?*

PB: (sigh). I honestly do not know the answer to that. I guess I will have to wait and see how I feel when the time comes.

SPC: *You enjoyed the writing process. What about the researching process? So many authors despise it.*

PB: I loved it because it was such a challenge. It became obvious fairly quickly that the "Secessionville Papers," so to speak, do not exist. I had to look in a variety of different places for material. The search was enjoyable, but I consistently ran up against a mind set that tended to dismiss the campaign and battle as nothing but a blip in the big picture. Secessionville did not even merit its own entry in the recently-published four-volume *Encyclopedia on the Confederacy*! Occasionally I began to question the whole process myself. But then, some outstanding manuscript account would surface and remind me that this is a story that has needed telling for a long while. And I would continue on.

SPC: *How do you respond today when you run into that mind set?*

PB: I tell them to read the book.